page 4 Spec

"   " The Baptist in
                    America

page 39 is of especial
                interest

See page 204 for W. M. Society

S0-BRZ-629

Francis E. Clark

MEMORIES

OF

MANY MEN IN MANY LANDS

AN AUTOBIOGRAPHY

CARL A. RUDISILL
LIBRARY
LENOIR RHYNE COLLEGE

BY

FRANCIS E. CLARK, D.D., LL.D.

PRESIDENT OF THE UNITED SOCIETY OF CHRISTIAN ENDEAVOR
AND OF
THE WORLD'S CHRISTIAN ENDEAVOR UNION

*A Gift of Love to.
Rev. J. Alonzo Yount.
Louise G. Yount
and
John L. M. Yount.
from
Clara Louise E. Dohme
of Baltimore Md
Sept 1927.*

UNITED SOCIETY OF CHRISTIAN ENDEAVOR
BOSTON   CHICAGO

G
440
.C 52
1923

Copyright, 1922, 1923

BY

THE UNITED SOCIETY OF CHRISTIAN ENDEAVOR

PRINTED IN UNITED STATES OF AMERICA

Second Edition

19613
Oct¹, 43

THE PLIMPTON PRESS
NORWOOD · MASS · U · S · A

Dedicated

TO A HUNDRED THOUSAND FRIENDS IN ALL LANDS

A FEW OF WHOM ARE NAMED IN THIS VOLUME, AND ALL OF WHOM HAVE
BLESSED MY LIFE; BUT ESPECIALLY

TO MY WIFE

WHO HAS SHARED WITH ME THREE OF FIVE JOURNEYS AROUND THE WORLD, AS
WELL AS MANY SHORTER VOYAGES; WHO HAS BEEN MY CONSTANT COMFORT
AND SUPPORT, AND WITHOUT WHOSE HELP AT THE TYPEWRITER, AND FREQUENT
SUGGESTIONS OF LITERARY VALUE, THIS VOLUME COULD NEVER HAVE BEEN
WRITTEN. TO HER I INSCRIBE IT ON
THIS FORTY-SIXTH ANNIVERSARY OF OUR MARRIAGE

OCTOBER 3, 1922

*This book was presented as
a gift on entering another
dwelling near the town
of Boone N. C.
Sept. 1927*

FOREWORD

HIS volume has been written in different lands during the last seven years, much of it in snatches of time caught between speaking engagements. The only comparatively free time I have been able to devote to it has been a month or six weeks in Honolulu in 1916, and nearly two months in Freiburg, Germany, in the spring of 1922. Even these months were frequently interrupted by unexpected calls for addresses and by demands for articles for different publications.

I have had to rely for dates largely on my memory, supplemented by Mrs. Clark's, and by a few of her "Line-a-Day" books. This may have resulted in slight inaccuracies in dates of minor importance. Yet on the whole I think my readers may congratulate themselves on the fact that I have not kept a careful diary, lest this volume might have swelled to an inordinate size.

Old Edmund Waller once wrote:

> "Poets lose half the praise they should have got;
> Were it but known what they discreetly blot."

So do autobiographers. In their case the last line might be slightly amended to

> "Were it but known what they, perchance, forgot."

My chief sins or chief virtues, as you may look at it, have been those of *omission*, for in spite of much forgetting, my embarrassment has been the embarrassment of riches. I have recalled so many incidents I wanted to record, and especially so many people I wanted to tell about, that my task has been

v

that of using an ever-sharp mental blue-pencil. I have constantly had to remind myself that my task was to write a personal autobiography, and not a history of our times, or a history of the Christian Endeavor movement. A multitude of my friends who have been most usefully prominent in Christian Endeavor will not find themselves mentioned in this volume, — not because I have forgotten them, or do not love them, but simply for lack of space in a book which, as it is, I fear is too large.

I have had equal difficulty in choosing the illustrations and have looked over no less than two thousand photographs to find a hundred which on the whole seemed most suitable.

It has been a genuine joy to write this book, in spite of its inevitable deficiencies and the difficulty of finding time for it, for it has brought to mind dear friends in every land and many happy scenes of fellowship and spiritual communion. I trust that in the future this book may be some contribution to the story of the movement with which my name has been connected, and which, I feel more and more, as the years go by, is not of man, or of the will of man, but of God.

FOREWORD TO SECOND EDITION

As I have read over a copy of the first edition of this book, I have become more keenly alive to its imperfections, and especially to its shortcomings and omissions.

Particularly have I mourned that I could not mention, even by name, one-tenth of the friends, nay, one one-hundredth of those who, by their zeal, enterprise, and wisdom, have done so much to make Christian Endeavor the power it has become throughout the world.

Limitations of space have obliged me to confine mention of Christian Endeavor workers in America to very brief notices of those who have been my past, or are my present colleagues in the Headquarters offices in Boston. We who are the officials of the United Society humbly acknowledge that we have been among the least of the agencies employed of God in building up Christian Endeavor, compared with the great mass of volunteer workers, who, during the two-score years past, have given their best of intellect, heart, and soul, without hope of money reward and without seeking renown of any kind.

The many trustees of the United Society and of the World's Christian Endeavor Union; the scores of faithful field-secretaries in different States and countries; the tens of thousands of State, county, and local-union officers, the equally faithful officers of local societies, and the rank and file who have followed such worthy leaders; the young lady secretaries and stenographers in the Home Office, and workers on our Christian Endeavor publications, — to all these, rather than to those that happen to bear some national official title, should praise be given. In such a movement, so providential, so God-directed from the beginning, it seems almost invidious to single out any for praise, however deserved. To God be all the praise!

Still, there are two or three names of those connected now or formerly with the United Society of Christian Endeavor, omitted by inadvertence, which I should like to mention here. One is that of Clarence C. Hamilton, whose picture appears in the page of United Society officers. As field-secretary of the Ohio Union, and as field-manager of *The Christian Endeavor World,* and as field-secretary of the United Society, he has long had an important place. He does double service in these capacities, and probably visits more union gatherings with the Christian Endeavor message than any other officer. At the same time, his ingenuity in advertising *The Christian Endeavor World,* and in obtaining new subscribers, has been invaluable to the paper.

Another conspicuous name on the rolls is that of Karl Lehmann, whose Christian Endeavor career began twenty years ago in Las Vegas, New Mexico. His resourcefulness and energy and his fine abilities as a speaker and organizer made him a power in the Christian Endeavor ranks in the West, and in the national work as Southern-secretary. He is now engaged in business, but still lives and works for the cause, as shown by his repeated election as president of the Florida State Union.

Another name of one who has done yeoman's service as president of a great State Union, trustee of the United Society, contributor to *The Christian Endeavor World,* and superintendent of Rural Christian Endeavor, is that of John R. Clements of Binghamton, New York. Perhaps his most signal service has been as a writer of popular hymns. By exercising this exceptional gift he has put the whole Christian world under obligation, for some of his hymns are found in almost every gospel hymn-book, and in many of the larger "standard" volumes. I am proud to share my name with one of his sons and one of his grandsons, as well as with the sons of many other friends whom I cannot mention.

My pen will run away with me if I am not careful, and another volume will be needed if I extend indefinitely the list of these without whose help, and God's blessing upon it, Christian Endeavor could not be what it is to-day.

CONTENTS

CONTENTS

ILLUSTRATIONS

Memories of Many Men in Many Lands

CHAPTER I

YEARS 1599–1670

MY EARLY ANCESTORS IN AMERICA

THE STRENUOUS CAREER OF REV. ZECHARIAH SYMMES —
ANNE HUTCHINSON AND THE QUAKERS — THE LAND OF
NOD — HOW MY FIRST AMERICAN ANCESTOR HELPED
ME THROUGH COLLEGE — THE CLARK BRANCHES OF
THE FAMILY TREE.

UTOBIOGRAPHIES, except by the most
distinguished of men, often appear to me to
savor of egotism, since they seem to imply
that the writer thinks that other people are
anxious to know what he has been, and done.
Nevertheless I am going to lay myself open
to this same charge, since many friends have asked me to
write down these reminiscences, and have assured me that
they would be of interest, not only to my own children, but
to the larger family of Christian Endeavorers, and, possibly,
to an even wider circle.

A further reason which I have in my own mind for these
reminiscences is the fact that the character of my work and
the organization that I have especially represented, have
brought me in contact, during the last forty years, with some
of the foremost men of our times, and other interesting char-

acters; and, however uninspiring a man's own life may be, his memories and his estimate of others who have helped to make the history of his generation are not without interest.

Now that I have more than reached the age of three-score years and ten alloted to man by the Psalmist, and have been reminded of the uncertainty of life by a severe illness and a more severe operation, as well as by two or three somewhat narrow escapes from a violent death, I have decided to write down, in as orderly a fashion as I can, the events of the last one and seventy years, so far as they have touched my little orbit.

It is the fashion of some autobiographers to begin with their remote ancestors, but few Americans care to go further back than to the days when their first forbears crossed the salt seas for a home in the new world.

Following this precedent, I will say that my first ancestor in America was Rev. Zechariah Symmes, who was born at Canterbury in England in 1599. He was educated at Emmanuel College, of the University of Cambridge, where he was graduated in 1620.

He was evidently of stern, nonconformist stock, for Cotton Mather tells us that Rev. William Symmes, the father, charged his sons, Zechariah and William, " never to defile themselves with any idolatry or superstition, but to derive their religion from God's Holy Word, and to worship God as He himself has directed, and not after the devices and traditions of men."

That Zechariah followed his reverend father's instructions, and perhaps improved upon them, is indicated by the fact that he was frequently harassed by prosecutions in the bishops' courts, of which the redoubtable persecutor, William Laud, was then the head. This was some twenty years before Archbishop Laud's own head fell on Tower Hill in London, " for his agency in subverting the liberties of England."

Without any premonition of what was to happen to him

when fortune's wheel should revolve again, Laud made it very hot for Zechariah Symmes, and compelled him to leave London, where he was lecturer at St. Anthony's, and to remove to Dunstable in 1625, where he acted as rector for the eight following years.

Of my visit to Emmanuel College and to Dunstable in 1920 when on the track of my ancient progenitor, I will speak later, and will only add at this point that Laud and his persecuting myrmidons followed Zechariah to Dunstable. Feeling that he could have no peace in England, he sailed with his wife and seven children in the ship " Griffin," for Boston, where he arrived September 18, 1634. This family counted nine among the two hundred immigrants on the " Griffin," among whom was the famous and somewhat cantankerous Anne Hutchinson, who made so much trouble for the Puritans in later years.

Very soon after his arrival in Boston, on a fast day appointed for the occasion, Mr. Symmes was elected and ordained the teacher of the church in Charlestown. This church already had a pastor, the Rev. Thomas James, who had been with it since its organization two years before, but after the coming of my ancestor he seems to have confined himself to pastoral labor, while Mr. Symmes did the work of preacher and teacher.

It is interesting to recall that the first church in Boston was originally formed in Charlestown, July 30, 1630, and for some time met for worship under the shadow of a great oak. It was soon found, however, that it was difficult for the large families of those days to cross the Charles River, especially in the winter, so the church was removed to Boston, on the other side of the Charles, where a majority of its members resided, and the new church of which I have been speaking was organized in Charlestown in 1632. This church is still in existence and not long since I had the privilege of preaching to its present day congregation.

Alas, there were ministerial differences in the seventeenth

century, as in the twentieth. It is often difficult for two clergymen of different temperaments, though equally good men, to work together in the same church. It was so in this case. The majority of the people sided with Mr. Symmes, while Mr. James sought fresh fields and pastures new in Providence, New Haven, and Virginia, and afterwards returned to England, a good and true man and faithful servant of Christ to the end of his long life.

Another distinguished member of the Charlestown church was Rev. John Harvard, who came three years later than Mr. Symmes, and who had graduated at the same college in Cambridge.

It is thought by some that he was for a time a colleague of Mr. Symmes. This is probably a mistake, for he died of consumption a year after reaching America, but not before he had immortalized himself, and perpetuated his name throughout all coming generations, by willing one-half of all his property, to the amount of 779 pounds, 17 shillings, and two pence, to the great college which bears his name.

I have a dim suspicion that my honored ancestor, strong and noble man though he was, was somewhat difficult to get along with, for he not only seems to have had some trouble with his colleague, Mr. James, but was one of the most militant of those involved in the celebrated controversy with Mrs. Anne Hutchinson and the Antinomians. He did not enjoy her company on the voyage, and did not believe in the special revelations with which she regaled him. Nor did he at all approve of the meetings which she held after reaching shore. But she gave as good as he sent, and denounced him and his confreres roundly for " holding to a covenant of works." The end was the banishment of Mrs. Hutchinson from the Massachusetts Bay Colony, as every one knows.

This Puritan pastor seems to have been involved also in the trouble with the Quakers. I am glad to say that, so far as I know, he had nothing to do with banishing any of them, though he seems to have annoyed them by his visits to them while in prison, for " religious conversation suited to their needs." For this and similar efforts, we read, " he was grievously reviled by the Quakers."

I wonder what these " similar efforts " were. I fear they may refer to something besides " religious conversation." But we must remember that some of the Quakers of those days were very unlike the delightful, peace-loving citizens who bear that name to-day, for we read that in some places their conduct was in the highest degree " turbulent and provoking." " Margaret Brewster," it is said, " went into a meeting-house with her face smeared with black paint. Deborah Wilson went through the streets of Salem naked, as a sign of her adherence to the naked truth. Lydia Wardwell went into a meeting-house in Newbury as naked as she was born." Many opened their shops on the Lord's Day in defiance of the laws, so that the Rev. Zechariah and his fellows had excuses for their harshness which are not generally recognized.

Toward the end of his life another controversy, which must have been painful at the time, resulted in the formation of the First Baptist Church in Boston. The evil tree of discord thus for once bore good fruit, in multiplying strong evangelical churches throughout all the confines of the city. It seems that one of the members of Mr. Symmes' church — one Thomas Gould — would not bring his infant child for baptism. In fact the boy lived to be ten years old, and still the symbolic water had not been sprinkled on his brow. The father was repeatedly admonished, and at length, in the year 1665, with others, was excommunicated, and they then formed the First Baptist Church in Boston. This unhappy, yet happy event, marks the contrast between the seventeenth and the twentieth centuries.

Mr. Symmes' salary during most of his ministerial life was ninety pounds sterling a year, a very good stipend for those days, for only one other minister, the eminent John Cotton of

Boston, had as much. Moreover the town of Charlestown was generous to this long-time and greatly honored pastor, and gave him a tract of three hundred acres of land now in the thriving town of Winchester " extending from the north end of Mystic Pond to the borders of Woburn." At another time it gave him three hundred acres more in the " Land of Nod," now within the borders of Wilmington. The latter gift received the name of the region to which Cain banished himself, because it was such a forlorn district and so far from any church, and as Mr. Symmes' twelfth part of the Land of Nod was valued when he died at only five pounds, the region probably deserved its name. A small portion of these original grants has remained in different branches of the Symmes family to the present day, and, when a boy, a number of these acres in so-called " Turkey Swamp " in Winchester, which belonged to me, were sold for a few hundred dollars which went toward my college education.

I have dwelt at some length on the life of old Zechariah, because of his unique personality, and because his life touched so many of the most interesting events in the early history of Massachusetts.

The Reverend Zechariah ended his useful and strenuous career February 4, 1670, having been pastor of the church in Charlestown for more than thirty-five years, and to the very end of his days. So much honored was he that he was buried at the expense of the town, and on his tombstone they engraved his eulogy, two lines of which run as follows:

> " A prophet lies beneath this stone,
>   His words shall live though he be gone."

He left behind him, besides a good name and a modest fortune, a devoted and noble wife and ten children, three others having died before their father. From this good man I am descended in the eighth generation, having for my forbears his son William, and his son William, then three Johns in succession, while my father broke the hundred-year line of Johns by being named Charles.

The militant spirit of Zechariah seems to have descended to many of his descendants, for not a few of them fought in the Revolutionary War. The second John in the series of my ancestors was Captain John Symmes of the Revolutionary army. He was one of the Medford Company, commanded by Captain Isaac Hall, which marched to Charlestown on the memorable seventeenth of June, 1775, but reached Bunker Hill just too late to take part in that fight. He made up for it, however, by enlisting for three years, and was doubtless engaged in many battles, though the particulars of his military career have not been preserved. At the close of the three years he came home, " ragged and emaciated," we are told. He was paid in the depreciated currency of the day, all of which he gave for a yoke of oxen. The oxen he sold and took his pay in the same currency, which he kept for a short time, while it constantly depreciated, and then paid it all for a bag of Indian meal, so that the net financial results of his three years in the Revolutionary War seems to have been one bag of corn meal.

Mahomet Ali, an old man who had served many years in the Turkish army, once told me that he received no pay at all, but when he was discharged was given a ragged red Turkish fez, — the only soldier of whom I know who fared worse financially than my ancestor, John the second.

Another descendant of Zechariah Symmes, though not in my direct line, married General William Henry Harrison, the eighth president of the United States. That his wife, Anna Symmes, had a strong religious influence over old " Tippecanoe " is indicated by the well-authenticated fact that during the presidential canvass of 1840 a company of politicians from Cincinnati visited the candidate at North Bend. " General Harrison met them at some place near by, and, extending his hand courteously, said, ' Gentlemen, I should be most happy to welcome you on any other day, but if I had no regard for religion myself, I have too much respect for the religion of my wife to encourage the violation of the Christian Sabbath.' "

So far as I know there have been no scalawags among the descendants of Zechariah Symmes, though had there been, possibly their misdeeds would not have been recorded in the family memorial. There was, however, one harmless but somewhat distinguished crank, who created a very considerable sensation in his day with his theory of " Concentric Spheres

THE PRESENT SYMMES HOMESTEAD IN WINCHESTER, MASS.
Built by Deacon John Symmes in 1806.

and Polar Voids." This was Captain John Cleves Symmes, who fought in the war of 1812 and received from his superior officer " honorable mention " for his bravery at the Siege of Fort Erie. After the war he had time to turn his attention to the interior of the earth, and he came to the conclusion that " the earth was hollow, habitable within, and widely open about the Poles." An elaborate book was written to prove this theory, and he did his best to induce Congress to fit out an expedition to explore these concave regions, and visit the inside of the earth. A hard-hearted Congress, however, would not make the appropriation, and he died a brokenhearted man with his fantastic theories still the ruling passion of his life.

In visiting the second President Harrison, a very distant cousin, at his home in Indianapolis we had a hearty laugh over the vagaries of our common relative.

Of the Clark branch of my family tree I do not know as much as of the Symmes branch, but I have no less reason to be proud of its honorable record so far as I know it.

The first ancestor of that name of whom I have any certain knowledge was Rev. Thomas Clark, who was born in Boston in 1652, the son of Elder Jonas Clark, graduated at Harvard in 1670, and was settled as pastor in Chelmsford, Mass., the same year. He died in 1704. As the Scripture genealogy would put it, Thomas begat Jonas, and Jonas begat Thomas, and that Thomas another Thomas, and that Thomas an Oliver, who was my grandfather. All the descendants of the first Thomas appear to have been sturdy and godly men. My own grandfather, Deacon Oliver Clark, was certainly a man of this type. He lived in the town of Tewksbury, Mass., on a farm lying on the edge of the city of Lowell, and now incorporated within its limits. For nearly half a century he was deacon in a church in Tewksbury, and afterwards in the High Street Church of Lowell. He brought up a family of five daughters and three sons, who lived to honor their father's memory, some of them to extreme old age.

At one time it was said that the old deacon had thirty-three descendants, all of whom were members " in good and regular standing " of the Orthodox Congregational Church, a distinction which meant something in those days of strict examination for church membership.

But I have written enough about my remoter ancestors. It will be a more congenial task to tell of those who were nearer and dear to me.

The fourth child of Deacon Oliver and Nancy Huse Clark, his first wife, was Lydia Fletcher Clark, my own dear mother, to whom I shall devote another chapter.

MY FATHER

MY BIRTHPLACE — PIONEERING IN CANADIAN FORESTS —
THE MIGHTY OTTAWA — AYLMER AND BYTOWN — A
TERRIBLE EPIDEMIC — A WIDOW'S GRIEF.

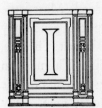 FIRST opened my eyes upon "this goodly frame, the earth," on September 12, 1851, in the little frontier village of Aylmer, Province of Quebec, or Lower Canada, as it was then called. How I happened to be born in the Queen's Dominions, rather than in the old Bay State where my ancestors had lived for more than two centuries, will appear a little later.

At that time Aylmer was very near the confines of civilization. Vast and almost untrodden forests stretched to the north and the west. The town itself was of considerable importance, the seat of a court-house, a jail, and three or four churches, and was the largest village in that vicinity. The city of Ottawa, now one of the most beautiful and flourishing capitals in the world, was then called Bytown, and a lumbering stage-coach every day ploughed through the mud of spring, or the dust of summer, or the driving snows of winter between Aylmer, the metropolis, and Bytown, the suburb. The tables have long since been turned, however, and now Aylmer is the suburb and watering-place of the beautiful capital with which it is connected by a fast trolley line.

My earliest memories are connected with the mighty Ottawa River, on whose banks Aylmer is situated, and the great rafts, sometimes twenty acres in extent, which went floating by day

CHERRY COTTAGE

My birthplace, or else the home to which I was moved when a few weeks old. Built by my father in 1850 or 1851, now to be used as Presbyterian manse

after day in the spring time. On these rafts whole families would live for weeks at a time, as they came slowly down the mighty current, for the Ottawa at Aylmer spreads out into a lake three miles wide. It was this great river, with the vast virgin forests which lined its banks, and extended for hundreds of miles into the interior, that led my father, Charles Carey Symmes, to leave his home in Winchester, Mass., and to seek his fortune in the untamed wilderness. Other enterprising young men of the Symmes family, and still others of the names of Wright and Eddy from Massachusetts, had preceded him.

It was intended at first, doubtless, as a temporary migration for business purposes, and my father was always an American citizen, so that when I came to be of voting age I did not have to be naturalized. My father's business was that of a civil engineer and timber locater, and his duties required him to spend weeks and months at a time in the heart of the wilderness, locating the claims of the owners of these vast forests. His companions were largely French Canadians and Indians, and I have learned that he was a great favorite with his men, friendly, and good-natured, and always ready to help them in an emergency.

The hardships of such a life would be unendurable by men of softer stuff, for it involved long marches, days spent in toil, and nights often with only the blue sky for a tent. The winters in those northern latitudes, when most of his work in the forests had to be done, were appallingly cold, the temperature sometimes marking fifty degrees below zero, so that the mercury in an ordinary thermometer would freeze solid, and could be fired like a bullet out of a gun; — a novel use of quicksilver, once made by my father, as I have been told.

To this frontier home in Aylmer my father took his young bride, Lydia Fletcher Clark, to whom he was married on November 10, 1840. She was the third daughter of the

Deacon Oliver Clark of whom I have before spoken, and in her veins ran some of the blood of the Daniel Webster family. Because of this she was given her middle name of "Fletcher." Daniel Webster's oldest son bore the same name.

Here I may as well stop to explain how my name happens to be Clark while my father's was Symmes. Before I was three years old my father died, and my mother before I was eight. At her request I was adopted by my uncle, her brother, Rev. Edward Warren Clark, for whom I was named, so far as my middle name is concerned. He was perhaps her favorite brother, and when she died, and at her request, I was legally adopted by him. To save complications and mis-understandings, which seemed to me far more important as a boy than they would now, my name was legally changed to Francis Edward Clark by the "Great and General Court of Massachusetts."

Old people in Canada still remember the terrible visitation of cholera which devastated the Province in 1853–1854. My father's business called him to Three Rivers, a large town on the St. Lawrence River, midway between Montreal and Quebec. The dreadful plague was at its height, having been brought from the Old World by the immigrants who were then flocking into the new. Hundreds of them died before they reached their destination. On a St. Lawrence steamer my father travelled with the infected immigrants, many of whom, from time to time, after a brief struggle with this frightful disease yielded to it and were immediately buried. I have heard it said (and, from his general character I believe the story is true) that he attempted to take care of some of these poor creatures and to assuage their sufferings. Just before reaching Three Rivers he himself became a victim to the same disease, and a few hours after being put on shore, so swiftly does the virulent poison work, he died, far away from his wife and children.

His older brother, Henry, however, was able to be with him

in his dying hours, and he is buried in the little Protestant Cemetery of Three Rivers. His comely marble monument, when I first saw it, many years after his death, was shrouded almost to the top in the deep Canadian snow. However cold his tomb, I believe that one of the warmest and noblest hearts beat beneath his breast. He died on August 4, 1854, shortly before my third birthday, and it is not strange that I do not remember him at all. Unfortunately this was before the days of photographs, and even ambrotypes were rare, so that I have never been able to find a picture of my father.

I cannot better close this chapter than by quoting a sentence or two from my mother's journal, written, as she supposed, only for her own eyes. She had reached Three Rivers shortly after his death, but not before his interment had become necessary. Again four years afterwards she made another pilgrimage to his grave and wrote as follows:

" I kissed the dear sod that covered him, and seemed almost to feel his loving arms about me." . . . " Four years ago today my beloved husband died. Oh, the sad, sad day, my beloved Charles, husband of my youth, thy kind and loving heart, that ever throbbed with love to wife and children, stilled on that sad day its beatings! Beloved of my heart, could I but have seen you, could I but have imprinted one kiss on that dear brow, could I have felt the pressure of those dear hands, and heard the last loving farewell! But it was not the will of my heavenly Father, and He doeth all things well; and though it seems dark and mysterious now, I am persuaded that I shall one day see that it was all for the best. Though our heavenly Father afflicts, yet He is a God of love, and oh! my soul, forget not all the blessings with which thy days have been crowned since that dark, sad day. Thou hast had health and strength. Thy children have been blessed with health. They are virtuous, intelligent, and happy. Thou hast been blessed in thy labors, so that thou hast not lacked for food or raiment. Bless the Lord, O my soul, and all that is within me, bless His holy name, who redeemeth thy life from destruction, who crowneth thee with lovingkindness and tender mercies."

CHAPTER III

YEARS 1814–1858

MY MOTHER

HER GIRLHOOD — HER EDUCATION UNDER MARY LYON —
HER CHARACTER — HER WONDERFUL JOURNAL — HER
STRUGGLE FOR SELF-SUPPORT — MY BROTHER CHARLES
— CHARLIE'S DEATH.

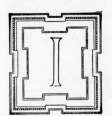I SUPPOSE most men think that their mothers were the best and noblest women who ever lived. I certainly share that opinion with other loyal sons, and believe that my estimate is not based solely upon partiality and affection. The testimony that has come to me from relatives and friends, and above all the testimony of her private journal, which I shall always thank God was preserved for me, tell of a woman unusually gifted in intellect and disposition, while the ambrotype which I have since had enlarged speaks to every one who sees it of a peculiarly sweet, serene, and gentle nature.

For the sake of personal friends and relatives, and for the larger circle of those who would learn how to bear affliction and unusual sorrows with a calm trust and beautiful resignation, I have published some parts of this journal in book form for private distribution, and I cannot perhaps do better than to quote in this chapter some paragraphs from this journal which especially reveal this character, and also from the preface in which I have told something of her life.

I have received, literally, hundreds of testimonies from those who have read this little volume, telling of the comfort

THE OLD CLARK HOMESTEAD IN TEWKSBURY, MASS.

Where my Mother and Adopted Father were born.

it has given them, of the new sense of the Father's presence in the midst of their own afflictions, and of the new revelation it has been to them of how a Christian may live and die.

Of course her journal was not written for publication,— far from it, — my mother probably never thought that even her own children would read it, for otherwise she could not have poured out her heart so frankly and ingenuously. She seems to be simply talking with herself and her God as she writes.

But after these nearly seventy years I am betraying no heart secrets in quoting some of it, and if it can help others to a higher Christian life, she herself would have me use it in this way. But first a few words about her life.

Lydia Fletcher Clark was born September 30, 1814, and was noted even in her girlhood for a peculiar faculty of endearing herself to family and friends. Brought up in the old New England *régime*, her father a Puritan deacon of the old school, a *régime* sometimes thought to have been stern and narrow, herself one of the older sisters in a large family of children, she added to sweetness, strength, and to gentleness, nobility of character, and to winsomeness, womanliness, and to innocent purity, unselfish love to God and man.

Even in these early days Lydia Clark was noted, not only for her gentleness and strength, but for a certain poetic gift to which her journal testifies, which led her partial brothers and sisters to call her "Mrs. Sigourney the Second." Mrs. Sigourney was then the fashion, and was considered a much greater poetess than future times have been willing to admit, so that then the compliment was a more thorough-going one than it seems after the lapse of three-score years.

Another formative influence of value in her life was her school life under the celebrated Mary Lyon, the foremost woman whom America has produced, in the old Academy at Ipswich, Mass., before Mount Holyoke Seminary was founded. I long preserved a diary, bound in an old bit of newspaper, written in my mother's school-girl hand, recording the words of Mary Lyon at chapel exercises. This diary I afterwards gave to Mount Holyoke College.

At about the age of twenty-five she married, as already related, the man of her choice, Charles Carey Symmes, and her life poem grew in depth and beauty and heart melody. It was, apparently, a perfect union of hearts. No harsh word, no unkind act, ever marred it, as she herself has declared, and it lasted, in all the intensity of its love and devotion, far beyond the grave.

I have already related how my father took his bride to the village in the wilderness on the banks of the Ottawa. Here their children were born. Charles Henry, Edward Carey, Katherine Noel, Francis Edward. Edward and Katherine died in infancy, but the eldest and youngest lived to grow up, the eldest a remarkable boy whose story of joyous life and triumphant death is told in the latter part of my mother's journal. The happy years flew by, — happy in spite of the two little mounds in the Aylmer churchyard: happy in spite of the fact that the loved husband was away from home much of the time, in the wilderness among the savage beasts and savage men, hewing a way for civilization.

The beautiful wife and mother interested herself in the affairs of the little town, took an active part in church life and the primitive society of the place, and left her impress, the impress of a sweet, womanly, Christlike nature, upon all whom she touched.

She spent one winter in Berthier, another frontier town of Quebec, and here, true to her instincts, at once began to make her little world brighter and better. Her light could not be hid; it shone as brightly in the wilderness as in the city. Full forty years after she left Berthier an old woman came to me one day with a worn, battered, old-fashioned Sunday-school book in her hand, saying, " Your mother formed the first Sunday school in Berthier. She collected a library for us, and we have cherished those books ever since because they came from her." She was only a few months in this little log-house metropolis, but the impress of her life is felt to-day.

Winters and summers sped away, bringing their alternate varied sunshine and cloud. There were many partings in the little cottage at Aylmer, as the loved and loving husband frequently set out for "the bush" on his long surveying and lumber-locating expeditions, but then there were just as many home-comings and happy reunions, when, for a few days or weeks, all too brief, the family at Cherry Cottage (for this was the name of the little house my father had built) was reunited again.

Just as many home-comings? Alas! there was one less, for once in the summer of 1854, the husband kissed his wife and left their home for the last time. It was the fatal cholera year. Old inhabitants still recall it with a shudder. The dread disease, imported from Europe with the immigrants as I have related, secured a dreadful and sudden grip upon the New World.

I have already given some details of my father's death, and of my mother's hurried journey to Three Rivers only to find her beloved one buried from her sight. She soon returned to the lonely home in Aylmer and to her two fatherless boys. But now we see the noblest part of a noble life, the four years and a half of struggle for independence that ensued. She had not come from sturdy New England stock for nothing. The blood of the Puritans, who loved independence, personal, financial, religious, and political, flowed in her veins. She had not gone to Mary Lyon's school in vain.

Necessity was laid upon her, and in meeting this necessity in the spirit of cheerful courage and abounding love to God and his children she found her great opportunity. She opened a private school. Pupils flocked to Cherry Cottage. They could not pay much, and she did not ask much; but enough to keep body and soul together, to pay her modest bills, to keep her children with her, and to provide something for the education of the older one. A few boarding pupils added to her slender income.

Cherry Cottage became the centre of mirth and youthful good spirits, — good spirits which were never unduly repressed by the gentle mistress, — as well as the centre of studious habits and noble character building. A second Mt. Holyoke was started in the wilds of Canada — on a very small scale, it is true, and with a very modest prospectus and

My Mother

curriculum, but a second Mt. Holyoke, because a spirit kindred to, and the peer of Mary Lyon, presided there.

More than three years passed away. Of the last two the journal tells in simple, eloquent, and pathetic words. One more great billow was to pass over this patient soul. Her son Charles grew up to be a manly, strong, wholesome, fun-loving, but gentle boy, the kind of boy that ripens into a true gentleman. Far and away the best scholar in his class at school, he was a boy who was not ashamed to help his mother in the kitchen and the garden. An earnest, active Christian and communicant of the same Presbyterian church with her,

mother and son walked hand in hand. At first he leaned the
more heavily upon her; but, as he grew toward manhood, the
weight began to shift, and she found herself leaning upon the
strong, filial arm of Charles the son, as she had before leaned
upon the arm of Charles the father.

He never disappointed her, but returned love for love and
answered unselfish care with a care as unselfish as the mother's.
Daily he grew to be her pride, her support, her joy. He developed literary tastes and gifts, and a long story of much
merit, but which in his modesty he afterwards burned, was
written by him. His future was full of the largest promise,
as his present was of the largest comfort to all around him.

He was almost seventeen, but care and responsibility
seemed to have added half a dozen years to his age. He was
a full-grown man in ability to share his mother's burdens,
though still a child in his tender love, when, suddenly, after
a few days of illness from typhoid fever, this staff was taken
from the frail woman, and the mother-heart was wrenched
from its last earthly support.

So much has been foolishly written in derision of precocious
young saints that have died in their teens, and of
their death-bed scenes, that I hesitate to print the account from
my mother's journal of the last hours of my brother Charles.
It must be remembered that he was not only an earnest Christian, but one of the most natural and healthy-minded of boys.
There was nothing sickly or morbid in his disposition; his life
was not only natural but even exuberant in its gayety.

"I will write a short account of my dear boy's sickness
and death," writes my mother in her journal, "it may at
some time be gratifying to his little brother if he is spared."

After describing at length the earlier days of his illness,
she continues, "Once as he lay upon his bed, he said,
'Mother, I think this sickness will do me good.' I said,
'Why, my son?' thinking he meant physically. He
answered, 'I have had a great many good thoughts, since
I have been sick. I think I see better what life is for; at

all events, I shall know how to sympathize with those who are sick.' Sometimes he spoke of the time when he should be better able to earn some money for me. Sometimes he would say, 'Perhaps God has sent this illness to teach us to be more grateful for our continued health.' But he always spoke as though he thought his own sufferings very light compared with others. . . .

"Early on Sabbath morning I became calm enough to ask him if he were willing to die if God saw fit. With great emphasis he replied, 'I am willing to go this minute if God wills.' I said, 'But would you not rather stay with mother?' 'Of course, mother, I would rather stay and help you if

MY MOTHER

The older boy is my brother Charles. I am in the centre.

God were willing.' I said no more then, except to ask him if he were happy, to which he replied, 'Perfectly happy.'

"About six A.M. the doctor came; and the moment he looked at him he said, 'Oh, Charlie, you are going to leave us.' He looked up and said, 'I am perfectly content, doctor. I am very happy.' The doctor wept like a child; and as he stooped to kiss the dear boy, Charlie said, 'Good-by, doctor, I am very happy.' Turning to me he said, 'We shall meet in heaven, mother. I shall see dear papa before you do.' Then again, 'God will be with you, mother.' To his little brother whose heart seemed breaking, he said, 'Frank must be a good boy; he must be a Christian. Oh, it is a glorious thing to be a Christian.'

"Many of his young companions had assembled in the room and were weeping around the bed. They came up one by one, and he kissed them and bade them good-by as calmly and composedly as if he had been going a short journey.

"When he had bid them all good-by I said, 'Will you bid me good-by now?' 'Oh, no, mother,' he said, 'I will bid you good-by a good many times yet.' He asked me what day it was. I said the Sabbath. 'Blessed Sabbath!' he exclaimed, 'Is it not a glorious death? Are you not satisfied, mother; are you not satisfied?' I asked him once, 'Are you afraid to die, my son?' 'Oh, no,' he replied with emphasis; then as if fearing I might think him self-confident, he added, 'I know that I have done a thousand things that were wrong, but I am sure God will forgive me'; then hesitating as if for breath, I added, 'through the merits of Jesus Christ.' 'Amen,' he responded, in a clear full tone. At another time, he said, 'Don't be at much expense about the funeral, mother, it will not help me any.' At another time he said, 'I couldn't write your epitaph, mother.' The last words I could catch from his dying lips were, 'Almost home.' Thus died my beloved son before he had completed his seventeenth year, ripe for heaven. O my son, my blessed, blessed son!"

Perhaps I may be permitted to call attention to some striking mental and spiritual traits which my mother's journal reveals, and which have been a source of inspiration and courage to many who have read it.

Her gratitude and thanksgiving for small mercies, as she recorded them for her own eye only, impress me most profoundly, and rebuke my own ungrateful life. Many a woman in her circumstances would have thought she had very little cause for gratitude. A widow thrown in early life upon her own resources; a family to support by the hard, grinding life of a schoolmistress; far from her childhood's home and hundreds of miles from most of her relatives and early friends, in a remote though not inhospitable frontier village; — what had she to be peculiarly grateful for?

Yet almost every entry is a psalm of thanksgiving. In the

smallest occurrence she found evidence of God's peculiar goodness.

The ability to lay in a winter's supply of wood, the payment of a just debt by one of her scholars, the kindness of a blacksmith who mended some kitchen utensils for her, the thoughtfulness of a neighbor in putting a load of tanbark under a loose foundation to keep out the cold, the faithfulness of the kitchen-maid, a kind note, a pleasant call, — all fill her heart with gladness and her lips with praise, and cause her to cry out, " Bless the Lord, O my soul! "

Let me transcribe a few lines:

> " February 7, 1857: I see much, very much, to be thankful for. Almost every one has paid his bills, and I have been able to pay all I owe, and have a little left. . . . I received a kind note from Mrs. Symmes and a pleasant call from Mr. Thompson."

How few would think such trivialities worth a grateful thought! Fewer still would think them worth recording as special mercies.

> " February 18 — . — To-day I was better, and this evening feel quite well. How much I have to be grateful for in my continued health! "
>
> " March 23. — To-day I paid for thirty cords of wood for next year's use. How thankful should I be that I have the means for my family when many a poor widow sees her children suffer with cold and hunger! To-day I received a letter from Mrs. S. with seven pounds for her daughter's board and tuition. Oh, for a grateful heart! "

Most people would think the collection of a just bill that barely enabled her to live, hardly cause for a sigh of gratitude.

> " November 13. — How much have I to be grateful for that I am surrounded by temporal blessings at this season of the year! Let me enumerate some of them. I have a good comfortable house, an abundance of good, dry wood; I have

on hand provisions sufficient or nearly so for three months, and my own health and that of my children is very good. Bless the Lord, O my soul, and all that is within me, bless His holy name."

"October. — I have taken a new bedroom over the kitchen, which is very warm and comfortable. . . . Truly the Lord is good and will not suffer the soul of those who trust in Him to want."

Could anything show more plainly the possession of the " merry heart " that doeth good like a medicine?

All things earthly, too, seemed to remind her of their heavenly prototypes. Spring comes with its budding flowers and reminds her of " What heaven must be, where no thorns and briers intrude among the flowers and fruits that bloom in the Paradise of God? "

The mild radiance of a summer night calls her thought beyond the stars, and, as she thinks of the loved one gone before, she cries out, " Oh, what exquisite scenery may he not now behold! My husband, my husband, when shall I join you? "

But why need I quote more when every page, almost every line, breathes an other-worldliness, a heavenly peace, a joy in God, a sense of His presence and of the absolute reality of eternal things? Thank God for such a mother!

Chapter IV
Years 1856–1869

MY BOYHOOD

EARLIEST MEMORIES — MY MOTHER'S DEATH — GOOD-BY TO
AYLMER — BEAUTIFUL AUBURNDALE — MEMORIES OF
THE CIVIL WAR — CLAREMONT — ACADEMY DAYS.

OME of my friends surprise me by telling
me that their early memories go back to the
time when they were only three years old,
or to two and a half years, and they relate
marvellous tales or traditions of being able to
read the Bible before their fifth birthday.
But not being a precocious boy, I have no such marvels to
relate. Indeed my first distinct memory is connected with my
fifth birthday, when, in honor of the event, my mother and
brother, and some young ladies from my mother's school, took
me out in a boat on the big Ottawa River, for an afternoon's
excursion. I probably should not remember this were it not
for the fact that the boat ran upon a submerged rock or a
shoal and was hung up for a little while, a circumstance which
frightened me very much, although there was really no
danger.

Indeed, the memories of all my days in Aylmer look dim
and hazy through the mists of more than sixty years. But
they are all, with the exception perhaps of the little episode
on the Ottawa River, and the death of my dear brother and
mother, exceedingly pleasant ones. I remember no hard word
or unkind speech or act in the little circle of Cherry Cottage.

The boy Francis

Francis at the age of Six

Francis at the age of Nine

The Lad at the age of Twelve

A Freshman at Dartmouth in 1869

A dignified College Senior 1873

Dr Clark as a Pastor 1889

Dr Clark Today

Dr Clark in 1895

Dr Clark in 1908

Always the atmosphere was cheerful, and usually merry. My mother kept her sorrows and heartaches for her private journal and hid them behind its covers. I remember no gloom or suspicion of melancholy in the little circle.

My brother, from all that I remember and all that I am told, was of an unusually frank and sunny disposition, a great favorite with the young ladies of the school, who contributed their full share to the joys of the household. Happy evenings with reading and music and cheerful games were the rule and not the exception, and the days were filled with wholesome work and study for all. Sundays were days of rest and worship, but by no means the gloomiest days of the week. In fact I believe they were the brightest and happiest of all, for then my mother had more leisure for her family.

Though church and Sunday school always engaged her attention, yet there was an hour left for a quiet walk in good weather. All of my boyhood was spent in two Puritan families, which to-day, in some circles, would be considered very strict; yet I have not the slightest recollection of a gloomy Sunday, or of any unhappy constraint in connection with the day. My mother and brother were members of the Presbyterian church, in which I, too, was dedicated to God's service, and I had a few years ago the great honor and pleasure of placing a modest stained-glass window in this church in loving memory of them and of my father. The church was recently burned in a great fire that swept Aylmer, as I shall relate in another chapter.

One early memory of church-going reminds me how cold were those Canadian winters, where the mercury, even in the towns, sometimes sank to forty degrees below zero, and more. Though our home was not more than five minutes walk from the church, I reached it one Sunday morning after church, with a frozen nose, to which a liberal application of snow soon brought a tingling circulation again. Another trivial early memory, which naturally left its impress.

In the later months of 1858 sad days came to Cherry Cottage. Then came the sickness and death of the talented and courageous boy who had become his mother's staff and stay, as I have already related. From this shock and sorrow my mother never recovered, and in six months she followed him. She made many more entries in her journal, it is true, almost every one of which breathes the trust and hope, the gentle resignation and thanksgiving for little mercies that always characterized her. Indeed, they grew more and more deeply spiritual as little by little her bodily strength failed. The following are the last records that I find in her journal:

"February 12. Sabbath evening. Another blessed Sabbath has gone. I have not been very well, but I went to the Sabbath school, but not to church. I hope I shall feel better to-morrow and have more energy.

"February 15. Our good, kind doctor called to-day. It does me good to see him, he is so kind and sympathizing. I think I feel a little better to-day; the weather has been glorious. I sat this eve and watched the calm and glorious sunset, and thought of my beloved boy in those mansions above, which our blessed Saviour has prepared for those who love Him."

Here the beautiful record of the beautiful life ends. She gradually grew worse; could not even persuade herself that she felt " a little better "; until on March 26, 1859, the gentle spirit took its flight beyond the " glorious sunset " to the dear husband and the " beloved boy," and to " those mansions above which our blessed Saviour has prepared for those who love Him."

I remember the last kisses and blessings which she showered on my little head, and then the labored, stertorous breathing, the silent room that followed, with the blinds closed and the shades drawn, the funeral procession to the little cemetery half way between Aylmer and Ottawa, where she lies beside her eldest son and the little children who were taken from life so early; the return to Cherry Cottage; the sympathy of kind neighbors and friends, of aunts and cousins, a number of whom lived in the vicinity, and the heart-breaking grief of a boy who now, though but little more then seven years old, had lost father and mother, two brothers and a sister, and was the only one left of the cheery Cherry Cottage family. I can hardly realize, as I write this, that I am already nearly thirty years older than the oldest one of my family circle when she died.

My Adopted Father, Rev. Edward W. Clark

Very soon after my mother's death, my uncle, Rev. Edward Warren Clark, of Auburndale, Mass., came to Aylmer to take me to his home. He was the favorite younger brother whom my mother had asked to take care of me in case anything should happen to her, a commission and a charge which he seems to have undertaken gladly, as he had no children of his own.

My last days in Aylmer I remember with considerable distinctness; the leave-taking and the "good-by" to cousins and kindly neighbors and sympathetic friends. But my most vivid memory is of leaving Cherry Cottage, and giving a farewell kiss, not only to its inhabitants, but to different portions of the house and gardens, which were particularly dear to me. As I could not kiss all the stones in the rocky yard, I remember bestowing a salute upon one little stone and throwing it at the others, as a farewell token; and as the trees were too numerous for such osculatory demonstrations, one cherry tree received the embrace for all the rest.

But in a child's mind new scenes soon chase away old impressions if not old memories, and the journey to "the States," where I had been only once before, and that as a very little shaver, was a perfect kaleidoscope of new impressions. From Aylmer to Ottawa, — then just beginning to assume dignities which awaited it as the capital of a great Dominion, — from Ottawa to Rouse's Point we went, and from Rouse's Point to Ogdensburg. There we spent the night, and I was almost frightened out of the little growth I had already achieved by finding myself alone as I awoke in the middle of the night, my uncle having gone out to see a fire which was exciting the neighborhood. Thinking that I was being deserted by everyone, I was captured in a distant corridor of the hotel by a kind-hearted chambermaid, who found me crying as though I had lost my last friend, as indeed I thought I had. But the fire was soon extinguished and with it my fears and anxieties on the return of my uncle, whose kindness and gentle consideration for the little orphan I shall never forget.

Auburndale, which we reached the next day, was not the populous and beautiful village that it now is; nevertheless it was a lovely quiet suburb with maple-shaded streets, and many comfortable mid-Victorian homes of the pioneer commuters of Boston. My uncle was the first pastor of the newly-formed Congregational Church of the village.

I cannot imagine a more ideal spot for a boy to grow up in. One of the old inhabitants used frequently to quote Goldsmith's lines, beginning,

"Sweet Auburn, loveliest village of the plain,"

and apply them to the new Auburn — dale. A good school, good neighbors, with a sufficient quota of boys and girls in their families to provide chums for the newcomer; the

MY ADOPTED MOTHER
A descendant of John Cotton and granddaughter of
General Artemas Ward.

Charles River to fish in, where the capture of a pickerel afforded joy and glory enough to last a week; the big city of Boston only a half hour away, where I was soon allowed to go on errands without any chaperon, — all these afforded a variety of joys sufficient to satisfy any normal boy.

My aunt, who received me with a welcome as warm and loving as my uncle had given me, was an unusual woman in many respects, a descendant like myself of the Puritans of

Boston, with the blood of John Cotton, Cotton Mather, and General Artemas Ward of the Revolutionary army, flowing in her veins. She was, perhaps, too insistent in earlier years that all around her should come up to her own high Puritan standard, but as the years went on she ripened and mellowed in a marvellously beautiful way, until when she died in my own home in Auburndale, nearly fifty years later, the most appropriate words which the officiating minister could find to base his funeral remarks upon were: "Let the *beauty* of the Lord our God be upon us," for in face and character all felt that the *beauty* of the Lord her God had long rested upon *her*.

My uncle's health failed in early life. Indeed before going to Auburndale he had been obliged to give up the ministry for two years after his first short pastorate in Reading, Mass., but in many ways he was of more than average ability. While in Auburndale he was elected chaplain of the Massachusetts Senate, and re-elected the next year, an unusual honor in those days, since previously the chaplain's term had been but for a single session. This honor carried with it his election as Overseer of Harvard College, but both the chaplaincy and the overseership he laid down at his country's call, when, in 1863, he was asked to become chaplain of the Massachusetts Forty-seventh Regiment of Volunteers. This was a nine months' regiment, and his service in the army was consequently brief, but sufficiently long greatly to injure his health, and he reached home after the regiment was mustered out, more dead than alive, and in the grip of the malarial fever then so prevalent in New Orleans where his regiment had been stationed. He was greatly beloved by the soldiers, and though in failing health, ministered to them physically as well as spiritually to the last.

Under these circumstances the events of the Civil War naturally made a deep impression upon my childish mind. Indeed I remember begging earnestly to be allowed to go with him, pleading that I could at least black his boots and perform such services, if they would not let me be a drummer boy.

I remember hearing the sad, indignant tolling of the bells when John Brown was hung. When Lincoln was shot I grieved as for my own father, going up into a little loft all by myself and bursting into bitter tears. It shows what a hold the great President had on the hearts of the people that even a fourteen-year-old boy (a rather tearless age) should cry.

When before this the news came of the surrender of Vicksburg and the Battle of Port Hudson, and these newspaper reports were supplemented by letters from " the Chaplain," it can be imagined how real and vivid were the scenes of those awful years of the Civil War.

What favorites the war songs were with the boys and girls of those days! " Tramp, tramp, tramp, the boys are marching," " Tenting to-night on the old camp ground," " We're coming, Father Abraham, three hundred thousand strong," " When Johnny comes marching home," " They've grafted him into the army," and even that somewhat lugubrious ditty, " Just before the battle, mother," all fired our enthusiasm and patriotic zeal. We even roared out at the top of our little voices, " We'll hang Jeff Davis to a sour apple tree." I am glad that this " hymn of hate " was the worst that we were allowed to sing, and I wish we had not sung that. As in these later years I visit the South, where many of my dearest friends sided with the " Lost Cause," I wonder at those days of bitterness and rancor, and rejoice that they are so buried in the kindly oblivion of the past that to-day the memory of those old songs excites only a smile.

A few months after being mustered out my adopted father had sufficiently recovered his health to enable him to take another pastorate, this time at Claremont, N. H., one of the most thriving and beautiful towns of the old Granite State.

Claremont will always be to me a name of happy memories,

not only because of the generous and comfortable home and kindly people, but because of the more spacious country attractions of lake and river and field and forest. My adopted father was a genuine lover of nature, versed in bird-lore and tree-lore, a good shot, and a lover of tramps and out-door expeditions. All these qualities he found it easy to transmit to me, as we often sallied out together with rod and gun. There were few ponds within a radius of twenty miles that we did not visit, with the aid of " Billy," the parsonage horse, and no imaginable joy seemed to me greater than these excursions.

The love of out-door life has remained with me to the present day, though the gun has been discarded of late years for the camera and the opera glass, for most of us grow more tender-hearted as we grow older.

Another thing for which I have reason to be especially grateful to my foster father is the care he took to insure my progress in reading and English composition. The best books were always at my disposal, and the worst were kept out of my way. A limited amount of novel reading was allowed, and of Dickens, who was my favorite author, I was permitted to indulge in only one chapter, or at most two, in the course of a day.

In still earlier years, next to " The Swiss Family Robinson," Grimm's " Household Tales " were my especial joy, and I became thoroughly intimate with " Rumpelstiltskin," and the little tailor (was it?) who killed seven flies and then went around with the legend on his hat band, " Seven at one blow."

When, many years later I was attending a German National Christian Endeavor convention in Cassel, I took great pains, in memory of those early loves, to hunt up the abode of the Brothers Grimm, where these wonderful tales were written. The quaint old house is marked with a tablet, and well deserves to be. Remembering my own boyhood, I felt kinship with the little girl who once brought ten pfennigs to the

Brothers Grimm, saying, " You said in your last story that if anyone did not believe that the tailor married the princess he must pay you a mark. Now I do not believe that a tailor ever, ever married a princess, but I haven't got a mark, so I have brought you ten pfennigs, and will bring you the rest when I get it." Surely no better tribute to the realism of a fairy story was ever paid than this.

As I have intimated, my adopted father took special pains, not only with my reading, but with my writing also, and encouraged me to launch out in venturesome ways on the troubled sea of literature. Though he himself never wrote much for publication he had a fine taste for good writing and a restrained literary style. One result of this encouragement was my ambitious attempt at a novel when I was about twelve, in the style of " Pickwick Papers," then my *beau ideal* of literature. I do not think it ever got beyond the second chapter, where the hero made his *début* among the Patagonians. Whether he was slain and eaten alive, or got back with a whole skin to his native land, I do not remember, and very likely the plot did not develop to this extent.

A more successful effort that I remember was a long letter of several pages to my father, urging him to allow me to camp out with some other boys on the banks of " Cold Pond," a dozen or so miles away. So skilfully did I array the arguments in favor of the expedition and bring up the objections which I knew were sure to be raised, only to knock them down like other men of straw, that my letter proved successful in securing the coveted excursion, while it so pleased my father that he preserved it among his family memorabilia to his dying day, more than forty years later.

I must not forget Mount Ascutney, glorious old Ascutney! which though on the Vermont side of the Connecticut, shows off to best advantage from Claremont on the New Hampshire side. Once a year, and sometimes twice we climbed to its top and spent the night in the little stone hut that crowned its topmost peak. What excursions those were! Though only a dozen miles from Claremont, to climb Ascutney seemed a rarer privilege than it would be to cross the ocean and stand on the peak of Fujiyama to-day. Never was there such a delicious ice-cold spring as that which you will find half way up the mountain on the left-hand side of the path; never was there such a magnificent view over the New Hampshire hills and the Vermont valleys, which lay stretched at our feet. If you do not believe it, dear reader, climb Ascutney for yourself, but you must do it with a boy's eager heart, and fresh impressionable imagination.

The spiritual surroundings of the Claremont parsonage were as helpful as the intellectual and material. Family prayers night and morning, portions of the Bible to be studied and learned, were part of my daily life, and I do not remember that these seemed monotonous or unwelcome tasks. Ruskin has told us that the 119th Psalm, the longest in the whole book, was the severest task in memorizing that his mother ever demanded of him, but that he received more help from that Psalm than from any other chapter of the Bible, though he committed to memory many other difficult passages. I was not required to learn that Psalm, or any chapters in Second Chronicles, as was Ruskin, but I only wish now that I had made better use of my opportunities and learned many more.

Every Sunday evening at the hour of family prayer I was expected to report both morning and afternoon sermons. I was naturally ambitious to give the longest and most accurate report possible, taking notes in church for that purpose. It was a splendid exercise for the memory and for powers of expression, and for the intellect and heart as well. I commend it to modern parents.

As a result of these wholesome religious influences, and moved, as I trust, by the Spirit of God, when thirteen years of age, I stood up, trembling and abashed, in the little prayer-meeting room of the Claremont church, and confessed my desire to be counted among the followers of Christ. No evangelist or season of religious excitement had brought me to a decision, but religious training and conviction.

While I believe heartily in revivals, and in many revivalists, and in special periods of religious awakening, I also believe that there is a place for the Timothy type of conversion as well as for the Pauline, and that Mother Eunice and Grandmother Lois may be as much used of God in bringing their children to Christ, as the most fiery and eloquent evangelist. The dingy little chapel of the Claremont church, now greatly altered and beautified, will always be a place of sacred memories to me.

My school days at Claremont were mostly passed in a so-called academy, for it was before the days of high schools. This academy was of moderate pretensions, but some of the teachers were of marked personality, especially the principal, a Miss Chamberlin. After all, the personality of a teacher is worth far more than buildings of brick and mortar, school, books and blackboards, and all the paraphernalia of modern education. Miss Chamberlin's academy was a smaller copy of the oft-quoted college with " Mark Hopkins at one end of the log and pupils on the other."

When little more than sixteen years of age my real academy days were begun, and one cold December day I drove with my adopted father to the hill town of Meriden, N. H., to be entered as a " middler " in famous old Kimball Union Academy, which was then one of the three largest and most important fitting schools in New England, with between three and four hundred students enrolled upon its catalogue. Meriden would not perhaps be considered the most attractive place in the world by a city boy, for it was and is remote from the railroad, with a lumbering stage-coach (now an automobile) connecting it with the outer world, and with only one new dwelling house built since the early days of the Civil War up to this time.

Nevertheless it had and has attractions all its own: — splendid scenery among the New Hampshire hills, green in summer and snow-clad in winter; Grantham Mountain and the Croydon Hills, Mount Ascutney, and the White Hills not far away; magnificent coasting in winter (for it is a village set upon a hill, a high and steep one at that), and glorious air and sunshine all the year round.

Here too, the teachers, if not all peculiarly eminent for their scholarships, were men and women who knew how to impress themselves upon their students and bring out the best that was in them. Dr. Cyrus Richards, the long-time principal of the school, was a Greek and Latin scholar of note throughout the country, who, if stiff and prim, and a martinet in some of his rules and regulations, was still one who commanded the respect of his students, and the impress that he left on their minds was always one of manliness and righteousness.

Rule twenty, which kept the boys and girls from speaking to each other, walking together, or if possible, from even casting sheep's eyes across the road, except on one or two red-letter days in the course of the year, would seem absurd enough in these days, but it at least fostered a respect if not reverence for the opposite sex, and never bred the contempt which the familiarity of the present day often engenders.

If Kimball Union Academy were not a place for high thinking on the part of all the students, it was certainly a place for plain living; for corn mush and milk, baked beans and oatmeal, meat two or three times a week, and " flap-jacks " that on certain memorable days appeared on the table, were the staples of our bill of fare.

At a recent Alumni reunion of the school, the old boys and girls, in " reminiscing," told how the board bills in the late sixties, when we were specially extravagant, mounted up to $1.37 a week, while one white-haired old gentleman who had been a student in the early sixties, declared that at his club (for all students boarded in clubs with a commissary of their own choosing), the board bill amounted to eighty cents a week for a whole term. He remarked, parenthetically, however, that the landlady's pig was very lean that year, there being no scraps left over for it.

Let no one think however, that we considered ourselves abused or half starved. We were healthy, hearty, and rugged, without a suspicion that we were not faring sumptuously every day, and we never imagined that we could be objects of pity on the part of ourselves or anybody else.

At the end of less than two years, I was graduated with some small honors and, with twenty-five of my classmates, took the easy examinations which Dartmouth then imposed upon its *Pœnes;* the " Meriden delegation " furnishing more than a quarter part of the Dartmouth class of '73.

The old school on Meriden Hill is comparatively flourishing once more after a long period of depression, when it became almost extinct, and I am glad to give some little time each year to its interests, as chairman of the board of trustees, though others on the board give far more both of time and money, especially my classmate and intimate friend, Alfred Hall, Esq., of Boston.

Meriden, in another way, is now being put upon the map, having become, through the efforts of Mr. Harold Baynes, the most famous bird town in America, with its " Bird Sanctuary " and " Bird Plays," in which the daughters of President Wilson, when their summer home was in Cornish, half a dozen miles away, thought it worth while to take part.

When a boy enters college, in his own estimation at least he leaves boyhood days behind, so I will close this boyhood chapter with my memory of that twelve-mile ride from Kimball Union to Dartmouth for matriculation in the class of '73, whose fiftieth anniversary is close at hand.

CHAPTER V

YEARS 1869–1873

DARTMOUTH DAYS

DARTMOUTH CENTENNIAL COMMENCEMENT — CHIEF JUS-
TICE CHASE AND GENERAL TECUMSEH SHERMAN — OUR
PRESIDENT AND PROFESSORS — PRIMITIVE DAYS AT DART-
MOUTH — FRATERNITY LIFE — LITERARY EFFORTS —
FOOTBALL IN THE OLD DAYS — TEACHING SCHOOL
WINTERS.

 WAS fortunate in entering Dartmouth Col-
lege at the beginning of the second century
of that noble old New Hampshire institution,
and the commencement of 1869, which I attended as a newly fledged *Pœne*, was the
most impressive perhaps which Dartmouth
had ever known. That was in the days of the old-fashioned
college commencements, which resembled a country fair quite
as much as the graduation days of an institution of learning.

The sideshow man was in full evidence; the man with the
educated moose was there; the pop-corn man and the vender
of pink lemonade were prominent on the campus; and if the
Wild Man of Borneo, the Fat Woman and the Human
Skeleton had been in that vicinity they would certainly have
put in an appearance. Country people flocked from all the
region round about, and many found greater entertainment
in the booths on the campus than in the two dozen stilted commencement orations of the young graduates in the college
church, and I for one do not blame them.

But there were other and more exalted entertainments on this occasion than either the campus or the college church afforded, for the Chief Justice of the United States, Salmon P. Chase, Dartmouth's most distinguished alumnus then living, presided at the alumni gathering in a great tent pitched on the campus, which was also graced by the presence of General William Tecumseh Sherman, then comparatively fresh from the glories of the battlefield, and acclaimed as the second greatest general of the Union army.

Of course Daniel Webster and Rufus Choate were eulogized, as they have been at scores of commencements since their graduation. On this occasion the glorious things which were spoken of Dartmouth and her distinguished graduates were cut short by a tremendous shower of rain, which caused the Chief Justice of the United States, the Lieutenant-General of her army, and as many others as could possibly do so, to take refuge under the speakers' platform from the deluge that poured through the dry canvas.

Alas, their last estate was worse than the first, for there were wide cracks in the platform, through which the rain poured upon their devoted heads, not in drops but in rivulets. If I remember rightly the shower soon abated and the exercises proceeded to the end without curtailment, in spite of the damp and dripping condition of some of the principal speakers. Owing to the somewhat meagre preparations for the appetites of a crowd which was larger than was expected, and with reference to the principal articles on the menu of the alumni dinner, the punsters declared that it was " merely a salmon, pea, chase."

My real college life of course did not begin until the next September. Though some might dispute my views on this point, I also think that I have reason to congratulate myself that I was a college student of the olden times, when Dartmouth was a comparatively small college. She was a college with slender endowment, a very moderate equipment and with few students according to the views of the present day, (when hundreds every year are trying in vain to enter her over-crowded academic shades), but men of great hearts, command-ing personality, lofty ideals and spotless characters graced the presidential and professorial chairs.

Not that such men are not found to-day in Dartmouth and all our colleges, but the personality of the professors has been in a measure, I believe, overshadowed by the excellence of the equipment, while the introduction of some younger professors on the score of specialized and technical scholarship rather than of character, has made the moral and religious tone of many of our colleges far less dominant than in days of old.

I cannot explain exactly what I mean unless I could intro-duce to all my readers the president and professors of that ancient time.   President Asa Dodge Smith was tall, impressive, courteous to the last degree, with a large expanse of shirt bosom, a long coat, and a well brushed silk hat always in evidence. Of course his suavity and his efforts to conciliate and please wherever possible, together with a middle name convenient to their hand, led the boys who had been disciplined, or who for some other reason did not like the president, to call him " The Artful Dodger " (Oliver Twist was then a special Dickens' favorite), but the great majority respected him, and those who knew him intimately loved him. Coming from an important New York pulpit, he brought with him a courteous dignity and grace which Dartmouth needed, but withal one of the warmest hearts that ever beat in a college president's bosom.

I remember that several years before I went to college he was marooned by a New Hampshire blizzard in our Clare-mont home, and that even then he inspired me by his gentle courtesy and personal interest with an unfaltering attention to matriculate some day as a Dartmouth freshman, an inten-tion which he fostered by various letters and remembrances. It was currently reported that no man-child was born in a New

Hampshire home that Dr. Smith did not get his eye on as a prospective Dartmouth student.

His kindness was continued throughout all my college course, and on one occasion at least, he talked with me very seriously about entering the ministry, and, before the interview was ended, dropped upon his knees and prayed that I might be led to give my life to such service. I am glad that his prayer was answered, and that he preached the sermon when I was ordained and installed as pastor of Williston Church, in Portland, Maine. This was one of the very last acts of his life, for he was soon after taken ill, and within a few months went to his great reward.

To think of a president of our great colleges of to-day praying with an individual student that he might be led into the ministry! Well I am afraid, that to some it might savor of the impossible, I hope not of the ludicrous. I am convinced, however, that there would be more graduates from our universities in the ministry to-day if there were more Asa D. Smiths in the presidential chairs, though I admit that Dartmouth has had greater presidents in these later years.

And then the professors! Their personality was scarcely less impressive than that of the president. Professor Edwin D. Sanborn, " Professor Bully " as every one affectionately called him, our teacher of English literature, what a noble character was his! Strong, rugged, tender, with a genuine appreciation and love for the best things of literature, he led his students to love them too.

Professor Parker, at the head of the Latin Department, polished, winning, and courteous, became our highest ideal of what a Christian gentleman should be, while Professor Noyes, nervous and intense, but enthusiastic for his department of moral philosophy and political economy, did not deserve the belittling name of " Peanuts " which was said to be derived from a story he once told of his " wild days " in college, when he went through " Bed-bug Alley " in Dartmouth Hall eating peanuts and saying " d ———." Professor Charles Young was the most distinguished of our teachers in a scholarly way, and had already made Dartmouth's little observatory famous by his discoveries of the sun spots, and the spectrum analysis of the sun's rays. I remember, many years after graduation, when he had returned to Hanover to spend his declining days after a distinguished service at Princeton University, he tapped me on the shoulder, as he sat behind me on the platform, on " Dartmouth Night," and, assuming his old professorial voice, asked me sharply, " Clark, what is the distance from the earth to Mars? " I had not known that he was there, and his amazing question was enigmatical until I looked around and saw his smiling face and twinkling eye.

Dr. John Lord, though not a regular professor, was a regular lecturer on history during my college days. His " Beacon Lights of History " are still standard books of which new editions are constantly appearing. His lectures were as interesting as his manner was eccentric, and he sometimes scandalized the other professors by lighting up his cigar after the lecture, almost before he had left the chapel door. He was the only one of our professors that indulged in the weed, so far as I know, and that indulgence was laid to his general eccentricity, and was condoned on that score.

I remember hearing from an uncle of mine who was also his college classmate, an amusing story concerning him; — how in a class prayer meeting he was called on to offer prayer, all the students being upon their knees. Being somewhat nervous and excitable he hitched his chair from place to place, until, when he was through, he was on the opposite side of the room from where he began. In the meantime he had unconsciously tied his handkerchief round his knees, so that when all the others arose from their reverential posture, he was quite unable to do so until he was unbound.

Professor Proctor, of the Greek chair, Professor Hitchcock

the eminent geologist, Professor Quimby, who took us
through the intricacies of conic sections and the differential
calculus, and the younger men, Tutors Lord, Emerson, and
Chase all deserve mention, for each one had a " personality "
that impressed itself upon the students.

Our class of '73, owing doubtless to the glories of the
centennial year, was the largest that had ever entered Dartmouth College, and numbered, all told, with those who entered later in the course, and counting the men in the Chandler
Scientific Department, though for some unexplained reason
they were not counted with the classicals in those days, fully
130 men, a very respectable number though scarcely a quarter
part the size of the present Dartmouth classes.

There were rough and tough men in the college classes of
those days, men who drank and cursed and whose virtue was
not immaculate. Many of these were weeded out in the
early years of the college course, though some managed to
graduate among the ninety or thereabouts who received their
sheepskins on a hot June day in 1873. In spite of these men
I am confident that the tone of the college as a whole was in
those days earnest, sincere, and genuinely religious. Those
were the days of compulsory chapel and compulsory church,
which we took for granted as we did the precession of the
equinoxes. It never occurred to us that in a well-regulated college anything less could be demanded, while the class prayer
meetings, though of course entirely voluntary, were usually
attended by fully half of our class, most of whom took part
briefly, according to the present Christian Endeavor custom.
I am not sure that these class prayer meetings did not give me
my first idea of what a church young people's society might
be. At any rate, I know that they were the most stimulating
religious feature of my college life, where, with other
Christian classmates, I in some way declared myself, week
after week, as on the side of Christ.

In the midst of our college course a genuine revival of

religion occurred, as was usually the case in those days at least once in four years. Some of the strongest men intellectually and socially in my class as well as in the other classes were thoroughly converted. It can well be imagined how this revival rejoiced the heart of President Smith, a religious awakening in which he and his daughter Sarah, and several members of the faculty, took a prominent part in personal work for the students.

No Dartmouth student of my generation and of many that preceded and followed, for a generation of students is only four years in length, will forget Dr. Leeds, the pastor of the College Church; scholarly, solemn, and uncompromising in the pulpit, but the very soul of geniality in his own home. This parsonage home and the homes of many of the professors were genuine havens of refuge in the limited social life of Hanover, for all the students who would avail themselves of their privileges, and largely made up for the lack of other social attractions which city colleges are supposed to enjoy.

Freshmen fraternities, which have since been abolished, were then in vogue, and it was not till the beginning of my sophomore year, according to the custom of that day, that I was initiated into the Zeta Chapter of the Psi Upsilon Fraternity, following in this respect in my adopted father's footsteps, for he was a charter member of the Zeta Chapter, and followed by two of my sons in the classes of 1901 and 1912 respectively. I was tempted to become an Alpha Delt, through a generous invitation urgently presented by a senior who afterwards became the president of the largest theological seminary in America, but family considerations prevailed, and of course neither in college days nor since, have I been willing to admit that any fraternity could be seriously compared with old Psi Upsilon.

But those were modest days for college fraternities, as for other college housings. We had no elaborate building with lounges and fireplaces and luxurious paraphernalia, but hired a modest room in the old "Tontine," Hanover's one business block.

Yet the fraternity spirit in those days ,was most admirable. It was a rare and genuine fellowship that was promoted, and a clean, sensible and serious view of life as well. A profane oath, or a glass of "booze" it was felt would have desecrated the sacred precincts of the fraternity hall; the meetings were opened with prayer, and a banquet provided by a local caterer once a year was the extent of our convivialities.

Much time and thought were put into our literary exercises, which were held every week, and the debates and papers furnished almost the only opportunity for practice in speaking and literary effort. Among other happy memories I recall a visit to the Amherst chapter as a Zeta delegate to the annual convention of 1872, and, as - - - of the fraternity, (how near I came to revealing an unrevealable secret!). I had much to do with the entertainment of the convention at Dartmouth the next year. This convention, like the previous one, passed off gloriously, though I remember that some of the brothers from the city colleges were inclined to turn up their noses at our country ways and country roads, when we took them for a ride to the Shaker settlement at Enfield.

I suppose that most college students to-day, whether from the country or city, would regard the surroundings of Dartmouth in the early seventies as exceedingly crude and primitive. We carried up our own water from the old-fashioned pump on the campus, and our own coal and wood from our private stock in the cellar. We chose our commissary and boarded in a so-called "club," making our bills of fare to suit our purses, few of which ever knew any superfluous cash. Dartmouth was then a poor man's college and drew its constituency largely from the New Hampshire farms, with a considerable contingent from Massachusetts, and a sprinkling from the West. Dartmouth men have always been famous for sending their sons back to the old college.

I may be allowed an old graduate's privilege, I am sure, to cherish the fond belief that just as strong, vigorous, and successful men were turned out in the days of the college pump and the kerosene lamp as in the modern times of shower bath and electricity.

I am tempted at this point to tell far more than my space will allow concerning my college mates and classmates, and as I think of Jack and Fred and Sam and Rich and Tom and Jim and Alf and George and Judge and remember the distinguished lawyers and ministers and professors and college presidents who would have to answer if I called the roll today. I find that it would be quite impossible, within the limits of this volume to tell what I would like concerning them. But these distinguished men were all there in embryo in that little New Hampshire village, and I could name scores of them who have made their mark upon their day and generation.

I was attacked by a genuine case of *cacoathes scribendi*, during my preparatory course at Meriden and it became more virulent during the college days at Hanover. How well I remember my first published article. It appeared in the *Manchester Mirror*, a weekly paper, during my early academy days, and related to the mysteries of the planchette, which was then exciting superstitious people and amusing saner ones. How I hugged that paper to my bosom! a volume of five hundred pages would seem far less important now. But my pride took a tumble, as pride usually does, when I wrote to the editor and asked for payment for the article, and received his reply saying, that he could buy any number of such articles for fifty cents apiece, and thought that the copy of the paper he had sent me was a quite sufficient reward.

However, I was not entirely discouraged from hoping that I could sometime earn my living with my pen, and, during my college course, made various other essays in the same direction. A number of articles published in the *Old Curiosity Shop*, a Boston magazine of somewhat ephemeral life, brought me in over one hundred dollars in the course of one year. I hope that my contributions did not hasten the death of the magazine, which expired the following season. These literary efforts, I suppose, were the cause of my election as one of the editors of *The Dartmouth Magazine* during my senior year, and also of a short-lived college weekly called *The Anvil*, which was started by a brilliant classmate, Fred Thayer by name, who afterwards served his apprenticeship on the *Independent* and the *New York Times*, and whose untimely death was mourned by all soon after he entered the ministry.

My first book, entitled " Our Vacations," though it related largely to the excursions and out-door life of college days, was not published until my junior year in Andover Seminary. What wonderful excursions those were! Two weeks in the White Mountains with half a dozen classmates at the close of sophomore year was a fortnight ever to be remembered. We walked from Hanover through the notches of the White Hills and the Franconias while an old horse and an impromptu prairie schooner which was just as good for the mountains as for the prairies, carried our tent, our blankets, and our cooking-kit. The yearly excursion of the newly fledged juniors was a regular feature of those college days, and was perhaps the progenitor of the famous " Outing Club " which has helped to make Dartmouth the great out-door college of the country.

Stories of other vacation weeks spent with classmates at Nahant and Cohasset on the Massachusetts shore, and excursions to the Maritime Provinces and Quebec, during which I was able to pay my expenses by correspondence for certain Boston papers, made up the substance of this little book, which, even in these days, I sometimes see kicking around, forlorn and neglected, on the ten-cent counters of second-hand book shops.

I must not forget to record the unique experience of the Dartmouth men of the olden days as student pedagogues.

Massachusetts in general, and Cape Cod in particular, were quite overrun with college boys who were practising on the unsuspecting youths and maidens of the Old Bay State. Six weeks' vacation in mid-winter was the rule for Dartmouth in the early seventies, while students who wished to teach were allowed six weeks more at the beginning of the spring term, whose studies they were not obliged to make up. As a matter of fact almost every boy either taught or told the faculty that he " wanted to teach," so that Hanover was a particularly lonesome place during the three months from January to April.

During my freshman year I taught in Topsfield, Mass., and in the sophomore winter in the adjoining town of Boxford, and during both of these winters had the privilege of living much of the time alternately in the charming homes of two of my uncles who had married sisters of my mother, and were spending their declining years in Boxford, a town which enjoys the unique distinction, according to a late census, of having exactly the same number of inhabitants as in the days of the Revolutionary War.

The same winter that I taught in the first district of Boxford where the classes ranged all the way from the a,b, abs, to the beginners in Algebra, " Sam McCall," recently a distinguished congressman and Governor of Massachusetts, taught in another district, and an eminent professor of New Testament Greek, Fred Bradley, (I give them their old-time names), in still another. Who imagined in those days that " Sam " and " Fred " would occupy these chairs?

At the end of my sophomore year the teaching privilege was taken away from Dartmouth students, or at least the winter vacation was cut short, and all were obliged to make up for lost time, so that few were able to replenish their lean pocket-books by the meagre twelve-dollars-a-week salary for school teaching, and few Dartmouth boys thereafter made love to the Cape Cod maidens, or pitched the unruly big boys of their schools into the snow drifts, an athletic feat for which the huskiest were frequently chosen in the earlier days.

While it would seem absurd to-day to take so much time out of a college course, I am not at all sure that those twelve weeks of teaching were not quite as valuable as any twelve weeks of being taught, and they at least enabled many a poor boy to finish his college course without too large a debt.

Our college was not visited by as great a number of distinguished men as at present, yet we had a course of lectures every winter, for those were the days when the "Lyceum" flourished, and the voice of the orator was heard in the land. Who was the lecturer among the coterie of Boston wits who declared that F-A-M-E spelt "Fifty And My Expenses"? I am inclined to think that it was Edward Everett Hale, though I remember that when I had something to do with the college lecture course, he decided that *one hundred dollars* was about the right stipend for him. It seemed to us a large sum, but when he explained that he could earn as much by staying at home and writing articles we concluded that we must have him, "irregardless" of expense. In those days we heard W. H. H. Murray, the brilliant meteor that flashed across the theological sky in Boston and soon went out in darkness. He gave us his tirade against "Deacons," with special reference to Park Street Church deacons. He was at that time also editor of *The Golden Rule*, and I little thought that I should follow him in the editorial office and actually inherit the wooden chair with a collapsible writing table on which he wrote his sermons and editorials and Adirondack yarns. Theodore Tilton, too, about the time of his memorable contest with Henry Ward Beecher, came to enlighten us about our political duties, and, if I remember rightly, he advised us to vote for Horace Greeley.

I recall, also at one commencement time, seeing the good gray poet, Walt Whitman, shuffling down the main street of Hanover, where he had come to deliver a commencement poem. He wore a blue flannel shirt open at the neck, his voice was muffled, and I could not hear his poem and probably could not have understood it if I had heard it, but I remember that as I afterwards passed him on the street he gave me a gruff but hearty " good morning."

My Psi U connections gave me the privilege of writing to the celebrated essayists, Brother E. P. Whipple, Brother Charles Dudley Warner, and others, asking for poems or addresses for convention days. I did not expect to get them, but it enabled me to secure some treasures for my autograph album. Charles Dudley Warner, I remember, whom I had modestly asked to write a poem to grace some occasion for his younger brethren, replied that he had never written a poem in his life and would have to decline " with thanks and tears."

While teaching school in Boxford I drove one bitterly cold night with Bradley to Lawrence to hear Wendell Phillips lecture on " The Lost Arts," a lecture which he gave some hundreds of times, and always with rare effect. I shall never forget that tall, graceful form surmounted by a splendidly symmetrical head, or that mellifluous voice which was rarely raised above the conversational tone, but always conveyed his exact meaning with a nicety of expression, which the orator who tears passion to tatters never knows. The anti-slavery cause was indeed favored by the advocacy of America's greatest orators and writers, and none was greater than Wendell Phillips.

Thus passed my college days, days which are always more likely to make a more profound impression on a boy's memory than any others. For the benefit of a few old Dartmouth men, who may possibly honor me by reading these pages, I would say that I roomed, as some of them did, first in the Haynes house on the main street, then at Barney McCabes' where the library now stands, and for the last year in No. 10 Reed Hall, with its splendid outlook over Balch Hill and toward Moose Mountain.

How crude and unscientific the Dartmouth sports of those days would seem to a baseball fan or a football enthusiast of to-day! Baseball was just beginning to be reduced to Medean and Persian laws, which were supplanting the " round ball " and " two old cat," of former days. Tennis was unknown, as well as basket-ball, and the football we played would to-day be considered a mere undisciplined scrimmage for the pigskin. Yet what rare fun was the old fashioned football, when half a dozen fellows would get out on the campus and shout with stentorian lungs: " Whole divisions! Whole divisions! " and the seniors and sophomores, the juniors and freshmen, would come streaming down from Dartmouth and Thornton and Wentworth and Reed and line up against each other for a furious combat! After " the warning " the man who could most often get the ball and do the most vigorous kicking was the best fellow. We never heard the mysterious numbers called out, or even knew the difference between a quarter-back and a half-back, but we were all in it, and no one thought of sitting on the bleachers while twenty-two men got all the exercise.

The annual cane rush might perhaps be counted among the athletic sports of the day, and one of my most vivid memories is that of the tall, dignified, and portly form of President Smith in spotless garments, getting into the midst of the fray, and shouting in classic phrase, " Disperse, young men, disperse to your rooms! " They finally dispersed, to be sure, after the sophomores secured the fragments of the cane, but not until the worthy president had been hustled (without the least intention of course), and his polished silk hat ruffled, I fear, beyond repair.

Those were rough old days in some respects when the freshmen's seats in chapel were once in a while drenched with a liberal supply of kerosene oil, and occasionally a corpse from the dissecting room of the Medical school was set up in their seats to frighten the new-comers fresh from their guileless homes. We may congratulate ourselves that such "rough-housing" is a thing of the past.

In the late days of June 1873, the seventy or more survivors of the classical department of the senior class were graduated, the Scientific students having a separate commencement day. The commencement exercises were comparatively simple. We had no caps or gowns, but every senior who could afford it, and there were few who could not, sported a tall hat in memory, perhaps, of Daniel Webster. Nor were there any gorgeously arrayed trustees and distinguished alumni upon the platform, declaring by their fine colored feathers whether they were M.A.'s or PH.D.'s, D.D.'s, or LL.D's.

But the commencement exercises always attracted a crowd, and each of the many speakers on the programme was assured of the sympathetic and often tearful attention of a father or mother, or perhaps a sweetheart, in the gallery. The red ribbon of the Phi Beta Kappa was not as great a distinction perhaps in those days, for it was given to all in the first third of the class. Otherwise I might not be entitled to wear "the key," though I graduated, if I remember rightly number 12 in the class.

The next day we separated, some to meet frequently, others occasionally at class reunions, but some never again.

Of late years Dartmouth has wonderfully expanded, far outstripping its old rivals, and equalling Harvard and Yale in the number of its undergraduate students in academic studies.

Freshmen classes of six hundred are the rule (all that the town can possibly accommodate), while fifteen hundred or more each year have to be refused admittance for lack of room.

Dartmouth's great President, William J. Tucker, during his administration started this wonderful advance in numbers and equipment, and the present President Ernest Martin Hopkins, is his worthy and eminently successful successor. I am glad to have a son (Eugene Francis Clark) as secretary to the college and Professor in the Department of German.

TWO GREAT THEOLOGIANS AND TEACHERS — SERMON CLUBS
— MISSION WORK — WHERE I MET MY FATE — MY
WIFE'S FORBEARS.

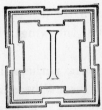DID not fully make up my mind as to what
my life-work should be until near the end
of my senior year in college, when the desires of my parents, the advice of President
Smith, and above all my own convictions of
duty, determined me to study for the ministry.

I had been wavering between journalism, for which I had
much liking and perhaps a little aptitude, and the ministry,
but the weightier sense of duty overcame boyish inclination.
I must also acknowledge that it was an easier thing in those
days for the graduate of an Eastern college to enter the ministry than it would be to-day, where prospective theological
students are often looked upon as " weirs."

Andover was then the great theological seminary of New
England, as it had been from the beginning, largely because
it had been presided over by the greatest theologians of their
time, a succession which perhaps reached the climax of its
intellectual and spiritual strength in Professors Park and
Phelps, who were then the presiding geniuses of the institution.

That this pre-eminence was recognized by many outside of

the Congregational denomination was indicated by the fact that Phillips Brooks, then in the height of his commanding power as rector of Trinity Church, Boston, sent many young Episcopalians to Andover to obtain the foundation of their theological belief, though they usually finished at some Episcopal Seminary. Among these Episcopalian students was William Lawrence, now the beloved bishop of Massachusetts, and the immediate successor of Bishop Brooks. The younger brother of Phillips Brooks, John Cotton Brooks, was my classmate and roommate during my junior year, though he spent most of his nights in his Boston home. For many years and until his death, he was the rector of Christ Church, Springfield. In his seminary days he was a fellow of infinite jest and high spirits, and he could never settle down for a " go " at the Hebrew lexicon or grammar without first throwing all the sofa pillows in the room at my head.

Of all the teachers whom I have ever known, perhaps I might say of all the men I have ever known, Professor Edwards A. Park was the most pre-eminent in his personality. It was no task to take his lectures. Students looked forward to them as to a rare treat, as they would to a lyceum lecture by John B. Gough or some other brilliant light of the lyceum platform. Professor Park's logic was unanswerable if we accepted his premises, as most of us did without hesitation, and every lecture was lighted up by a rare humor, which never seemed to lose its edge as do the oft-repeated humorous interludes of many teachers.

Professor Park's physical proportions were as impressive as his intellectual. On no other man did I ever see such a braindome. Yet his smile was as winning as a child's, and before a specially good story his mouth would pucker up charmingly and we knew that something extraordinarily good was coming. His humor was saved for his lectures however. In preaching he was serious, exalted, majestic. In hearing him we could imagine how Jonathan Edwards, from whom he was directly descended, as his first name indicated, must have swayed his audiences. He preached his famous " Judas " and " Peter " sermons in Andover once every two or three years, and those were great occasions, not only for the students but for all the people who could crowd the old seminary chapel.

In the earlier years of his connection with the seminary, when he was professor of Homiletics, he had the reputation of being unduly severe. I have heard my father tell about a

DR. EDWARDS A. PARK
Professor of Systematic Theology, Andover Theological Seminary.

young man in his seminary class who preached a sermon on total depravity, taking the ground that every unconverted man was as bad as he could be, and using for his text the story of the swine that ran violently down a steep place into the sea and were drowned.

Professor Park listened as patiently as he could to the end of the sermon, which was preached as a trial sermon before the students. The only criticism he made was, " I advise you, young man, to throw that sermon where the hogs went."

But whatever may have been Professor Park's pungency of rebuke in his earlier days, I never saw anything of it during my seminary course, nor ever heard a harsh word of criticism for any one of the students. His geniality and good humor were as marked in the home as in the classroom, and his quiet jokes will be long remembered. I recollect calling upon him a few years after graduation, when he related a story of how easily some men can be imposed upon by a solemn face. It was at the time of the American Board controversy over missionaries who believed in the possibility of a second probation, and there was some question about returning to his field Rev. Robert Hume, who harbored the possibility of some such hope for some heathen. "Yesterday," said Professor Park, "a caller asked me if I supposed the Board would send Mr. Hume back. 'No,' said I, 'they would no more send him back than they would send his uncle back.'" "Who was his uncle," said the caller. "Why, didn't you know," answered Professor Park, with his peculiarly serious and guileless expression, "that his uncle was David Hume, the great infidel historian?" "No," said the visitor in amazement, "was he?" The Professor enjoyed a hearty laugh over his visitor's credulity, imposed upon as he was, for the moment at least, by the professor's solemn air. It showed me also that the professor did not take Mr. Hume's case quite so seriously to heart as did some other defenders of the faith. It is needless to say that Mr. Hume was sent back, and became and is one of the most honored, beloved, and eminent missionaries of the American Board.

It was inevitable that many stories, most of them probably apocryphal, should circulate in Andover about this professor. One of the most popular of these stories was to the effect that he turned up on one occasion, without any previous announcement, in the classroom of a German professor, and that by his questions and the inevitableness of his logic he completely floored the theologian who at last refused to answer his questions. When asked afterwards who the stranger was he is said to have answered, " I don't know, but I think it was either the devil or Professor Park of Andover."

A more likely story, which accords with the Professor's quiet New England humor, related that, when on a foreign hotel register he signed his name " Edwards A. Park, Andover," the hotel clerk desired to know where Andover might be. With solemn and weighty assurance Professor Park said impressively, " Sir, it is just seven miles from Tewksbury," a small town, chiefly noted for a great State almshouse. " Oh," said the clerk, " I was not aware of the location of your city."

Professor Phelps's reputation was scarcely less than that of his distinguished colleague, but of a different sort. His choice English diction, a style that has never been surpassed by an American author, and his deep spirituality, made impressive by a benignant, if somewhat sad face, impressed all who came under his influence.

Professor Churchill, teacher of Oratory and Elocution, who in Professor Phelps's absence because of illness, read many of his lectures to us, was of a still different type, but was immensely popular with the students. Genial, jovial, and kindly to the last degree, he won all our hearts, as well as golden opinions and golden dollars, by his inimitable public readings. He especially excelled in his portraiture of Dickens' characters, and was for many years one of the most popular men on the lyceum platform.

Professor Thayer deserved the reputation of being one of the greatest Greek scholars in the country, but his exegesis was so minute and critical that in the seminary course we managed to study but very few chapters, and scarcely got an adequate idea of the teachings of the New Testament.

Professor Egbert C. Smyth and Professor Charles M. Mead were also very widely known for their scholarship, though it was not of a popular character, and impressed only the like-minded scholarly few.

The intellectual life of Andover was stimulating, not only in the classrooms but in the student gatherings. The Rhetorical Society, familiarly known as the "Porter Rhet," was especially valuable for future sermonizers and preachers. The weekly critic neither gave quarter nor asked it. He often tried to see how completely he could flay the essays of the other men, and, when their turn came, their knives were always whetted for the scalp of the critic of the previous week. Yet it was all done good naturedly, and I never knew of any hard feelings that resulted.

Our sermon clubs were another means of intellectual attrition, and every week we tried to prove the truth of Solomon's proverb, as "iron sharpeneth iron, so a man sharpeneth the countenance of his friend." Many a sermon plan was consigned to the scrap-heap after it had been presented to the club, and many a beautifully finished discourse, the pet production of the young theologue, was never preached after his classmates had had their say about it.

I belonged to two of these clubs, one in my own class, and another in the class ahead of me, whose other members were Harry P. Nichols, later an eminent Episcopal rector of New York City, C. J. H. Ropes, for many years a well-known professor in Bangor Seminary, and James L. Hill, a breezy Westerner, of whom I shall have occasion to speak later in these pages.

The professors did not encourage the students to preach during the earlier years of their seminary course, though many strained the rules because of their desire to do good along the lines of their chosen profession, a desire accentuated, perhaps, by their lean pocketbooks. My first sermon, I remember, was preached in the old Presbyterian church at New Boston, N. H., and six services a Sunday since, have often tired me less than that maiden effort amid the New Hampshire hills. "Were you not very tired after your long sermon?" said a Scotch parishioner to his pastor. "Ay, mon," was the reply, " but it would ha' done ye good to see how tired the people were." I hope my audience was not as much exhausted as was the preacher; at any rate they asked me to come again and settle there, but it was too early in my seminary course to accept this invitation.

Franklin, N. H., was another favorite " supply " for Andover students of those days, not only because of the fairly

HARRIET ELIZABETH ABBOTT, MRS. CLARK
As a school girl of thirteen in Abbott Academy, Andover, Mass.

good honorarium, but because of the kindly audience and generous hosts, and when the theologues came back to Andover, they would tell with a conscious glow of satisfaction how a United States Senator was in the audience, and a railroad president started the wood fire in the air-tight stove in their room before they rose in the morning. Let us hope that a more august Presence still was in those audiences, and that a benediction was left behind in the home of the Senator and the railroad president as well as of all others in the audience.

My literary activities during my seminary course brought me in some money from *St. Nicholas* and other papers and magazines, and enabled me as a newspaper correspondent to take my adopted father on a vacation trip to Prince Edward Island and Cape Breton, which we both greatly enjoyed. While in the Seminary my first book " Our Vacations " was published by Estes and Lauriat of Boston, and had a fair sale.

Voluntary and unpaid mission work was not neglected by Andover students. It fell to my lot to teach a Sunday-school class in the Abbott Village Mission School, and here I met my fate, for another teacher in that same school was Miss Harriet Elizabeth Abbott, who taught the primary class, played the cabinet organ, and was generally the life and inspiration of the school. I shall not go into particulars or tell how on a rainy evening under the same umbrella, on our return from Abbott Village to Andover Hill, a question of very considerable importance to us both was settled. As she is manipulating the typewriter while I dictate these words, it has been difficult for me to write what I have already dictated and I am not allowed to say anything further on this head, except that now it is more than forty-seven years since that rainy March evening in Andover, and that I have thanked God more fervently each year for Abbott Village and Andover Hill.

She will, however, allow me to add that her father was a pastor in Hampton Falls, N. H., and that her mother, for many years after her husband's death, mothered a multitude of students in the big square three-story house at the corner of Main and Phillips Streets in Andover.

My wife's grandfather was for fifty years pastor of the old church in North Hampton, N. H., and was known and loved as " Father French " throughout the length and breadth of the State. He brought up a family of eleven children on a salary of four hundred dollars a year, gave all his children a good education, and left to them and to his grandchildren a blessed memory.

Her great uncle, Samuel Farrar, or " Squire Farrar," as he was generally called, was famous in Andover for his devotion to the seminary, of which he was treasurer for many years. He

HARRIET ELIZABETH ABBOTT
The girl I married, October 3, 1876.

gave all his time, and eventually all his money to the seminary, and his benignant portrait can be seen in the " Farrar Room " in the splendid new Andover Hall at Cambridge. What the old gentleman would have thought of Andover's " new departures," and of her close attachment to Harvard, to whose theology he was bitterly opposed, I will leave it to my readers to conjecture.

My future wife's descent on one side of the family was from that couple distinguished in song and story, John Alden and Priscilla Mullens. I have always rejoiced that John " spoke for himself " on a certain occasion that Longfellow has made memorable.

We were married on October 3, 1876, in the beautiful Seminary Chapel whose dedication had been hastened that the ceremony might take place there. The knot was tied by Professor Egbert C. Smyth, before a large assembly of Andover citizens and students, and the next day we started on a brief tour to Montreal, Quebec, Ottawa, and Aylmer, my early home. A perusal of that charming idyl, " Their Wedding Journey," by William D. Howells, then recently published, whose characters took nearly the same honeymoon trip, will sufficiently describe the joys of that journey, which ended at Portland the day before my actual entrance upon the gospel ministry.

Near the end of my senior year at Andover I had been called to the pastorate of the Williston Church of Portland, Maine, an offshoot from State Street Church, which held its services in a humble chapel on the corner of May and Danforth Streets. Here a church of some fifty members had been gathered, together with a vigorous Sunday school. Among these fifty men and women were some of the rarest Christians I had ever known, — men and women who in spite of the fewness of their numbers and the scantiness of their resources would inevitably form the nucleus of a strong and vigorous church. Its story must be reserved for another chapter.

WILLISTON DAYS

A YOUNG PASTOR'S FIRST CHURCH — THE RAPID GROWTH OF
WILLISTON — THE " BEAUTIFUL CITY BY THE SEA " —
MAINE'S GREAT MEN — PERSONAL RECOLLECTIONS OF
THOMAS B. REED.

OW much a young minister's first pastorate
has to do with his future success or failure!
He may be discouraged, disheartened,
made almost disgusted with the ministry by
an unresponsive, captious, or quarrelsome
people; or the opposite kind of a church
may lead him to feel that there is no profession so exalted and
so well ,worth while as the gospel ministry. It is the fashion
of many modern novelists to depict the former kind of church,
rare, and by no means typical, as it is, and to give the impression that all the good people are outside of the church,
and all the mean people within its communion.

Williston Church was emphatically of the right sort. It
was only four years old when I became its pastor, and had all
the enthusiasm, buoyancy, and hopefulness of youth. Its
membership of about fifty was largely composed of young
men and women who desired in this new church to find larger
scope for their activities than they could easily find in the
old, staid State Street Church, from which they had come.
Moreover the church was in a new and growing part of the
city, not far from the beautiful Western Promenade with its

view of the White Mountains in the distance, and Deering's Oaks, of which Longfellow wrote so lovingly, near by.

Though largely composed of poor people or those in very moderate circumstances at the beginning, the location of the church soon drew to its membership several of the wealthier class who were very soon able to make the church self-sustaining. This happy mingling of rich and poor, a commingling which had no trace of servility

WILLISTON CHAPEL
Out of which grew Williston Church.

on one side, or condescending patronage on the other, was another most happy element which made for the immediate success of the church. Indeed, so rapidly did it grow in its membership, its congregations, and its Sunday school that some other churches began to look askance upon this new enterprise.

"What has become of our cat?" a neighboring minister's wife is reported to have asked her husband concerning a stray feline. "I don't know," answered her spouse, "unless it has gone over to Williston with the rest of the folks." The great majority of new members, however, were not drawn from other churches, but came into our church on confession of their faith, and, during the seven years of my pastorate, more than fifty on an average were received each year.

Before I accepted the call I was convinced that the limit of growth had been nearly reached if we remained in the little wooden chapel on the corner of May and Danforth Streets, a chapel which would hold perhaps two hundred people when crowded, and one of the conditions of my accepting the call was that, within a year, the church should make an effort to " move to a more eligible location and build a new edifice."

This seemed indeed at first a " large order " for the fifty church members with their scanty resources, but, before the year was out, it seemed much more feasible, and, within less than two years a beautiful new brick church was erected and dedicated on the corner of Thomas and Carrell Streets in the most attractive and rapidly-growing section of the city of Portland.

A ten thousand dollar debt when the church was completed looked colossal indeed, since we supposed that every one had strained himself to the utmost in building the church. But the very first Sunday of its occupancy the debt was fully subscribed, and the church was dedicated entirely free from any encumbrance. One happy feature of this first Sunday in the new church was the presentation of nine babies, whose parents consecrated them to the Master's service, among them our own little daughter, Maude Williston Clark.

I have often wondered at the generosity and considerateness of my parishioners. As I look over a few of the sermons of those older days I am amazed that they should have been received with such kindly appreciation. I imagine, however, that the earnestness and enthusiasm of a young preacher often makes up for defects in thought and style which would not be so easily condoned in an older man, and that this fresh and eager enthusiasm largely accounts for the popularity of the young " theologue " in our pulpits.

The prayer meetings of Williston Church were from the beginning famous for their numbers in proportion to the church membership, and for genuine vigor and spirituality, I have never known them to be surpassed. The Christian Endeavor society, which was formed in the fifth year of my pastorate, was a constant recruiting-ground not only for the young people's meeting, but for the mid-week meeting of the church. I have been told that during a recent interregnum of pastorates, when, for a year, Williston Church was without an ordained leader, more than forty laymen were found who were ready to conduct the mid-week meeting, so that for almost a full year the meeting had a different leader each week.

Portland well deserved, even more than its larger sister, Brooklyn, the name of " The City of Churches." In those days there were nine Congregational churches, three Baptist, three Methodist, two Episcopal, two Universalist, and two Unitarian churches, as well as two large Catholic churches. These, with various conventicles for the smaller sects, certainly furnished spiritual opportunities sufficient for a city of 30,000 people.

In many ways Portland was an ideal city for home-makers. It was neither so large that one was lost in it and his influence unappreciable, nor so small as to be concerned only with provincial matters and neighborhood gossip. It was a country-city, combining the advantages of both city and country. In the late seventies it was introducing the telephone, which was just beginning to come into use, but it had not yet attained to electric lights, and the infrequent street cars were pulled by horses. In the winter wheels were exchanged for runners, and the snow, trodden down hard in the middle of the street, was heaped up on the sides so that persons on opposite sidewalks could scarcely see each other because of the snow ramparts which divided them.

WILLISTON CONGREGATIONAL CHURCH, PORTLAND, ME.

The church of the First Christian Endeavor Society formed February 2, 1881. The Parish House at the left has been added since, during the pastorate of Rev. Smith Baker, D.D.

Portland, and, indeed, the whole State of Maine was at that time famous for the influence of its leading citizens in nation-wide affairs. William Pitt Fessenden, who loomed so large in national concerns during the Civil War, was living in retirement in his beautiful colonial home on State Street. Neal Dow's home on Congress Street was pointed out to all visitors, and the little old gentleman with his halo of white hair and beard, though well on toward the eighties, was still prominent in municipal and State affairs, and as fiery as ever in his denunciation of the saloon, and in his support of the prohibition law which he had fathered so many years before.

James G. Blaine was a name to conjure by. He lived in Augusta, but he was frequently in Portland on political and other business. Though I was never personally acquainted with him, I remember well his handsome face in which were set two of the most piercing black eyes that I ever saw; eyes that commanded attention as well as his melodious voice and persuasive utterance. More than any other man I have ever seen he cast the spell called " magnetism," for want of a better name, over all who came within sound of his voice or reach of his eye. He was literally a " spell-binder," and his marvellous memory for names and for little details in the lives of the people he met, added to his remarkable personal and political influence.

One of the deacons of the Williston Church was in the railway mail service of the Post Office Department. As he was walking along Exchange Street one day, someone from behind put his arm over the deacon's shoulder and said in a cheery tone, " Hello, Jefferds, how is the P. O. D.? " Looking around he saw that it was none other than the Secretary of State of the United States, James G. Blaine, who thus familiarly addressed him, and it can be imagined that Deacon Jefferds voted for Blaine whenever he had opportunity, whoever might be the opposing candidates.

Another prominent statesman just coming into power was

Nelson Dingley of Lewiston, the Speaker of the House for many years, and author of the Dingley Tariff Bill. He was prominent in religious circles as well as in national politics, was occasionally seen at the annual meetings of the Congregational State Conference of which I was moderator during three years of my pastorate in Portland. Mr. Dingley was afterwards moderator of the National Congregational Council.

Of all the coterie of famous Maine statesmen who made that era so distinguished in the history of the State, and gave to the commonwealth more influence in national affairs than was accorded to a dozen other States combined, Thomas Brackett Reed had, in many respects, the most interesting and original personality of all of them. It so happened that I knew him better than any of the others, for his mother-in-law and brother-in-law were members of Williston Church, and for many years he was a summer neighbor at Grand Beach on the shores of Casco Bay. My wife and I were his guests in Washington before he became Speaker of the House, but not before his ready repartee and caustic wit had made him a power to be reckoned with by both parties.

But it was at the seashore that I knew him best. His great bulk could have been seen any early morning, rolling, sailor fashion, along the boardwalk, usually followed by my dog Duke, who seemed to be as fond of him as were his human neighbors. Mr. Reed and I were both trying to learn to ride the bicycle at the same time, an art in which neither of us became proficient. He succeeded better, however, in amateur photography, and took several pictures of my dog and his master. In one of these I was seen riding towards Old Orchard in a wobbly fashion, while the picture, owing to some defect in development, was light-struck immediately over my head. In sending me the picture afterwards from Washington, he wrote that if he were not afraid of being irreverent he should label this picture " Paul on the Way to Damascus."

He had a large store of Bible quotations ready to his hands

as his speeches proved, and was much exercised over theological questions. Indeed, during his early years he had intended to study for the ministry, and was partially supported in his college course by State Street Church on that account. His views having changed while in college, however, he decided to study law and honorably paid back to the church all that it had advanced for his education. His political opponents garbled these facts in various circulars and pamphlets when he first ran for Congress, branding him as a dishonorable religious renegade, a misrepresentation which I was able to refute in one or two religious papers of influence. But when I casually mentioned that his father-in-law had been an honored Congregational minister, the harmless item of information acted as a boomerang, for the Democrats at once charged him with trying to " ride into Congress on the backs of his wife's relatives."

Years afterwards, on my return from one of my visits to India, he had a serious talk with me about the mysterious ways of Providence which he could not understand, and which allowed millions of harmless natives to die in the awful famine which was then raging in India.

The last conversation with him that I remember related to the Filipinos. It was after his retirement from Congress, prompted largely by his disagreement with the McKinley administration on the Philippine question. Naturally he was not fond of " the little Major " as he called McKinley, who had snatched from him the presidential nomination when it was almost within his grasp, and he totally disagreed with him in regard to the retention of the Philippines. With the characteristic drawl, which marked every utterance in public or private, he said, in answer to the suggestion that it was our opportunity to enter the Philippines and convert and civilize the natives, " I don't think it's the business of Uncle Sam to set up a kindergarten for the Filipinos, or to be their wet nurse."

In those days there were no particularly famous literary

men in Portland though J. M. Neale, the story writer and essayist, was living when I first went there, and Portland was particularly proud to have been the birthplace of Longfellow. The house in which he was actually born had become a poor and dirty Irish tenement, now redeemed, I am glad to know, and to be preserved for the loving reverence of future generations. Portland will never forget that she has been immortalized in more than one of Longfellow's poems, as he wrote of the " beautiful town that is seated by the sea," of " Deering's Oaks," of the " black wharves " where lay the ships from distant lands, and the swarthy sailors who manned them.

Every line of " My Lost Youth " is full of memories of Portland. I can quote but two verses:

" Often I think of the beautiful town
    That is seated by the sea;
Often in thought go up and down
The pleasant streets of that dear old town,
    And my youth comes back to me.
    And a verse of a Lapland song
    Is haunting my memory still:
' A boy's will is the wind's will,
And the thoughts of youth are long, long thoughts.'

" I can see the shadowy lines of its trees,
    And catch, in sudden gleams,
The sheen of the far-surrounding seas,
And islands that were the Hesperides
    Of all my boyish dreams.
    And the burden of that old song,
    It murmurs and whispers still:
' A boy's will is the wind's will,
And the thoughts of youth are long, long thoughts.' "

THE BEGINNING OF THE CHRISTIAN ENDEAVOR MOVEMENT

FEBRUARY 2, 1881 — PRE-CHRISTIAN ENDEAVOR SOCIETIES — COOKIES AND A CONSTITUTION — A WONDERFUL TRANSFORMATION — GROWTH OF CHRISTIAN ENDEAVOR THROUGHOUT THE COUNTRY — DENOMINATIONAL OPPOSITION.

HE most important incident of my life in Portland, though it seemed of small consequence at the time, was the formation of the first society of Christian Endeavor. This took place on February 2, 1881 in the parlor of my home at 62 Neal Street, where I was then living. The society was an evolution, rather than a creation by the fiat of the minister. For more than four years, as was natural in such a church, my thoughts and prayers had centred around the development of the young people. Every year there had been seasons of special religious interest among them in connection with the "Week of Prayer," in the early days of January, which we religiously observed; a week which, I regret to say, has largely lost its significance in most churches.

During the four months previous to the Week of Prayer, after the re-gathering of the church when the summer vacation was over, my aim was to make my preaching and pastoral work lead up to that week, as the culminating season in the church year. Then special meetings were held every night, the claims of Christ for an immediate decision to serve Him were urged, an opportunity was given for all to declare themselves, and without exception, each year a religious awakening was the result, which usually brought from twenty to forty new members, most of them young people, into the church.

But I had increasingly felt each year that it was not enough to lead them to declare themselves upon Christ's side, and then to join the church. Though in the " Pastor's Class " I had tried faithfully to prepare them for church membership, I still felt that much was left to be desired. The young Christians, naturally diffident in the presence of their elders, took little or no part in the prayer meetings of the church, when there were others who could speak and pray so much more fluently; nor were they prominent in its social and benevolent activities, when overshadowed by others of more experience.

The great task which confronted Williston Church, as it has confronted so many others, was how to give these young converts duties and responsibilities, suited to their powers, that would train and develop them for larger duties and responsibilities. Even before this Williston Church had not been especially lacking in resourcefulness in its efforts for the young. We had tried the debating club, and the musical society, and attractive social gatherings had been frequent. The minister's wife had been particularly active in her efforts to interest the boys and girls in missionary lore, and to increase their interest and their contributions for the missionary societies, and her " Mizpah Circle " of boys and girls had become one of the most important features of the church life.

Still none of these efforts seemed to accomplish the desired result of training up a company of devoted, earnest young people, outspoken among their companions in their acknowledgement of Christ's claim and ready to work for Him along all practical and systematic lines.

All such efforts as I have described for training in debate, in singing, in temperance, and missionary zeal failed, not because they were not good in themselves, but because they did not go far enough in developing an all-round, symmetrical Christian character. Because of this defect there have been a multitude of failures in young people's societies of various names since that day, and I doubt very much whether regalia

THE MIZPAH MISSION CIRCLE

Of Williston Church, of which Mrs. Clark was superintendent. This Circle was merged into the first Christian Endeavor society when it was formed. This picture was taken on the steps of Dr. Clark's first home in Portland, at 42 Pine Street.

and passwords and secret formulas which the rest of the church are not supposed to know, or even a khaki uniform, would have developed these young Christians of Portland into stalwart champions of the church which most of them became. This is not saying that I am not heartily in favor of the Boy Scouts and similar organizations, but something more is needed in a *church* for training young *Christians*.

The second of February, 1881, was a clear, cold day, typical of a Maine winter, and the pastor's wife had invited the boys and girls of the Mizpah Circle to the parsonage on Neal Street for the afternoon, providing for them, besides the usual missionary meeting, plenty of games and a supper, of which an abundance of home-made cookies was an out-standing feature. After supper the younger children went home,

WILLISTON PARSONAGE IN 1881

Parsonage of Williston Church, Portland, Me. The first Christian Endeavor society was formed in the left-hand front corner room of the lower floor, and there the constitution was signed. The upper left-hand corner front room was the pastor's study, where the constitution was written earlier in the same day, February 2, 1881.

while the older ones were joined later in the evening by their still older brothers and sisters, until a company of fifty-eight had gathered in the parsonage parlor.

While the minister's wife had been making cookies in the kitchen, the minister, in his study in the third story, had been framing a constitution for the Young People's society which he hoped to form that evening, and which he decided to call the

" Williston Young People's Society of Christian Endeavor." This society was different from others that he had started, chiefly because it laid the greatest stress on the *religious* features. It was to be an *out-and-out* Christian society. The pastor had become tired of half-way measures for training his young people, and while he doubted the efficacy of the new plans, he decided that they were well worth trying.

On this account the activities of the new society were to centre around the weekly young people's prayer meeting, though of course they were not to end there. In order to make this meeting a real power each member was to promise to attend and take some part in it, not to preach a little sermon by any means, or to deliver a Pauline exhortation, or to offer a prayer as long as Solomon's. A Bible verse, if it expressed his thought, was to answer the requirement of " taking some part aside from singing," and a sentence of prayer, which might also be one of the thousand Bible prayers, would fulfil all requirements.

There was naturally some hesitation about accepting these stringent rules, but, led by the teacher of the Young Men's Bible Class, Mr. W. H. Pennell, all the young people present signed the new constitution, after it had been carefully explained, and the first society of Christian Endeavor was launched with Mr. Granville Staples as its first president.

It made no stir, however, even in Williston Church circles. Nothing was said about it in the morning papers, and probably half the church members knew nothing about it, for this church had a fashion which might be commended to others, of letting their pastor, whom they trusted, do about what he thought best without criticism, but with much encouragement if the plan worked out well.

The immediate transformation of the young people's prayer meeting, which in Williston and in many other churches had been for years a dead-and-alive affair, was as surprising as it was gratifying. The new members did as they had promised.

Instead of a few of the older, gray-haired "young people" (young people by courtesy) monopolizing all the time, the forty or fifty members of the new society all took their part. The pastor had only to sit back and enjoy the meeting as a grateful and blessed surprise, summing up at the end, perhaps, the chief lessons that had been brought out.

The committees that had been provided for in the constitution at once organized for service; the lookout committee to

MR. GRANVILLE STAPLES
First President of the first society. Still in active business
in Portland, Me.

secure new members and to make sure that they knew what they were doing when they joined the society; the prayer-meeting committee to provide topics and leaders for each meeting, and to see that it was the best possible meeting that they could arrange for; the social committee to make the young people thoroughly acquainted with one another, and the music committee to turn the musical abilities of the society to the best account. Several other committees were soon formed.

I shall not go into particulars or relate here the history of the Christian Endeavor movement, since that has already been written in more than one large volume. I need only add that the society was an increasing joy to the pastor, and an ever-increasing strength to the church, and that, though half a dozen generations of young people have since come and gone, the activities of the Williston society have never been interrupted. It is now especially prosperous under the guidance of its popular pastor, Dr. Turk.

If the new society was at first little known in the church and community of Portland it can well be imagined that it was utterly unknown for months in the wider church circles outside of the city. Articles, however, written by the pastor for *The Congregationalist* and *The Sunday School Times* in the following summer, telling how one church sought to train its young people, attracted considerable attention, and were copied in several religious papers in America and Great Britain. As a result the second society was started in the North Church of Newburyport, Mass., in October, 1881, by the enterprising young pastor, Rev. Charles Perry Mills, who, by the way, was an inveterate punster. He fastened upon me in these early days, as a pure piece of facetiousness, the soubriquet " Father Endeavor," for which he pretended my initials stood. This joke was taken in earnest by people all over the country and has led many whom I had never seen, to suppose, for many years past, that I am only slightly under a hundred years of age.

Before the end of 1881 two or three more societies of Christian Endeavor were formed, and during the next five years they multiplied, slowly at first, but with increasing momentum, until at last thousands in all Protestant denominations, were formed every year.

It is needless to say that this surprising development of the first little society has been as amazing to me as it could possibly be to any one else. No such design or dream was at first entertained, and the growth of the movement has always been a source of genuine humility to me as I have thought how little I have had to do with it, and how purely Providential the work has been, from its insignificant beginning to its present development throughout the world.

While I feel profoundly how little credit I deserve for this growth, I have been deeply grateful for the testimony that has come literally from thousands of pastors, missionaries, and lay workers that their first impulse to give themselves to religious service, and the first realization that they could actually speak and pray and work for Christ came to them in a Christian Endeavor prayer meeting, or when appointed on a Christian Endeavor committee.

At the same time many amusing incidents concerning my own life and my family history, of which I was totally unaware, have come to me from many sources. Several persons whom I have never met have written me that they knew me well as a boy. At least a score of people have told me that they have heard me preach in some place that I have never visited, or that I was pastor of some church of which I had never heard. Several scores have informed me that they had Christian Endeavor societies long before 1881. To be sure they were not called "Christian Endeavor," nor did they have the distinctive features or constitution of the society, but then ".they were practically Christian Endeavor societies." The printed report of an ecclesiastical conference of a denomination other than my own even gave a circumstantial account of how I had said at a public meeting, " Gentlemen and ladies, I am not the founder of the society of Christian Endeavor. That honor belongs to one of your own ministers, Rev. ——— to whom I am glad to make this acknowledgment even at this late day." Since, as a matter of fact, I had never spoken at the meeting referred to, and had never heard of the good brother alluded to, I have often wondered at the vivid imagination of the scribe who made up this report.

As a matter of fact the rapid growth of the society is not to be wondered at, for tens of thousands of pastors were thinking along the same lines and desiring the same results, and were eager to adopt any plan that promised well, without any itching desire for originality or notoriety.

Name This Society shall be called the Williston Young People's Society of Christian Endeavor. (Portland, Me.)

Object. Its object shall be to promote an earnest Christian life among its members, to increase their mutual acquaintance, and to make them more useful in the service of God.

Membership. The members of this society shall consist of all young people who sincerely desire to accomplish the result above specified. They shall become members upon being elected by the society and by signing their names on this book.

Officers. The officers of this society shall be a President Vice President and Secretary. There shall also be a Prayer-meeting Committee of five a Social Committee of five, and a Lookout Committee of five.

Duties of Officers. The duties of the President, Vice President, and Secretary shall be those that usually fall to those officers. The Prayer-meeting Committee shall have charge the Friday evening prayer meeting; shall see that a topic is assigned & a leader provided for each meeting

The Prayer-meeting. It is expected that all the members of the society will be present at every meeting unless detained by some absolute necessity and that each one will take some part however slight in every meeting. The meetings will be held just one hour and at the close some time may be taken for introductions and social intercourse if desired. Once each month an experience meeting shall

ORIGINAL COPY OF THE CONSTITUTION

Accepted by the first society of Christian Endeavor, Williston Church, Portland, Me.

Thousands of young people's prayer meetings were already in existence and thousands more young people's societies of various kinds, were readily transformed into Christian Endeavor societies when its methods became known and the spiritual capacities of young people were fully realized.

Of course there was opposition, as there always must be to a new idea, and some conferences and some newspapers teemed with such expressions as " The society for the development of young prigs," " an organization for the growth of hot-house green peas," etc., while some contended that Christian Endeavor stood only for " Courting Endeavor." Other jibes of this character were not infrequent, but they became less and less common, as the churches came to see that the societies were made up for the most part of devoted young Christians who were growing in grace from week to week, and were developing constantly the finer traits of active Christian character and life.

All the denominations at first seemed to accept the society as their common denominator, and it was not until nearly eight years had passed that the bishops of the great Methodist Episcopal denomination proclaimed that their young people must have a denominational society of their own, with a denominational name, that the two thousand Christian Endeavor societies in their churches must be changed into " Epworth Leagues," and must withdraw from the fellowship of the Christian Endeavor unions which had sprung up all over the land. This they gradually did, greatly to the grief of many pastors and a multitude of Methodist young people.

Several denominations at once followed the lead of their Methodist brethren in forming distinctively denominational societies, and it looked at first as though this movement which had already brought together hundreds of thousands of young Christians in friendly interdenominational fellowship, while at the same time they were thoroughly loyal to their own churches and denominations, would be frustrated. But the interdenominational fellowship finally prevailed except in the great ecclesiastical body already referred to. Many of the denominational young people's organizations were changed to Christian Endeavor societies. The unions, State, county, and local, grew constantly stronger, representing as they now do, more than fifty denominations in the United States alone, while the society as a whole, and in all parts of the world, has grown steadily in numbers and influence with each succeeding year.

The seven years of my pastorate at Williston, though as happy as any one could desire, did not pass without temptations to go elsewhere at a larger salary and to what seemed at the time more commanding pulpits.   During the early months of my pastorate the North Avenue Church of Cambridge extended a call which I was at first minded to accept, but the claims of my own struggling church prevailed, as they did in later years when calls, or negotiations which I was told would . if I consented, result in calls, came from churches in Manchester and Concord, N. H., Brockton, Mass., Auburn, Me., and other places.

An invitation in the early months of my pastorate to become one of the editors of *The Congregationalist* was also very attractive, as it was in line with my strong inclinations in college and seminary days, but again the needs of Williston Church seemed to forbid.   But when, in 1883, a hearty and unanimous call came from Phillips Church, South Boston, I felt that Williston was so thoroughly established, its membership so large and aggressive, and its place in the community so well recognized that someone else could carry on its work to a larger success than I might be able to do.

So, with many sad and affectionate farewells, and substantial tokens of the love of our people for both Mrs. Clark and myself, my request for a council of dismission was acceded to, and I was released from my obligations to Williston Church and almost immediately was installed pastor of the historic Phillips Church of South Boston.

During these seven years my salary had been gradually raised by a generous people, as their prosperity, increased, from $1,800 to $2,500 and though there was much sorrow on both sides at the separation, there were, so far as I remember, no heart burnings, and none but happy memories of the seven years we had spent together as pastor and people.

IN SOUTH BOSTON

AN UNUSUAL INSTALLATION — SOUTH BOSTON IN THE
EIGHTIES — A GENEROUS CHURCH — PHILLIPS CHURCH
SOCIETY OF CHRISTIAN ENDEAVOR — THE GOLDEN RULE
— FAREWELL TO THE PASTORATE.

PHILLIPS CHURCH was of a very different type from Williston. It had a notable history of sixty years behind it, and a line of distinguished ministers to whom the people looked back with reverence and love. It was the leading Protestant Church on the peninsula of South Boston, both in numbers and influence. Its audience-room was one of the largest in the whole city, and had recently been renovated and decorated at large expense.

It was not without some misgivings that I became the successor of Rev. R. R. Meredith, D.D., famous in those days and for many years afterwards for his pulpit oratory and for his gift in teaching great normal Sunday-school classes, for I felt that I could not equal him in either of these respects.

However, I soon found that again my lines had fallen unto me in pleasant places, and no pastor could ever wish a more loyal, devoted, and affectionate people than made my lot a happy one during the nearly five years of my ministry in South Boston.

An unusual event occurred at the very beginning of my pastorate, for the same council that dismissed Dr. Meredith, on

Rev. S. Winchester Adriance
First General Secretary
Oct. 14–Dec. 1, 1885

George M. Ward, D.D.
General Secretary
1885–1888

William Shaw, LL.D.
Publication Manager, 1889–1899
Treasurer, 1886–1906
General Secretary, 1906–1920

John Willis Baer, LL.D.
General Secretary
1890–1903

Von Ogden Vogt
General Secretary
1903–1906

Hiram N. Lathrop
Treasurer, 1907–1915

Clarence E. Eberman
National Field Secretary
1901–1903

Former Officers
United Society of Christian Endeavor

the same afternoon and evening examined and installed me as his successor, a celerity of ecclesiastical procedure which I have never known equalled.

But Dr. Meredith had co-operated with the church in the choice of his successor, and it was his desire that the double service should take place on the same day. This Boanerges of the pulpit, with his massive, lion-like head and tremendous voice, had attracted large congregations to Phillips Church, which, however, did not perceptibly fall away as I feared they might, for the loyalty of the people to the church of their choice was unusual, and in this they had been trained by the very successful seventeen-year pastorate of Dr. E. K. Alden, afterward the home secretary of the American Board, who had preceded Dr. Meredith. I saw at once that more pastoral work was needed, and that more attention should be given to training the young people of the church, as indeed I had been repeatedly told by my predecessor; and, putting time and strength and heart into these congenial tasks, as well as into pulpit preparation, the church, with the blessing of God, seemed to prosper, and an average of more than one hundred each year was added to its membership.

Though the exodus from South Boston to the suburbs had already begun, and the influx of Irish Catholics was increasing year by year, yet many of the old families were still left, and the officials of the church were especially prominent in the social, industrial, and philanthropic life of the community. I shall never cease to love and reverence the memories of Deacons Simonds and Burnham, who so completely took their young minister into their hearts' love, while the two Junior deacons, Messrs. Gallagher and Lincoln, eminent educators and graduates of Harvard, were as loyal and efficient as deacons could be.

The prayer meetings of Phillips Church were famous during all these years for their numbers and their genuine spiritual power, and during the Week of Prayer they often overflowed the large vestry, crowding the wide platform, as well as filling every seat upon the floor.   The same plans of preaching and evangelistic effort were followed as in Williston Church and were rewarded each year in early January by a genuine religious awakening and the conversion of many young people and others.

After a few weeks, as can be imagined, a Christian Endeavor society was formed, and became even more of a power in Phillips Church than the first organization was in Williston. There were many more young people to be reached, and an unusual corps of efficient leaders was soon raised up.   Among these was William Shaw, the first president of the society, a young man of much executive ability, as well as of much readiness and cogency of speech.   He was then employed as salesman in a carpet store in Boston, and had recently graduated from " The School of Hard Knocks " in a cotton factory in Ballardvale.   By a singular coincidence, he had been a pupil of Mrs. Clark's when she taught a grammar school in that village just after her graduation from Abbott Academy.

Mr. Shaw at once became my chief lieutenant for work among the young people, and when, a few years later, the United Society of Christian Endeavor was formed, and *The Golden Rule* was purchased, he became, step by step, the advertising solicitor for the paper, the business manager of the United Society, treasurer of the same, and finally general secretary.   He is now a Doctor of Laws, that honor having been conferred upon him by Occidental College of California, whose successful president for ten years was John Willis Baer, Dr. Shaw's predecessor as secretary of the United Society.

Other young men and women were scarcely less efficient than Mr. Shaw, and the Christian Endeavor society of Phillips Church flourished apace.   It became so large that though the society met as a whole once a week, the different divisions also had their weekly meetings for prayer and conference.   These divisions were called the Christian Bands of the society, and as far as possible, I met with them all every week, which gave me an opportunity to obtain a personal insight into the spiritual needs and aspirations of each member.

To return to family affairs; we had brought with us from

WILLIAM SHAW
When he entered upon his Christian Endeavor career in 1883.

Portland two small children, Maude Williston, four and a half years old, and Eugene Francis, three years old.

Soon after reaching South Boston, " Faith Phillips," who lived but little over a month, was born, and the devoted kindness of the people in our affliction endeared them to us still more.

A serious breakdown in health in the first year of my pastorate proved even more conclusively the love and generosity of the people of our new church, for they insisted on sending me to Florida at their expense during the winter, and as that trip seemed to accomplish little good, they again insisted on three months' vacation, before the first year of my pastorate was over, and on a trip to Europe with my wife, a trip whose expenses they also paid.

There was nothing specially memorable about this journey, which took us over the beaten paths of the ordinary tourist, through England, Scotland, Ireland, Belgium, Holland, Switzerland, and France. It effectually restored my health, however, and of course it was a great event in our lives, as the first trip abroad always is to Americans, who have been fed from their childhood on the history and tales and legends of the Old World.

During these years in South Boston I preached three series of sermons to young people, based, in part, upon letters that I had solicited from prominent Christian business men and others concerning true success in life. One of these series had also been preached in Portland, and was published serially in *Wide Awake*, a popular magazine for young people, and afterwards in book form. Two others series preached in Boston to large evening congregations were also published by " Lee and Shepard " and by " Lothrop " during my Boston pastorate. One of these, meant especially for boys and young men, was called, " Danger Signals," and one particularly intended for girls and young women was entitled, " Looking out on Life."

I recollect, too, that the gifted wife of Cyrus K. Curtis, publisher of *The Ladies' Home Journal*, had been a member of Phillips Church, and at her solicitation, several of my sermons were published in that magazine, which had not then attained its country-wide popularity and the enormous circulation of the present day. It will probably excite a smile, if not something broader, to think of *The Ladies' Home Journal* publishing a series of sermons for the delectation of its readers.

Especially during the years of 1886–87 the number of Christian Endeavor societies increased at a remarkable rate. Local unions began to be formed in many cities. State Christian Endeavor unions were talked of and actually inaugurated. The Massachusetts State union was formed in Phillips Church one cold wintry day when a snow blockade prevented a large attendance, but did not interfere with the organization.

In the meantime, in the summer of 1885, the United Society of Christian Endeavor, the international organization for all America, was formed at Ocean Park, near Old Orchard, on the coast of Maine, where the convention of 1885 had been held.

From the beginning the conventions of the society, though small at first, had been remarkable for their enthusiasm, and for engaging the genuine interest of the young people. The first one was held in Williston Church in the summer of 1882, less than eighteen months after the formation of the first society; the second in the Second Parish Church of Portland, of which my dear friend, Rev. Charles A. Dickinson, D.D., was pastor; the third in 1884 in Kirk Street Church of Lowell, to which Dr. Dickinson had gone in the meantime; and the fourth, the most significant of all, at Ocean Park, as I have already said. Here were gathered several young pastors who afterwards became especially prominent in the work; Rev. Howard B. Grose of the Baptist Church, Rev. Ralph Brokaw of the Dutch Reformed, Revs. Nehemiah Boynton and James L. Hill, Congregationalists. Of this

quartette, Drs. Grose, Brokaw, and Hill have remained
Trustees of the United Society and the steadfast friends and
advocates of the movement to the present day. Dr. Grose

GEORGE B. GRAFF

For a number of years the successful publication manager of the United
Society of Christian Endeavor. Mr. Graff was a charter member of the first
Christian Endeavor society formed west of the Mississippi River — the Pilgrim
Congregational Society of St. Louis — and was the first delegate from the West
to a Christian Endeavor national convention, the fourth, held at Ocean Park, Me.
His pastor, the eminent Dr. Goodell, wrote the introduction to Dr. Clark's first
Christian Endeavor book, entitled, "The Children and the Church."

has also been for many years, the Vice-President of the United Society and a valued helper on many important occasions.

Mr. W. H. Van Patten, afterwards mayor of Burlington, Vt., and one of the first friends of the society, was elected president of the new national organization. He it was who had printed at his own expense a large edition of my first little book about Christian Endeavor, entitled " The Children and the Church," some two thousand copies of which he distributed gratis, at the same time putting paid advertisements in many papers, offering free information concerning the principles of the society to any who would apply. He was a rarely sympathetic man, gifted in the conduct of meetings, having had much experience in Y. M. C. A. work, and the society owes much to his early friendship.

It can be imagined that my correspondence concerning the society had increased rapidly during these years. Letters were beginning to come from far away India and China, telling of the success of the experiment in these mission lands. The demands upon my time as speaker at many conventions and local-union meetings, and in churches that desired to form societies, also greatly increased, and I began to feel that I could no longer support the heavy burden of my pastorate and at the same time be an exponent of Christian Endeavor principles and plans.

In the meanwhile my friends, Charles A. Dickinson and James L. Hill, and myself, had been able to borrow enough money at a bank in Lowell on our individual notes to purchase the almost defunct *Golden Rule* which, financially considered, had been going from bad to worse since Rev. W. H. H. Murray's collapse. It had for some time given a column or two to Christian Endeavor news, and had frequently published my sermons, but we felt the necessity of an organ especially devoted to the interests of the society, and, supposing that the paper had several thousand subscribers, hard cash was paid for it. We soon found that many of the subscribers whose names appeared upon its list were "deadheads," and for a time we greatly regretted that we had not started our Christian Endeavor paper *de novo*.

Of this journal, whose name some years afterwards was changed to *The Christian Endeavor World*, I was chosen editor-in-chief, and my companions in the ownership associate editors. For a long time before purchasing the paper, thus risking our little all, we had tried to persuade some benevolent people of large means to contribute enough money to enable the United Society to own the paper, but, being unsuccessful in this, we decided that there was nothing else to do but to become responsible ourselves for the risky enterprise.

At first it was a hard struggle to make both ends meet, but, gradually the paper gathered headway, and finally it attained a circulation of nearly a hundred thousand copies a week. The owners felt that they held it in trust for the United Society, to which they agreed it was eventually to belong, and that the proceeds should be used largely for the benefit of the Christian Endeavor cause. My share of these proceeds together with what I have been able to earn with my pen in other ways has enabled me to take during the last thirty years some nineteen journeys to distant lands, five of them encircling the globe. I no longer have any financial interest in the paper, having sold my life interest for a small sum to Dr. Shaw, the present publisher, in 1911.

With these many new duties pressing upon me I felt that sooner or later I must resign the pastorate of Phillips Church. This I did after about four years, though I remained with the church for nearly another year, as stated supply, either preaching myself, or exchanging with brother ministers. To the very end I cherished nothing but love and respect for the good people, which I have reason to believe was returned in some measure, and which my wife, who had developed unusual powers as an "assistant pastor," shared to a larger extent than I.

CHAPTER X

YEARS 1888–1891

TRAVELLING DAYS BEGIN

MY FIRST FOREIGN CHRISTIAN ENDEAVOR JOURNEY — THE
KINDLY SUNDAY-SCHOOL UNION — AN OBJECTION AN-
SWERED — WILLIAM E. GLADSTONE — AUBURNDALE
AGAIN.

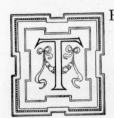HE last line of the old hymn which reminds
us that we must continue our work " till
travelling days are done " I have always
felt might have a special application to
myself, though, as I write these words, the
days are apparently not quite " done," for
I am revising this chapter in a modest hotel in Paris, while I
am planning for another long journey to the new republics of
Europe.

Whenever these travelling days may be *done*, they were
practically *begun* in the year 1888. I had reluctantly severed
my connection with Phillips Church, but was still living in
South Boston, supplying the pulpit of my old church, when
an invitation came to me from the directors of the British
Sunday-School Union in London to attend the " May Meetings " of the union and tell its members something about
the new organization entitled " Christian Endeavor," which
was beginning to be known in the United Kingdom.

It is true that my wife and I had made a portion of the
" Grand Tour " of Europe previously, but the journey had
been for health and sight-seeing alone, the only journey of that
sort which I have ever undertaken. On that occasion we made

few acquaintances, and I made no public addresses. The trip in 1888, was a very brief one, only for the work I had been asked to do, and I scarcely went outside of London, and returned home as soon as the May Meetings were over.

It began rather inauspiciously, for I found, when the old " Cephalonia " was sailing out of Boston harbor, that my trunk, with all the worldly belongings that I expected to take with me, barring the clothes in which I stood, was left behind upon the wharf, though I had been assured by the ship's officials that it was safe on board. Even my tooth-brush and razor were left in America, for I had put my hand-bag in the trunk, and I was stranded with only a " top hat," which was more in vogue as head-gear in those days than now, without even a steamer cap to meet the gales of the Atlantic. However, the barber was able to supply me with a tooth-brush and a paper collar which admitted of being turned, and my fellow passengers, taking pity upon me, supplied one or two other necessary articles, until I was able to replenish my wardrobe and toilet case at Liverpool. My trunk followed me on the next steamer, and I received it on my return to Liverpool just in time to bring it home with me, its contents quite undisturbed.

The only distinguished passengers on this ship were James Russell Lowell and some members of his family, but being shy, I did not attempt to scrape an acquaintance with the great author and diplomatist. Chance brought us together, however, at the same table in the Northwestern Hotel in Liverpool, soon after we landed. When I ventured to remark that it was a fine hotel, he rather squelched my advances, by declaring " There are no decent hotels left in Liverpool." Possibly his steak was tough, or his coffee muddy, for I have an impression that usually he was one of the most genial of men.

I reached London early in the morning after our steamer docked in Liverpool, having travelled all night by rail, and had hardly time to draw a long breath before I was ushered into the council room of the Sunday-School Union at 56 Old

Bailey, and was expected to tell my British brethren something of the ins and outs of the Christian Endeavor movement, and how the society might help to stop the leak between the Sunday-school and the church, a problem which greatly perplexed them at that time.

The reception they gave me was kindly, but not particularly cordial, for the society did not at once commend itself to conservative Britishers, who very likely said to themselves, as did the conservative Peter, when told in the vision to arise and eat of the ceremonially unclean things in the sheet let down from heaven, " Not so, Lord, for I never have."

However, a beginning was made, and the Sunday-School Union decided to take the society under its fostering care. Soon the prejudices largely disappeared, and the societies multiplied almost as rapidly as they had in America, until London became one of the largest Christian Endeavor centres in the world. It has now about five hundred societies.

I was asked to speak at other meetings during the next week or two, either public meetings of the Sunday-School Union or of the Congregational Mission Boards. At one of the latter, where only a committee of ministers was present, many objections were raised to the new plan, especially to the pledge which required the members to attend and take some part in each meeting, unless, for not doing so, some conscientious reason existed.

One of my auditors, who has since become a very good friend and advocate of the movement, declared that he would as soon think of asking his young people to *pledge* themselves to play lawn tennis as to go to a prayer meeting. An honored American missionary, Dr. Tracy of Turkey, who happened to be present, came to my rescue by saying that in his opinion, the churches of Great Britain as well as those in other parts of the world, had " too much lawn tennis and too little prayer meeting "; that they did too much to amuse the young people, thus cajoling them into becoming church members, and too

CARL A. RUDISILL
LIBRARY
LENOIR RHYNE COLLEGE

little to develop an outspoken and active Christian life. After he was through I did not feel the necessity of giving any further answer to that objection.

On this visit to England, if I remember rightly, I was asked to speak at a young people's meeting in the City Temple, the most noted Free Church edifice in the United Kingdom, where I have several times since addressed similar gatherings. Joseph Parker was then the famous pastor of City Temple and presided over the meeting. He had recently returned from a rather unfortunate visit to America, where he had gone to deliver a eulogy on Henry Ward Beecher, but did not altogether succeed in pleasing his American audiences on that and other occasions. I felt that my effort in the City Temple was not far from being a failure, for I had tired myself out with sight-seeing during the early part of the day, and was naturally apprehensive upon appearing before my first large British audience, an audience which filled the Temple. Dr. Parker, however, praised my effort in glowing and unstinted terms, and, had I not known better, and had I not been conscious of comparative failure, I should have supposed it was the greatest address ever made in his church. At the same time he took occasion to praise Americans in extravagant terms and to tell how fond he was of them and they of him, so that I more than suspected that he used the occasion of my presence to square himself with the congregation as to his American visit, and to counteract some prejudicial reports of it that had appeared in the London papers.

On the whole I think that Joseph Parker was the greatest preacher of his time. I heard him a number of times on other visits to London, and he always impressed me with the cogency and originality of his thought, his dramatic powers, and his tremendous oratorical abilities, which allowed him to play upon the sympathies and emotions of his hearers, as a skilful musician upon the strings of a harp. Other memories, more characteristic of the man, I must reserve for another chapter.

It ,was on this visit to London that I heard William E. Gladstone for the first and only time. He addressed a great congregation of nonconformist ministers in the Memorial Hall on Farringdon Street, on the issues of the day. As the ministers practically all belonged to the Liberal Party, of which he was the exponent and leader, they literally went wild with enthusiasm, if ever an audience did, punctuating every sentence, whether important or commonplace, with rounds of applause.

Mr. Gladstone was famous for having trouble with his old-fashioned neck-gear on public occasions, and, this time, too, his dickey and necktie got away from him, while he tried unavailingly to get them back where they belonged. Even this was a subject for uproarious applause, actuated perhaps by the kind intention of giving him a breathing spell, wherein he might adjust his cravat. I do not remember the points of his address, but the whole scene gave me a vivid impression of the extraordinary love, devotion, and admiration which his Liberal contemporaries felt for this greatest British statesman of the age. One statement of the venerable premier made a profound impression upon the audience, when he intimated that his opponents were hoping to prevent his Home Rule bill from becoming law until after he should have finished out his short remaining span of life and could no longer advocate it. The emotions of the audience are hard to describe, for anger at his opponents, grief, and admiration for the speaker were so involved that his hearers could scarcely contain themselves. I never saw England's Grand Old Man again, but a few years later, when I happened to be in London, I followed the throng which crowded into Westminster Hall to pay their last respects as his body lay in its casket upon the great catafalque. His face was not shown, but we knew that all that was mortal of the noblest Briton of the century lay within those narrow, oaken walls.

Returning to America and to my family, which shortly before my departure to England had been increased by the birth of our second son, " Harold Symmes," we soon removed from South Boston to Auburndale, where I had built a home on a street that is now called Williston Road; a house now occupied by my esteemed associate, the prolific and well-known author and editor of *The Christian Endeavor World*, Dr. Amos R. Wells. I was attracted to Auburndale by the happy memories of my boyhood there, and, though I found it much enlarged, and that it had become an important suburb of Boston, and one of the most beautiful villages of the city of Newton, I also found the same kindly atmosphere and neighborly good-will that I remembered in the earlier days. It was dubbed " The Saint's Rest," because of the number of ministers and missionaries who had made it their abode, but most of these saints were very busy people and did very little resting, unless to " rest in the Lord " is the meaning of the phrase.

Here our youngest son, " Sydney Aylmer," was born in 1890, and here we spent nearly twenty-five happy and busy years, interrupted by many journeys abroad and to all parts of the American continent.

EARLY JOURNEYS IN LANDS AFAR

THE AMERICAN QUARTETTE — " NEW YORK '92" — A ROUND-
THE-WORLD COMMISSION — SIX WEEKS IN AUSTRALIA —
CHINA, JAPAN, AND INDIA — IN THE CENTRE OF A TY-
PHOON — A SORE DISAPPOINTMENT.

 HAVE neglected to mention that at the sec-
ond of the two memorable annual conven-
tions of the Christian Endeavor Society held
at Saratoga Springs, N. Y., in 1886 and 1887,
I was chosen president of the United Society
of Christian Endeavor, a new responsibility
which hastened my decision to give up the pastorate of Phillips
Church. The movement grew with phenomenal rapidity
year by year in America, and foundations for a large expansion
of its work were laid in India, China, Japan, Turkey, and
Mexico, to which lands our American missionaries had carried
the new ideas of Christian nurture. In the Kingdom of
Hawaii, as it then was, where the first society outside of the
United States was established in 1883, the movement grew as
rapidly as in the home land.

In Great Britain its growth was slower, but was sufficiently
encouraging to lead the Endeavorers of that country to invite
some of their American brethren to cross the Atlantic at their
own expense for a short campaign in the different cities of the
United Kingdom. This was three years after my visit described in the last chapter. Three of my ministerial companions, Charles A. Dickinson, James L. Hill, and Nehemiah

Boynton, with myself, accepted this invitation in 1891, and each of us addressed meetings in a dozen or more of the cities of the United Kingdom.

I do not now distinctly remember all the places that I visited that year, but one of them was Birmingham, where the meeting was held in Carr's Lane Chapel, of which the celebrated Dr. Dale was then the pastor. He was in some respects the greatest power in the Free Churches of Great Britain at that time, and, though he was absent from Birmingham when the Christian Endeavor meeting was held in his church, I have cherished a warm letter of sympathy and approval of the movement, and regret for his absence, which he sent to me shortly afterwards.

Occasionally, at intervals between the meetings, the American quartette got together to compare notes, to recount their adventures, and to smile at peculiarities which, in our provincial Americanism, we considered provincial Britishisms. Before the arrival of the others, for we sailed on different ships, Dickinson and I attended the first British National Christian Endeavor convention in Crewe, and after the campaign was over he and I extended our journey as far as Rome, indulging in a few days of sight-seeing before returning home.

This journey helped the Christian Endeavor cause very considerably. I have heard since that there was more or less scoffing by the unsympathetic, at those "young American preachers," who had come to teach the Britishers better ways of training the young people, but on the whole our audiences were remarkably cordial and friendly.

The National Christian Endeavor convention of 1892 in New York City was a record-breaker in more senses than one. No such religious convention had ever been held in America, nor, for that matter, in any other part of the world. Some twenty-five thousand young people attended it and Madison Square Garden was crowded day after day, while the overflow filled many churches and out-door spaces besides. It

was almost as much of a surprise to the leaders of the movement as to the outside public, though we did not share the
diminutive ideas of the New York hotel-keeper, who offered
to take in the whole convention, in addition to his other guests.

One minister assured me before the convention began that
it " would not make a ripple in New York City, since conventions came and went and nobody knew they were there."

But the people of New York were very well aware before
the meetings were over that twenty-five thousand eager and
earnest young people, with their songs and badges and banners
and bright faces, were taking the city by storm. The New
York papers which began by giving scanty reference to the
convention, ended by devoting many columns to it each day,
and even the cynical *New York Sun*, whose reporters at first
came to scoff, remained to praise if not to pray.

Such men as Whitelaw Reid, John Wanamaker, afterwards
a trustee of the United Society, and Chauncy Depew were attracted to the meetings, and though not on the programme
spoke brief words of good cheer. Mr. Depew declared, with
a covert smile, that " New York never looked so fresh and
green before," a remark which might or might not be attri-
buted to the verdure induced by recent rains. He also assured
us on that occasion (a remark which I have heard him repeat
once or twice since) that the New York Central Railroad, of
which he was then the president, transported an immense
throng, such as it had never before handled, with promptness
and despatch and without a single accident; — an admirable
occasion for an advertisement of the great railway system.

This convention, with reports concerning the spread of
Christian Endeavor in many lands, led us to realize, as we had
never done before, that it was becoming a world-wide movement, and that something should be done to unify its forces
and lead Endeavorers everywhere to feel their kinship one with
another. So it was decided in New York that I ought to make
a journey around the world, accompanied by Mrs. Clark, to

accomplish this purpose so far as we could. Some two months later we started on the first of our long pilgrimages, which took us on this occasion across the continent, and then across the Pacific to Hawaii, New Zealand, Australia, China, Japan, India, Egypt, Syria, Turkey, Spain, and Great Britain; a journey which occupied some eleven months, and was a memorable one, at least to those who made it.

The United Society, being more flush with funds at this early period than it has been since, because of its fewer responsibilities and contributions in mission lands, paid a part of our travelling expenses on this journey. Since then, however, for thirty years I have paid all our expenses when going to missionary lands, and have in large part earned the money by articles and books inspired by these travels and largely written on steamships and railroad trains.

Australia was the first land where we made any prolonged stay; though, while the steamer stopped for a few hours in the harbors of Honolulu and Auckland, meetings were held on shore. In the harbor of Appia in Samoa we saw the pathetic relics of the memorable typhoon of a few years before. Two German men-of-war, and one American, were cast up on the shore by this tremendous storm. Their bones were bleaching in the tropic sun, and we recalled the story of the British steamer, Bellerophon, which was able to steam out of the harbor in the teeth of the typhoon, while the sailors of the doomed American cruiser manned the yards, and gave them a ringing cheer, though they knew that they themselves were being driven by the gale straight to destruction. There, too, we saw in the distance the site of the grave of Robert Louis Stevenson on the top of a conical green-clad hill. Near this spot the natives had with great exertions built the " Road of the Loving Heart."

The steamer on which we sailed for Australia was small, and the unending swell of the Pacific was heavy, and few and joyous were the days when my wife escaped seasickness. As we sailed into the magnificent Bay of Sydney, which constitutes the most spacious land-locked harbor in the world, we saw a steam launch coming out from the city bearing a great streamer, on which the letters Y.P.S.C.E. were conspicuously displayed. We appreciated the abounding hospitality and cordial greetings of our friends, but what was the dismay of Mrs. Clark, who was longing to put foot on *terra firma,* to find that we were expected to step from the steamer, not on to the dry land, but down into the little launch, for several hours sail around the harbor.

Still, if any other city in the world possessed such a magnificent harbor as Sydney, its inhabitants would be equally proud of it, and would be quite willing to endure the chaffing which their pride engenders; as for instance, when the sailors of a British man-of-war on shore-leave, are said to have paraded the streets of Sydney with high collars on which was printed conspicuously the legend, " *Yes, we have seen your harbor and admire it.*"

Our six weeks in Australia were busy ones indeed. Meetings morning, and afternoon, and evenings, the only rests being the long railway journeys between the cities; journeys facilitated by free passes over all the Australian railways. Our itinerary included Sydney and Melbourne, Ballarat and Adelaide, and back again across Victoria, New South Wales, to Queensland, some three thousand miles in all to Brisbane. From Brisbane we sailed for China on the " Ching tu," and luxuriated, during fifteen days, in the calm tropic seas, behind the Great Barrier Reef, which encircles a large section of Australia; through the Arafura, Sulu, and the Celebes Seas, dotted with islands as they are, until at last, we reached Hong Kong, the famous British city of southern China.

Before leaving Australia I must tell of some of the famous Australians whom we had the pleasure of meeting. One of our fellow-passengers on the " Mariposa " was Sir George Dibbs, then the premier of New South Wales, who had left

Australia a few months before, as I was told, a roaring republican, despising kings and queens and royalties and nobilities of all sorts. But while in England, he had knelt before good Queen Victoria, and, at the tap of her sword, plain George Dibbs had risen as Sir George Dibbs. With pardonable pride,

A BUSY STREET OF SYDNEY, NEW SOUTH WALES

but with a very subdued type of republicanism, he showed us the decoration, " the bauble " as he called it, which represented his knighthood.

He had the reputation of being by no means a religious man, but at the Sunday-evening song-services on the steamer, which Mrs. Clark persuaded him to attend (his first religious services for many years, he declared), he frequently called for his favorite hymn, " Nothing but leaves," by which he perhaps hoped to do a mild penance for a non-religious life. When boasting to Mrs. Clark one day of winning the pool on the ship's run, she suggested that it would be a pretty good plan for him to put a tenth of it into the box which stood in the companion way for the benefit of the widows and orphans of sailors. He at once handed over to her a tenth part of his ill-gotten gains, and after that he compelled the winner of the pool each day to do the same, so that the widows and orphans profited more by that voyage than by any previous one for many a long year, since the pools were seldom less than a hundred dollars a day.

One of the famous ministers of Australia was our host in Melbourne, Dr. Llewellen Bevan, well known in three continents, Europe, America, and Australia, where he had held notable pastorates. He was one of the best *raconteurs* who ever told a good story. After the late evening meetings came a late supper, and afterwards a round of good stories from the doctor until one o'clock in the morning.

While pastor of the Brick Church in New York City he criticised in public a woman for coughing unnecessarily during the service. This subjected him to severe criticism in the press, and he was accustomed to speak of it jocosely as " the cough heard around the world." His imitation of the high-brow English accent was side-splitting, and, being a Welshman, he did not hesitate to take off his English fellow-countrymen. Relating how a public meeting was broken up he told, amid peels of laughter, how the chairman of the meeting attempted to eulogize Mr. Spicer, the candidate for Parliament, whom he called " Mistah Spisah."

" I have great pleashah," said the chairman, " in advocating the election of Mistah Spisah." " Heah! Heah! " said the solemn voice of a political opponent in the gallery, and the audience tittered. " We cannot do bettah than to elect Mistah Spisah," continued the chairman. " Heah! Heah! " came the monotonous echo from the gallery. " I am glad to announce," continued the chairman, when the laughter had subsided, " That we shall soon have the pleasure of hearing from Mistah Spisah." " Heah! Heah! " again came from the gallery god. By this time many of the audience took up the refrain, while the rest roared with laughter, and the chairman was unable to complete his address.

Dr. Bevan recently died in Adelaide, where he had served as principal of the Congregational Theological College for many years. He was mourned by all who knew him.

There were many other dear friends whom we met in Australia, whose affection I cherish, and from whom I have frequently heard during all these later years, but of whom I cannot speak in this chapter. In all my travels I have never seen a more genuine and delightfully warm-hearted people than one finds in those great islands of the South Pacific, New Zealand, Australia, and Tasmania. The meetings in all the cities were great in size, usually crowding the largest halls, and were enthusiastic almost beyond description.

The next meetings after leaving Australia were held in Hong Kong and Canton, after which we sailed for Yokohama. This voyage came near being our last, for our little steamer, "the Peru," of three thousand tons burden, was overtaken after a day or two by a terrible typhoon, which, on its way from the Philippines gradually overhauled us. For days the storm had been increasing in volume, and finally burst upon us with terrific force. All one night the storm raged, except for about an hour when we were in the centre of the typhoon.

A typhoon (as is well known) is a circular storm revolving with tremendous velocity around a comparatively calm centre. While in this calm centre numerous exhausted sea birds dropped upon our deck, and remained with us until better weather returned. The outer edge of the storm was even worse than the first contact, and it seemed as though our ship would surely founder. Our own stateroom was on deck, while our thirteen year old son, Eugene, was below in a cabin room. Many of the passengers, finding themselves unable to stay in their berths, lay on the saloon floor, holding on to the pillars or chairs. Eugene could not get to us or we to him, but so far as he was concerned it made no difference, for he was too sleepy to know how severe and dangerous the storm was, and slept through the most of it.

At length day dawned, and the worst of the storm was past. In the distance the snow-capped peak of Fujiyama looked down upon us benignantly, and we knew that our troubles for the time were over. Mrs. Clark, searching amid the wreck of toilet articles and various kinds of *débris* on the floor of our cabin, found a " Friendship Calendar," which home friends had written out for her, and thinking to find a word of comfort and help she looked for the message for the day, which proved to be this:

" The Lord is able to give thee much more than this! "

We sincerely hoped He would not, however.

This day was the American Thanksgiving Day and it may well be believed that we ate with more than usual gratitude the Captain's Thanksgiving dinner with " turkey and fixin's."

In Japan the rough ways of travel were made smooth by my friend and classmate, Rev. James H. Pettee, whose long and eminent service in that country was afterwards recognized by the degree of D.D. from two American colleges. In his home in Okayama we obtained our first genuine glimpse of every-day life in Japan, while his gifted wife took us to the homes of some of the Christian Japanese who inducted us into the mysteries of Ceremonial Tea, and other things Japanese. Until his sudden death in America in the rooms of the American Board in Boston, just as he was about to return to his work in Japan, he had been the leader, among the missionaries, of the Christian Endeavor forces of that country, where a national union now exists.

After a few weeks in Japan we returned to China and enjoyed some pleasant meetings in Shanghai and Ningpo. While in Shanghai we were invited by a missionary friend to visit the native Chinese city. Any one who has been there knows how crowded those little narrow streets are with jostling, pushing coolies and men intent on all kinds of business of their own. We had been travelling so rapidly that our letters could not keep up with us, and we had found nearly two months accumulation of mail matter awaiting us.

I had crowded some fifty or more letters just obtained at the American consul's office into my overcoat pocket, but had not had time to read one of them.

When we had finished the novel and interesting rounds of the queer old city, I felt in my pocket and found, to my dismay, that every one of the letters had been stolen, with the exception of one that had dropped out of the package. All the home news covering those two months, all news from my office, and from neighbors, was irretrievably gone. We advertised and made every effort to get them, but it was useless, and in a day or two we had to sail away again, for another long voyage, with no information concerning the welfare of children and home friends. Few disappointments could have been more poignant.

From Shanghai we sailed for India by way of the Straits Settlements and spent some memorable weeks with the missionaries of the Arcot Mission of the Dutch Reformed Board, where Christian Endeavor first took root in India, and afterwards in the Madura and Marathi missions of the American Board, and in the Baptist mission among the Telugus where I enjoyed a few interesting days. Rev. Robert Hume, D.D., of whom I have before spoken, one of the most eminent missionaries whom India has known, was the leading spirit in the Marathi Mission. He was not at first greatly impressed with the value of the Christian Endeavor movement, but afterwards came to regard it as one of the leading agencies for the evangelizing of India, and has frequently thus expressed himself in public.

Some years later at a great public meeting in Tremont Temple in Boston, when he was at home on a furlough, he told of his conversion to the merits of the organization, and regretted that he had "poured cold water on Dr. Clark on his first visit to India," though, to tell the truth, I had not been aware of any douche of that sort.

The late Dr. P. S. Henson, the ever witty, who was then the pastor of the Tremont Temple Baptist church, was the next speaker, and created much amusement by declaring that Dr. Hume had made a great mistake in *pouring* water on Dr. Clark. The missionary ought, he said, to have put him clear under, and then he would have come out a thorough-going Baptist.

One of the most interesting men who ever went to the mission field was Dr. Jacob Chamberlain of the Arcot Mission, a member of a celebrated missionary family. He had had many adventures during his life in India, adventures which he knew how to recount with much literary grace and vividness. Soon afterwards he asked me to write an introduction to one of his volumes of missionary adventure entitled, "In the Tiger Jungle." Another commission of the same sort which I was glad to perform was the writing of an introduction for an admirable *resumé* of missions throughout the world by Mrs. William Scudder of the same Arcot Mission.

The rest of this eleven months' journey held incidents enough to fill another chapter.

IN PALESTINE, TURKEY, AND EUROPE

THE TERRORS OF JAFFA — TURKISH OBJECTIONS TO LITERA-
TURE — UNSUCCESSFUL ATTEMPTS AT SMUGGLING —
THE BIRTHPLACE OF ST. PAUL — CILICIAN GATES AND
TAURUS MOUNTAINS — A PERILOUS JOURNEY — CON-
STANTINOPLE AND HAMID II. — SPAIN AND ENGLAND.

FTER leaving India this first round-the-
world journey took us across the Indian
Ocean, through the hot Red Sea and the
Suez Canal to Ismailyeh and Cairo. A
short stay in Cairo gave us an opportunity
to see something of the work of the splendid
United Presbyterian Mission in Egypt, of which I may speak
further in connection with later journeys. In this mission the
Christian Endeavor movement has long flourished.

We were obliged to hasten on to Palestine, and the landing
at Jaffa was all that our most vivid imagination had painted
it. We were on the edge of a storm during which no other
landings were possible for some days after our ship discharged
her cargo. The story was still fresh of the landing party
which was held up midway between the ship and the shore by
the rascally boatmen, who demanded backshish, until the small
boat was overturned and all the passengers were drowned,
while the crew saved themselves. This story did not add to
our comfort as our small boat surmounted, one after
another, the big waves which rolled between us and
the slippery landing place which at Jaffa does duty

for a pier. Modern travellers can now go comfortably by rail all the way from Cairo to Jerusalem, one of the few blessings resulting from the war.

Our stay in Palestine was necessarily brief, and we went little further than Jerusalem and Bethlehem at this time, for we knew that a missionary friend was coming across the Taurus Mountains in a wagon, a long seven-days journey,

SOME LEADING CHRISTIAN ENDEAVORERS OF CAIRO ON A PICNIC
TO THE PYRAMIDS

to meet us at Mersin, and take us back with him to his home in Cesarea, in the centre of Asia Minor. I will speak later of a longer journey in Palestine.

The journey across Asiatic Turkey was, in some parts of it at least, as exciting as it was interesting, for in the early days of 1893 the Turks were on the verge of one of their periodical outbreaks against the Armenians, and massacres and rumors of massacres were in the air, though they did not break out in their full bloody horrors until later in the year.

When our steamer reached Mersin, as we expected, our missionary friend, Rev. James L. Fowle, was waiting on the wharf to receive us. We had been informed of the exceeding anxiety of the Turkish government to prevent the contamination of its subjects with western literature. Some stories were rife at that time, which were at least good enough to be true. One was to the effect that a text-book on chemistry was forbidden entrance to the Empire because the formula for water, " H_2O," might be interpreted to mean, " Hamid II is nothing." This I believe to be an actual fact, though I am not so sure that a school geography was objected to because it referred to the " union " of the waters of the Missouri with the Mississippi, since the Sultan did not wish his subjects to know anything about unions or combinations of any kind.

A whole edition of one English book relating to Turkey was seized and burned upon its arrival and when an eminent classical scholar of Constantinople remonstrated with the authorities, they declared that it was utterly impossible that such a book should be allowed in the Empire since it contained a reflection upon the Turkish government. " Did you ever realize," replied the scholar, " how large a vacancy would be left in the world's literature, if every book containing anything derogatory to Turkey were eliminated? "

Knowing something of this antipathy to English literature, my wife, not wishing to be deprived of her Bible, had placed it with one or two other books under a pile of soiled linen in a travelling bag which had been hitherto entirely devoted to laundry purposes.

Going ashore we found the Turkish custom-house official in bad humor, and with some excuse, for it was the time of the Fast of Ramadan, and he had had nothing to eat since the night before. My wife went on to a missionary home near by, leaving Mr. Fowle and myself to struggle with the official.

" Open that thing," he said gruffly, pointing to the laundry bag. "I assure you," I said, "it contains nothing but soiled clothing," for my wife had not told me of her attempt at innocent smuggling.

At this my missionary friend spoke up, saying: "You can believe what he says, for he is a minister of the Gospel, and I am a missionary." "How do I know but what you are both lying," the unmannerly official replied. "Missionaries don't lie," said my friend. "Open that bag!" was the only answer. Glowing with conscious rectitude, I opened the bag, took off the first layer of shirts, and there lay the incriminating Bible. It can be imagined with what scrupulous care the rest of our baggage was examined, and that every scrap of printed and written matter was taken away from us.

The only one who rejoiced in this conscientious work of the official was our son, Eugene, whose Latin grammar and other text-books which he was expected to study more or less every day, were taken with the rest of the plunder. We did not see them for another six weeks, when, through the exertions of the American Minister to Turkey, our books were returned to us, together with several others that did not belong to us, but not until we had reached Athens, and were well out of the Sultan's domains.

We were delayed several days in Adana and Tarsus, waiting for a *bouroultoo* or safe conduct from the Vali of Adana. At last it came, written in bold and straggling Arabic characters which seemed to say by their vigorous uphill slant, "Let these people go on their way in safety or else your head will come off as a penalty." In fact it did say something to that effect, though not being proficient in Turkish I cannot give an exact translation.

Adana, it will be remembered, was in 1908 the scene of one of the most horrible massacres of history, until it was eclipsed by the much more horrible persecutions of 1915–1918. Indeed, a few weeks after our arrival in Mersin, and shortly after we had left Turkey, the whole country was red with blood and lighted with the torch of the incendiary, while the great Powers of Europe looked on supinely, saying " What can we do about it? " If they had done something about it then, the more awful horrors of later years might have been largely averted.

The delay in waiting for our safe-conduct from the Vali gave us several days to visit Adana and Tarsus, the birth-place of St. Paul. While we were there the good news came to the principal of St. Paul's Institute, a high-grade mission school for the boys of Tarsus and vicinity, that Mr. Elliott F. Shepard of New York had given a hundred thousand dollars to the endowment of the school; — welcome news indeed for a struggling missionary institution. Good use has been made of it and ever since the school has taken high rank among the educational institutions of Turkey.

The morning that we left Tarsus for the long and perilous journey through the heart of Asia Minor, the boys of the two Christian Endeavor societies, Senior and Junior, met to give us a " send-off," and their kindly good wishes for the journey. The president of the Junior society, who voiced the feelings of the younger boys, soon had a chance to test his faith, for in the persecutions that followed he was called upon to re-nounce his allegiance to Christ or " suffer the loss of all things," even life itself. Like the great Apostle of Tarsus for whom the school was named he chose the better part and would not so much as hold up two fingers, as he was urged to do, to show that he had accepted the doctrines of Mohammed. In the political trouble of 1921–22 I understand this institu-tion like every other in the land of the Turk, has suffered from new persecutions, has indeed been closed and the city destroyed.

The journey across the great tablelands of Asia Minor was full of interesting adventures. Our conveyance was one of the few spring-wagons in all Turkey. It looked not

ONE OF THE GREAT MOSQUES OF CONSTANTINOPLE
The boatmen of the Bosphorus in the foreground.

unlike a "prairie schooner" and carried our provisions, our beds and bedding, while a springless wagon of native manufacture carried our trunks and other belongings. A Turkish zabtieh, or soldier, was detailed as our guard, but whether he was more of a protection or a peril I was never quite able to determine, especially when he was caught red-handed carrying off some of the property of the villagers in whose houses we had lodged. They came tearing after us hot foot, searched and found in the saddle-bags of our soldier guardian the Joseph's cup (a pair of gloves) which was lost.

The nights were usually spent in stuffy, filthy khans or in worse village "guest-rooms," and the days in the wagon, which was able to make some thirty miles between daylight and dark over the execrable roads which still characterize every part of Turkey. Indeed in some places there were no roads at all, and we struck off across the fields. The only decent stretches of highway were the remains of the old Roman roads. We were often obliged to ford the streams as best we could, though sometimes the Roman bridges, built two thousand years ago, were still intact. From others the Turks had carried off the stones of the noble arches to build their huts or their sheepfolds.

The "Cilician Gates," so called, is not far from Tarsus, the name being applied to a famous narrow pass through the magnificent Taurus Mountains which was widened and made passable for heavy transportation by the enterprising Tarsians hundreds of years before the Christian Era. This is a world-renowned engineering feat of the ancients, and resulted in making Tarsus one of the most important of commercial centres for many centuries.

A village that rejoiced in the unhappy name of "Graveyard Spout" was our first stopping place for the night, but the "spout" furnished an abundance of clear cold water for our wayside ablutions the next morning, and that first night was by no means the worst of our experiences.

At Nigdeh, two or three days' march further on, our missionary friend was arrested and imprisoned for a few hours until he could prove his harmless intentions, and here we were the guests of the Armenian pastor, whose cool, clean house was a great contrast to the filthy unventilated public " guest-room " where we often lodged.

To come out at last after a week's journey on the plains of Cesarea under the shadow of the mighty Ali Dagh was a welcome event, and still more glad were we to find ourselves the guests of Dr. and Mrs. Farnsworth, the veteran missionaries of Cesarea, and afterwards of their daughter Mrs. James L. Fowle of Talas, a near-by suburb of Cesarea.

After the long, cramped journey in the missionary wagon, and the nights in the unsavory guest-rooms, a genuine Turkish bath was an event to be remembered. It was none of your fake Turkish baths of our big cities, with steam radiators and gilded ceilings, and Hibernian Turks to rub you down, but the original thing, with hot stones plunged into the sizzling water to raise the steam; lusty Turks to massage your cuticle until it seemed that they would rub it to ribbons, and a fountain of pure, cold, spring water for the final douche. The only baths that I remember as superior to the one in Cesarea are the more famous establishments at Broussa, Turkey, where natural hot springs make the hot stones unnecessary.

A week in these mission homes of which I have spoken freshened and heartened us for another week in the wagon on our way to Constantinople. One incident of the latter part of this journey I shall never forget. We had come to the town of Istanos where was a vigorous Armenian church housed in a comfortable building, a Christian Endeavor society being one of its auxiliaries. As usual, under such circumstances, I was asked to make an address, which the Armenian pastor was to interpret into the vernacular. I noticed his nervousness and hesitancy and the blank expression on the faces of his audience who seemed to be able to make nothing out of his translation.

THE CEREMONY OF SELAMLIK

The Sultan of Turkey, Abdul Hamid II. The Great Assassin going to Mosque guarded by 10,000 soldiers.

The trouble was explained later, when he told me that just as I began to speak he saw a Turkish soldier take a seat in the back of the church, whom he knew to be a spy upon our proceedings, while he also knew that if he made a slip and pronounced a forbidden word, we should all find ourselves in a Turkish prison, in which the reform principles of Mr. Mott Osborne are by no means enforced. I had known before that many words were on the Index Expurgatorius of the Sultan, among them " union," " fellowship," " brotherhood," " Christian Endeavor," etc. I tried to avoid them as far as possible, though it was difficult to do so, but in his nervousness and fright my interpreter succeeded completely in not only avoiding them, but also in making such a hodge-podge of my speech that no one knew what he was talking about.

In Angora we looked for Angora cats but saw none, a fact which confirmed my impression that the last place to find an animal or an article is the place that has given its name to it. Thus in Neuchatel I have inquired in vain for Neuchatel cheese, and for Apollinaris Water on the Rhine steamers that sail by Apollinaris. When in the Isle of Man I looked diligently for a Manx cat, and after some search and many inquiries was rewarded by the sight of one small tailless kitten, one of a brood of four, all the others of which had the usual caudal appendage.

However, if we saw no Angora cats in Angora, we saw the beautiful fleecy Angora goats on the plains near by, and, what rejoiced us more, we found a railroad train, which in two days took us to Constantinople, including a night's stop at Eski-Shehir. Turkish trains then travelled only in the day time, tying up at night when darkness overtook them at some station where the traveller could find meagre accommodations.

No unusual experiences were enjoyed or endured during the rest of our journey to America. A few days in Constantinople enabled us to visit those splendid institutions of which all Americans should be proud, Robert College and the American College for Girls.

That marvellous missionary and administrator, Dr. Cyrus Hamlin, was then living in extreme old age in America. He had left an undying impress upon Turkey, not only in the founding of Robert College, but in the establishment of industrial and sanitary reforms in Turkey. To know him in retirement was to know one of the stalwarts of the century, a genuine Yankee, inventive, resourceful, indomitable, and courageous, a man whose religious convictions were a part of the very fibre of his being. His autobiography, " My Life and Times," is a book that deserves to be reprinted in a new edition for every generation of Americans.

After a short stay in Athens, where we recovered the books which were so offensive to the Turkish government, we made our way as rapidly as possible to San Sebastian at the invitation of Mrs. Alice Gordon Gulick, the beloved educator, who had adjured us to follow out the intention of St. Paul and " make our journey into Spain." The famous International Institute for girls was then located at San Sebastian, the beautiful summer resort of the royalties and the *elite* of Spain. As we entered the main building of the school, the pretty Spanish girls in the balcony above showered rose leaves upon us, a delightful welcome which was borne out by the reception given us by Dr. and Mrs. Gulick and the teachers and pupils during our short stay.

The Christian Endeavor society had already become an important element of religious training among the girls of the school, many of whom in future days went out to establish little centres of light and learning in the darkest districts of Catholic Spain. Ever since, the society in the school, now removed to Barcelona, has been an important factor in the life of the Protestant church of Spain, and, as we shall see later, the largest religious gathering of the Reformed churches ever held in the Iberian Peninsula was in connection with the Christian Endeavor convention in Barcelona.

All these influences had their start in Mrs. Gulick's heart

and brain.   She deserves to rank with Mary Lyon as one of the greatest of American woman educators.   Like Mary Lyon she was not afraid to have it known that her school was distinctively a religious and Christian institution, as, I regret to say, are the principals of some institutions which started as missionary schools and received the money for their endowment from Christian people.

Mrs. Gulick went to her great reward a few years ago; her husband, Dr. W. H. Gulick, who was the Nestor of all the missionaries of Spain, and for many years one of the leaders of the Christian Endeavor movement of the Kingdom, passed away in 1922.

A short stay in London enabled us to attend the British National Christian Endeavor convention in Bradford, after which we sailed for home, in June of 1893, rejoiced after these long wanderings in many lands to greet our children, relations, and friends, and to see the Stars and Stripes floating over us once more.

One result of the adventures and experiences of this journey was a large and fully illustrated volume, chiefly written during the journey on steamships and railway trains and published by A. D. Worthington of Hartford, the well-known subscription book-publisher of that day.

At the earnest request of the publishers it received the somewhat banal title, " Our Journey Around the World."   To this volume Mrs. Clark added some impressions of our experiences from a woman's standpoint.   From the viewpoint of its circulation, this was one of the most successful books I have published, some fifty or sixty thousand copies being sold, the royalties from which enabled me to take still other journeys in the interests of the movement which it seemed my duty to promote.

CHAPTER XIII

YEAR 1893

CHRISTIAN CITIZENSHIP AND
CHRISTIAN ENDEAVOR

PARTISAN POLITICS — A TRAGEDY TURNED INTO COMEDY —
AN UNEXPECTED COLD DOUCHE — THE PRUDENTIAL
COMMITTEE.

OON after our return home from this first journey around the world in 1893, the annual International Christian Endeavor convention called us to Montreal, where for the first time the United Society held its annual meeting outside the borders of the United States. By this time the principles and methods of the movement were pretty well understood, and I had begun to feel that the time had come to voice each year, if possible, in my annual presidential address, some message that might be the keynote, or at least *a* keynote of the work for the coming year. It was to be adopted, of course, only so far as it appealed to the common sense of the young people of the society, and was approved by their pastors and churches.

Already the insistent whisperings of an aroused civic conscience were being heard throughout the land, whisperings that have gained in volume each year since, and have sometimes developed into loud and even strident shouts for reform. It seemed to me that the time had come for the young people of our churches to take a new and keener interest in public affairs, not only in temperance, to which they were already committed, but in all lines of good citizenship. So I proposed in my annual address that the unions form good-citizenship committees, and that the topics relating to civic righteousness should find a place upon our convention and local-union programmes, and sometimes, when appropriate to a religious meeting, in our prayer-meeting topics.

The idea was very generally taken up, and now few meetings of large importance are considered complete if such topics are left entirely out.

The tragedy of Robert Ross, an Endeavorer of Troy, New York, who was killed while defending the polls from the ballot-box stuffers, added the good oil of righteous indignation to the flames already kindled, and the society has been known ever since to stand foursquare for temperance, good citizenship, and civic righteousness.

Some attempts have been made to use it for political purposes, on the plea of its identification with moral reform. But these attempts have come to naught, for common sense has taught us that to ally the society with any one political party, however noble its professions and platform, would defeat the very purpose that we had in mind and introduce unending wrangling and dissension. This attitude has sometimes cost us dear for the time being, and I have personally been the object of violent vituperation by good men who failed to see that there was any salvation for the individual or for the country outside of their party, and who believed that all who thought otherwise were " cowards " and " poltroons."

A possible tragedy which ended in comedy, if not in roaring farce, was one of the incidents of the convention in Montreal. An educated and eloquent Hindu, Mr. Karmarkar of India, long one of the Endeavor leaders of that country, in an address before the convention, unwisely compared the Roman Catholic religion with Hinduism, not altogether to the disadvantage of the latter religion. The speech was reported in the Montreal paper of Catholic proclivities and the priests in various addresses added to the indignation of the people. So some " lewd fellows of the baser sort " determined to clean out the whole convention. They assembled in great numbers from the lower wards of the city, and were marching in strong force upon the great tent where the meetings were held, when the police, who had got wind of their proposed attack and were prepared for it, turned a mighty stream of water upon the advancing mob from sections of fire hose which had been connected with hydrants at strategic points.

The rout of the enemy was immediate and complete. They could not stand cold water, though they might have faced the billies of the police officers. The angry crowd melted away, and the students of McGill University, ardent and aggressive Protestants as they were, who had come to fight the mob and defend the Endeavorers, found that their chief duties consisted in escorting the pretty girls to their homes and boarding-houses.

That no real ill-feeling was created by the incident was shown by the address of the mayor of the city, himself a Catholic, who had welcomed the Endeavorers to Montreal, and who, afterwards, at a farewell banquet on Mount Royal, congratulated them on the success of the convention, and the good which he believed it had done the city.

Though it was natural that, during all these years, I should find the duties of my office as president and editor largely absorbing my time and strength, I was able to give some attention to other duties as well, and for nine years, at two different times, I was a member of the Prudential Committee of the American Board, a committee which has under its care the vast interests in all the world of this great missionary undertaking. The weekly meeting of the Prudential Committee occupied the whole of every Tuesday afternoon, and my only regret is that frequent absences and other absorbing duties when at home prevented me from giving more help to the important tasks of the committee.

My personal acquaintance with the missionaries on the field, in frequent journeys in almost all parts of the world, however, made up in some degree for the scant time I could give to the regular meetings in Boston, for at the time of my first journey around the world no officer of the Board or member of the

HON. SAMUEL B. CAPEN

The most eminent Congregational layman, President of the Prudential Committee of the American Board of Foreign Missions, Chairman of the Committee of Thirteen, Boston Convention of Christian Endeavor, which numbered over 56,000 delegates.

Prudential Committee had visited the mission stations on the far foreign fields of India for more than thirty years.

I have always been glad to have been associated during these years with the Christian statesmen who managed the affairs of the American Board. Though this was largely the period of theological controversy and high, and, sometimes, bitter feeling between the older elements and more " advanced " (theologically) constituents of the Board, I recognized in these men who then had control, not only sterling Christian character, but a genuine self-sacrificing devotion to what they believed were its best interests.

Dr. Thompson, the chairman of the committee, Dr. Alden, the able financial secretary, Dr. Plumb, and Dr. Webb, all were genial and courteous, but unbending in their devotion to the evangelical, orthodox doctrines which they believed the Board was founded to establish.

With the administration of the missionary statesmen who have succeeded them, Dr. James L. Barton, whose experience on the field so well fitted him for his present post, the honored and beloved Samuel B. Capen, a constant and enthusiastic friend of the Endeavor movement, the greatest layman of his generation, and others, I had a shorter experience on the Prudential Committee, but one no less valuable to myself. One of the advantages of an interest in foreign missions, which is not always recognized, is the broad and sympathetic outlook that it necessarily gives of the world, its needs, its sufferings, and its only means of healing and health.

Chapter XIV

Years 1885–1922

TRUE YOKEFELLOWS

some of my fellow-workers — god's chosen men —
where and how they were found — what they
have done — many unnamed workers — the hand
of providence

F THIS were a history of the Christian En-
deavor movement I should have much to
say about my colleagues in the United Society, in the State unions, and in many foreign
countries, who have done so much to make the
society a powerful factor in the religious life
of the world. I cannot even mention a hundredth part of
them by name, but I cannot fail to speak of a few who have
been closely associated with me for years in the office of the
United Society. No stronger token of the favor of God upon
the movement could be asked for than the Providential way
in which a number of young men have been led to associate
themselves with our work: young men of keen intellects, wide
sympathies, large executive ability, and unusual devotion to
the Master.

In 1890 we were in great need of a general secretary. The
first secretary, my classmate, Rev. S. W. Adriance, a most devoted and lovable Christian man, was unable to leave his
church, and continued in office but a few weeks. He was
succeeded by a brilliant young layman, George M.
Ward. When he resigned after a short term of office, we

CHARLES F. EVANS
Southern Secretary

PAUL C. BROWN
Pacific Coast Secretary

IRA LANDRITH, D.D., LL.D.
Extension Secretary

CLARENCE C. HAMILTON
Field Secretary of the United Society
and Field Manager, C. E. World

W. ROY BREG
Southwestern Secretary

RODERICK A. WALKER
Manager Western Office

SECRETARIES AFIELD
United Society of Christian Endeavor

DANIEL A. POLING, LL.D.
Associate President and Citizenship
Superintendent

AMOS R. WELLS, LITT. D., LL.D.
Editorial Secretary, 1906–1916.
Editor C. E. World

EDWARD P. GATES
General Secretary

ALVIN J. SHARTLE
Treasurer and Publication Manager

STANLEY B. VANDERSALL
Alumni Superintendent

ROBERT P. ANDERSON
Editorial Secretary

OFFICERS
United Society of Christian Endeavor

knew not where to look for his successor. The work was new, and there had been little time to develop expert Endeavorers.

I had heard of a young man in a small city of Minnesota, who had had a remarkable religious experience, and was devoting himself heart and soul to the Christian Endeavor cause in his own church, and especially to the work among the Juniors. I had a strong impression, an impression that came from above, I believe, that he was the man of all others whom we needed at that crisis of the society's affairs. I journeyed

Secretary John Willis Baer, and Mrs. Baer. Also their children, Francis Shaw, George Van Dusen, and Mildred.
Photograph taken about 1890

1,500 miles on purpose to see him in his home, came back with my impression confirmed, and soon John Willis Baer was inducted into the secretarial office. The choice proved most happy, and the ready gift of speech, interesting personality, and real devotion of Mr. Baer made him for eleven years not only one of the most popular young men in the country, but a successful leader of the rapidly growing Endeavor hosts.

In the year 1892, it was "borne in upon me," according to the phrase of the old theologians, that we must have an efficient man in the editorial office of *The Golden Rule*, as managing editor. My necessarily frequent absences made it out of the question for me to give the time that ought to be given to the details of the paper, and though we had had one or two efficient young ladies as my assistants, the growing circulation and importance of the paper demanded still another editor. Before my journeys abroad, or to the far west, I had been accustomed to write up a large number of editorials and weekly articles in advance, but these could scarcely have the timely appropriateness to all conditions that might arise.

I had been much interested by the articles of a prolific young writer named Amos R. Wells, who had contributed, not only to *The Golden Rule*, but whose articles I had seen in *The Sunday School Times*, and other papers. There was a brightness and pungency to his articles, and they indicated a fund of common sense as well, which seemed to me to promise large things for the future. I had the opportunity of meeting him at a convention at Yellow Springs, O.; he was a professor of the Greek language and literature in Antioch College, living on what he called a "small and precarious salary."

However successful as professor of Greek, his destiny evidently lay along the line of literature, and he was soon persuaded to become the managing editor of *The Golden Rule* and to be my neighbor in Auburndale. The seventy book-titles that Mr. Wells, now Litt.D. and LL.D. Wells, has to his credit, and his multitudinous articles of all kinds in periodicals, grave and gay, serious and humorous, have spoken for themselves to a host of readers, and I need not characterize him further. He is now editor-in-chief and part owner of *The Christian Endeavor World*, while I have relegated myself to the honorary editor's shelf, with no responsibility for or interest in the financial side of the paper.

The same good hand of Providence has been shown in the

advent of many others in the official ranks of Christian Endeavor. I have already spoken of Dr. William Shaw, and, were there space, I would write more at length of Arthur W. Kelly, Rev. John F. Cowan, noted for his Sunday-school lessons, and Rev. R. P. Anderson, our editorial secretary, a prolific writer on many subjects, whom I first met in Christiania in 1905, as related elsewhere; of Charles S. Brown, who has furnished many excellent Christian Endeavor tunes; of George B. Graff, who efficiently managed the publication department of the society for many years; of Hiram N. Lathrop, who was also for many years our genial treasurer. I would also like to write at length of Mr. A. J. Shartle, the present treasurer and publication manager, reliable, conscientious, and enterprising in managing the finances of the society; of our Associate President, Dr. Daniel A. Poling, eloquent, winning, and popular as are few young men in America, who combines within himself so many sterling and attractive qualities, and who, I rejoice to say, in the ordinary course of nature, has most of his life before him, instead of behind him, as in my case; of Dr. Ira Landrith, one of the latest accessions to our official forces, known far and wide, in the East and West and North and South, as one of the most persuasive orators of the day, welcomed on every Chautauqua platform, as well as at every Christian Endeavor convention. All these men are still in the active service of Christain Endeavor, and it is too soon to write their biographies.

Some of the men of whom I have spoken when, as they thought, they had finished their best work as Christian Endeavor leaders, have been called to other distinguished tasks. George M. Ward, the first secretary, became president of Wells College, New York State, and afterwards of Rollins College, Florida. John Willis Baer was for ten years the successful president of Occidental College in California, and is now a financial magnate of the Pacific Coast. He was the first lay moderator of the Presbyterian General Assembly.

Von Ogden Vogt is the honored pastor of a church in Chicago, and author of a notable book on church architecture. William T. Ellis, once assistant editor of *The Christian Endeavor World,* is known throughout the country as a traveller, writer, and lecturer of unusual merit; while George W. Coleman, for many years advertising manager of *The Christian Endeavor World,* is the well-known founder of the " Ford

GEORGE W. COLEMAN

Hall Meetings," and the " Father of the Open Forum," as well as a rising statesman, whom the reform element of Boston sent to the city council, of which he soon became president. He was at one time acting mayor of Boston.

Another most fortunate choice was that of E. P. Gates as general-secretary in 1919. He had long been the very successful secretary of the Illinois union, and his promotion to the position of general-secretary, when a vacancy occurred, was inevitable. Keen, alert, popular with all, indomitable in energy, he cultivates no side issues, but makes Christian Endeavor the passion of his life. Rev. Stanley Vandersall, too, attends conscientiously and untiringly to the new Alumni Department of which he is the head.

The hand of Providence has been equally shown in the choice of field secretaries in many States. I need only mention the names of a few such long-time workers in these lines as the devoted Paul Brown of California, now the national Intermediate secretary of the United Society; Roy Breg of Texas, who has done so much for Christian Endeavor in the Southwest, and Charles Evans of Kentucky, the beloved Southern field secretary, who have already devoted years not a few to this service. Other names come readily to my pen's point, — of those who have done and are doing much for Christian Endeavor: — Eberman, the deeply spiritual secretary of the United Society, who gave his life to the cause while travelling in its interests; Farrill of Wisconsin, and others who have gone to their reward.

I cannot make my book a catalogue of names though I might, were there space, record hundreds of those who in office or out have not spared themselves and who have contributed largely to the success of Christian Endeavor also; young ladies not a few in the headquarters office as personal secretaries or workers in various departments, and a multitude in the field who have served as State and local-union presidents, secretaries, and chairmen of committees. How can I express the gratitude of the cause to these voluntary, unsalaried, unwearied workers? I believe I have proved my point that the men and women whom God has called to the front, prove that the Endeavor movement during all these years had been the object of His special care.

It has often seemed as though the one man of all others who was capable of establishing and extending the movement after it had been inaugurated in the different countries, has been found, and, did space allow, I could point to more than a score of such instances, where we have been led to approach exactly the right person for leadership.

The fact is, I suppose, that the principles and methods of the society have attracted to it a certain type of men and women who, when approached, have been willing to give their time and strength to its development, but in this I see no less clearly the hand of God. To these men and women the success and rapid growth of the movement are due.

The board of trustees of the United Society, representing the different denominations, is a proof of this same natural and divine selection. Dr. Floyd Tomkins, the eminent rector of the Church of the Holy Trinity, Philadelphia, is the one man in all the country who can best lead young people to the spiritual table-lands of entire consecration and devotion, as he has done at hundreds of conventions and local-union meetings. The eloquent and lamented Drs. Wayland Hoyt and P. S. Henson, leaders in the Baptist denomination, were never too busy to travel long distances to our conventions and to give us their ripest thought. Dr. Howard B. Grose, of the same denomination, the vice-president of the United Society of Christian Endeavor, has often contributed of his wit and wisdom to many conventions. Dr. David James Burrell of the Dutch Reformed Church, has contributed both poetry and prose and eloquence of the highest order to our conventions. Dr. John Henry Barrows, the president of Oberlin College, and one of the " spell-binders " of the American pulpit, was seldom absent from our great gatherings, and I shall never forget how, at a consecration meeting, the settee at which we were both kneeling, shook with his unrestrained emotion, as, one after another, the young men and women renewed their consecration to the Master.

Two or three so-called " retreats " will also long stand out in my memory, especially one at Lakewood, N. J., where we

SOME OF THE EARLIER TRUSTEES OF THE UNITED SOCIETY OF CHRISTIAN ENDEAVOR

Front row left to right: Canon Richardson, Dr. H. B. Grose, Dr. Charles A. Dickinson, Mr. W. H. Pennell, first signer of Christian Endeavor pledge, Dr. McMillan, Dr. J. Z. Tyler. Among the back row will be recognized Dr. William Patterson, Dr. Derby, Dr. Shaw, Dr. Brokaw, Dr. Rufus Miller, Dr. James L. Hill, Dr. Rhodes, Secretary John Willis Baer, Dr. Cowan, Mr. Kidder, Auditor, Dr. Teunis Hamlin. This

gathered as trustees of the United Society, and where such men as Dr. Tomkins, and Dr. Burrell, and Dr. Stewart of Auburn Seminary, Dr. Dickinson of Boston, and other eminent leaders of different denominations, told in that intimate and sacred service their hearts' deepest experiences.

Dr. Cleland B. McAfee, one of the well-known brothers to whom the Presbyterian denomination and American Christianity generally are indebted, is also one of our active trustees, as are Dr. E. Bourner Allen and President Henry Churchill King, honored Congregationalists. The venerable Bishop Fallows, recently deceased, was beloved of all Americans. Up to the time of his death in his eighty-seventh year, he was active in every good cause. John Wanamaker, known wherever the English language is spoken, is also a distinguished member of this body. The latter was chosen when he was Postmaster General of the United States. I might, if there were space, mention many others no less distinguished, who ornament and strengthen our board of trustees.

One of the most versatile and interesting of the men with whom I was thus brought in contact, as a trustee of the United Society of Christian Endeavor, was President William R. Harper of Chicago University, so honored in life, so heroic in his lingering illness and death. At the time when I knew him best he was a professor at Yale. He was the only man I ever knew who could make the study of Hebrew interesting. An hour in one of his class-rooms was more entertaining than — what shall I say — an hour at the movies? The comparison seems trifling. He was a man who apparently could do without sleep, who could work twenty hours a day, and yet was never driven by his work, or seemed too busy to see a friend. I remember calling on him once at New Haven, and as the train for Boston did not leave till one o'clock in the morning, I prepared at a reasonably early hour, to go to the station to wait for my train. But he would not hear of it, but insisted on my staying at his home, saying that he never went to bed before one or two o'clock, and he wanted to have our talk out. Then he went to the station with me, and would not leave until my train started for Boston.

In foreign countries, too, the good hand of the Lord has been no less evident in the choice of leaders for the Christian Endeavor cause, but of these I shall often speak in connection with my journeys in these lands.

CHAPTER XV

YEARS 1876–1922

A SHORT CHAPTER ON RECREATIONS

THE MAINE WOODS — A MEMORABLE CANOE TRIP — THE
LITTLE BACKWOODS GIRL

OR the successive editions of the biographical dictionary called *Who's Who?* that is published in London, I am asked year by year what is my favorite recreation, and formerly I had no hesitation in replying that it was camping in the Maine woods and fishing in the Maine lakes. Perhaps if I should go into particulars, I should have to confess that the humble game of quoits is, in my opinion, quite as good as fashionable golf, and does not take nearly so much time, though perhaps my opinion may be partly accounted for by my lack of proficiency in the latter sport. Lawn tennis became popular after my youthful days, and I have never understood it well.

I think I might in my youth have made a baseball " fan " had time and opportunity allowed me more frequently to visit the bleachers, for there are few things more genuinely exciting than a game of baseball between two well-matched and proficient teams. The alertness of the players, their eagerness and marvellous skill, and the fact that every nerve of their bodies, and every drop of blood in their veins, seems to be commandeered for the game, makes of it an exhibition of a certain kind of human prowess which can scarcely be excelled. In my early days, " Two Old Cat " and " Barn Ball " were thought to exhaust the possibilities of baseball. However,

this game, too, has been developed in later years when many
cares and duties have prevented me from becoming proficient
in its technicalities or even its nomenclature.

Of late years I have found abundant joy and recreation on
my old farm, in watching " green things growing," in the
idiosyncracies of hens and chickens, cow and calf, pigs and
goats, and in the lovelier antics and flirtations of the " fowls of

CAMPING IN MAINE

Crossing Pleasant River to our camp in the Maine woods.   Dr. James L. Hill, Rev.
S. W. Adriance, Dr. C. F. Bradley, and Dr. Clark and Guide on buckboard.

the air." For six months in the year ocean bathing and swim-
ming is a daily recreation with me up to the present, and one
which I hope never to get too old to enjoy.

To return to the Maine woods, I cannot do better perhaps
than describe one vacation trip which was typical of a score
of others which gave me renewed vigor, year after year.

The most memorable trip of all was one with Dr. Charles

A. Dickinson, my old friend and colleague in Portland and Boston, and President Charles F. Thwing of Western Reserve University and Adelbert College. We started from the further side of Moosehead Lake on the West Branch of the Penobscot for a canoe trip of two hundred miles through the many lakes of the Allegash waters and down the St. John River into New Brunswick. Three guides, three canoes, and a sufficient store of eatables, together with a tent, constituted our outfit. A more delightful fortnight I never spent. Sometimes our canoes would take us down the still waters of an almost stagnant thoroughfare. Again we would have to cross a large lake in the teeth of a gale of wind, but most exciting of all was the running of the rapids, when it seemed every minute as though the canoe would be swallowed up in the boiling water, or dash itself to destruction against some gigantic boulder, only to be turned, just in the nick of time, by the flexible wrist of the guide who handled the paddle in the stern.

At one clearing, forty miles from any other habitation, a woman in distress came down to the shore and begged us to carry her out to civilization. This we could not do of course, not wishing to be arrested for wife-stealing, but, when she changed her plea, and asked us to take one of the children out with us we agreed to do so if the father was willing. It proved that he " did not care a hang," though I am not sure that " hang " was the word he used, and we took her in one of the canoes. It must have been that we did this at the instigation of Dr. Dickinson, whose warm heart always prompted him to relieve those in distress, especially the children, however much it might cost him. He gave his address to the mother, letting her know how she might always hear from her child, and with this addition to our passenger list we started on the last hundred miles of the voyage. The little girl proved to be an apt scholar, and learned her letters before the trip was over from an illustrated handkerchief which happened to be in our baggage.

When she saw her first train of cars, on the New Brunswick shore, as we paddled down the St. John, and heard the engine shriek, she was struck dumb with amazement, and cried out, " Do you suppose that thing will ever holler again? " evidently thinking it was some bull of Bashan that had invaded the solitudes of New Brunswick.

CAMP DEAN
In the Maine Woods on the Carrying Place Pond.

We were able to add something to her exceedingly scanty wardrobe before we reached our summer home on the coast of Maine, where the ladies of our families took charge of " the little heathen," who had never heard the name of God except " when Daddy damned him." For some time Dr. Dickinson kept her in his own family together with other orphan children whom he had adopted, and afterwards placed her in a happy and very comfortable home where she grew up to be an intelligent and well-favored young woman.

CONCERNING INTERPRETERS AND INTERPRETATION

HOW CHRISTIAN ENDEAVOR STARTED IN CONTINENTAL
EUROPE — INTERPRETERS OR INTERRUPTERS — A LUDI
CROUS TRANSLATION — THE ABILITY OF JAPANESE IN
TERPRETERS.

HE early days of 1894 found me in the grip of the Grippe, a persistent enemy that has more than once laid me low, and brought a long list of ills in its train, chiefly a nervous exhaustion which I have often tried to fight too long and have had to acknowledge ignominiously at last as the victor. This prevented me from attending the International Christian Endeavor Convention in Cleveland that year, and made me for months an unwilling and somewhat rebellious prisoner in my Auburndale home. But there was perhaps a Providence in this as well as in so many other seeming ills, for it sent me to Europe in the early fall in search of health, a journey which resulted in the beginning of the Christian Endeavor movement in many of the continental countries.

While gaining health and strength in the delicious bracing climate of Switzerland, a letter came to me from a young German pastor, Herr Blecher by name, who desired to know more of the Society, something about it having already appeared in the German papers. As in so many other instances, he proved to be exactly the man of all others to spread the idea throughout his own country. With flaming enthusiasm and apostolic zeal, and a face shining with the joy of his message, he went everywhere and enlisted everybody who would listen, as he told of this method of Christian nurture.

From Germany the news of the work spread to the Scandinavian countries, to Russian Poland and Russia proper, to Austria and Hungary, to German Switzerland, and to some of the Balkan states, though the American missionaries in Bohemia, Bulgaria, and Macedonia were most efficient in establishing the societies in those countries.

In the Latin countries, France and Italy and Spain, the work had a different origin. Mrs. Gulick, Spain's great American educator, of whom I have already spoken, was responsible for its development in the Iberian Peninsula, while the first societies in France were started in the McAll Mission.

Either on this visit or an earlier one, I forget which, I was invited by the venerable Dr. McAll to visit him in his home in Paris to explain the working of the society. It was toward the end of his life. He was old and feeble, and seemed harassed with a multitude of the details of his mission, but his first assistant and successor, Mr. Greig, warmly welcomed the society and declared that it was the exact thing that he had been especially longing and praying for on the very day of my visit, of which he had not been previously informed.

Theodore Monod, the eloquent preacher and beloved pastor of the then Established Reformed church, Henri Merle D'Aubigne, the nephew of the eminent church historian, and Père Hyacinthe, whose name was at that time a household word throughout France because of his break with the Catholic church, were all friends of the movement, though Father Hyacinthe seemed to keep much of his interest in his wife's name, where the Jew kept his religion. I fear, also, that Madame Hyacinthe's interest largely centred in her anti-tobacco crusade, and that it cooled when she found that the society could not be used exclusively to this end.

This development of the work throughout the continent has called for many visits to its different countries during the last twenty-five years or more, visits which I cannot describe in detail lest my narrative prove wearisome, but I shall pick out a few incidents here and there, which may prove of interest.

My visits to Germany were full of joy before the war, so hearty and enthusiastic had been the reception of the cause that I represented, and again they were resumed, I rejoice to say, in 1922, with equal pleasure to myself and friendliness on the part of the people. " *How the hats blew up* and the hand-kerchiefs waved," wrote a German friend, struggling with English, in describing one of the conventions. Writing of another convention speaker, he declared " we were delighted to have Rev. F. B. Meyer in our middles." But these very natural slips in " English as she is wrote " only warned me of the far more terrible blunders that I should make if I attempted to speak in a foreign tongue. Wisely I have never attempted it, but have always addressed my audiences through interpreters, except in English-speaking countries, and have had occasion to seek the kind offices of interpreters *in some forty different languages,* twenty of them in Europe alone. Until one counts them up it seems difficult to believe that so many languages are spoken on that little continent.

On the whole I have not found my interpreters " interrupters," as Joseph Cook was accustomed to call them, though I have sometimes had occasion to recall Maltbie Babcock's definition of speaking through an interpreter as " a compound fracture of speech, followed by mortification."

For the most part my interpreters deserve my sincerest thanks and warmest praise, for the heartiness and enthusiasm which they have thrown into their translation, often leading me to feel that they were making a far better speech than I myself could have made. Sometimes however the experience is excruciating as when one's interpreter attempts to give a literal, word-for-word translation, with little regard for the

connection, or the idioms of his own language. Sometimes he
has had the barest nodding acquaintance with the English
language, but has attacked his job as though he had the vocabulary of a Shakspeare. In such cases the blank and wearied
look of the audience, or their interpolations; " he did not
say that, he said this," and etc., and etc., tell me what a mess he
is making of the whole thing.

Sometimes the mistakes of the interpreter are ludicrous, as
when in Japan an eminent professor was translating an address of Mrs. Clark's. In the course of it she remarked that
we were like a couple of carrier pigeons flying around the world
and alighting here and there, with messages from friends.
Not being acquainted with these birds, and supposing they were
some kind of gallinaceous fowls, the professor gravely told his
audience that we were " like a rooster and a hen, flying around
the world and lighting here and there." The missionaries who
understood both languages were audibly amused.

As a rule I have found that the more remote the language
is from English, philologically, the better the interpreters.
Thus the translators that I have had in Japan, Russia, and the
other Slavic countries have often been better than in the lands
whose languages are allied to English. I have stood in my
stocking feet on many a platform in Japan while the wind
whistled through the paper walls, but happy and content,
knowing that the brother by my side would enter into the very
heart of my address, would gesticulate and perspire with his
task, and would make a deeper impression upon his audience
than I could hope to have made, even if all had understood
English.

Thinking I would test my friend, Rev. Mr. Miyake, who
interpreted for me in various parts of Japan, I inserted in the
middle of a long paragraph (for he had asked me to speak for
five minutes or more at a time without interruption), a verse of
a familiar hymn, which had been translated, as I knew, for the
Japanese hymn book. I wondered how he would struggle

A JAPANESE CHRISTIAN ENDEAVOR LEADER AND FAMILY

One of the best interpreters, Rev. T. Makino, his mother, wife, and seven children. Mr. Makino was formerly President of the Japanese Christian Endeavor Union.

with the rhyme and metre of poetry. Quick as a flash he picked up the Japanese hymn book, turned to the familiar hymn, and, when he came to the right place in the translation, read the verse in its flowing Japanese version. From that time I never doubted Mr. Miyake's skill and accuracy as an interpreter. Rev. T. Sawaya, long the efficient secretary of the Japanese Christian Endeavor union, was an equally good and even more dramatic interpreter.

The art of speaking through an interpreter consists in knowing exactly what you want to say, and saying it in simple, concrete terms, avoiding involved and obscure sentences, imaginative flights and great attempts at eloquence. I have seen interpreters perspire and grow red in the face and then give it up altogether when a speaker involved him in some metaphysical distinction, quoted a Browningese poem, or attempted a pun which had absolutely no equivalent in any other language. Anyone who indulges in such efforts ought to be indicted for cruelty to interpreters.

To speak with the aid of *one* interpreter is by no means a harrowing experience, but when one has to have two or more for the same sentence the task is more wearisome. Once when in South Africa, visiting the famous Chiefs' School at Lovedale at the invitation of the beloved Doctor James Stuart, I was obliged to have not only a double-barreled interpretation, but a regular repeating rifle, for, as the sons of the chiefs understood three different languages, and had no one language in common, three interpreters stood by my side, and gave what I had to say in three languages to different portions of the audience. A better way was that followed in Constantinople, when, in different parts of the same large room, Armenian, Turkish, and Greek girls were gathered, while Mrs. Clark addressed them, and the teachers interpreted her remarks to each group in their own tongue. After all, a better substitute for the gift of tongues is a good interpreter of one tongue.

Chapter XVII

Years 1884–1922

GREAT BRITAIN AND GREAT BRITISHERS

A SCORE OF THE WORLD'S MOST ELOQUENT PREACHERS — DRS. MEYER, CLIFFORD, MACLAREN, PARKER, SPURGEON, AND MANY OTHERS — IN SPURGEON'S CLASS-ROOM — DR. PARKER'S HUMOR — A GOOD IRISH STORY — WILLIAM T. STEAD.

Y ACQUAINTANCE with some outstanding people of Great Britain must be crowded into one chapter, regardless of chronological order, for I have made fourteen or fifteen visits to Britain's " right little, tight little island," within twice as many years.

" We like Americans but detest America," said a plain-spoken Britisher, in one of the very frank moods for which his countrymen are famous, to an American; the latter answered with the retort discourteous, " We like England, but we detest Englishmen." This American, unless led away by his desire to get even with the Britisher, could not have gone behind the barriers of reserve which many Englishmen put up between themselves and all strangers. He had not become accustomed to the " brutal frankness " and " a certain condescension " of which Americans complain, and which, after all, really mean so little. When one does get behind the barriers he finds that there are no more delightful hosts and cordial friends in all the world than the descendants of our own forbears who stayed in the motherland.

Among the ministers and religious leaders now living (in

162

1922) whom I have rejoiced to call my friends, are Dr. John Clifford, the Grand Old Man of the Free Churches of Great Britain, Rev. Frederick Brotherton Meyer, D.D., known throughout the world for his evangelistic labors and writings; Dr. J. H. Jowett, Dr. R. J. Campbell, Dr. James Stalker of Scotland, Rev. Thomas Yates of London, Rev. John Pollock of Ireland, pastor of the largest Presbyterian Church in the United Kingdom, Rev. James Mursell, Rev. Thomas Phillips of London, Rev. Lionel Fletcher of Cardiff, and of course I have met many others whom I greatly esteem, but I am limited by lack of space, from mentioning all the names I would like to record.

Of those who have passed away, Dr. Joseph Parker, Charles H. Spurgeon, and Alexander Maclaren are the most eminent.

Many others whom I have met more casually, were or are stars of the first magnitude in their own ecclesiastical firmament, like Dr. Horton of London, Dr. Jones of Bournemouth, Dr. George Adam Smith, Hugh Price Hughes of blessed memory, Bishop Gore, Henry Drummond, Dr. Carpenter, Bishop of Ripon, Dr. Creighton, Bishop of London, Silvester Horne, who was no less worthy of a bishopric, and many others, living and dead, well known to American readers.

On my first Sunday in London, more than thirty years ago, like nine Americans out of ten who are religiously inclined, I went to hear Charles H. Spurgeon in the morning, and Joseph Parker in the evening. Mr. Spurgeon's burly form and homely face, — homely in both the American and English sense of the word; his resonant, beautifully modulated voice, and the spiritual exaltation of his sermon, made a deep impression upon me, as upon all his auditors. This was in the later years of his life, but his bow of eloquence still abode in strength, and his natural force was but little abated, for some years to come.

On a later visit, he kindly invited me to speak to his congregation for a few moments before his sermon, and it was an experience to be remembered, — standing in that high pulpit with something like a score of deacons underneath, some of whom I feared would be sadly mangled if the pulpit should fall, — while all around, on the floor and in the two great galleries, right and left and before, and even a few behind, was a great audience such as Mr. Spurgeon had gathered Sunday after Sunday for many years. Such a weekly example was this, as the world has scarcely ever seen, of the personal power of a speaker, united with the glowing presentation of the Gospel message.

My most vivid memory, however, of Mr. Spurgeon, was in the class-room of his students, where he invited me on another occasion to tell the young theologues something about the Christian Endeavor movement. I was struck with the eager, tiptoe attitude of expectation with which everything he said in his brief introduction of me was greeted by the students. It seemed as though they were ready to weep or laugh at every sentence, and were confident that something worthy of tears or smiles would be forthcoming. The smiles, however greatly predominated, for Spurgeon was by no means a weeping preacher. His allusion to a picture on the wall of the class-room which represented the angel spirits of the martyrs hovering over the dead bodies in the arena where the lions were tearing them to pieces, in spite of the gruesomeness of the picture, evoked considerable laughter, as he told how one of his little grandchildren, looking at the picture and the fluttering angels, exclaimed nonchalantly, " Huh, pigeons."

I have forgotten the connection, or how it aided in the introduction of a humble American visitor, but the students being in the mood, seemed equally on the *qui vive* when I came to speak, and when I began to tell about the different committees in the American Christian Endeavor societies, the lookout, the prayer-meeting, and the social, they began to smile; the music, the temperance and the sunshine committees, and they began to titter; the good literature, the flower, and the

Rev. John Pollock and his Wife and Son Paul, who was Killed in the World War, on the Right. Rev. James Mursell on Left. Miss Elsie Pollock, Now a Missionary in Formosa, with Dr. Clark. Both Mr. Pollock and Mr. Mursell have been Presidents of the British Christian Endeavor Union, and the former is President of the European Union.

evangelistic committees, and they broke into quite a guffaw. I saw nothing funny in it, but they seemed to think that I was perpetrating some American joke, at which it was their bounden duty to laugh, or that, perhaps, I was drawing a long American bow in regard to the actualities of young people's work. This, it is needless to say, was in the early days of the Christian Endeavor movement, for now they have in Great Britain all these committees and many more in their societies.

Afterwards I received from Mr. Spurgeon permission to use every week in *The Golden Rule*, extracts from his sermons, which were specially reported for us by Mr. Charles Waters, a deacon of the Tabernacle, and one of the earliest friends of the Endeavor movement.

Since Mr. Spurgeon's death I have had the privilege of knowing his successors, Rev. Thomas Spurgeon, Dr. A. T. Pierson, another eloquent American pastor of the Tabernacle, Dr. A. C. Dixon, and of addressing several great audiences of young people within its hospitable walls.

Probably of no London preacher are so many good posthumous stories told as of Dr. Joseph Parker. I have already written of my first introduction to the City Temple and of Dr. Parker's over-flattering introduction of myself. It was far more interesting to sit in the pews and listen to the doctor's mighty, reverberating voice, as he denounced some evil of the day, or to his flute-like tones as he touched on lighter themes, or led his congregation in an uplifting prayer. No such born actor, I believe, ever mounted pulpit stairs. He could not help being theatrical. It was as natural and necessary to him as breathing.

In private conversation, however, he could be kindly and genial as a politician, or brusque and savage as a bear, as he deemed either mood a fitting reception to his visitor. He received strangers for a few moments after the morning service in his little study back of the pulpit, where he held court for half an hour, each visitor sending in his card and being strictly limited in time. " When can I have an hour's conversation with you, Doctor, on an important subject? " asked one boresome visitor after the morning service. " Never, sir, never to all eternity," roared the Doctor, but I think he did accord him the regulation five minutes.

A minister now in South Africa has told me about attending a party of brother clergymen among whom was Dr. Parker, who prided himself on his enormous head, as well he might, considering how much it contained. Greatly to the annoyance and chagrin of some of the brethren with smaller craniums, Dr. Parker would take from the hat rack, one after another, the tall tiles which they had worn to the party, place them on his own shaggy brows, and show how the hat tottered around, several sizes too small, on his head.

Perhaps my most amusing personal experience of Dr. Parker's astounding oratory came in connection with the World's Christian Endeavor Convention in 1910. The meetings were held in the great Alexandra Palace, in one enormous hall in which twenty thousand auditors gathered for some of the mass meetings. Other halls and tents, were, however, used for the smaller meetings, and in one of these an interdenominational programme was provided, with the leading representatives of each of the great denominations as speakers. The celebrated Dr. Creighton, Bishop of London, spoke for the Church of England, Hugh Price Hughes for the Methodists, Dr. Watson of Birkenhead, for the Presbyterians, Dr. Greenough, chairman of the Baptist Union for that year, for the Baptists, and Dr. Joseph Parker for the Congregationalists. Truly a more distinguished platform would have been hard to find in the five continents.

The Bishop of London made a splendid twenty-minute address, friendly and fraternal, and dwelling especially upon the *temper* with which we should do Christian work. As I was presiding at the meeting, I next introduced Dr. Parker to speak for the Congregationalists. His opening words were astonishing: " Mr. President, I think that you introduced the last speaker as ' the Bishop of London.'   I had an impression that *I* was the Bishop of London; for a man who has stood in the pulpit for twenty-five years, preaching the Gospel of Jesus Christ week after week to a great congregation, has some right to consider himself the Bishop of London."

Such unspeakable bombast made us want to hide our Congregational heads, but Dr. Parker knew how to get out of a difficulty, or rather he often made a seeming oratorical blunder for the sake of getting out of it.   He continued, " But, Mr. President, though I may have had the impression that I had some right to be called a Bishop of London, since I have heard the magnificent address of Dr. Creighton, I have come to the conclusion that, after all, he has the better right to be called *the* Bishop of London."

This relieved the tension, and he went on to say, " I have been asked to speak for Congregationalism.   I would not be wet through for any ism in the world."   The peculiar significance of this remark was evident as we saw the perspiration oozing through his thin alpaca coat, for it was a frightfully hot day, and the glass roof over this particular audience room seemed to focus the sun's rays upon the devoted speakers on the platform.   However, Dr. Parker was fully able to occupy his twenty minutes on the broader theme of " Endeavor," without much reference either to Congregationalism or to Christian Endeavor.

The other speakers were all eloquent and impressive, but none gave such successive shocks and counter shocks to the audience as did Dr. Parker.

On this occasion, Hugh Price Hughes told me privately after the meeting that he was greatly desirous that the Wesleyans should join the Christian Endeavor movement as the other denominations of Methodists in Great Britain had done, but, he said, he had only been able to " keep his toe in the doorway " to prevent its being entirely shut in the face of the movement, referring to the fact that the Wesley Guilds of Great Britain and the Epworth Leagues of America were the only young people's societies whose denominational authorities forbade the interdenominational fellowship. In spite of this fact, however, since all the other Methodist bodies, and there are many, are in this fellowship, there are probably more Methodist Christian Endeavor societies throughout the world than are found in any other one denomination. Not a few, indeed, among the Wesleyan Methodists.

Two other eminent divines whom I have seen at many conventions, and who always seem as eager and interested in the meetings as the young people of a quarter of their age, are Dr. F. B. Meyer, and Dr. John Clifford.

Dr. Meyer has been president of the British Union, as well as of the great London Federation of Christian Endeavor societies and has found them a real aid in his evangelistic work. I was much impressed by his answer to a nominating committee from the British Union, who came to ask him to serve as president for the succeeding year. They had not much hope that he would accept, knowing how busy he was as pastor of the great Christ Church on Westminster Bridge Road, as a voluminous writer of books and religious articles, and as a frequent traveller to America and other lands on evangelistic tours, so they said to him: " We will not ask you to do very much work, Dr. Meyer, but the use of your name as president will be a great help to us."

He answered, " My dear friends, if you want me to be a figure-head president, I cannot accept; but if you want me to be a genuine working president, I will consider it one of the greatest privileges of my life, and will give every Thursday to the work of the society, going from Land's End to John O'Groat's, wherever I may be called." It can be imagined how delighted the delegation was with his reply, and still more delighted, when, in the course of the year, he fulfilled his promise to the letter.

Dr. Meyer is the most genial and companionable of men, full of good spirits and good humor in private life, and on suitable public occasions, and untiring in his capacity for work; writing on railway trains and motor busses, taking on task after task, but never, apparently, too hurried to do each duty well. If there was a beehive church in all the world it was Christ Church under his administration. Under Dr. Poole, his American successor, it still retains this distinction.

Dr. John Clifford is a man of a somewhat different type, though earnest for the spread of the kingdom, equally eloquent in the pulpit, equally busy out of it, and equally a born leader of men.

On two or three occasions he has asked me to preach in his famous church, Westbourne Park Chapel, when I would much rather have sat in the pew and listened to him, a preference which doubtless his congregation shared with me. On the last occasion of this sort in 1914, he invited Mrs. Clark and myself to his pleasant home to meet his invalid wife and to take dinner with them. You need to get into a great man's home really to know him as he is, and Dr. Clifford shines there as well as in his pulpit. Genial, friendly, unassuming, he makes his guests feel that they are conferring a favor as well as receiving one, and he is not above the small pleasantries of life. On his table, I remember, was a large box of chocolate creams which he passed to us, remarking that though he had lost many of his teeth he still kept his " sweet tooth." I think it speaks well for a man of eighty to retain his boyhood's predilections.

I was much interested in the originals of several cartoons that had appeared in *Punch* and other papers, which had been presented to him, and which he had framed and hung on the wall of his stairway. One of them represented him in one of his reform crusades as Davy Crockett, while Prime Minister Balfour was the coon up the tree, crying out, " Don't shoot, Dr. Clifford, I'll come down."

One of his good stories related to an occasion when Dr. Dwight Hillis had been advertised to preach for him. For some reason Dr. Hillis did not turn up at the hour for the service and he had to preach himself at a moment's notice. As he was going out of the church, after the service, he heard one stranger say to another, neither of whom had known of the substitute: "The old man did pretty well *for an American,* didn't he?"

The late Dr. Alexander Maclaren, and Dr. Jowett of Birmingham, afterwards of New York and London, are two more of Great Britain's preachers, with whom I have had some personal contact.

In Doctor Maclaren's church in Manchester, during his lifetime, I preached two or three times, and have had the honor of spending a night under his hospitable roof. Among all the expository preachers, living or dead, in my opinion he stands at the head. His marvellous aptitude of illustration opened windows into the truth as does no other preacher whom I have heard or read. His illustrations were always apt and pat, never strained, and are strewn as thickly through his sermons as jewels in a king's crown. A young preacher needs scarcely any other commentaries in his library than Dr. Maclaren's volumes on the many books of the Bible. His English was as pure, simple, and limpid as that of the greatest masters of our mother tongue.

In his home, too, he was a charming host, and I looked with reverence and almost with awe, when, as a comparatively young man, I was his guest and remembered how his books had seemed to me the supreme volumes of Biblical lore. The last time I saw him was near the very end of his life. He had asked me to preach for him in the evening, while he took the morning service, and I was privileged to listen. Though feeble in body his mind was as clear, his points as telling, and his illustrations as forcible as when he was in his prime. But when I went to his study after the sermon he was utterly exhausted, his face incredibly wrinkled by age and by studious days and nights, while he seemed to take some comfort in occasional whiffs from his long " church warden." With his permission I soon afterwards compiled a volume of " Similes " from Dr. Maclaren, Rev. F. B. Meyer adding an estimate of Dr. Maclaren's life and work.

Dr. Jowett represents the present generation of great preachers, and perhaps there is no one either in Great Britain or America who by simple, quiet, but most forcible appeal to the best that is in his hearers, can so hold and entrance them. In his old church in Birmingham, Carr's Lane Chapel, I have seen great gatherings of young people, all of whom seemed to feel at home in a sanctuary made famous by the pastorates of three of the greatest preachers of the last century, — Dr. James, Dr. Dale, and Dr. Jowett.

Rev. John Pollock, pastor of St. Enoch's Church of Belfast, Ireland, for many years past, is even more widely known in Christian Endeavor circles than these eminent preachers, for he has been president of the Irish Union, of the British Union, and of the All-European Union as well, and has made many journeys to America and other lands in the interests of the movement. We have spent many happy vacation days together in Scotland, Ireland, and America, when I have been sometimes guest and sometimes host.

The dry humor of Scotland and the more rollicking fun of Ireland both find a place in this genial friend who is Scotch by birth and training and Irish by adoption, and the long tramps we have had around the shores of Nantucket and Martha's Vineyard, some sixty miles or more in less than a week, and other shorter rambles, as well as our common tastes and tasks, have endeared him to me. He has written also some of the best Christian Endeavor hymns in the hymnals of Europe and America. " For Christ and the Church " is especially stirring.

Another Irishman after my own heart was the late Rev.

J. G. Lamont, who according to the itinerant system of the
Methodist Church to which he belonged, vibrated between
Belfast, Dublin, and Cork.   Very tall, impressive in figure
and bearing, a fine preacher, and a most devoted Christian,
there was yet a twinkle in his eye which told one before he
spoke what a rare *raconteur* he might be.   His Irish stories
were inimitable, especially his favorite tale of the ignorant
countryman who was so under the dominion of the priest that
he took for law and gospel everything that the priest told
him.

Pat was a sad drunkard, and his confessor had labored with
him many times.   At last, after an unusually bad spree, the
priest said to him, " Pat, if you ever get drunk again, I'll
turn ye into a rat."   The poor fellow, in mortal terror of
this fate, kept straight for quite a while, but at last his appetite overcame him, and he reached the drivelling state of
maudlin tears and self-pity, and confided to his wife,
" Bridget dear, I couldn't help it.   I've been drinking again,
and Father Maloney is going to turn me into a rat."   Between his sobs he blubbered out, " Bridget, when you see the
tail growing on me, and me eyes growing smaller, then,
Bridget, *for heaven's sake, look out for the cat!* "

Such a story seems tame enough in print, but when told
with Mr. Lamont's rich Irish brogue, and when he pictured
out poor Mike thinking he was gradually turning into a rat,
his tail growing longer and his eyes growing smaller, it was
irresistible.

On one occasion I was attending a convention in Cork when
Mr. Lamont was stationed there, and I was his guest.
Taking an afternoon for a holiday, we went together to
Blarney Castle.   Mr. Lamont, before we started, pinned on
to his under coat a long and imposing row of Christian Endeavor badges which he had worn at various conventions, and
which looked very much like military decorations.   When
we reached the gate to the Castle he threw back his overcoat

and, assuming a military air, displayed his badges to the wondering eyes of the old soldier who collects the shillings which allow entrance to the castle grounds. The old veteran looked with amazement at the supposed evidence of military prowess, and exclaimed in awe-stricken tones, " It was the Lord's own mercy, Sor, that ye got back alive! "

Rev. James Mursell, now pastor of a large Baptist Church in High Wycombe, England, is another of my choice British friends. A distant relative of William Carey, the pioneer missionary, he exhibits something of Carey's adventurous spirit, and has had fruitful pastorates in Scotland and Australia, as well as in England. In all these countries, as well as in America, we have had happy days together.

It can be imagined that when, at the great Boston convention of 1895, Mr. Mursell, Mr. Pollock, Mr. Lamont, Rev. Knight Chaplin, then the secretary of the British Christian Endeavor Union, Rev. Mr. Montgomery, an eminent Presbyterian pastor of Belfast, and Rev. J. L. Closs of Australia, all came as delegates, and were all guests at our home in Auburndale, we had many a lively hour of relaxation after the strenuous duties and innumerable meetings of the convention.

Rev. James Stalker, whose " Life of Christ " and other books have been so popular in America, has been our kind host on more than one occasion. He once invited Professor George Adam Smith to meet us at his home. Dr. Smith had just come from an evangelistic service in a mission, and I was delighted with his warm, evangelical spirit, especially as he was at that time under suspicion in conservative circles for his liberal views regarding " the second Isaiah " and the other prophets.

Professor Drummond sent word at the last minute that he was ill and could not come. This was, alas, the beginning of the long two years of mysterious illness, which at last ended in his seemingly untimely death. I had before met Mr. Drummond at a Christian Endeavor convention in Hamilton,

Ontario, where I was charmed with the impromptu little speech that he made to the young people, for his presence was unexpected. His simplicity, sincerity, and naturalness are reflected in his books, and his very face showed forth the love which he declared was the greatest thing in the world.

He was travelling with Lord and Lady Aberdeen on this occasion, and I was struck then, as I have been since with their simple friendliness and cordiality of manner, so like in its quality to that of their friend, Drummond.

To return to England after this little character-sketch excursion to Scotland and Ireland, a minister who has filled a large space in the eye of the public, and has figured in many newspaper headlines, is Rev. Reginald John Campbell, Dr. Parker's successor in the City Temple. There could scarcely be a greater contrast than between these two men, the one big, burly, dramatic, with a voice of thunder, the other slight, spirituelle, with an impressive halo of white hair, which gave the impression that he was about ready for translation; without any histrionic gift, and with a thin, high voice. Yet Dr. Campbell crowded the City Temple through all his theological wanderings, as Dr. Parker had done before him, until he decided to leave the Congregational fold for the Church of England.

He came to America on his first visit in 1903 to speak at the International Christian Endeavor Convention in Denver, Col., and while on this side of the Atlantic was our guest for two or three days with his good wife at our home in Auburndale.

I cannot close this chapter without speaking of two eminent laymen whom it has been my privilege to know intimately. One of these was Mr. W. H. Hope of Liverpool, a wholesale commission merchant, whose equal for unselfish and untiring religious work I never knew. His days and nights were literally given to the poor children of Liverpool. This was his business in life. He engaged in trade as William Carey cobbled shoes, " to pay expenses." I have seen the little ragged, dirty, homeless children in Liverpool's slums crowd around him and fight for a chance to hold his hand, while joyous cries of " Mr. 'Ope," " Mr. 'Ope," " Mr. 'Ope," echoed from every side as he went down the long mean streets to his mission work.

One of the beautiful memorials which he has left behind him is the Christian Endeavor Holiday Home at Kent's Bank, which he was largely instrumental in establishing, and which was so successfully carried on by Mrs. Jennie Wareing, the beloved " mother " of a multitude of young people, and a poetess of no mean order as well. She has just passed to her great reward, mourned by a great host of young people.

Another gentleman who was greatly interested in this home, was in many respects, I think, the most eminent Englishman I have ever known, Mr. W. T. Stead, the great editor, reformer, and publicist. He was a many-sided man.

In the early days of our acquaintance he did me the honor of publishing a character sketch of myself in his magazine, *The Review of Reviews,* and I wondered that he could find so much to say of a somewhat obscure American clergyman, though of course it was the Christian Endeavor society, then in its earlier years, that chiefly engaged his pen. From that time until his lamented and tragic death in the wreck of the " Titanic " I saw him many times in his office in London. When the World's Endeavor convention was held in London in 1900, he was invited to speak but refused to do so, on the ground that he was expected to address young men alone, while, if he spoke at all he wanted to address both sexes, for one of the chief benefits of the society, was, in his opinion, that it brought the sexes together, and gave the best of them a chance to get acquainted and form lasting ties of companionship and love. Thus the early sneer that Christian Endeavor stood for " Courting Endeavor," became, in his mind, one of its chief glories.

Though he would not deliver an address he entered into the

convention, and especially its social features, with great heartiness, and invited a large number of American delegates and others to an excursion up the Thames in motor boats, for which he provided a most bounteous collation, spending hundreds of dollars on the trip.

Among the other guests on this occasion were Silas and Joseph Hocking, the well known authors, Marianne Farningham, the writer of beautiful hymns, and others of the literary ilk, together with many young aspirants for the honors of the pen and the ink-pot.

Mr. Stead was the life of the party, and when the conversation bore upon literary matters he gave the young quill-drivers a recipe for becoming authors. " In order to become good writers," he said, " you must fall in love with a woman twice your age, and be so dead in love with her that you will insist upon writing to her every day of the week. You won't write drivel to such a woman, and your respect and love for her will soon make you masters of a good style." Whether there was a touch of autobiography in this advice he did not tell us.

As is well known, Mr. Stead believed that he was in communication with the spirits of the dead, a belief that was a great comfort and inspiration to him, though he said it had not changed his theological views, and that he still believed in all the great truths that were taught him at his mother's knee. He read me long letters which he thought came from his beloved son who had been his colleague on *The Review of Reviews,* and who had passed into the other world. The letters were full of religious fervor and most beautifully expressed, and showed an especial interest in the great Sunday-school class of young men, which he had taught when on earth.

Mr. Stead also told me about " Julia," from whom, as well as from his son, he thought he had received many communications by automatic writing. As I remember it, " Julia " was a Boston school-teacher whom he had never seen, but who had managed to establish communication (Mr. Stead being the writing medium) with a friend who was still living.   A little book called " Letters from Julia," of which he gave me an autographed copy, is an interesting story of life in the other world, particularly to those who accept Mr. Stead's premises.

In this connection I must tell of an incident which occurred in the year 1900 on our return from a long journey across Siberia after escaping from Peking just before the Boxer massacres, of which I shall tell in another chapter.   Mrs. Clark and I were perhaps the last people who left Peking before the siege, and the newspaper editors of London were naturally anxious to find out all that we knew about the situation in Boxerland, which after all, was not very much.   It was supposed at that time to be certain that the missionaries and diplomats were all dead, and it was known for a fact that the German Ambassador had been killed, and a memorial service had been appointed in St. Paul's Cathedral in memory of the English martyrs.

Mr. Stead came to me and said that though he believed most clairvoyants were fakirs, yet there was one in Paris that he believed did possess second sight, and he would like to consult her about the fate of the besieged in Peking.

He added that before going into a trance the clairvoyant must have in her hand something that had recently come from the place she wished to see, and asked me what I could give him that had recently come from Peking.   I handed him a letter of introduction from M. de Giers, the Russian Minister, and one from Mr. Conger, our American Minister, with some other little things from my suitcase.

He took them over to Paris and in two or three days brought them back to me telling me that when the clairvoyant held them in her hand she went into a dead trance, and told him that she could see the people of Peking, that they were for the most part alive and well, that the German Ambassador was killed, but that the British Ambassador was well, though his

wife was afraid that he might kill her if worst came to worse,
rather than allow her to fall into the hands of the Boxers.
Moreover she said that the allied armies were on their way to
the rescue and that the siege would soon be raised. She went
on to say further, that this trouble would soon be followed by
a great war of the nations, in which Russia would particularly
suffer.

When she came out of the trance and Mr. Stead told her
what she had said, she declared, " I must have been mistaken
this time; it cannot be possible that they are not all dead."
A few days afterwards it was found that the clairvoyant,
whether by a happy coincidence of circumstances or otherwise,
had spoken substantially the truth, and the memorial service
in St. Paul's was called off. I leave my readers to draw their
own inferences, and will only add that whatever they may
think of Mr. Stead's spiritualistic leanings, which I could not
sympathize with, he was one of the kindliest, keenest,
brainiest, bravest, and most generous men I ever knew.

MEXICO, JAMAICA, AND CUBA

MEXICO TWENTY-FIVE YEARS AGO — ZACATECAS — LOVELY
JAMAICA — AN UNUSUAL GREETING — CUBA AND THE
SPANISH WAR.

I N SPITE of our proximity to Mexico, I have made but two journeys to that Republic, not because of lack of interest in our neighbors, but partly because the calls from lands across the seas have seemed more insistent than those from the southern Republic, and partly because, for years, that distressed country, with its constant revolutions and counter-revolutions, has afforded little scope for religious meetings, or other activities of the sort.

But my visits to this land have given me some idea of its extreme wealth in natural resources, and its large opportunities for Christian service among the people who have been so long exploited by the church and by greedy land-holders. In its earlier days Mexico owed not a little to the Church of Rome for such civilization as it enjoys, and the priest, Hidalgo, who inspired Mexicans with a desire for liberty, and led the way, is one of the noblest characters in modern history. Protestant missionaries, however, are doing much to bring a purer faith to the people who are throwing off the shackles of ecclesiastical and political serfdom.

Our first journey to Mexico City was interrupted at several places where we stopped for public meetings. One day in

San Antonio was memorable to us, at least, because of a cyclone which did great damage in Texas, and swept the edge of the city, but without making any great havoc there. I could realize, however, as never before, as I saw the black storm-clouds gather and break in their fury, the terrible power of the wind as it marshals its forces and levels everything before it, snap-

THE ORGAN CACTUS OF MEXICO

ping big trees like pipestems and planting houses or wrecks of houses many rods away from their original foundations.

The journey from northern Mexico to the capital was hot and dusty and most uncomfortable, as such a journey on the edge of summer is likely to be, but was relieved by a halt with our missionary friends, the Eatons, in the thriving city of

Chihuahua, — a city which has figured so largely in the later troubled history of the Republic.

Mexico City, after the heat and dust of the lowlands, seems charming indeed with its four o'clock shower every afternoon in summer time, and its distant view of lofty snow-clad Popocatapetl and Iztaccihuatl. When peace shall be really established and a stable government shall have been able fully to cope with the bandits, as now seems likely under the Obregon *régime,* this great upland plain of our southern neighbor, with its many beauties and unusual attractions for the naturalist, the archaeologist, and the lover of magnificent scenery, will become one of the most attractive spots of the twin continents.

The chief Endeavor gathering of this journey was the national convention at Zacatecas, a famous mining town, some 7,000 feet above the sea. It was a good meeting, and gave us an introduction to many of the missionaries and native workers, who are doing their best to make Mexico the splendid, prosperous country of vast resources, which Providence designed her to be.

Zacatecas was, I think, at that time the most arid and parched city that I ever visited. No rain, it was said, had fallen there for seven years, the city water was running low, was of a poor quality, and had to be used sparingly. Clouds of dust whirled through the streets, and dreadful epidemics caused by the long drought were feared. When we arrived there seemed no certainty that the drought would not continue for seven years more, but toward the end of the second day, strange to say, a welcome drizzle began, and late at night, as we took our departure, a drenching rain set in which let loose every evil smell that seven years of drought had bottled up. Evidently the Lord had opened the windows of heaven, and I can only hope that the spiritual blessings of the convention were as large and fruitful as the abundant shower that watered the earth.

One of the most charming islands lapped by any ocean is Jamaica, whose name, unfortunately, has been chiefly associated in the minds of many Americans with the fiery liquor that in the olden times demoralized many a community. This reproach she shared with New England, as the two chief centres of the rum trade, but she no longer deserves it, to the same extent as formerly at least, for with the decadence of the sugar plantations, rum and molasses are going more and more to the shades of forgotten traffics, and bananas and oranges and other tropical fruits are taking their place.

Jamaica is one of the shining examples of the beneficence of British rule. Here ten thousand whites live together in peace with seven hundred thousand blacks. The communities are orderly and self-respecting, and though there is a sad lack of education in many of the black districts, there is little abject poverty.

The roads throughout Jamaica, as in most British possessions, are admirable for carriage or automobile, and there are few more lovely drives in all the world than half a dozen which can be taken over the hard white highways, under the magnificent tropical foliage, with splendid palms of all descriptions towering toward the skies, while trees and shrubs covered with brilliant flowers meet the eye in every direction. Frequently, too, we pass vast groves of banana trees that furnish a cheap and succulent fruit for uncounted thousands in our great cities, and a fruit that is equally appreciated by the well-to-do. Captain Baker of Cape Cod who introduced this fruit to North Americans half a century ago was a benefactor of mankind.

The negroes of Jamaica are a happy-go-lucky people, for our brothers in black in that fortunate isle do not have to exert themselves, at least to obtain a bare living. Just laws are well administered, and the religious life of the negroes is more intelligent and sensible than in many other places. They have large and substantial churches in several cities and towns, and the work of English missionaries has evidently not been in vain.

THE LEADERS OF CHRISTIAN ENDEAVOR IN JAMAICA IN 1898
The Tall Man in the Back Row is Mr. John Randall, President of the Union.

Christian Endeavor societies have long flourished among them, and it was often my pleasure to speak to great audiences of most attentive listeners. A church in old Spanish Town I particularly remember, with a high pulpit nearly on a level with the second gallery. The stairs leading to it are built around a mast which seemed to sway perilously as I ascended to my perch at the top. I took comfort in the thought, however, that there was no danger of its falling over, since for scores of years the old pulpit had been thumped vigorously by my colored brethren of the cloth.

The loyalty of the Jamaican negroes to the mother country is most interesting, and sometimes touching. They often speak of " going home," meaning England, though neither they nor any of their ancestors were ever within three thousand miles of the " home " country, and probably their descendants will be quite content to stay in Jamaica. Some of them even assume an exaggerated Cockney accent, and I have had an itinerant vendor of walking-sticks ask me, " Will you 'ave a horange or a hebony cane, Sir? " On one occasion I was introduced to a large audience by a Brother in Black, who made a very flowery speech of welcome, and ended by saying, " We are very glad to welcome to Jamaica, our cousins from America, as we English say." The " cousins from America " appreciated the welcome and at once felt at home.

Of all the extraordinary introductions I ever received, and they have been many, the most extraordinary was given me in Jamaica, and I think I must quote it entire for the benefit of my readers:

" The Society of Christian Endeavor greets Dr. and Mrs. Clarke with happy greetings, and extends to them the warmest welcome of ecstacy jubilant with gratitude to Almighty God in bringing them across the main of the mighty deep and safely landing them in the haven of this popular American city on the shore of the isle of Springs, " The Queen of the Antilles," as it is called.

"We think ourselves highly favoured to be privileged first of all the societies in Jamaica to receive the long-looked-for visit of Dr. Clarke the world-wide renown of Christian Endeavor, as also the pioneer and champion of the great Endeavor vehicle, and to welcome him and Mrs. Clarke in our midst.

"Hail, to the father of Endeavorers in every part of the world and the founder of so great an auxillary for Christ and the Church!

"The little leaven is permeating the whole lump, and with mingled feelings we agree that the endeavour movement is a tree planted by the rivers of water that bringeth forth its fruit in its season; its leaf also shall not wither, being an evergreen of longevity to all intents and purposes, which is a fruitful source of blessing in the economy of grace to attract the young into the gospel net, and win them for Christ and the Church.

"As a society we are keenly sensitive and alive to the fact that much good has been, is being and will be achieved in connection with this busy hive of Christian activity, fraught with dear desire of every nation to establish universal righteousness, as a means to an end, and to hasten the glorious time when the kingdom of this world shall have become the golden age of the kingdom of God and His Christ, to the joy of every longing heart."

This first journey to Jamaica was made in 1898, shortly after the Spanish War, and we returned home by way of Cuba, sailing from Kingston for Santiago. As we sailed into Santiago harbor we saw wrecks of three of the Spanish battleships piled upon the shallows, and the castle where the brave Hobson was imprisoned when captured after his perilous attempt to prevent the Spanish fleet, which was bottled up in Santiago harbor from escaping through the narrow channel. Never was a great naval victory so decisive and so comparatively bloodless, and Admiral Cervera, the Commodore of the Spanish fleet, was, after his surrender, far more popular in America, and fêted much more royally than on his return to Spain.

Santiago was then in the early days of its reconstruction. It was a dismal, dirty city, which offered few inducements to the traveller to remain, and after a single meeting, we took a Spanish steamer for Havana, as the railroad between the two chief cities of Cuba was not then completed. This voyage took us around two thirds of the coast of Cuba, and we were glad enough when it was completed.

Havana, too, still showed the effects of long centuries of Spanish misrule, and gave little promise of the delightful winter resort it was soon to become. We had the pleasure of meeting General Leonard Wood, recently Presidential candidate, and now governor of the Philippines, who was then the military governor of Cuba, and were struck by his quiet, dignified, and refined bearing, an American soldier of the best type.

There were few inducements in Havana, as in Santiago, for a long stay, at that period of the country's history, and the special errand which took me to Cuba did not detain us very long. So it was not many days before a Ward Line steamer landed us under the shadows of the skyscrapers of New York.

One of our genial fellow-passengers on this journey was General Greely of Arctic-exploration fame. It was hard to believe that the kindly, handsome, well-fed companion of our voyage had been reduced to live upon his old boots while on his disastrous but fruitful expedition in the far north, and we realized again the old truth that a genuine hero is as modest as he is brave.

DISMAL DAYS IN INDIA

TWO WONDERFUL CONVENTIONS — EN ROUTE TO INDIA —
LORD NORTHCLIFFE — A TERRIBLE PLAGUE — AN AWFUL
FAMINE — WILLIAM CAREY FIRST AND THIRD — A CHAIN
OF LOVE — OFF FOR AFRICA.

HE journey to Europe in 1894, alluded to
in a previous chapter, largely restored my
health without requiring any long period
for rest or recuperation, and I was able to
accomplish more in different European countries than I had dared to hope for at the
start. Most of 1895 and the last half of 1896 were spent in
America. These years were memorable in Christian Endeavor
annals for two enormous conventions: " Boston '95 " and
" Washington '96." Both will be long remembered. Those
were the days of extremely low rates by rail and boat for conventions of all sorts. To conventions of unusually large
proportions half rates or less were granted.

It is safe to say that never before or since has Boston been
so crowded with visitors as in July, 1895. No less than 56,425
Christian Endeavor delegates were registered. They came
from every State in the Union, and from several foreign lands,
Great Britain and Australia being particularly well represented.
Boston made unprecedented preparations for the oncoming
hosts. The streets were ablaze with flags and pennants and a
wealth of bunting such as I have never seen in any city. All
the railroad stations within twenty-five miles of Boston were

handsomely decorated with the convention colors. A large section of the " sacred Common " was set apart as the chief meeting-place, and two enormous tents, holding ten thousand

PERCY S. FOSTER

The beloved musical director of many Christian Endeavor Conventions.

people each, were pitched upon it, while the parks were full of Christian Endeavor emblems in living flowers.

The Boston papers vied with each other to give verbatim

reports of the addresses, issuing special colored supplements, and containing little else for a week than the news of the meetings. The celebrated Lord Northcliffe, then plain Alfred Harmsworth, who happened to be in America at the time, and whom I met a year later on a journey to India, told me that he had never before realized the " news value of religious copy," that he never saw a convention so well and fully set forth as in the *Boston Herald* and *Boston Globe,* and that his papers in London would be more hospitable to such gatherings in the future than they had been in the past.

The convention in Washington in 1896 was scarcely less memorable, and the song service held at the East Front of the Capitol, where it was said that 75,000 people were gathered together, will never be forgotten by those who heard it. It was led by Mr. Percy Foster, who has been during all the years since the beloved convention song-leader.

" Tom " Reed was then the Speaker of the House, and though Congress had adjourned, and he was not at the convention, he facetiously offered me, on account of the extreme heat, the use of his Kentucky homespun suit, which had been exploited in the papers as the regalia of the presiding officer of the House of Representatives. Since Mr. Reed tipped the scales at not less than 250 pounds, the ample proportions of his suit would scarcely have fitted my more meagre form.

A furious storm the night before the convention opened wrecked one of the three great audience tents which seated ten thousand people each, and water-logged the others; but with incredible energy on the part of Mr. W. H. H. Smith, the chairman of the Washington committee, and his colleagues, the wrecked tent was repaired, the wet seats were dried, and the convention was in all respects one of the greatest and most successful ever held.

Very soon after this, with my wife and four children, I sailed for Europe, intending to make an extended journey to India and Africa, leaving my family in Germany for the educa-

CHRISTIAN ENDEAVOR CHORUS OF FIVE THOUSAND, WASHINGTON, D. C., 1896

East front of United States Capitol. Percy S. Foster, Muscial Director.

tion of the children. In those days the cost of living in Europe was very considerably less than in America, and as the ocean fares were cheap, it cost no more to pay the fares of the family and their living expenses in Europe, than to live for the same length of time in America. At the same time it gave us all much more of united family life, and my children a wide experience in travel in many lands which they would not otherwise have enjoyed. On these accounts, on several different occasions they accompanied me to Europe, and, incidentally, on my return from longer or shorter speaking trips, we enjoyed many a happy holiday together, in Switzerland, Germany, Holland, or Great Britain, before college days and the later, sterner duties of life, kept the young folk continuously in America.

It can well be imagined that one of the great drawbacks of the wandering life which for more than thirty years I have been compelled to live has been the breaking up, more or less, of the home and its traditions. This has been compensated for, however, in large measure, by the family flights to which I have alluded, and by the further fact that my wife and my daughter have, one or the other, usually accompanied me on the journeys around the world, and on my more extended travels.

In 1896, however, there seemed to be no other way than that we should separate for many months, since we could not all go together and the children were too young to be left without their mother. So, having placed the two elder children in the family of a German pastor in Berlin, and having seen the younger children established with their mother in pleasant apartments on the Linden, I started off alone on a journey which proved to involve many interesting episodes. Going overland to Naples, I sailed, after an exasperating delay, on a dirty Italian steamer for Alexandria, since my round-trip ticket required me to go by a certain line that shall be nameless.

It was a dark and stormy night when our steamer pushed its

murky way out through the Bay of Naples. Vesuvius had recently been in a tumult, and a great red cross of molten lava gashed its side, a portent which, in earlier days, would have been considered most auspicious for one on such an errand as mine. Little cups of oil in which were smoky wicks served to make the darkness of the passages of the ship visible, and I wondered if we should reach the other side without foundering or burning up. However, a good Providence guided the voyage, and I was able at Ismailyia to transfer to a fine British ship for the journey through the Suez Canal and the Red Sea to Bombay.

On this ship, among other interesting passengers, I made the acquaintance of Alfred Harmsworth, to whom I have before alluded. He was then a young man at the beginning of his remarkable career as the greatest and most successful newspaper publisher in the world's history. Alert, clean cut, and affable, he evidently had a wonderful power for acquiring knowledge and extracting information from all comers. He was not then Lord Northcliffe, or even Sir Alfred, but he told me that he already owned three daily newspapers and twenty weeklies, whose preferred stock, if I remember rightly, he had just sold for five million dollars, keeping the common stock and the control of the syndicate in his own hands. Before he died the number of his papers and magazines increased, I understand, to over one hundred, while he owned vast tracts of forest land in Newfoundland, where the pulp for the paper of his numberless publications was grown.

Many a hot, sultry night on the Red Sea or the Indian Ocean we paced the decks together, while he unfolded his plans for a high-class religious monthly, of the same grade as the *Century* or *Harpers* in its illustrations and in the value of its articles, proposing that he should furnish the capital for an international edition, while I should look after its interests in America. The scheme never came to anything, for before either of us reached home, Sir George Newnes, the enterprising publisher of *The Strand Magazine* and other periodicals started the *The Sunday Strand*, which seemed to take the place of the proposed publication and make it unnecessary.

Mr. Harmsworth did not strike me as a man of high religious principle, but as an opportunist of remarkable force and sagacity. One reason that he gave for desiring a religious magazine, and for publishing cheaper religious periodicals that were already in his syndicate, was that he wanted to " please his old mother, who was very religious." This was certainly a good reason, as far as it went.

He also told me how a few years before he had been working for ten dollars a week in a publishing office, when it occurred to him that an interesting but not too substantial weekly for the masses, and costing only a penny, might be successful. So he made up a dummy and called it *Answers*, which he presented to a publisher who agreed to finance it. It is of the same character as the still more famous *Tit-bits*, and twenty years ago even, brought him an income of thousands of pounds every year. This was the beginning of his fortune and of his rise in public life, which ultimately made him, especially with his ownership of *The Times*, the Thunderer, one of the most influential, one of the most feared, and at the same time one of the most courted men in Great Britain. After reaching London on my return I lunched with him in his elegant home, but I remember nothing of the interview.

At last the weary hours of the long voyage were over, and we sailed into the harbor of Bombay. News of the great plague which was then prevailing had reached us before we left Europe, but we had no thought of finding the city in such a condition of fright and dismay. Something like a thousand people a day were dying of the plague. Many of the principal stores were closed. A great exodus from the city of panic-stricken people had already taken place; four hundred thousand, it was said, had already left, and thousands more were struggling to get away. They besieged the railway station, crowding the third-class cars to suffocation, and often encamping for days in the open spaces around the station before they could get aboard the train which would take them into the country and comparative safety.

At night the sad wailing of the hired mourners in the funeral processions, and the beating of the native tom-toms, was almost continuous, as the funerals passed by the missionary home where I was staying, while double the usual number of vultures were seated solemnly on the edge of the Towers of Silence, where the Parsees bury their dead; the unclean birds waiting for the frequent corpses which were left for them to dispose of.

After a few days I left Bombay for a mission station of the Disciples of Christ in one of the central provinces. Here the horror was of a different kind, but no less acute, for poor India was suffering from famine as well as from plague in that dreadful year. This particular province suffered more than many of the others, and all day long a gaunt procession of men, women, and children came to the mission compound to receive what little aid could be given. At times they would line up around the fence which surrounded the compound, stretching out hungry hands for any dole they might receive. They were half naked, and their out-standing ribs told of weeks of semi-starvation, and of constant hunger; their sunken cheeks and eyes, too, and the protruding wind-filled bellies of the little children told their own sad tale. All we had to give them was handfuls of coarse grains mixed with some wheat. This they often could not wait to carry home or to cook, but, as we filled each pitiful hand, the grain would be carried raw and unground to their mouths to satisfy the craving which had become intolerable.

The hearts of the missionaries as well as that of their visitor were wrung, but what more could we do for the ever increasing throngs?

Since those days means of transportation of food have been

THE PRESS TENT OF THE CHRISTIAN ENDEAVOR CONVENTION IN DETROIT

improved, tanks for the storage of water have been multiplied and enlarged, and it is not probable that another such famine will visit India, even though there may be years of scarcity, for always in Burmah and in some parts of India the crops are good, and the famines have arisen from a lack of transportation, rather than from a lack of supplies.

It is also true that no such visitation of the plague as that of 1896-7 will again devastate India, for in recent years it has been found that the germs of the plague are carried by fleas, and fleas are carried by rats, and thus the contagion spreads from house to house. A serum has also been discovered which renders those inoculated with it largely immune. Twenty-five years ago, however, the cause and the prevention of plague were not known, and I saw many little ineffectual fires of wood with sulphur sprinkled on them, burning before the infected houses in Bombay, a supposed mitigation of the evil which was absolutely of no value.

In those days, too, the lepers were far more in evidence in India than they are to-day. One frequently passed them on the street where they were allowed to roam at large. I remember riding one long afternoon in a second-class compartment with a leper, most of whose fingers had been eaten off by the dread disease. What other parts of his body were infected I do not know, since he had the considerateness to wear cotton gloves and a veil. However, it has been found that there is very little danger of contagion from casual contact with a leper, and medical science has done much, and will do more, to mitigate the horrors of this dread disease.

This journey was not altogether so gruesome as my readers so far may have imagined. It included many interesting scenes and many delightful visits to my missionary friends who had invited me to Ahmednagar and Sirur, to Calcutta and the villages of Eastern Bengal, to the Punjab and the Lodiana Mission, to Madras and the wonderful temple city of Madura.

Two or three happy incidents especially stand out in my

memories of this journey. One of these relates to a visit to the Beals of Bengal with my friend Rev. William Carey, the great-grandson of the pioneer Protestant missionary of the world. William Carey, the third, resembles his great-grandfather in face and figure, and an oil painting of William the first would answer very well for his great-grandson to-day.

Before starting for the rice fields, I renewed my missionary zeal by visiting the Baptist College at Serampore, near Calcutta, founded by the original William Carey, where are treasured many mementoes of him. What impressed me most were the forty great tomes, each one containing the translation of the Bible in one of the many different languages of India, all translated by this wonderful scholar and linguist with the help of his native pupils. It seems incredible that one man could have accomplished so much literary work even if his life were lengthened to twice the usual span, but the fact is that William Carey was as great a linguist as he was a missionary. The poor shoemaker of Kettering became one of the world's great scholars along certain lines, a scholarship which was recognized even in his own day, for he was a professor in the government college for many years, and earned, if I am not mistaken, something like $200,000 as salary, all of which he turned into the coffers of the missionary board for work in Bengal.

I shall never forget how the original hammer, used by Mr. Carey when pegging shoes in Kettering, was revered, almost as a sacred object, by the young people at the International convention in San Francisco in 1897, where it was used as a gavel to call the convention to order. It was loaned to me by Rev. James Mursell of England, a relative of the Carey family, and I took it home with me on my return from India for use at this convention. How the young people crowded around the rude hammer, eagerly desiring to touch it, as though they might receive some inspiration from the cold iron! Afterwards I returned the precious relic to its owner, but not before some *fac similes* were made, which have been greatly prized.

Afterwards in telling of the incident to Rev. F. B. Meyer of London, he said to me with real emotion, " Oh, that I could live so and do such work for the Master that some common article of daily use which had belonged to me, — a pen, a pencil, a hammer, or anything of that sort, might be deemed precious by future generations." I know of few men for whom such a prayer is more likely to be fulfilled.

Not far from the college at Serampore is an old ruined pagoda, where it is said that Henry Martyn, an almost equally famous missionary, used to retire for his private devotions, and there is a tradition that on one occasion, Henry Martyn, William Carey, and Adoniram Judson met for prayer in this old pagoda, which even then was in ruins. What a prayer meeting must that have been!

William Carey's tomb is here, a large four-sided monument, on three sides of which are inscribed the names and virtues of his three wives, and on the fourth his own name with this humble confession of his faith carved beneath:

> " A worthless, weak, and helpless worm,
>   In Thy kind arms I fall."

I left Calcutta with the modern William Carey late one evening by rail for one of the branches of the Ganges River, where we found a little boat with steam up, waiting to begin its voyage by daylight. On this craft we sailed for several hours, and were then transferred to a mission house-boat for a narrower section of the river. After some hours more the house-boat became too large for the water-way, and, up a long canal, in a kind of canoe called a dinghy, towed by stout coolies on the bank, we made our way until even the dinghy could go no farther. Then we stepped out upon the bank and, under the glorious Indian moon walked for about two hours more, while tales of tigers and cobras in the vicinity kept us alert, until at last we came to a little village of some forty or fifty houses, called Chabikapar.

It was about two o'clock in the morning when we reached there, and Mr. Carey and I, bending low, crawled on hands and knees into one of the huts belonging to a Christian, and therefore a little cleaner than the others, and stretched ourselves upon the straw for a few hours of sleep. Long before daylight we could hear the soft pattering of bare feet as the delegates to the Endeavor convention we had come to attend made their way through the jungle by the borders of the canal, under the great leaning cocoanut trees and the broad-leaved bananas, to the little chapel where the meetings were to be held.

Many scores walked all night to attend this meeting, and all the next night to get home again, for there was no accommodation for so large a throng in the little village of mud houses, only half of which belonged to the Christians. When daylight fairly arrived the singing had begun. Some of the songs were the ordinary gospel hymns, others the weirder native music, with the accompaniment of tom-toms and a few one-stringed or two-stringed instruments.

When we had taken our places in the chapel the delegates followed, but not in any such fashion as I had ever seen before. Instead of straggling in by ones or twos or threes they danced in in groups, each group representing one of the sixty societies in the vicinity, but it was most orderly and highly proper dancing, and I never understood so fully before how David danced before the Lord. One of the leaders, who was considered especially expert in this practice, led in each little group, dancing backwards himself with a rhythmic swaying of his body, while the rest followed him, keeping time with his motions. Reaching the interior of the chapel, they squatted on the ground as closely together as possible, to make room for the societies which followed them.

The meetings throughout the day were most interesting and of a highly practical character, showing how better work might be done, indicating faults of administration, and promoting larger spirituality as well as effectiveness. Toward the close of the day Mr. Carey said to the assembly, nearly a thousand strong, which not only filled the chapel, but overflowed into the outside regions that were within sound of the speaker's voice: " Let us make a chain of love for our friend from America! "

I was interested in his remark for I had never heard of a chain of love before, and awaited further developments with curiosity. At once he called for Bible verses bearing upon the subject of God's love to man, the love of Christians for one another, and so on. They came thick and fast from the audience, and were quickly written down on colored pieces of tissue paper. Then, by the deft fingers of the Bengali maidens, these pieces of paper were pasted together until they made a long chain. Whereupon a good deacon in the church threw off, as a sign of respect, part of the scanty garments in which he was clothed and came forward to the desk. His brown skin shone like old mahogany well rubbed with cocoanut oil, and with all the dignity of a Lord Chesterfield, he placed the chain around my neck, and told me that he wished me to carry the chain home to America as a token of Christian love and fellowship, because in all lands we were one in Christ.

There seemed nothing odd or *outré* in the incident in those surroundings, but I thought, with a smile, how it would look to my friends at home to see me standing there, not only with this tissue-paper chain, but with half a dozen garlands of beautiful flowers around my neck, while I was sprinkled with rose water, a little attar of roses rubbed on the back of my hand, three small limes put in either palm, and a plate of bananas and a piece of betel nut done up with lime in a green leaf provided for my refreshment. Yet all was done in the heartiest spirit of comradeship, and it seemed to me that the idea of a chain of Christian love was as beautiful as it was unique.

Another memorable visit was that to the Arcot mission. The venerable Jacob Chamberlain, famous missionary and author, was still alive, doing splendid work with his two sons and members of the Scudder family for the Telugus of the region. One of the many convention gavels which I treasure was made by his own hands and given me at that time. It consisted of a beautiful piece of teakwood, with a block to strike it on, the gavel as well as the block inlaid with many rupees and sixteen anna pieces of the ancient native *régime*, coins no longer in general use. Dr. Chamberlain was one of the best *raconteurs* in the world, and his stories of missionary adventure, to which I have before alluded, did much to popularize the knowledge of missionary heroism in the home land.

Another pleasant incident of this journey to India was an occasional visit with my old time friend, President John H. Barrows of Oberlin College, who was then touring India on the Haskell Foundation, and was lecturing in all the prominent universities. We happened to meet at several centres, and his eloquent voice was heard at some of the conventions which I had gone to attend.

At last came the time for me to depart from India for Africa, sailing from Madras. The only means of transportation was by a so-called coolie-ship, for which I had a ticket on the round trip from Boston to Boston. But when I attempted to claim my passage I was amazed to find that there was much red tape to be untied before I could go on board. The ship was not expected to carry white passengers and did not care to do so. There were no fit accommodations, and the little steamer was crowded fore and aft with a great load of coolies who were going over to work on the sugar plantations of Africa.

I labored long and earnestly with the agent of the company, and demanded the right of passage which my ticket guaranteed. He told me that all the passengers on the ship had to be quarantined for two weeks before sailing, and then disinfected, their clothes burned and a new strip of white cloth given each of them in lieu of their old clothes. I naturally would not submit to such treatment, and after considerable argument he told me I might sail if I would bring a physician's certificate of good health. This I did and at last the agent reluctantly made out a paper to this effect: "*In my opinion Rev. F. E. Clark may be allowed to sail on the Congella without fear of infecting the other passengers.*" Never was I more glad of a clean bill of health, though I had a dim suspicion that I might be more in danger of infection from the other passengers than they from me. The humor of the situation mitigated the annoyance of the delay and inconvenience.

SOUTH AFRICA BEFORE THE BOER WAR

ON A COOLIE SHIP — AMONG THE ZULUS — PRESIDENT KRUGER
(" OOM PAUL ") — IN THE DIAMOND FIELDS — A RE-
MARKABLE SCHOOL — ANDREW MURRAY AND THE MUR-
RAY FAMILY.

HE voyage from Madras to Durban, of some five thousand miles, proved to be an uneventful one, but not so tedious as I had feared. My cabin in the after part of the ship was next to the rooms of the captain and the mates, with whom I messed, and I had a kind of cockpit with an awning over it, mostly for my exclusive use during the day. Though it was immediately over the propeller, the smooth seas made it a comfortable place for reading and writing.

The food was abundant, but not of the daintiest. As there was no ice, there could of course be no fresh milk or fresh meat, and the butter in those tropic seas could always be served better with a spoon than with a knife. One bunch of bananas was hung from the ceiling of the upper deck at the beginning of the voyage, but it dwindled rapidly and after the first two or three days out there was no more fresh fruit.

Knowing what was before me I organized my time, which I have always found it a good thing to do on shipboard as well as elsewhere, and resolved to devote so many hours a day to reading, and so many more to writing since I had a weekly article and sundry editorials to write for *The Christian En-*

deavor World. This voyage, too, produced a little devotional volume, called " The Great Secret," which has had a steady though by no means a phenomenal sale, ever since. During many long voyages I have found it wise to set before myself what the boys would call " a stunt," to be accomplished before the voyage should end, a habit which, first and last, has resulted in a number of volumes and many articles for magazines and newspapers. A book entitled " Fellow Travellers " was also in part an outcome of this voyage.

No land was touched during this long journey, though the tip of India was seen as we sailed between the continent and its beautiful daughter-island of Ceylon, whose " spicy breezes," however, we did not approach near enough to smell. Skirting the Seychelles Islands ,we sailed across the long stretch of the South Indian Ocean on even keel, until, after twenty-three days, I was rejoiced to hear the man at the lookout cry out, " Light on the port bow! " Sure enough the good news was true, and I could see through the blackness of the tropical night a flickering, waving flame on an African headland, which told that we were not far from Durban. This was not a lighthouse, as might be expected, but apparently a bonfire or perhaps an out-door kitchen where some Zulus were cooking an evening meal.

When we reached the quarantine station I was distressed to hear the officer in charge arguing with our captain about a two-weeks quarantine. The latter plead earnestly with him, however to allow " his white passenger " to land, as well as himself, which, after a day's delay, was permitted. At the wharf some ministerial friends welcomed me, and I was soon in the thick of a speech-making campaign which took me to most of the larger cities of South Africa.

Natal is a beautiful colony, with the softest of climates, the most charming tropical foliage, and a large population of husky Zulus, who do the hard work of the colony. This is the finest race of black men that I have seen. Their forms are symmetrical and stalwart and they seem to have an unending flow of good spirits. Jinrikishas are commonly used in Durban, as in other South African cities, and the jinrikisha men, all of them Zulus, get themselves up in the most grotesque and *bizarre* fashion. Their costume consists largely of beads, with barely enough cloth to fulfil the demands of decency, and many of them wear cows' horns, strapped on to their heads in some way, which give them the look of Diabolus himself. Their shining eyes, gleaming teeth, and good-natured grins are anything but Satanic, however, and they run and cavort, and draw up their big baby carriages for a passenger with a flourish, as though existence was a long, huge joke.

It was my privilege to go some forty miles from Durban, partly by rail, and partly by a cart drawn by six oxen, with my friend Rev. Charles N. Ransom, to the mission station in Amanzimtote. It was an interesting trip to my unaccustomed eyes. The curious African trees and foliage, and the many kraals on the hillside, a big kraal for the chief in the centre, and smaller ones for his numerous wives, clustered around it, were conspicuous features. The deep, dry gullies through which the oxen had to plough their way with the lumbering cart, and the neat and comfortable mission houses at the end of the journey, all were interesting and novel. The Zulus are a strong race mentally and physically, and though inclined to be independent, and sometimes top-lofty in their attitude to white men, on the whole make faithful converts.

My engagements allowed me only a day or two in Zululand, when I took the comfortable train, provided with sleeping-cars, for the Transvaal, stopping for a minute in Ladysmith, a town which afterwards became famous in the Boer War. Reaching there very early in the morning, the hospitable Dutch pastor refreshed me with an enormous bowl of hot, black coffee, the universal drink among the Boers, while the British indulge largely in tea almost as strong and black, either beverage being sufficient to destroy an American digestion in a short time.

Johannesburg, which twenty years ago had the reputation of being the wickedest city in the world, seemed like one of our biggest and rawest western boom towns. There were some substantial and really fine brick blocks, approaching the height of modest skyscrapers; great stretches of streets lined with poor shacks, some fine homes in the outskirts, and thousands of little cabins made of corrugated iron, or at least roofed with it, for wood is scarce on the Veldt.

The show places of Johannesburg are of course the mines on the Rand, the richest ridge of earth in all the world, with possibly the exception of Coolgardie in Western Australia. I went down in one of these mines, but there was little to see. No tempting nuggets, no sparkling specks of gold visible in the rich quartz, at least to the careless eye, but when the quartz is crushed and washed, the wealth of the Indies, or it is more proper to say, the wealth of golden Africa, is found in it.

An interesting relic which my Christian Endeavor friends gave me in Johannesburg, at the close of the meeting, is a cane made of the horn of the Jemsbok, which I have added to my large collection of gift canes from all parts of the world. It is black, and light, and unbreakable, and its peculiar distinction is that it belonged to the species of antelope which gave rise to the fable of the unicorn, for the hunters who first saw it bounding across the Veldt saw the two horns which stick out at an acute angle from the animal's head, and thought it had but one, since they are exactly in line.

At Pretoria, the capital of the Transvaal, as it then was, I had an interesting interview with old President Kruger. His pastor accompanied me and translated for me to the president and from the president to myself. The old gentleman was sitting on the stoop of his modest, white cottage, a stoop adorned with two famous white marble lions, given him, I believe, by Cecil Rhodes. A beard of a week's growth adorned his cheeks, and a long Dutch pipe depended from his mouth, while, through the window, I could see good Frau Kruger knitting away industriously on a stout pair of socks, doubt-less meant for her lord and master. It was said that the president understood English fairly well, but so disliked the language, and also those who spoke it, that he insisted on always speaking Dutch, and on being interpreted.

When his pastor introduced me, the president tapped me on the shoulder, in a semi-playful, semi-serious mood, and said, " Are you one of the Yankees that always run to the Queen when they get into trouble? " His allusion was to the report that John Hays Hammond, the eminent American mining engineer, who was then in the Pretoria jail, charged with incit-ing an insurrection against the Transvaal government, because of some connection with the Jameson Raid, was said to have put himself under British protection when threatened with arrest. I have since laughed with Mr. Hammond over the president's insinuation, and he assured me that he never thought of putting himself under British protection; that his arrest was a mistake of the Transvaal government; and that he kept the American flag flying over his bungalow thinking that it would give him more protection than the Union Jack.

After Oom Paul's (for he was called Oom, or Uncle by all the burghers) humorous introduction of the conversation, he settled down to more serious things, and I found him especially interested in the progress of evangelical religion in other lands. Before I went away he assured me that any one who came to his republic to advance the cause of Christ and of Christian education and efficiency was welcome. Speaking of his own religious experience, he told me how much he was indebted for his conversion and his start in the Christian life, to a mis-sionary of the American Board named Lindsay, who was sent out to the Zulus, but who, when the Zulu wars made it im-possible for him to continue his work, turned to the Boers, and was most helpful in holding revival meetings among them. " Oh, he was a good man; he was a good man," repeated Oom Paul twice over, " there were few like him."

My impression of this famous character in African, and indeed in the world's history, was that he was a rough diamond, but a real one; ignorant of letters, bigoted, superstitious perhaps, but genuine in his religious belief, unrivalled in his knowledge of the burgher heart, and sincere in his devotion to the right, as God gave him to see the right.

I was told that the Bible was one of the few books that he could read fluently, a statement which seems strange in view of the fact that it would seem that if one could read any book " all print would be open to him," as Silas Wegg would say. But Paul Kruger was so familiar with the Bible that when once he got started he could go on indefinitely, verse after verse, and in some parts chapter after chapter. It was said that he was often heard praying very early in the morning, and reading the Scriptures which he loved so well. I cannot believe that he was the mercenary, double-minded man that his enemies considered him, and I have not changed my opinion that the war which he fought, disastrous as it was to him, was an unjust and cruel war, though it eventually brought many blessings to the conquered republics.

Another interesting place that the conventions to which I was scheduled carried me was Kimberley, the great diamond region of the world, which has brought untold wealth to the members of the De Beers Company, and unnumbered jewels to sparkle in the rings and the coronets of beauty. A number of years before my visit a little child was seen playing with some bright white stones which he had picked up in the sterile country that surrounded his father's home. One of these stones was built into the mud wall of their little home. A passing traveller was attracted by its brilliance, and took it to a jeweller, who pronounced it to be a diamond of the first water, and one of the largest ever discovered. At once the rush began, and the Kimberley diamond fields were soon the centre of a great population. Few of the diamonds however were found upon the surface but in the hard, blue clay beneath, even to the depth of thousands of feet. This blue clay is hoisted from the depths of the mine and spread out upon the " floors " as they are called, great stretches of level land, to disintegrate in the sun and rain.

These floors are guarded day and night by armed men, and one is not allowed to pick up even the smallest lump of blue clay, for it may contain a Kohinoor. The Zulus in the mines, who dig the clay, virtually endure voluntary imprisonment during the time of their contract, and when they are allowed

ACRES OF DIAMONDS

A scene in the diamond room of one of the large mines at Kimberley, South Africa.
One of these parcels of diamonds is worth $300,000.

to leave they are searched most diligently for diamonds which they may have tucked under their lips, or in their nostrils, or hidden in a flesh wound made on purpose for its reception, or even swallowed. The two crimes of I.D.S. and I.D.B., " Illicit Diamond Selling," and " Illicit Diamond Buying," are the most serious in the Kimberley Decalogue.

In the office of the company I was allowed to see piles of diamonds of different weights and different qualities. Great shining heaps of stones, some dull and looking like any piece of quartz, and others glistening with something of the sparkle which they will emit after they have been in the hands of the Amsterdam lapidaries.

Bloemfontein, the capital of the Orange River Free State, was another interesting town in this South African tour. Here I happened to be on the day of the assembly of the legislature of the Republic. As I went into the hall of the House of Representatives the legislators marched in in procession for the opening session, headed by President Stein. I never saw such a company of giants in any other legislative hall. Every one looked six feet tall or more. Every one was stalwart in proportion to his height, and each one was " bearded like a pard." No wonder that a race represented by such men gave the great British army plenty of trouble before it could subdue them. I afterwards had an interview with President Stein, who struck me as an agreeable and polished gentleman. He had been educated in European universities, unlike his brother president of the Transvaal, and though opinions differ in regard to his career, I believe him to have been honest, conscientious, patriotic, and a worthy president of the little republic of the Orange River Free State.

A visit on this journey which I shall long remember was the one to Lovedale, a famous school for the sons of African chiefs, founded by Dr. James Stewart of the Free Church of Scotland. Dr. Stewart has since died, and no more fragrant name than his, not even excepting Livingstone and Moffat, is found in the missionary annals of Africa. He was a man of remarkable intellectual power and much personal charm, and his school was a thoroughly Christian institution whose influence reached far and wide among the leaders of many African tribes.

I happened to get to Lovedale in the time of a religious revival. Many of the boys who would thereafter have a large influence in wide sections of Africa had found, as they believed, the way of life. Dr. Stewart and all the teachers were doing their utmost to deepen the religious conviction, and to strengthen the character of the new converts, as well as to give them the elements of a good education. I was particularly touched, after one of the evangelistic meetings, to see the little fair-haired youngest daughter of Dr. Stewart sitting beside a black boy, Bible in hand, telling him in simple language what it was to be a Christian.

It was at this school that I had the experience of Gatling-gun interpreting, to which I have already alluded, where, after I had spoken a sentence, three different interpreters in as many different languages took it up, one after the other, while I waited patiently for the third to finish before resuming my discourse.

Dr. Taylor, a famous Methodist bishop, who had striven so valiantly to establish self-supporting missions throughout Africa was visiting Lovedale at the same time. Though in failing health, and with a greatly weakened voice, he was a most entertaining companion. I was particularly interested in his exposition of Psalm 103 at family prayers. In his some-what breathless, jerky way, for he had no breath to spare, he read the Psalm, commenting as he went along. " David talked to himself, — speaks to his soul, — tells himself to bless the Lord, — gives his reasons for doing it, — tells him-self of the bigness of the love of God, — states its perpendicu-lar measurement, — " as high as the heavens above the earth," its horizontal measurement, — " as far as the east is from the west," — its affectional measurement, " as a Father pitieth his children," and so on with a pithy comment on each verse.

Soon after I saw him the good bishop died, mourned by thousands in two continents.

Dr. Stewart was as genial as he was wise and strong, and had many interesting anecdotes of his journeys and of his life in Africa, a life which has been ably set forth in all its unusual richness and power in a recent biography. One of Dr. Stewart's characteristic stories related to a voyage on a steamer of the Peninsular and Oriental line (P. & O. for short) from Africa, a steamer of a line which I have had occasion to know is more extreme in its Church of England rules than Canterbury Cathedral itself.   On this voyage Dr. Stewart was returning home with a large number of other missionaries when the captain came to him one Sunday morning and asked if there was a clergyman on board to conduct the morning service.   " Certainly," said Dr. Stewart, " here is my friend Mr. A., an eminent Methodist missionary, and Mr. B. of the Baptist Church, and Dr. C. a well known Presbyterian preacher, and I am one myself."   " Oh, I meant a *clergyman*," replied the captain, and went off to seek one of his own denomination.

This proved to be a curate with a stomach as weak as his preaching powers.   Scarcely had the service begun, when the wind arose and the waves became somewhat boisterous.   The poor man could not continue the service beyond the Psalter, and Dr. Stewart remarked that the only verse of poetry he could think of at the time were the lines on the burial of Sir John Moore:

> " Few and short were the prayers we said,
>   As his corse to the ramparts we hurried."

The most interesting of all my visits on this journey to South Africa was the one to what might be called " The Murray Belt," a region of Cape Colony which has been especially influenced by the life of Dr. Andrew Murray, the great devotional writer, his ancestors, and his descendants.   Andrew Murray doubtless influenced and deepened the spiritual life of more Christian people than almost any other man of his century, and yet his pulpit was a somewhat obscure one, among the Boer farmers of Wellington.   But his books have " gone forth into all the earth," and he surely has " a goodly heritage " in the lives of a multitude who rise up and call him blessed.

A decided difference in the spiritual atmosphere can be felt as one travels south from Johannesburg and Kimberley.   The prevailing idea in those quarters twenty years ago, at least, was to get rich, and to " get rich quick." People had gone there to seek gold and precious stones, and to raise sheep on the wide Veldt. The sturdy, homely virtues of the Boers were gradually being overshadowed by the rush of immigrants from different parts of the world, who sought only material things, and of whom it might be said that religion was not even a by-product of their lives.

PARSONAGE OF THE FIRST ANDREW MURRAY, GRAAF REINET, CAPE COLONY
In this house all the seventeen children of the first Andrew Murray were born.

But as one drew nearer to Capetown, one felt the difference in the spiritual atmosphere. Things of the other world had more significance, and righteousness, charity, and good will had a larger meaning. Not that there were not many earnest Christians and much religious work done in the neighborhood of the gold mines and the diamond fields, but I am speaking of the general atmosphere.

It is worth while to tell briefly the story of this remarkable family that has largely brought this change, and has made many parts of Cape Colony centres of genuine and deep religious interest.

Something over a hundred years ago the Dutch farmers of Cape Colony became distressed at the rationalistic teaching of their pastors, who had been educated in Holland. Fearing for its effect upon their children, they sent to Scotland for a preacher who was sound in the faith, who believed in the Bible and would preach earnestly the accepted truths of evangelical religion.

A young man named Andrew Murray was sent out to them. He had a particularly youthful face, and the old Dutch farmers said one to another. " They have sent out a girl to preach to us." But the first Andrew Murray proved to be a man, and a man of stalwart stuff, who soon showed by his preaching, strong and courageous and earnest, that he was the man they needed. While in the Adderly Street Dutch Reformed Church, a church which is still flourishing, and where I have spoken on more than one occasion, the young preacher from Scotland saw a fair Dutch girl who attracted his attention. He was at the impressionable age which sooner or later comes to most young men, and, to make a long story short, he wooed and won this fair girl, and, as a bride of only sixteen years of age, carried her off to the parsonage in Graaf Reinet, a flourishing village in an oasis of the Karoo, or desert lands of South Africa.

Here a family of seventeen children were born, twelve of whom lived to grow up, and I was told, when in Graaf Reinet, that each of these children *averaged* twelve children of their own, though some had several more. Most of them grew up to manhood and womanhood, and became preachers or preachers' wives, missionaries, or teachers, or religious workers of eminence in some sphere, scattering all over South Africa and making their influence felt for good wherever they went.

The most eminent of the first Andrew Murray's children

was Andrew Murray the second, of whom I have already spoken, the world-renowned preacher, writer, and religious leader. All the children, however, inherited, and, apparently, chiefly from their mother, unusual spiritual qualities. She was one of the rare women with a heavenly vision, a mystic of the best type, who could see far into the skies, and genuinely commune with her God.

A homely but touching incident was told me of Grandma Murray, as she was affectionately called, who had died but a few years before my visit to the " Murray Belt." When a visitor would say to her, " How did it happen, Grandma, that you brought up such a large family, and that they have all turned out so well? " She would say, " Oh, I do not know; I never said much, and I never did very much, but just tried to live as well as I could! " That was all so far as she could tell it perhaps, but how much it involved of gentleness and lovingkindness, of prayer and righteous living, and personal communion with God!

The youngest of the seventeen sons and daughters, and the last survivor of this wonderful family was George Murray, who died in the early days of 1921. I have recently seen a picture of him and his wife and their fifteen interesting children, taken about the time when I was in South Africa. All of those boys and girls and young men and women, were bright, interesting, good-looking and well dressed, and almost all are now full-time Christian workers. Blessed is the man who hath his quiver full of such children. I am glad there was no birth control in that family.

I felt honored to spend a night or two under that roof in Graaf Reinet, where all of the Murray children of the first generation were born, and to be the guest for a short time of Andrew Murray of Wellington. This is the Northfield of South Africa. Here Dr. Murray established a splendid school for the higher education of women, a school in which Americans may well take pride, for it was inspired by the life of Mary

Lyon, and was modelled after old Mount Holyoke Seminary. Its chief building was given by a philanthropic American of Worcester, Mass., and its earliest teachers and many of its later ones have been Americans; Miss Ferguson and Miss Bliss, both graduates of Mt. Holyoke, I think, being the pioneer teachers. Miss Bliss, too, is the pioneer Endeavorer of South Africa and long the secretary of the South African Christian Endeavor Union. Other similar schools have been

GEORGE MURRAY'S FAMILY WITH FIFTEEN CHILDREN
Photograph taken some years ago.

established at Worcester, Stellenbosch, the Paarl, and Bloem-fontein, all receiving their inspiration from the same source, and many of them employing teachers from America.

Dr. Murray's influence was not only that of a great evangelist and devotional writer, but of an eminent educator as well. Though nearing ninety when he died, he was, when I last saw him, still bright and sprightly, his face shining not only with a heavenly light, but with genuine, human good fellowship. The last time I went to South Africa, though I could not visit Wellington, he journeyed to Capetown on purpose to give an address of welcome at the impromptu convention that was held there, and it was an address as cordial, genial, and witty as one could wish to hear.

Soon after my visits to the Murray Country I sailed from Capetown, a most interesting city, superbly situated; up the long, long coast of Africa, into the Solent and Southampton harbor, and there, on the pier, after seven months' absence, a mother with two larger children and two smaller ones waited to welcome husband and father, back from his long voyage.

CHINA IN THE GRIP OF THE BOXERS

A CALL ON COUNT OKUMA — CHINA'S INTERESTING CONVEN-
TION — REASONS FOR THE BOXER UPRISING — A PRAYER
FOR RAIN — BRAVE MISSIONARIES — THE MASSACRES AT
PAOTINGFU — HORACE PITKIN — MARY MORRILL.

T HAS been our lot to visit many countries both before and since the journey of which I am about to write, on the eve of critical events or during the course of troubles and disasters which have been regarded as world-wide calamities. For example, the visit to Turkey, which I have already described, took place just before the Armenian massacres; the journey to India during the year of plague and famine; a visit to Jamaica which I will describe later, while the earth was still trembling with one of the greatest earthquakes of recorded history; a visit to Europe within two months of the breaking out of the Great War, another soon after its conclusion; and a journey in China in 1916 when the rebellion against Yuan Shi Kai's imperial plans was going on, and province after province was rising against his rule.

This journey to the Far East at the beginning of the present century was no exception to the rule, though when we left home to attend the national Christian Endeavor conventions of Japan and China, early in the year 1900, there were no unusual clouds in the sky so far as we knew, and we had no idea of the terrible scenes of massacre and pillage which were soon to rock China to its foundations, and which we barely escaped witnessing, if not sharing.

On this occasion we were accompanied by our second son, Harold, who was the only one of the trio who, without responsibilities or forecast of danger, thoroughly enjoyed the unusual experiences that awaited us.

I recollect nothing of special moment connected with our visit to Japan on this occasion, except that we renewed the acquaintance of many dear friends of the past belonging to the missionary boards, and enjoyed many delightful meetings with Japanese Christians.

I recall a delightful interview with the late Count Okuma, who was always especially hospitable to Americans. This pleasure has twice been repeated since, and I always found him the same genial, courteous, and interesting host as have hundreds of others. He showed us on this occasion his famous collection of Chrysanthemums and of dwarf trees, some of which were a hundred years old, and yet not too large to grace a dinner table, while little evergreens of six or seven years found ample room in a flower pot not much larger than a lady's thimble.

His beautiful villa is built in two sections, one with lofty rooms, elegant furniture, and costly bric-a-brac, in the European style, another part in the plain, and charmingly simple Japanese fashion, with soft mattings on the floors, sliding partitions which serve for doors as well, paper walls, and the severe simplicity which rules in the ordinary Japanese households. Here pictures are not hung in profusion, remaining year after year in the same place on drawing room walls as with us, but a simple Kakemono or scroll, particularly appropriate to the season, is hung for a month at a time, and then rolled up to give way to a more appropriate scroll.

The year 1900 was "the Year of the Dog," for every year in Japan is named in cycles for some animal like the dog, the pig, the horse, the dragon, or the snake and the Count gave our twelve-year-old son two little ivory dogs exquisitely carved, taking them from the mantel-piece in his drawing room. I was surprised on visiting him sixteen years later to have the Count inquire for the lad whom he still thought of as a little boy, who was with me on the first visit, showing that this great statesman had something of the quality which has made some of our own statesmen famous and beloved, the quality of remembering not only names but little events and small items in the lives of their constituents.

Count Okuma was then out of office, and had long been in opposition to the government, but whether in office or out, he always seemed to be the same genial and friendly personage, a rare conversationalist, but never too busy or too intent to listen to what his visitors might have to impart.

After leaving Japan the journey from Shanghai to Foochow was one to be remembered, and especially the return voyage, because of the misery involved on a little cockle-shell of a steamer in a rough sea. Shortly after that the steamer went to the bottom, and as I believe no lives were lost, no tears were shed for the departure to " Davy Jones' Locker " of this chief instigator of seasickness.

A prayer meeting held on the way down with the Chinese delegates in the cabin was attended by the English captain, who was an earnest Christian and who showed his colors, and spoke some earnest words to the delegates gathered in the little cabin.

I remember an interesting story that he afterwards related, to show how difficult it is for a foreigner to tell from a China-man's looks whether he is an ordinary coolie or a grand Mogul in his own district, since, in every-day business, their clothes are much alike. On one of the voyages down the coast, a certain English captain was much annoyed by the many questions and apparent officiousness of one of the Chinese passengers, who seemed to be anxious to know about everything on board, and who was finding much fault with conditions as they were. The captain endured it as long as he thought he could, but at last, his wrath getting the better of his judgment, he kicked his inquisitive passenger down the companion way, only to learn before the voyage was over, that he had kicked one of the chief owners of the steamship line.

The most memorable meeting we attended in China was held in Foochow. Endeavor had taken root there in 1884, and had greatly increased in the years intervening before our visit. I shall never forget that great audience of blue-gowned Chinese men who stood up as one man when I first rose to speak, and putting their hands high over their heads, shook them silently but vigorously at me, without a sound of any description. Of course I did the same, and in half a minute we had all shaken hands, and were presumably introduced to each other.

A unique gavel was given me at this convention by Rev. George H. Hubbard, a young missionary who had formed the first Christian Endeavor society in China in 1885. The head consisted of a piece of a beam of the house in which the first society met, a building which had since been torn down, while the handle was a stout twig from a mulberry tree planted in the yard at the inauguration of the society. Beam and tree had been carefully preserved as memorials. He also presented me with a small Chinese drum on which to strike the gavel, as a reminder of the name first used for the society, a name which in English signified " *The Drum-Around-and-Rouse-up Society.*" Not a bad name for others to remember.

At that time all the missions, Methodists, Church of England, and American Congregationalists, united in Christian Endeavor, but before long the Methodist societies were notified by the home bishops that they must withdraw from this fellowship and form Epworth Leagues and unions of their own. It seemed to me at the time, and still seems, exceedingly strange, to say the least, that in missionary lands if nowhere else, a fellowship among the comparatively few young Christians should be thus ruthlessly uprooted.

OLD EXAMINATION CELLS, NOW ABOLISHED

In such cells Chinese students used to take their examinations.

I am glad to report that in Japan, on the contrary, the Methodist Episcopal Young People's societies have always retained the Christian Endeavor name and fellowship, owing largely to the good Bishop Harris, and also to other leaders in union work in that land.

One incident impressed itself upon my mind particularly, as showing the language difficulties which missionaries and others have to meet, where, as sometimes happens, entirely different dialects are spoken on different sides of the same river. Most of the delegates at this convention understood the Foochow dialect, which however was " all Greek " to some. Others understood only the Mandarin, while some missionaries understood both languages, so while one of the native delegates was speaking in Mandarin, an American missionary translated it into English, while another missionary interpreted his translation into Foochowese.

A pleasant incident was a journey up the charming Ing Hok River to the mission station of Ing Hok, a journey partly by house-boat, partly by bearers, until we reached the river bank; then by house-boat up the stiff current of the river; then by sampan, sitting on the bottom of the little boat under an arch of matting; then by bearers again along the bank of the river, in a rough home-made country chair, to our destination. It was very difficult in those days to obtain stalwart chair bearers, for the opium habit had made such inroads on the population, and so many of the coolies spent their days and nights in opium dens, so weakening their constitutions that it was sometimes impossible to obtain bearers enough for a large party.

Those that could be obtained always picked for the lightest members of the party, fat women being at a special discount among them. Now however, the opium curse has been largely stamped out, owing to the vigorous measures adopted by the Chinese government, in spite of the fact that much of the drug was for years forced upon China by the iniquitous insistence of British India.

The scenery on the Ing Hok River and the lower waters of the River Min on which Foochow is situated is among the grandest in the world. Indeed there is magnificent scenery enough, as one has said, if it were well distributed, to serve all the continents of the world.

It was with reluctance that we left our kind friends of Foochow and turned our faces northward, voyaging to Shanghai on the same little steamer that took us down the coast, but on a far rougher voyage.

At Shanghai we took another steamer and enjoyed a pleasant trip to Taku, the Port of Tientsin and Peking. There the first full realization of the storm that was about to break over China came to us. The missionary friend who was expecting to meet us at the wharf was delayed for some reason, and we were attacked by a horde of scowling, yelling coolies who seemed to menace our lives. It is true that these particular coolies only wanted the privilege of carrying our baggage for a sufficient remuneration, but hatred of foreigners was in their eyes and deepened their ugly scowl, though the time had not quite come for them to put their evil designs into execution.

Not being able to speak a word of their language, we found it difficult to negotiate terms with this howling mob, but at last made it plain what we wanted and were soon bowling in jinrikishas to the railway station, where the waiting train shortly landed us in Tientsin. We found the state of affairs there far more serious than we had supposed, or than any one outside of China then knew. The faces of the non-Christian Chinamen in the presence of foreigners was one vast scowl of hatred, throughout northern China. Most absurd stories were in circulation about the foreigners. " Western railroads were desecrating the graves." " Under every sleeper a Chinese baby was buried." " The eyes of Chinese children were plucked out to make foreign medicine." " The dragon god was dreadfully offended by the encroachment of the foreigner."

Heaven knows that the Chinese had reason enough for hating many of the foreigners who came to their shores. They had filched from them some of the richest portions of their fatherland. They had forced treaties upon them against their will and to their disadvantage. Individual Europeans had treated them with indignity and contempt times without number. I had myself seen in the French Concession at Shanghai a foreign policeman brutally kick a poor, timid Chinaman whose jinrikisha was a few feet across a boundary line near the steamship pier, and then smash his jinrikisha, his only means of living, into kindling wood. Such abuses had taken place every day for years in some parts of China.

Though the Boxers did not ascribe their uprising to the real causes, their indignation against Europeans which the wily Empress utilized with such deadly effect, was natural enough.

Added to these causes for the inevitable uprising, a most serious drought affected the whole of north China, and famine stared the coolies in the face. It was so dry that they could not plough their fields, so they had the more time to give to local politics, and to planning the revenge which they had so long cherished.

In the course of our first evening in Tientsin the missionaries gathered for prayer in view of the ominous events which threatened, and I remember especially the prayers of Dr. Arthur Smith, the gifted author, and his wife, that rain might speedily come to turn the attention of the Boxers away from thoughts of vengeance and to their ploughed fields. Before the meeting was over, as if in answer to our prayers, the heavens grew dark and a light rain began to fall. But alas, it was not enough thoroughly to wet the soil, and ploughing could not be begun. Even then, many of the missionaries, accustomed to the kindly attitude of the Christians for whom they worked, could not believe that serious trouble was coming, and assured me that they had little fear of it. Hon. Lionel Drew, who, next to Sir Robert Hart, was then the chief man in

Chinese financial affairs, told me that to him the outlook seemed very dark, and he thought the Boxers would soon do their worst.

This opinion, however, was not shared by the officials in Peking. Mr. Conger, then our minister plenipotentiary to China, told me he thought there was very little danger of an uprising, while Mrs. Conger told us of her recent visit to the Empress who had been particularly gracious and kind, and showed us rolls of rich silk, and a curious and very expensive ring which the Empress had just given her. Doubtless that astute old ruler was trying to put to sleep the suspicions of the foreigners, that she might work her evil purposes more securely.

In Peking a lull before the storm prevailed. The ill feeling, perhaps because of the instructions of the Empress, was less outwardly manifested. Still, the Boxers were practising their curious gymnastics in all parts of the city, and brandishing their spears and their long knives when they came together for their nightly evolutions.

There was little secrecy about these meetings. Indeed one of the Christians offered to bring a company of Boxers into the missionary compound that we might see their gymnastics and their drill. This honor, however, the missionaries declined with thanks, but in an open space not far from the compound I saw them perform, and there seemed to be nothing very dreadful or startling in their practice. They were for the most part fanatics, and of the lowest type of coolies, who believed that their exercises would make them impervious to foreign bullets, a belief that was dispelled as soon as fighting actually began.

I was impressed during my stay in Peking by the fearless courage of the missionaries. Realizing, as many of them did, the perils which beset them, they went about their ordinary work calmly and cheerfully. To the meetings I addressed, at one of which Minister Conger presided, some of the lady missionaries came in jinrikishas or on bicycles, travelling several miles through the dark streets in order to get to the meeting.

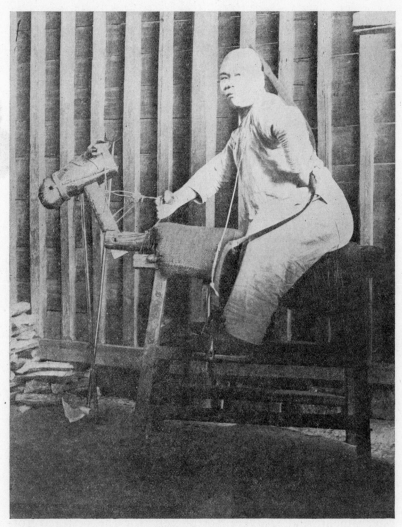

A CHINESE SOLDIER IN THE REGULAR ARMY IN 1900, JUST BEFORE THE BOXER REBELLION

This man belongs to the cavalry and is practising his craft on a wooden horse.

At a gathering in Tungcho, one of the principal mission stations, a few miles from Peking, a native pastor while I was speaking broke into the chapel, all excited and breathless, and said that he had been attacked and beaten by Boxers at the city gate. He was naturally afraid to go home alone, so one of the missionaries accompanied him, and met with no mishap.

While all were courageous, two or three names stand out as heroes of the siege which soon followed. Among these was my dear friend and interpreter at many a meeting, Dr. W. S. Ament. He proved to be one of the generals of the occasion, and, as Mr. Squires, the Secretary of Legation afterwards told me, was worth more than any professedly military man belonging to any of the legations. Dr. Ament was afterwards cruelly attacked by Mark Twain, and charged with looting the helpless Chinese, whereas the true facts were that he did more to help the homeless Chinese after the siege was over, to restore order and good feeling, than almost any other man.

Mark Twain's absurd and baseless charges were founded upon a newspaper falsehood, and when he was informed of the fact, and the charges were disproved, he did not have the manliness or the magnanimity to retract them, but said that if a man was fool enough to be a missionary he believed he was fool enough to do any other unaccountable deed.

Another hero of the siege was Dr. Gamewell of the Methodist Board of Missions, who was even more conspicuous in the public eye than Dr. Ament. He had intended to go home in a few weeks, and, as ordinary means of travel by sea were likely to be interrupted, he proposed to me that we should make up a little caravan and cross the Desert of Gobi together until we should reach the Trans-Siberian Railway. He found difficulty, however, in getting his passport from the Russian government, and so, very fortunately for the besieged foreigners in Peking, we were not able to carry out our plans, and he was caught in the besieged city, from which I barely escaped.

A memorable visit of these days in north China was to Paotingfu a large city situated about a hundred miles to the west of Peking.   This soon became known as "the city of the martyrs," for *every* missionary of the three boards, the Congregational, the Presbyterian, and the China Inland Mission, with their families, some twenty people in all were murdered a few days after our visit.

The story of Horace Pitkin will always be a classic in missionary annals. He was young, handsome, and brilliant, with considerable property of his own, while his wife was also well-to-do. One of the most popular men of the Yale class of which he was a member, a good scholar and prominent in athletics, he seemed to have everything that heart could wish in his own land. But feeling the call of the Master, he gave his life to China, and had been there but a very few years when the troubles of which I am telling broke out, and, in defending the ladies of the mission from the Boxers, he was himself slain. It is said that his head was displayed on the city walls.

An equally noble spirit of that same mission was Miss Mary Morrill who had come from Portland, Me., my old home, together with her comrade, Miss Anna Gould. Miss Morrill was a favorite in missionary circles in America from her interesting and winsome addresses, and we learned the secret of her power both with her audiences at home and with her Chinese converts, as we spent a few days in the same missionary compound at Paotingfu. It was the secret of a gentle, loving, Christian heart, and was well illustrated by an old Chinese woman, homeless and friendless, who had been ostracised by her family and friends when she became a Christian. One day she came to Miss Morrill and asked her if she thought friends would know each other in heaven. "Yes," answered Miss Morrill, "I think they will." "Well," replied the old woman, "I want to sit near you in heaven and take hold of your hand once in a while," a wish which I believe may soon have been fulfilled, for both were massacred by the Boxers.

Miss Morrill was seized and carried out of the mission compound after the death of Mr. Pitkin, and it is said was taken to a heathen temple where she was murdered, with what cruelty and indignities we do not know. But the Boxers afterward said that she was courageous and thoughtful for others until the very last, giving away the Chinese cash she had in her pocket to the little beggar boys who always swarm about one in China, saying to them, " You can have these; I shall not want them any longer." So thoughtful and considerate was she to the very end. I have recently been told that the famous Chinese Christian General Feng, who has won so many victories for the side of law and order, witnessed Miss Morrill's martyrdom, and, because of her courage and steadfastness, became a devoted Christian. He has introduced Christian Endeavor into his army and formed societies among both officers and men.

Miss Gould died with equal heroism, as did also the Presbyterian missionaries in the compound on the other side of the city, which we also visited more than once. The buildings of this mission were set on fire by the Boxers, the missionaries driven out and killed before the very eyes of their little children, who soon suffered the same fate, and it was said with as much genuine heroism as their parents displayed.

On our last day in Paotingfu we made a final visit to the Presbyterian compound.

Miss Morrill had provided a Sedan chair for Mrs. Clark, as being more comfortable than the Chinese cart. The regular chair coolies who belonged on the compound being away that day, she had sent out for some street coolies to act as bearers. They came in, two rough, coarse-looking men, with their trousers hanging down, loose and untied, and their queues rolled up into a pug on the back of their heads, and a scowl on their faces.

Miss Morrill said that they did not look right, and their trousers must be tied neatly around their ankles, and their queues hanging down as usual. The coolies, with cross looks, objected, and Mrs. Clark said it was no matter, let it go; they could carry her just as well one way as another and if they were more comfortable with their hair bobbed up in that way and their trousers loose, it did not make any difference. But Miss Morrill, who knew Chinese custom, said it must not be; that this was a mark of disrespect and discourtesy; that it was rude and impolite and the men knew it and knew that she knew it. She talked with them a little, pleasantly but firmly, and in a few minutes they had not only made themselves neat and tidy as she desired, but had done it pleasantly, and started off with a laugh, and good cheer. It was a remarkable example of the power of mind over matter, that that quiet, gentle little woman could not only make those rough men do her will, but could make them do it *pleasantly* and *cheerfully*.

The cart in which my little son and I were riding broke down while going through the city, and Mrs. Clark's bearers, pretending to be tired, set her down near the river bank, and began to jeer at her as a foreign woman, and make unpleasant remarks to their companions who gathered around. After a while, much to her relief they took her up again, and delivered her safely at the Congregational Mission compound, though not before her husband and the missionaries had become thoroughly alarmed for her safety, since processions of Boxers with long knives and spears had been passed by us on the way.

The governor of the city, who still pretended to protect foreigners, sent a guard of soldiers each night to the mission compound, who were supposed to defend us all against the Boxers should they attack us. It is more than likely however, that some of these soldiers were themselves Boxers, or that they would have run as fast as their legs could carry them if the Boxers actually appeared. They were supposed to fire their guns at nine o'clock each evening, to let us know that they were on duty. One evening no guns were heard, and when Mr. Pitkin inquired the next morning why the salute was not fired, the captain of the guard told him that they had no powder. The next night, after the same omission, he was informed that they had no wadding and so could not fire their guns. These were evidently their excuses to let him know that they did not take their duties seriously.

The day of our departure arrived, and very early in the morning we took the train back to Peking, over the railway which in a few days more was utterly destroyed by the Boxers, so that no trains could go or come, and the doom of the missionaries was sealed. At that early hour, a few Chinese were strolling about the platform, giving their birds, which they carried in cages, an airing, a favorite custom of these bird-loving folk. A few Chinese Christians and missionaries had come to see us off, and the last glimpse we had was of the stalwart form and white hat of Pitkin as he waved us adieu, and of the others who were soon to become martyrs of their faith.

Shortly after that we sailed from Taku on a small Japanese steamer commanded by a diminutive captain, who seemed greatly to enjoy playing rope quoits with our twelve-year-old son, whose stature was about the same as the captain's. However, he was a skilful captain, and, through the fog, steered his craft between the numerous islands which dot the coast of Korea, stopped for a few hours at Chemulpo, and at last landed us safely at Fusan.

ACROSS SIBERIA IN FORTY-TWO DAYS

PICTURESQUE KOREAN MONASTERY — LANDING IN RUSSIA — THE SIBERIAN RAILWAY — DANGERS AND DIFFICULTIES — FOURTH-CLASS CARS — LAKE BAIKAL — BLAGOVYESH-CHENSK — IRKUTZK — MOSCOW AT LAST.

S I have intimated in the previous chapter we were in serious difficulties as to how we might best return from China to Europe and America. I was anxious to get to London in time for the World's Christian Endeavor Convention of 1900, which was to open about the middle of July. The journey by water would be a long and tedious one. We had to give up our plan for crossing the desert of Gobi from Peking, since Dr. Gamewell could not go, and the caravan could not be formed. At last, with many misgivings, we decided to attempt the journey across Siberia from Vladivostok to London, a journey which by steam power had never before been undertaken by any one. Some said it could not be done. Others, who were more optimistic, said it could be accomplished in twenty days. The Russian ambassador to China said he thought it could surely be accomplished in twenty-eight days, and kindly gave me a letter of introduction "to whom it might concern." So we decided at last to attempt this new route, armed also with a letter from Mr. Conger, our American minister.

I have already described the beginning of this adventurous journey as far as Fusan. Only a few days after we left the port of Peking, its forts were fired upon by the Boxers, and the beginning of the end of China's ancient *régime* had come.

At Fusan we had to wait several days for a steamer to Vladivostok, and were kindly entertained in the home of a well-known Presbyterian missionary, Dr. Irvin. A memorable trip was one that we took with Dr. Irvin and some of our other friends to a famous old Buddhist monastery in the green clad hills some twenty miles from the port of Fusan. There were then no railroads in that part of Korea as there are now, and indeed no carriage roads of any kind, only bridle paths, or narrow footways, trodden by the Jickey men with immense packs upon their backs. Most of the transportation in Korea was then done by what children would call pick-a-back, though sometimes donkeys, ponies, and water buffaloes were pressed into service, with an occasional horse.

The people of Korea, who had not then become sophisticated by the Japanese, greatly interested us. White was the universal color of their costumes; at least, this was the color the first day the costume was worn, a color that for working people changed its complexion, becoming dingier and dingier as the days went on. The Korean gentlemen and ladies, however, wore spotless white, sometimes of an expensive material. The Japanese edict " top-knot come down," had not then been proclaimed, and all the men wore their hair twisted up into a little pug on top of their heads and fastened with a big metal hair-pin, while over the top-knot they wore a horse-hair hat something like the steeple-crowned headgear of our early pilgrim ancestors. Some of these hats are very expensive and cost their owners as much as thirty dollars apiece.

We made our way on donkeys, the ladies in chairs, across the broad plain, which follows the seacoast, and soon turned off among the hills, with rice-fields on either hand, and delicious-looking water gurgling on every side. This water, on pain of death, we were not allowed to drink, as it had come through the rice fields, where the fertilizer used had filled it with innumerable noxious germs of typhoid and other dread diseases.

As we kept getting higher the scenery at every kilometer became more strikingly beautiful. Great oak and pine trees lined our pathway. Charming waterfalls dashed down the hills, and many lovely flowers brightened the roadside.

At last the buildings of the old monastery came in sight, and we were heartily welcomed by the monks, who knew and respected our missionary doctor for his gifts of healing, which they had themselves experienced. The monastery was a rambling old structure, and to it belonged many of the ricefields, which had been a large source of wealth for generations. Altogether, it was one of the most picturesque, interesting, and unusual places that I have visited in all my travels.

Though we had brought provisions with us, the monks insisted on our sharing their evening meal, which consisted largely of rice on a large lettuce leaf, with some condiment like soy, and a relish made of fried bark and toasted seaweed, which tasted far better than it sounds.

They also taught us a good lesson in hospitality, for while we were all eating, a company of Korean pilgrims arrived, who were taken right into their refectory, and seated on the floor with the rest of us. As the cooked provisions had all been served to monks and guests, there was nothing to do but to take a collection; so one of the monks passed around a platter while each one put a spoonful of rice and some of the condiments from his plate on the common dish from which the new-comers were to be served.

This grace of hospitality, was, I fear, one of their few virtues, for I understand that they live a lazy and useless life. After supper they took down their gods from their pedestals to put them in a good light, so that Mrs. Clark might take their pictures, while they themselves were not averse to being immortalized by the camera. The whole surroundings were most unusual. The primitive yet ingenious way of pounding their rice by their water mills was most interesting. These worked automatically, and brought down, about once a minute, a heavy pestle in the mortar filled with rice, day and night, and day after day.

When night came the monks assigned us to some of their cells as our sleeping apartments, they themselves having moved out to other and perhaps less comfortable quarters. For a time all went well, and we fell into a comfortable slumber, but were awakened after a little by a sense of suffocation and burning heat and itching as well. We found on investigation, that the floor on which we were lying was really a stove, heated by flues underneath, in which our kind hosts had built fires in order that we might not suffer from the night chill. The innumerable living creatures which naturally inhabit such places, when they got thoroughly warmed up, went about their usual business, and added much to our discomfort. However we were able to ventilate our cells by opening the doors, and succeeded in getting some needed rest before a new day dawned in this secluded paradise of the hills.

We were soon on our way back to Fusan, and the next day found a Japanese steamer sailing for Vladivostok, on which we took passage, making only one stop on the way, and that at Gensan, or Wonsan, the Korean name, on the northern coast of Chosen, as Korea is now called.

The fine harbor of Vladivostok was reached early in the morning, and in a sampan with all our baggage we were conveyed to the wharf, expecting to find an eagle-eyed corps of custom-house inspectors waiting for us, and perhaps an order from the Imperial Government forbidding us to land, for we had heard much of the strictness and inhospitality of the Russian Czarist government to foreigners. However, no formidable officials awaited our landing, and I strolled up and down on the wharf for some time, trying to discover an inspector who would examine our luggage, and prepared for all kinds of trouble in the process.

A few years later on trying to enter Russia from the European side my expectations of trouble of this sort were fully realized, but in Vladivostok I could discover no inspector of customs of any sort, and after waiting a sufficient length of time, we loaded our trunks into a tarantass and ourselves into a droschky, and drove to the best hotel in town, a hotel by no means too good, "best" though it was.

Vladivostok was then a raw town on which an immense amount of money was being spent in docks and fortifications and improvements of all sorts, for it was not only the eastern terminus of the great Trans-Siberian Railway, but the capital of the vast province of Primorskaia, and the most important Russian seaport on the Pacific Coast. It is a hilly town with the streets at that time in a rather chaotic condition. The droschky men all drove with one or two horses between the shafts, and another running free outside the shafts, but able to pull when necessary. The drivers are all Jehus, and race through the streets at a furious pace, the free horse cavorting and prancing, and adding much style to the outfit.

My first call was upon General Tchickachoff, the Governor of Primorskaia. He received me very graciously, and especially, when he had read the letter of introduction from the Russian Ambassador to China, was exceedingly kind and painstaking for our comfort. He at once engaged sleeping-car accommodations for us to Khabarovsk, five hundred miles away, telegraphed for a stateroom on the first boat leaving Khabarovsk, and indeed his courteous thoughtfulness followed us half the way to Moscow.

I had always thought of a Cossack as a sort of cowboy, a rough rider of the Russian Steppes, with no undue regard for human life, from whom it would be well to keep away as far as possible. But here was my first Cossack, the general and governor, whom I found to be an educated, polished gentleman, with a most kindly and generous heart, and my boyhood ideas of Cossacks changed for the better.

The next morning we started from the railway station, over whose portals was the almost terrifying sign, " Petersburg 9,375 versts." A verst is about two thirds of a mile, and one can easily reckon the vast distance that lay between us and our goal. Moreover it was a distance beset with unknown dangers and possibilities of disaster. No one before had taken the new all-steam route across Siberia. Even then the railroad was not within 1,800 miles of completion, and that long stretch had to be made on the Amur River.

There was, however, in June, 1900, when we started, a possibility of going all the way by steamboat or railway train and for the first time in the history of the world, for the railroad to the upper waters of the Amur had been completed that winter, and on June 1, for the first time that season, the great river was free of ice, and the first boat was to leave Khabarovsk the next day.

We had read dubious accounts of the new railway in the papers. It was said by its traducers to be merely two streaks of rust across Asia, that the roadbed was in horrible condition, and that the trestles and bridges were flimsy and insecure affairs. This was an exaggerated story but nevertheless partially true, as we soon found.

Khabarovsk was then another raw pioneer town, beautifully situated on a high bank overlooking the mighty river, which was here some three miles wide, although still several hundred miles from its mouth.

Through a cloud of dust, which prevented us from seeing the beauties of Khavarovsk, if it had any, we were driven furiously to the wharf, and there, to our surprise and delight, found a fine, large boat, the " Baron Korff," with steam up, waiting to take us for the first stage of our journey on the Amur. It was well that Governor Tchickachoff had wired for accommodations for us, for scores of people who could get no chance to sail had long been waiting for the boat. It seemed selfish that the last should be first, but feeling the great importance of reaching our destination as soon as possible, we accepted what the gods had provided, and found ourselves installed in a large and comfortable stateroom, which we occupied for more than a week.

A FLASH OF LIGHTNING

On the Amur River.   The Manchurian shore is seen in the distance.
From a photograph by Mrs. F. E. Clark.

The Amur is a lordly river indeed, and for much of its course it flows with such a mighty and majestic, yet silent sweep, that it gives the impression, more than almost any other river, of resistless power and might.   There are few settlements on its banks, and what there are, are for the most part of the most primitive kind; log huts chinked with moss and mud being the prevailing type of architecture.

For a long distance Siberia lies on one side of the river and Mongolia on the other. Sometimes the river winds its way through beautiful meadows, which in June are bright with flowers of various kinds. Lilies of the valley, with the same sweet scent with which we are familiar, can be picked by the bushel. Orchids of various kinds and colors, but of general shape like our familiar lady's slipper, hide under the pine trees. Sometimes the river flows through great forests, though more often we see these forests of birch and oak and pine at a little distance; often looking like the park of some vast estate, so open are these forests and free from underbrush. Huge piles of wood are found at every landing, and usually two or three times a day our steamer stopped to wood up, while the roustabouts made lively work of piling up cords of four foot logs upon the lower deck to feed the ever-gaping maw of our furnaces. Thus passed eight or ten pleasant, though monotonous days, which gave us ample opportunity to read and write and enjoy the ever-changing scenery.

About eleven o'clock on a June evening our boat stopped at Blagovyeshchensk, and we were told that we could go no further on the " Baron Korff," since she (or he), drew too much water for the shallows above. It was still light in that northern latitude, and we wandered from hotel to hotel in this considerable city, seeking a place where we might lay our heads for the night.

A very bright and intelligent young lady, a correspondent of the New York papers, in whose behalf she was seeking unusual adventures, had joined herself to our little party, and at last we found one vacant room where the two ladies and the small boy could bestow themselves. But what should become of the grown-up male member of the party? He had about made up his mind to spend the night on the curb stone, when a Russian officer, a perfect stranger, came out of another hotel near by, and invited him to share his own room for the night. In the morning, when I tried to pay my share of the bill, he absolutely refused to let me do it, saying that I was his guest, and he could not think of such a thing. Was there ever a more perfect example of genuine hospitality, — to take an utter stranger, at midnight, into one's own room!

A Siberian bill, in those days, was a lengthy document for, as many people carried their own beds and bedding, and apparatus for their ablutions, every sheet and blanket and pillow case and towel furnished by the hotel was a separate charge, as well as the milk and sugar used in the coffee, the butter that we spread on the bread, and every last item for which we found any use. When all was reckoned up, however, the sum total was not extravagant, however long the bill.

The next day we took passage on a smaller steamer, and, when we reached the Shilka River, were transferred to a still smaller boat, or barge, towed by a very light-draught tug. So shallow was the water, for the season was an unusually dry one, we often ran aground, and frequently it would take hours to get us off the sand bars. The quartermaster was constantly casting the lead, while the little craft was in motion, and singing out in monotonous Russian the depth of the water beneath our keel. Occasionally, all the passengers and baggage had to be transferred for a time to another boat in order to decrease our draught.

The scenery grows more picturesque and beautiful as the journey up the Shilka proceeds, and the country becomes more mountainous. In one place the river cuts through a solid bed of coal, which years ago, caught fire, and for aught I know, is burning still.

Thus days and days passed, the monotony being relieved by frequent stops at the great wood-piles, where usually some Siberian woman awaited us with bottles of fresh milk, small loaves of bread, pieces of fried chicken, or roast lamb, with which we varied the monotony of our steamer's bill of fare.

Occasionally we would stop at a small village with a single street of log houses, a general variety store, and a big Russian Orthodox Church. Sometimes, while the boat was wooding up, we had time to explore the village to make sundry little purchases, and perhaps to attend a service, where we always found the priests arrayed in most gorgeous vestments of cloth of gold, which would have done credit to a metropolitan cathedral.

At one place, my boy and I, desiring to try our hands at fishing, saw a man digging in the field, and applied to him for bait. Whereupon, divining that we were Americans, he began to repeat the names of our sovereign States in the same order that I had myself learned them in the school geography: "Maine, New Hampshire, Vermont, Massachusetts, Rhode Island, Connecticut," etc. I found that he knew few other English words, but that he had a son in America and he doubtless beguiled the long evenings of a Siberian winter by studying the map of the country to which his son had gone, and imagining, perhaps, something of the wonders of the New World.

After twenty-two long days and nights we reached Stretinsk at the head of navigation of the Shilka, the longest tributary of the mighty Amur. We thought that we had had sufficient tribulation before this, but we found when we left Stretinsk that if we had tears to shed it was time to shed them then, for it took something like a week longer by rail to reach the banks of Lake Baikal, though it was only a thousand miles distant.

Troops were being hurried to the Chinese border to have their share in quelling the Boxer uprising, and we often had to wait for hours for the arrival and passage of a troop train. Soon after leaving Stretinsk a long railway bridge burned down just as we approached it, which caused a delay of many hours while all scrambled across a dry river bed to a train which had been brought up to the other bank. Up to this point the thoughtfulness of our good Cossack angel in Vladivostok had followed us, and we had obtained a tolerably comfortable car, much like a caboose on a freight train, but this train could not get across the river, and on the other side there was a general rush for the best seats.

The best seats that we could secure were hard boards in a car that was marked on the outside, " For Twelve Horses or Forty Men," a car used for the transportation of soldiers or

OUR FIFTH-CLASS CARS ON THE TRANS-BAIKAL TRAIN
Prisoners carrying water.

of horses, as the case might be. Indeed all the cars on this second train were of this character, and there were fully forty men, women and children in the car which fell to our lot. This part of the railway was still a military road and passengers were not desired, but taken on sufferance, so one could not complain.

With towels and rugs we managed to screen off a little family apartment, and got what rest we could at night on the boards which formed the impromptu seats. It was a trying

journey, but we made the best of it, and were glad enough
after six or seven days to reach Lisovitchnia on the eastern
shore of Russia's great inland lake.

Our fellow travellers, however, were most kind and considerate, and we came to have a real regard for the Mujiks
who travelled with us, even though cleanliness was not their
chief characteristic.   Nothing could be kinder than their attempts to reduce the discomforts of our journey.   They would

PRISON BARGE

A prison barge on the Amur River carrying prisoners to the Saghalien Island
before the Russo-Japanese war.

help us get our baggage down from the shelf near the roof
of the car.   They would also offer to divide with us their
black bread and curds and whey, though we were not often
obliged to accept their hospitality, since at the railway stations
there was always a small buffet, and outside the station a
line of native women behind a long table, selling the products
of the country.

Eggs and milk and bread were almost always available.

Then, too, at every station there was a steaming samovar, filled with boiling water, from which we all made tea as often as we wished. No product of the cup that cheers but does not inebriate is finer than that which one gets in Russia, for it is " Caravan Tea," which is brought across the desert, and

A PRISON CAR ON THE TRANS-SIBERIAN RAILWAY

Before the war nearly every ordinary train included one or more prison cars. Prisoners and criminals were often allowed to take their wives and children into exile. Note the woman and baby at the window.

has never known salt water. No nation is more fond of the tea-cup than the Russian, so that every railway station might be called a life-saving tea station.

All the way across Siberia a prison car was attached to our train and a prison barge had been towed up the long stretches of the Amur by our steamer. We were told that the prisoners behind the bars were not political prisoners but criminals, though they looked no more vicious than most of our fellow passengers. We could not speak the language and could have little communication with them, but their prison life did not seem terribly irksome so far as we could see, since wives and children often accompanied them.

Occasionally we passed long trains of emigrants, going to some spot in Siberia where the government had given them a grant of land, for the Czar was doing his best to people the waste places of that vast province. It was pathetic to see the gratitude of these poor emigrants for any little favor we could give. A kopeck tossed to a child, a half a loaf of bread to a family party, or an old garment which had outlived its usefulness so far as we were concerned, seemed to call forth an unending stream of blessings. I was much embarrassed to have one poor woman to whom I had handed some little gift through the window, come out of the car, and down the steps, kneel at my feet, and kiss my travel-stained shoes. Such a gift, in most countries, would have called forth scarcely a "thank you."

A lady friend in Vladivostok had given us a vocabulary of the most important words that we would be likely to need, some two hundred of them, spelling them out in the English equivalents for the Russian letters, and also giving us the sounds of the Russian characters. Before the journey was over we were able to spell out the signs as well as the headlines in the Russian papers, in spite of the silent letters, which seem to have no use in the language except to confuse and exasperate the foreigner. This little vocabulary was a great boon to us, and enabled us before the journey was over to ask for almost anything we desired.

At last the hard week in the military car was over, as well as our long stops of two hours or more at each little station. But a longer wait still was before us, at Lisovitchnia, the village

on the shores of Lake Baikal, while waiting for the great ice-
breaker which was to carry us to the other shore. There
seemed to be no earthly reason for the delay, while we sat
upon our trunks in the dreary railway station for nearly a
whole day waiting for the boat that apparently would never
come. We learned afterwards that a Minister of Justice of the
empire (minister of injustice, we preferred to call him) was

OUR FELLOW PASSENGERS ON THE TRANS-SIBERIAN RAILWAY
Waiting for the boat at Lisovitchnia on the borders of Lake Baikal.
From photograph by Mrs. Clark.

delaying the ice-breaker for his own convenience, and to the
inconvenience of two or three hundred passengers. My son
and I beguiled a part of the tedious day with short rambles
and with a bath in the icy waters of the great lake.

Baikal is one of the largest and most famous fresh-water
lakes in the world. It is about the size of Lake Erie, and is
noted for short but terrific storms that sweep down upon it

from the surrounding hills. "A man never prays till he takes passage on Lake Baikal" is one of the proverbs of the vicinage. All winter long the tremendous ice-breaker forces its way through the ever-thickening ice, keeping a passage open from shore to shore. Toward the last of June the ice had gone out of the lake, and its great iron beak was no longer of so much use. Just at nightfall the ice-breaker reached the shore where we were waiting, and the whole long train made its way into the bowels of the big ship, while our little family of three was fortunate enough to secure a comfortable stateroom and enjoy the first good night's sleep which we had had for nearly three weeks, since we left the "Baron Korff."

A comparatively short railway ride on the other side of the lake brought us to Irkutsk, the thriving metropolis of central Siberia. Our company of through foreign travellers on the journey from the Pacific Coast consisted of the four Americans already introduced, a Dane, a Swiss consul, a German baron, a Scottish merchant and his wife, a couple of Frenchmen, and, most congenial of all, Mr. John Jordan, the consul-general and chief diplomatic agent of Great Britain in Korea. His faithful service, soon after this, gained him the title of Sir John Jordan, and the high diplomatic post of Ambassador to China, where I had the pleasure of meeting him some years later in the marvellous old Chinese temple where the British Embassy to China is located.

When we reached Irkutsk there was a great rush for the weekly through train for St. Petersburg (which had not then changed its name to Petrograd). There were but a limited number of first-class compartments and naturally each of our fellow passengers, as well as ourselves, was eager to get one of them. We were handicapped, however, as some were not, by a lack of knowledge of the language, and when it came our turn to secure sleeping-berths, we found that only second-class compartments were left. However, we made the best of it, and consoled ourselves with the thought that a second-class compartment cost only half as much as the first-class. So we secured a large compartment with four berths for less than the price that our travelling companions in the first-class paid for two berths. When we reached the train, we found, to our surprise, that the second-class compartments were in the same car as the first class, and precisely the same in every particular except in the label stuck upon the window. So we proved the saying true, " he laughs best who laughs last," for we certainly had the best of it.

This last lap of our journey lasted eight days and was comfortable and uneventful, and the fares were only about a cent a mile. A good dining-car was on the train, and we were landed in Moscow on schedule time. Here we spent but a day, seeing as much of the city as we could, of its curious churches, its wonderful Kremlin, and its devout and superstitious people, for we had to hurry on to St. Petersburg, and then by the fastest possible train to London.

We had been forty-two days upon the road from Vladivostok, instead of twenty, or twenty-eight, as we were told would be the case. The World's Christian Endeavor Convention began the very next day after our arrival in London, instead of leaving us two weeks for rest and recuperation as we had expected. Nevertheless we had come through these trying experiences in good condition. The convention was all that we had expected, with some fifty thousand delegates and friends in attendance. For the first time in its history, many of the gray old buildings of London were decorated for a religious gathering, and we were greeted by hundreds of Endeavorers who had come from America as well as from other parts of the world to attend this great gathering.

A happy summer in Switzerland followed, since our older children had come across the ocean to join us.

The autumn found us in our own home, while I attempted to catch up with the arrears of work and writing which awaited me at Endeavor headquarters in Boston.

As I review this journey and its scenes, more than twenty years afterwards, I am tempted to moralize on the events that have occurred since that time: the seemingly impregnable monarchy overthrown, the weak Czar and his superstitious wife, the little Czarevitch and all his sisters murdered in cold blood in the Siberia to which the Czar had sent so many innocent subjects; a Bolshevist government set up and now apparently tottering to its fall; millions of people starving to death; a vast and once prosperous country racked and wrecked, and seemingly on the verge of eternal ruin! All these things have been brought to pass in half a decade! Who is bold enough to predict Russia's future?

THE CHARM OF SCANDINAVIA IN WINTER

AN INTERVIEW WITH KING OSCAR — PRINCE BERNADOTTE —
A LOVE MATCH — LOCKED IN THE ICE — FINLAND'S
WOES.

 HE most notable event of the year 1901 from the Christian Endeavor standpoint was the twentieth anniversary of the movement, especially celebrated on Feburary 2 in Portland, Me. This meeting brought together many leading ministers and laymen from different parts of the country, and emphasized the growth of the movement in two decades. By this time it had spread to every continent and to most of the nations of the world, and though the opposition of some denominationalists still continued, the marvellous Providential growth of the society during the first twenty years gave boundless hope and courage for the future.

By the beginning of 1902 I felt that I should again answer calls from across the seas, and on January 4, with my wife and three of our children, I set sail for Naples, with the intention of leaving my family in Italy while I should devote my time largely to meetings in the northern countries of Europe.

This plan was carried out and mid-winter found me in the Scandinavian countries, attending such meetings as I had been invited to in Denmark, Norway, Sweden, and Finland.

It may seem that mid-winter was an unfortunate time to choose for such peregrinations, but, as a matter of fact, no countries are more comfortable for winter travel than these northern lands. While tourists shiver in the cold marble palaces of Italy, which now serve as hotels or *pensions*, the traveller in Scandinavia finds comfortable, steam-heated railway cars, hotels warm in every room and corridor, heated by great, porcelain, wood-burning stoves, while the cold, though often intense, is of the dry, crisp variety, which makes far less drain upon one's vitality than the moisture-laden cold of more southern latitudes, even where the temperature is half a hundred degrees higher. I remember writing to my wife, whose room in a Florence *pension* was warmed, when heated at all, by a smoky little stove not much larger than a peck measure, that if she wished to be really comfortable she should have come with me to the Arctic Circle and beyond.

" Northern Travel " always exercised a strange fascination for me since reading, as a boy, Bayard Taylor's book with that title. His journeys in Sweden and Norway, his descriptions of the winter landscape in these cold countries, and his ride in a reindeer-sledge I deemed more fascinating than the adventures of Robinson Crusoe. The exploits of Dr. Kane, and the ill-fated Sir John Franklin expedition had also fired my imagination, and I found when visiting these Arctic regions that their winter glories had not been overdrawn.

A peculiar characteristic of Sweden in winter is the windless, frosty weather, lasting for days at a time, when every branch and twig on every tree, every fence rail and telegraph wire, is loaded inches deep with a feathery rime which sparkles in the sun like the jewels in a king's crown, while all the fields are covered with " acres of diamonds."

The glories of the sunset and the sunrise too are incomparable in these northern latitudes, where sunrise glows until noon-day and fades again into the marvellous sunset lights, all within the space of two or three hours.

On this journey I was a little too late in the year to find a night of twenty-four hours without a glimpse of the sun, but on a subsequent trip I got far into the Land of the Mid-day

Moon early in January, a memorable experience which I may describe in a later chapter. My five journeys to Scandinavia have all been made in the winter time or early spring, a season more favorable for the meetings which I went to attend, than for sight-seeing. But I do not regret the fact, for, though Scandinavia is supremely beautiful in the summer time, with its green fields, placid lakes, and rushing rivers, winter is after all the characteristic season, as it is in Canada, our own "Lady of the Snows."

The charm of Scandinavia lies not altogether in its beautiful winter and summer landscapes, its tonicky atmosphere, and the warmth and good cheer of its homes and hotels; the people themselves are worthy of the beautiful land which they inhabit. Brought up in the kindly school of a gracious democracy, they are genial and friendly beyond the generality of mankind, and being somewhat removed from the great arteries of travel, their hospitality is more generous and unstinted. The Swedes are a particularly suave and polite people, more nearly resembling the French in their manners than any other continental nation. The Norwegians, somewhat more bluff and brusque, perhaps, are none the less genuinely hospitable, and their sterling honesty has not yet been tainted in spite of the great influx of summer visitors, which has spoiled the primitive simplicity and genuine kindliness of so many other peoples.

Our American minister in Sweden at that time was Hon. William Widgery Thomas from Portland, Me., one of the most genial and jovial of men, who was a favorite with all, from King Oscar to the humblest servant of the legation. He had conferred a real benefit upon his native State by sending a large colony of industrious Swedes to Aroostook County, where they had greatly prospered. Some of them are now among the "Potato Kings" of the county. His father and mother I had known in Portland where they were much esteemed both in social and religious circles. Mrs. Thomas had been very anxious that William Widgery should become a parson, but

his tastes evidently did not lie in that direction. When he was
sent as our representative to Sweden one of the *bon mots*
at the farewell banquet which was given him in Portland, was
to the effect that now " Mr. Thomas's saintly mother would
have her heart's wish at last fulfilled, for William Widgery
had become a minister."

While I was in Stockholm he kindly offered to arrange an
audience with King Oscar for me, and I had the pleasure of
a twenty-minute talk with that democratic monarch in a beautiful little cabinet in the enormous palace of Stockholm. The
palace outside is as bare and to the ordinary eye as homely as
most king's palaces, though it is said by architects to be quite
in a class by itself so far as the beauty of its lines is concerned.
It is a vast building, capable of entertaining the King's fellow
monarchs with all their suites, even when they number hundreds of individuals. King Oscar had the reputation of being
the handsomest of European rulers, as well as one of the
wisest and most gracious. Considerably over six feet tall,
with an erect military bearing, and a benignant face, he at
once put his visitors at their ease and chatted as familiarly
as though he had not worn the royal purple.

Our conversation naturally turned on the Scandinavians in
America, and while he was gratified that they had given such
good account of themselves, and were considered as among
the most valuable elements of our population, he regretted that
America had proved such a powerful magnet, especially to his
Norwegian subjects. Not long after this the Norwegians concluded to set up a kingdom of their own, and to separate
themselves from Sweden, with King Haakon as their ruler.
It was a bloodless revolution, but a sore blow to King Oscar.
It was said that the old monarch never recovered from it,
though even in Norway he was to the end respected and loved
by most.

An interesting fact about this royal family is its descent
from one of Napoleon's generals, Marshal Bernadotte,

whom, on the death of Charles XII, the Swedes elected as
their king. It proved to be a wise choice, though the Hohenzollerns and the Hapsburgs were inclined to look down upon
the royalties of Sweden as *parvenues.*

In speaking of religious conditions in Sweden the king told
me that he left such matters largely to his second son, Prince
Oscar Bernadotte, on whom I afterwards called and found
exceedingly interested and sympathetic in all things relating to
the spiritual conditions of the country. Indeed he was one of
the most religious men whom I ever met, being especially
devoted to the work of the Y.M.C.A. in Stockholm, but
willing to speak for the cause of his Master wherever he was
invited and his other duties allowed. Though the state church
of Sweden is Lutheran, Prince Bernadotte seemed just as much
interested in other churches, especially in the Floragatan Independent Church, which he occasionally attended.

I have been told that he sometimes has preached to the
washerwomen, as they were bending over their tubs in a
public washhouse, and has even been to the far north to carry
the Gospel to the nomadic Lapps in their frozen wilds. I have
enjoyed three or four calls at different times at his modest
home, — that is, modest for a royal prince, — and have been
struck with the simplicity and beauty of the family life.

His union with the princess was a pure love match, since she
did not belong to a royal though to a noble family. In taking
Ebba Monk he at the same time gave up the possibility of
ever being king of Sweden. As I met the princess and their
charming family I felt that he had made no mistake in re-
signing the possibility of a throne for such domestic happiness.
The dominance of his religious life is indicated by his correspondence, as well as by his words and acts, for more than
one letter that I have received has been signed " Yours in the
Master's service," or words to that effect. This deep religious
character he perhaps inherited from his mother, who was known
far and wide as a peculiarly devout woman, delighting espe-

cially in the books and sermons of F. B. Meyer, and preachers of a peculiarly spiritual tone.

Crossing the Baltic to Finland, in mid-winter, was an experience to be remembered. For some miles from the city of Stockholm the ice on the landward side served for wharves for loading and unloading merchandise.

It was a picturesque sight, under the flaring torches, with stevedores on skis drawing great sleds, hurrying back and forth. Soon our ship was out in the Baltic, and then our troubles began, for the cold became more intense, and the strong wind from the north drove the floating ice down upon our little ship with tremendous force.

Through a few inches of ice we could cut our way as a knife goes through a cream cheese, but, when the ice became a foot thick, it was a decidedly different proposition, and we made but little headway. At length the ice closed in around us fully two feet thick, and further progress seemed hopeless. Our captain did not give up in despair, however, but sent out his crew, who, with axes and saws, attempted to cut a passage for the ship. It proved a hopeless undertaking, for the ice closed in more rapidly than it could be cut away. There was nothing to do but to send a message to the Finnish shore for help, and endure our imprisonment with what patience we could, waiting for a change of wind, or for an ice-breaker from the further shore.

It was a truly arctic scene that surrounded us, as for thirty-six hours we lay there, fast embedded in the ice. I made one or two short excursions from the steamer, and saw the great, jagged masses heaved up by the impact of the ice from the north, and could imagine what the heroes of my boyhood, Franklin and Kane, and other Arctic explorers had experienced. Here and there seals were playing upon the ice, and it was amusing to see the mother seals poke the little ones into the air holes, out of harm's way, when they saw their supposed enemy, man, approaching. We were in no danger except from

possible starvation if held in the ice too long, and I thoroughly
enjoyed the experience.

At last our cry for help was heard, and an ice-breaker put
off from the Finnish shore to help us; but she was not powerful enough, and soon she, too, was stuck in the ice, within

THE ICE-BREAKER OPENING A PATH FOR OUR STEAMER

plain view of the " Wellamo." After thirty-six hours, another
ice-breaker came to our rescue. She was the most powerful
vessel on the coast, and succeeded in breaking a channel
through which the " Wellamo " and our would-be rescuer
following closely in our wake, were able to reach the icy
wharves of Hango.

FROM THE BALKANS TO ICELAND

A MISSIONARY CAPTURED BY BRIGANDS — MANY RACES AND
LANGUAGES — ISOLATED ICELAND — THE ANCIENT AL-
THING — THINGVALLA — FISHING ON THE SOG.

FTER the visit to Scandinavia related in the
last chapter I returned to my family in
Florence, and after a few days of rest
started with Mrs. Clark for Bohemia, Bulgaria, Macedonia, and Greece, leaving three
of our children in Italy. One or two incidents of this journey stand out in my memory, though
later visits to these countries have somewhat dimmed the per-
spective.

This was the year in which great excitement prevailed
throughout the United States because of the capture by brigands of Miss Ellen Stone, an eminent American missionary,
and Mrs. Tsilka, her travelling companion. Shortly before I
left Boston, the news of her capture reached America, and
strenuous efforts were made to raise the sixty thousand dollars
which the brigands demanded.

Being then upon the Prudential Committee of the American
Board, of which organization Miss Stone was a missionary, I
had, with many others, sought to arouse the churches to the
necessity of speedy action, that her life might not be sacri-
ficed.

The capture and release of Miss Stone and Mrs. Tsilka,
the birth of the Tsilka baby in the wild mountain wilderness

on the border between Bulgaria and Macedonia, the dexterous way in which the money was at last made over to the wily brigands, and the captives released, form one of the most thrilling and romantic stories in missionary history, — a story which might well have resulted in a triple tragedy. For three months, if I remember rightly, they were in captivity, and it so happened that we reached Salonica very soon after the release of the prisoners. Miss Stone had already departed for

MRS. TSILKA AND HER BABY ELENCHE

Who was born in the wilds of Bulgaria when her
mother was imprisoned by brigands.

America, but we had the pleasure of seeing Mrs. Tsilka, a charming Albanian lady, and the beautiful baby which was born under such harrowing circumstances, in a robber's hut, the exact location of which they will never know, since the little party was transported by night, and with the utmost secrecy, from one trysting-place of the bandits to another.

A few months after our return to America Mrs. Tsilka and

little Ellenche were our guests in Auburndale, where they excited great interest among all our neighbors. A famous English clergyman, who was visiting us at the time, humorously declared that for the first time in his life he was quite thrown in the shade by a mere baby.

Another interesting visit on this journey was to Samokov among the mountains of Bulgaria, a station of the American Board, long an educational centre for all that region. The religious influence brought to bear upon the students greatly impressed me, for a genuine revival was in progress, and scores of young men and maidens were professing their devotion to the Saviour. The mighty influence which faithful teachers can exert for good upon their scholars, when they are themselves men and women of deep religious conviction was never more forcibly illustrated, for scarcely a boy or girl escaped its uplifting influence, and I was glad to have a small part in the joyous meetings.

Another interesting city which we visited was Monastir, then in Macedonia and under Turkish rule. It has since changed hands three or four times, for it fell to the Serbians after the first Balkan war, was taken by the Bulgarians in 1915, and again came under Serbian rule, when, later in the World War, the Allies from their base at Salonica captured the much beleaguered city.

It was a centre of military operations in 1902, and we saw hundreds of Turkish cavalry manœuvering on the plains that surround the city. Albanian brigands were no strangers to the harassed town, and often swept down upon it from the mountains, but, during all these thrice troublous times, American missionaries stuck to their post. We were glad to see something of their noble work; their church, their schools, their four Christian Endeavor societies, and their philanthropic efforts for the many nationalities, Turks, Greeks, Serbians, Bulgarians, and Albanians of this cosmopolitan city.

One of the missionaries whom we then saw, Miss Mary

Matthews, was not daunted even by the horrors of the world at war, but through those dreadful days of siege and counter siege, when bombs dropped into the mission compound, and even upon the mission houses, maintained her spirit of calmness and good humour, rejoicing that they had a " nice little dining-room in the basement," where there was small danger of the Bulgarian bombs, as they would have to crash through two stories before reaching her school-girls and herself.

In all these cities which we visited, it is needless to say that meetings were held, and we realized the confusion of tongues wrought at the Tower of Babel, which obliged me in the course of a few months to rely upon the services of nearly twenty interpreters in as many different languages in Europe alone.

Returning from these journeys in southeastern Europe, we found our three children, who had come with us from America, happily established in Venice, where after a short visit, I left them with their mother while I went to attend some important meetings in Switzerland, Germany, and Great Britain.

It would be wearisome to describe all these " journeyings oft," but one of them, which took me to Iceland in the summer of 1902, was somewhat out of the ordinary. My oldest son, who, the year before, had graduated from Dartmouth College, being as anxious to join the family as we were to have him, willingly accepted my proposition, that if he would work his way over on a cattle steamer I would pay his way back in the first cabin.

It was then a popular thing for college boys, theological students, and even young ministers to ship as cattle-men on the trans-Atlantic liners; receiving little more than their passage back and forth for ten days of hard and disagreeable work. It was considered quite a lark, and hundreds of American college boys who otherwise could not have afforded the expense, got more than a glimpse of Europe by thus enduring hardships for a few days. I considered it a well-worth-while experience, though some of my European friends have told me that in their country it would be considered below the dignity of a young man of good family to engage in such menial employment. I am glad that it never seemed to strike Americans in that way.

Meeting my son, Eugene, in the north of England we spent a few days in Cumberland, the loveliest of all the Lake regions, and soon sailed from Leith, the port of Edinburgh, on the steamer " Laura," bound from Copenhagen to Reikjavik. It was a rough passage and the little steamer of only a thousand tons burden was heaved about like a cork on the great swells of those northern seas. A dense fog covered the sea much of the time, and our captain, in trying to find the port in the Faroe Islands at which he wished to call, poked the nose of the " Laura " into more than one bay, which proved to be a wrong lead. At length, without mishap, however, he found the right harbor, and we lay for a day in the storm-begirt port of Thorshavn. An ancient and fishy smell pervaded the whole atmosphere. It was a quaint, primeval little town which reminded me of what our own Marblehead must have been in the early days before fashion invaded its streets.

Off again on the bounding billows (bounding is an adjective that peculiarly applies to these uneasy northern seas), we came, after three or four days more, to the harbor of Iceland's capital and only considerable city, Reikjavik.

Just before midnight we dropped anchor, and though the sun had set, it was still almost as light as noonday. Proof of advanced modernity was not wanting, for, scarcely had the anchor-chain run out, before a reporter scrambled aboard, and, standing at attention before me, in his best English, plumped out the question: " Sir, how do you like Iceland? " I felt at home at once in the face of this indication of American-like enterprise.

Reikjavik has about 6,000 inhabitants, and, compared with any other place on the island, is a metropolitan city indeed,

STREET IN THORSHAVEN, FAROE ISLANDS

for the farmhouses are some ten miles apart on the average and only a few other places could even be dignified by the term hamlet.

But the people are most interesting, strongly individualistic, democratic in their manners, acknowledging only the slightest tie that binds them to the mother country, Denmark. They are proud, as they have a right to be, of their long history, their bold navigators and discoverers, their literature and their language, which has preserved to the world a very early type of Norse letters.

Naturally, as this is the only considerable place in the island, there was little opportunity for an extensive Christian Endeavor campaign, but I had an interesting meeting and a large and attentive audience, in which were many members of the Althing, or legislature, then sitting in Reikjavik. A most excellent interpreter, Miss Johansdotter, supplied all my deficiencies in the Icelandic. She is a charming lady, well educated, and had travelled extensively in Europe and America, where she was known as prominent in the circles of temperance women.

I also had a very pleasant call on the Bishop of Iceland, and had a booklet on Christian Endeavor translated into the Icelandic tongue which had a considerable circulation.

Then as the " Laura " was to remain a week in port before returning to Denmark, my son and I determined to try our luck in one of the famous trout streams of Iceland to which anglers resort from far and wide. On our way to the Sog, which lies some forty miles from Reikjavik, we spent a night in Thingvalla, by far the most interesting spot in Iceland. Here on the green turf, under the open sky, for hundreds of years, the Althing, or legislature of Iceland, met, year after year. Here nearly a thousand years ago Christianity was first proclaimed, here criminals were tried, and when found guilty, were promptly thrown over a cliff into a deep ravine which is still shown.

As many as five thousand people attended the sessions of the Althing, in the old days, either as legislators or spectators, and it was probably the most democratic assembly of law-givers that ever convened, since the voice of the people, so many of whom were on the spot, could easily make itself heard.

The only carriage road in Iceland runs from Reikjavik to Thingvalla, and a small tourist hotel, almost the only one in Iceland, makes the visitor comfortable. Twenty miles from this historic spot lies the short but swift river Sog, and thither we had to travel on the backs of hard-bitted little Iceland ponies. Across seemingly endless wastes of volcanic cinder we made our way, around the base of extinct volcanoes which in past ages have devastated the land, seeing only one or two farmhouses, in sheltered spots, during all the journey.

At last we came to the farmhouse which was our destination on the banks of the Sog. The house was a very modest structure, banked up with sods half way to the eaves, a reminder of the terribly long and stormy winters. Around the house were a few acres of grass land which a husky girl was mowing. The spare room which was assigned to us was clean and comfortable, but the rest of the house seemed dark and dismal. A very small kerosene stove, and a smoky fireplace in which some small twigs were smoldering, seemed to afford the only opportunity for cooking and heating.

Though Iceland used to be well wooded, it is said that only one tree now exists and that in the north of the island. Some slender birches, little larger than a lead pencil, creep along the ground, but never dare to lift their heads to the cold blasts. In some parts of the island there is abundant peat, and some coal is brought from Scotland. It is a mystery to me why 80,000 people should choose to live on this barren, wind-swept outpost of the north seas, when the fertile prairies of the United States and Canada are open to them, as settlers. However the ties of home and kindred are compelling everywhere, and, be it ever so dreary, there is no place like home. Some ten thousand or more Icelanders however, have already settled in the Canadian northwest.

The trout-fishing in the Sog was superb. Indeed the great

DR. CLARK AND HIS SON FISHING FOR TROUT IN ICELAND
Veiled to protect them from mosquitoes.

iridescent beauties were caught rather too easily for the highest style of sport. We very soon had all we could eat, and were enabled to stock up the larder of our hosts. These fish are the staple food of the farmers in summer and winter, and even the ponies, when hay gets scarce, as it often does, do not object to frozen trout as an article of diet.

A BIT OF ICELAND SCENERY

As there is no night in that latitude in July the trout would bite as well at midnight as at noon, and an English sportsman who shared the farmhouse with us caught his last trout for the day shortly before the clock struck twelve, midnight.

The only serious drawback to the enjoyment of fishing was the persistent attention of the innumerable midges and mosquitoes which compelled us to wear gloves and mosquito-netting veils over our faces. Before many hours were gone we had had our fill of this too-easy fishing, and the next day we made our way back to Reikjavik, forty miles on our back-breaking ponies, and in due time found ourselves again on the staunch little "Laura," bound for Scotland. We later made our way to Switzerland where we had left the rest of the family.

Soon after this we sailed for America, having completed a long, zigzag journey, or indeed several of them, which had taken us through nearly a score of countries, from Salonica to Reikjavik, and from Dublin to Helsingfors, and had enabled me, I hope, to do something for the Christian Endeavor cause during six months in England, Ireland, Scotland, Spain, Portugal, and Italy, in France, Germany, Austria-Hungary, Bulgaria, Turkey, Greece, Norway, Sweden, Denmark, Finland, Switzerland, and Iceland.

NEW ZEALAND, THE TOURISTS' PARADISE

DEFINITE GOALS FOR ENDEAVORERS — OFF FOR NEW ZEALAND
— GEYSER WONDERS — A BOILING LAKE — A TERRIBLE
EXPLOSION — ENDEAVOR MEETINGS IN LEADING CITIES.

HE latter part of 1902 and most of 1903 were spent in America. These were busy months with numberless conventions to attend in the United States and Canada, but their story belongs rather to the history of the Christian Endeavor movement than to my personal reminiscences, if I would keep this volume within bounds. One or two events, however, seem to find appropriate place in these pages.

Among the conventions which I attended in the fall of 1902 was the Ohio State convention in Zanesville. At this convention it occurred to me that the time had come for a definite and specific effort for increase in the Christian Endeavor movement. It had now passed its twenty-first year. " Coming-of-age " conventions were being celebrated all over the country, and there was some danger that the young people might rest content with past achievments. At this convention, therefore, I proposed that the Ohio Endeavorers should strive to add ten per cent to the number of their societies. The idea was taken up with enthusiasm, and at the next International Convention I proposed that we make it nation-wide. As a result of this effort nearly seven thousand new societies were added to the ranks of Christian Endeavor.

The value of the idea lay in its definiteness in suggesting a specific goal which should appeal to ardent young people. Since then I have carried out this idea to a still larger extent, feeling that it was my duty at each national convention to suggest some practical measures appropriate to the special needs of the movement and the times. These ideas have been taken up with wonderful enthusiasm by the young men and women, and have been widely endorsed by pastors and denominational authorities with great cordiality.

A "Betterment Campaign" in 1905 followed the effort for a gain of ten per cent in 1903. In later years an "Increase Campaign" resulted in a gain of ten thousand new societies in two years. An "Efficiency Campaign" followed this, from which came a greatly increased development along many lines of Christian Endeavor work, while the "Millions Campaign," which called for a million new members, a million converts to the churches, a million new dollars for missions, etc., was successful in most important particulars, — the million new members being more than reached. A "Standards Campaign" followed this, which proved to be an efficient method of bringing a multitude of unions and societies up to a high standard of service and efficiency. The "Loyalty Campaign," putting great stress upon devotion to church and denominational interests, in 1919 and 1920 was equally fruitful. The "Foursquare Campaign" of 1921–1922, re-stating and re-enforcing the many-sided mission of Christian Endeavor for people of all ages, and for all needs of the young, which, as I write, is in full swing, promises to do more for the cause than any of its predecessors.

In 1903 the International Christian Endeavor convention was held in Denver, Col., and a providential escape from what might have been a very serious calamity is worthy of notice. The great tent in which the chief meetings were held was pitched on an open square where there was little depth of earth for the tent-pins. It was a hot July day, and the sides of the enormous canvas auditorium, which seated ten thousand people, were lifted to admit the air.

Though the ushers had been carefully instructed, and were prompt in lowering the sides when the wind threatened, a sudden small hurricane surprised them and, getting under the canvas, lifted it bodily from the earth, since the tent-pins in the shallow ground were unable to hold it. Then it settled down on the heads of the 8,000 auditors, who were listening to the address of a British delegate. It seemed at first as though a terrible loss of life was inevitable, but the canvas settled down so slowly that the people under it were able to dodge the many great tent poles, and the heavy electric arc lamps, which happily had not yet been lighted, and, cutting their way through the enveloping canvas, all soon found themselves on the outside, where they gathered together and sang with a sense of gratitude which is not always felt,

" Praise God from whom all blessings flow."

No one was seriously hurt, and though the great tent was destroyed past repair, temporary headquarters were found for the convention, which was hardly interrupted by the accident.

On Christmas day of 1903, with my daughter Maude Williston Clark, I started on my second journey to the Antipodes. It was hard to leave the family Christmas festivities for this long journey, but time and tide are imperative, and a week later we sailed from San Francisco on the good steamer " Sierra," a great improvement in size and comfort over the " Mariposa," on which, with my wife and son Eugene, I had made the same journey eleven years before.

Beautiful, hospitable Honolulu detained us for one day, and the charming tropical harbor of Pago Pago gave us a glimpse of this important coaling station that Uncle Sam has established in the mid-Pacific, and also of some of our Samoan fellow-citizens. Pago Pago furnishes a perfect specimen of a tropical island. The intensely green and exceedingly lush vegetation clothes the hillsides to the very top. Brilliant birds add a touch of vivid color to the landscape, and the blue sky and intense sunlight bring out the lights and shadows with unusual sharpness, while the brown inhabitants in their wattle huts add a touch of human interest to the scene.

A few hours, however, were all that were allowed to this Paradise of the mid-seas, and a few days later we steamed into the harbor of Auckland, and began a long and interesting series of Endeavor meetings which took us to all the large towns of New Zealand; Auckland, Wellington, Christchurch, Dunedin, and Invercargill, as well as to a good many smaller places. The New Zealanders surely lived up to their well-established reputation for hospitality. The meetings which I cannot attempt to describe in detail, were all that could be desired in numbers and enthusiasm.

I must not forget to tell of an excursion that our friends provided for us through the Geyser regions of the North Island. Most of it was over excellent roads, in old-fashioned coaches drawn by four horses, and our journey took us from one natural wonder to another in quick succession. Even the glories of our own Yellowstone Park pale before these greater wonders.

Here are geysers almost innumerable. Some playing like artificial fountains every twenty minutes or half hour, and keeping to their appointed minute as though regulated by a stop watch. Others send up huge columns of water, mud, and stones like the great geyser of Waimangu, which, if I remember rightly, explodes every thirty-six hours. This is more like a volcano than an ordinary geyser, for huge stones and oceans of mud are flung up hundreds of feet into the air, while the steam, which rises five miles towards the zenith, after one of the great upheavals, can be seen for scores of miles around.

A few years before our visit the whole top of the mountain had blown off, covering the country for miles about with *débris* many feet in depth. The country is very scantily inhabited, and so but few lives were lost, but some houses were buried ninety feet deep by the volcanic ash.

Since our visit another tremendous explosion has occurred, burying the little hotel, or "accommodation house," where we stayed, near the edge of the geyser, and spreading desolation still further around this vent hole of Hades.

Unfortunately we arrived at the edge of the crater a few minutes too late for the great diurnal explosion, but we saw many eruptions which in any other geyser would be considered by no means insignificant.

All of the phenomena in this region, however, are not of this terrifying order, for there were many little lakes, or ponds, most beautifully colored, some of an emerald green, some red as blood, and some that look like a great vat of whitewash. Purling streams go rippling over stones like a Vermont brook, but beware that you do not dabble in this brook, for the water is boiling hot. Little geysers abound that present many idiosyncracies in the time of their "shots," in the color of their water, and the shape of their fountains.

One of the most interesting experiences was a boat-ride over the hot lake, Rotomahana. On the side where we embarked the water was comparatively cool, but as the Maori oarsman carried us towards the farther shore the water grew hotter and hotter until it boiled around us, and thumped on the bottom of our boat. We found ourselves rowing through a veritable witches' caldron toward an abrupt hill on the farther shore from which wicked-looking spurts of steam issued from a hundred vents. This is the lake where once were the remarkably beautiful "crystal terraces," of pink and white, one of the wonders of the world, which were destroyed in the great eruption of Waimangu.

One especially pleasant memory of this thermal region will long remain with me. We had been riding all day since

LYELL BRIDGE, UPPER BULLER RIVER, NEW ZEALAND

early dawn, over rough roads. Night overtook us before we
reached the hotel which was to be our abiding place in the
Weiraki Valley. We were cold and stiff from the long journey in a cramped position. The proprietor of the hotel, wisely
suspecting my weariness, at once took his lantern, and guiding
me through his flower garden, led me to the edge of a natural
swimming-pool where the water was just over blood heat.
Six feet away was another pool that felt as cold as ice, and by

MANGAPAPA FALLS, NEW ZEALAND

jumping from one pool to the other I had all the benefit of
the hot and cold douche, on which the hydrotherapist sets so
much store. It was certainly a most delightful preparation for
the bountiful supper and glorious night's sleep that awaited me.

If New Zealand were only more accessible to the great
centres of population it would become, even more than Switzerland, the playground of the world, for here we find not
only such natural wonders as I have described, but unsurpassed
fishing to tempt the angler, and, in the South Island, mighty

Alps which rival any in Europe, and deep, placid fjords as fine as anything that Norway can boast.

The people, too, are most interesting, because of their bold adventure in a moderate socialism, and as political pioneers along many lines. They have good reason to be satisfied with their lovely and fertile islands, whose abundant rains never fail, and whose fertile soil could easily support ten times the million people who now call New Zealand their home.

The Maoris, or native New Zealanders, are among the most interesting of all aboriginal tribes. Though closely related to the Hawaiians and Samoans, they are in some ways superior to their cousins in the other islands. Their totem posts, or the images that answer the same purpose, their assembly houses, and their great canoes, show much artistic as well as mechanical skill. Some Maoris are well educated and a number of them have been elected as representatives to the New Zealand parliament.

Their curious method of salutation affords a stranger much amusement, for the Maoris of to-day, despite their advance in civilization, stick to the custom of their ancestors, and rub noses, instead of bowing or shaking hands when they meet a friend. On a little steamer on one of the lakes I was much amused to see a greeting between two of our feminine fellow passengers, one of whom had a proboscis of ordinary size, while in the other that facial ornament was entirely wanting, and only a depression showed where the nose should have been. However the ceremony was not omitted, and the two ladies did their utmost to fulfil the requirements of politeness.

I am tempted to dwell much longer on the beauties, glories, and thousand charms of New Zealand, but with these very inadequate descriptions must hasten on to her greater neighbor, Australia.

AUSTRALIA AND SOUTH AFRICA REVISITED

THE VASTNESS OF AUSTRALIA — A FRUIT-GROWERS' PARADISE
— GRAPES OF ESHCOL — THE "GOLDEN MILE" OF WEST
AUSTRALIA — ACROSS THE "ROARING FORTIES" — BOERS
AND BRITISH TOGETHER IN CHRISTIAN ENDEAVOR — A
REMARKABLE CAPTAIN.

 OST people in northern lands think of New
Zealand and Australia as close neighbors,
with only a strait between which a night's
run would cover. But when one reaches New
Zealand he finds that the journey from there
to Australia, in time at least, is almost as long
as from America to Europe by the fastest steamers, for by the
ordinary passenger ship it is a five days journey from Wellington or Auckland to Sydney or Melbourne, and a stormy,
uncomfortable voyage it often is.

We did not altogether escape the lashings of Neptune, but
reached Sydney in good condition, ready for a very strenuous
but interesting series of meetings in the states of Queensland,
New South Wales, Victoria, Tasmania, South Australia, and
West Australia, covering all the large cities like Brisbane,
Sydney, Melbourne, Ballarat, Bendigo, Hobart, Launceston,
Adelaide, Albany, Perth, Coolgardie, and some smaller places.

Nowhere does one find a more generous and kindly people
than in this vast island continent. Nowhere are there larger
Christian Endeavor audiences in proportion to the population.
Nowhere is there more unbounded hospitality, but I have

described many of these characteristics in a former chapter, and need not repeat the experiences of the second journey at any length.

The meetings were even larger than those I attended on my first visit, since the Endeavor movement during these intervening years had expanded in Australia, as well as in the rest of the world. The largest halls in the different cities were requisitioned, and very large audiences assembled.

Compared with our own country the population of Australia grows but slowly, but it has the advantage (if it is an advantage), of being more homogeneous and almost entirely of British descent.

Its comparatively slow growth is accounted for by several causes. The vast interior deserts of Australia which occupy so large a section of its surface will probably never be inhabited. A wide fringe of fertile soil along the shores is the only part of the great island that can support a numerous population, and though Australia is larger than the United States, excluding Alaska and our outlying territories, but a fraction of it can probably ever be the abode of man.

Nevertheless there are still vast tracts, especially in Queensland and West Australia, that invite the hardy settler; tracts which doubtless would have been taken up long ago, were Australia nearer the centres of European population, and had not the labor leaders who so largely control the destinies of Australia been so much opposed to what might be called promiscuous immigration. The laws against the coming of Orientals have been stricter than our own, and even the Kanakas or South Sea Islanders, who alone can work in the sugar-cane fields of tropical Australia, have been deported, though some of them had made their homes there for many years.

Australia, like America, too, has suffered from the congestion of its population in the great cities Sydney and Melbourne, which, combined, contain more than a quarter part of the people of this vast territory.

The Australian people themselves complain that far too much attention is given to sport; horse races and football and cricket-matches seeming to occupy the constant attention of a large section of the population. The balmy climate, contributing to the year-round out-door possibilities of most parts of Australia, makes such dissipation unusually tempting.

Nevertheless in spite of certain drawbacks I am inclined to think that these great islands of the South Pacific, New Zea-

IN THE FERN FORESTS OF QUEENSLAND, AUSTRALIA

land, and Australia, are, all things considered, among the happiest and most desirable parts of this world of ours. There is little poverty, except occasionally in one or two of the largest cities, though on my first visit, owing to an exceptional drought, soup-kitchens and bread-lines were established in Melbourne, and long queues of down-and-outers were waiting for their daily crust and coffee at the doors of several of the churches. This is not the common lot, however, of Australasians, and it seemed to me that New Zealanders especially, more than any other people, had obtained the answer to Agur's prayer, " Give me neither poverty nor riches," for there are few wealthy, and all are well-to-do.

Australia, like New Zealand, has been called the " Political Experiment-Station of the World," and well deserves the name. Untrammeled by the traditions of the ancients, by hereditary rights, or vested interests, these great dominions have been able to work out some problems whose solution America has not been the last to accept. These very experiments, however, have created new problems which, if we may believe the Australians themselves, are still far from a completely happy solution.

Our journey embraced many delightful episodes which space will not allow me to record. The reunion with old friends, the making of many new ones, the enthusiastic and undeserved welcome from the great audiences, have all left most pleasant memories. How I would like to dwell upon the visits with such friends as Mr. John Spencer, Mr. Bush, Mr. Harry, and many others who have been so largely responsible for the progress of Christian Endeavor in Australia, if only my space would allow!

The civic welcomes to my daughter and myself were unusual experiences in some of the smaller places. On one occasion the mayor and councilmen welcomed us as others had done, at the railway station, and then with a somewhat elaborate lunch. Not understanding, probably, the object of our journey, various viands, including whiskey, gin, wine, and beer, were provided, drinks which are not often seen at Christian Endeavor banquets. However, some soft drinks enabled us to partake of their hospitality, and at the same time to hold fast to our principles.

In another considerable town we were the guests of the Lord Mayor and the Lady Mayoress. We noticed that the table was bountifully heaped at every meal with all sorts of good things, and that they were pressed upon us far beyond the limits of our capacities. At the last meal our good hostess remarked, somewhat untactfully, " I was afraid I could not get enough for you to eat, for I have always heard that Americans were such gormandizers."

On this visit we saw two sections of Australia which we had not before visited, the beautiful fertile state of Tasmania or Van Dieman's Land, as it was called in our boyhood's geography, and the new state of West Australia. Tasmania is a wonderfully attractive island, well watered and fertile in every part, the very paradise of the fruit-grower, for apples ripen in February and March, when the markets of the northern hemisphere are bare, and when this delicious fruit (and no finer apples are grown anywhere) brings its highest price.

Tasmania, like New South Wales, was in the early days a convict colony, but few traces of those cruel old days are left in either state, and even Botany Bay, so unfragrant in the early days of Australia, has now been redeemed from its old associations. Here is established a colony and mission station of native Australians who are well cared for by the government. They are comfortably housed, and are instructed in agriculture and other simple arts of which they are capable.

One of the most interesting Christian Endeavor meetings which I attended during all these weeks was held in an aboriginal settlement, at a place called La Perouse, New South Wales, on the shore of Botany Bay. Here Black Charlie gave the address of welcome, while Black John presided over the meeting, and the little jet-black Juniors sang their Endeavor hymns. Afterwards John and Charlie entertained us with a rare exhibition of boomerang throwing, demonstrating how these curious missiles fly off at a tangent, circle around through the air, and obediently come back to fall at the feet of the thrower. These Australian natives, low as they are rated in the scale of civilization, have contributed at least one curious out-door sport, or art, shall we call it, and a very useful word, especially to our political vocabulary. A boomerang!

Tasmania is not the only extraordinary fruit-producing section of Australia. Queensland raises the finest pineapples that I have ever tasted, not excepting the delicious product of Hawaii. Its other tropical fruits are equally famous, while South Australia rivals Tasmania in its production of apples and grapes. Apple orchards of thousands of acres are grown in this favored state, and any one who finds himself in Adelaide in grape season may well thank his lucky stars, for veritable grapes of Eschol, bunches heavy enough to be " borne of two," of many different flavors, tempt the appetite. In South Australia the " grape cure " can be no hardship.

West Australia, the newest of all the Australasian states, offers the largest opportunities for new settlers, and in many respects is quite as interesting as its older sisters. Several kinds of trees, and many other products which are not grown elsewhere, are found in this little-known state. Among the many canes which have been presented to me in different parts of the world, I prize two beautifully mounted " raspberry-jam-wood " sticks, which were given to me in West Australia. The wood is of the finest grain, and takes a remarkable polish. It is by no means as sweet and sticky as its name would indicate, but, when recently cut is said to have a distinct odor of the delicious jam so dear to boyish palates.

Our most interesting journey in West Australia was to the famous gold mines of Kalgoorlie and Coolgardie. Far off in the desert, hundreds of miles from any adequate water supply, these wonderfully rich gold mines were discovered. The " Golden Mile " is said to be the richest spot on earth.

For years it was impossible to work the mines to advantage, for the scanty rains furnished little fresh water for man or beast, and none at all for the necessary hydraulic mining. Some flakes and nuggets could be retrieved from the unwilling earth, but it was not until an enormous pipe-line, carrying an abundant water supply from near the coast, was built through hundreds of miles of inhospitable desert that gold could be obtained, as at present, in vast quantities. All day and all night on a railway train we travelled beside this great pipe-line, writhing its way, like some huge boa constrictor, over hill and dale and prairie, and delivering its delicious life-giving fluid to the thirsty cities, hundreds of miles from the fountain head. I have seldom been so impressed by the pains that men will take and the labors they will undergo in their search for gold.

Our reception in the gold cities was most kindly, and the meetings were large and impressive under the auspices of my friend, Rev. Mr. Miles, afterwards the president of the West Australian Christian Endeavor union, and later still an honored chaplain of the gallant Australian forces in the great World War. One little incident of our journey to the gold-fields afforded us much amusement. Stopping at Narrogen, a small town on the Great Western Railway, a mass meeting was held by the Endeavorers in the evening, where I repeated what I had recently heard said in Adelaide, that the kangaroo was a typical Christian Endeavor animal, because it was going forward in Australia " by leaps and bounds." My friends there, at a typical tea meeting, where it was said that two thousand sat down at the tables, had given me a stuffed wallaby, a small species of kangaroo, as a specimen of " the Christian Endeavor animal."

The next morning after this meeting in West Australia, at which I had spoken, as I was preparing to go to the early prayer meeting, I was amazed to see an " Old Man Kangaroo," five feet tall, hopping along sedately behind a family who were on their way to church. He followed them in and entered one of the back seats, and stayed patiently through the service.

He proved to be a pet kangaroo, but the family remarked that he must have heard what I had said on the previous evening, and wanted to live up to his reputation, for he had never followed them to church before.

It was at this meeting that I heard a good brother pray: " God bless the Y.P.S.C.E. of the G.W.R.U. of W.A.," which, being interpreted, meant "the Young Peoples' Society of Christian Endeavor in the Great Western Railway Union of West Australia."

A few days after this we sailed from the thriving port of Perth for the long journey across the "Roaring Forties" to South Africa. But long sea journeys are the order of the day in these latitudes. Even the great Australian Bight, which looks on the map like a very modest piece of water, involves a journey of several days, and nearly 2,000 miles in going from the port of Adelaide to Perth on the West Australian coast.

I was told as we were leaving Perth that that strange boastful pretender, Alexander Dowie, "Elijah II," had just sailed from the same port for Europe, but that he was so displeased with the coolness of his reception and his lack of success in Australia that he showed his displeasure by sitting on the seaward side of the vessel, and never turning his eyes toward the land which, a few years before, he had left to practise his hypnotic arts on the great multitude of people he was able to gather at Zion City in America.

His life-story is a most singular one, and shows to what lengths fanaticism can go. A short time before this, his disastrous campaign in New York had exposed him to the ridicule of Americans, and hoping to recoup himself, he had returned to Australia, where he had formerly lived as a humble but useful shoe salesman. From the beginning the Australians refused to be beguiled by his blandishments and took no stock in his religious camouflage. Public halls were everywhere refused to him, and when he could manage to hire a private hall, students would often make it decidedly uncomfortable for the audience, with snuff and asafœtida. Yet all the time he was sending back to America cables about the millions of dollars that he had secured in Australia, and the thousands of converts who would follow him to Zion City.

Our journey to Natal, some 5,000 miles from Perth, was

uneventful, but varied by the many deck sports and entertainments, which, on these long voyages the passengers always
provide for themselves, in self-defense against the tedium of
travel. Personally I have always had another method of
making a long journey short, for articles for *The Christian
Endeavor World*, and for many other journals have always
occupied many hours every day, and more books than I perhaps

THE PRINCIPAL STREET IN DURBAN

Note the Zulu jinrikisha men in uniform, with cows' horns bound to their
foreheads.

ought to confess to have been the result of such steamship
hours when there was nothing else to do but read and write.

Unfortunately the " Marathon " was a day or two late in
making the port of Durban and my friends of Natal, expecting to meet me on a certain day when the boat was due,
came together in large numbers, but found no guest to
welcome at the welcome meeting. However they welcomed
each other and enjoyed a happy gathering, though most of

those who came from a distance had to return to their homes before the steamer arrived. Nevertheless a sort of addendum to the welcome meeting was held during our short stay in Durban, and I was able to renew some prized friendships made on my previous visit.

While dining at the house of a missionary I was called out into another room by a mysterious message, and there found a young man whom I had known slightly as one of our fellow-voyagers, who abruptly and uncompromisingly shot at me the question, " Dr. Clark, may I court your daughter? " I was rather taken aback, for I knew him but slightly, and I knew that my daughter had scarcely spoken to him. But he went on to tell me of his fortune of two thousand pounds a year, of his well-known family connections in England, etc.

Not wishing to decide so momentous a question, and knowing very well what the answer on my daughter's part would be, I paraphrased Priscilla's speech to John Alden, and said, " Why not speak for yourself, John? " A short interview with my daughter followed, and as a result our young friend decided to take another steamer to London, and we saw him no more.

An inch or two on the ordinary map of South Africa means several days of steaming from Durban to Capetown, though both seemed to be near the tip end of the Dark Continent.

Here in the capital of Cape Colony we had two or three days before the steamer sailed on which we had engaged passage to Southampton, and I attended a memorable meeting which my friends had arranged in the Adderley Street Dutch Reformed Church, where I had also spoken on my previous visit. The Boer War which was only a few months in the future when I was first in South Africa, was now a few months in the past, but the exceedingly bitter feeling generated by this unjust war had by no means had time to cool down. No meeting of any kind, I was told, had then been held between Boers and British. They were scarcely yet on speaking terms with each other, since Great Britain's generous policy toward the former Boer Republic had not been formulated.

But the Christian Endeavorers, both among the Boers and the British, had determined to bury the hatchet, and to have a union meeting. I was greatly surprised and gratified to find a large audience of both races, and to see the walls of the church decorated with the familiar mottoes in the two languages: "For Christ and the Church," "One is our Master, even Christ, and all we are brethren," "Welcome to South Africa," etc.

The president of the Boer union gave the address of welcome, while the president of the British union was the chairman of the meeting. After the addresses the chairman proposed that we should all rise and repeat Psalm 23, each one using the language with which he was most familiar. Then we repeated the Lord's Prayer, some in Dutch and some in English, and then, most remarkable of all, we stood and sang the old hymn of Christian fellowship,

> " Blest be the tie that binds
> Our hearts in Christian love."

It was sung most heartily in the two languages to the old tune of " Dennis," and was one of the most thrilling expressions that I had ever known of what Christian fellowship can do to bring together former enemies.

Many of the young men in the audience were Boers who had just been released from the prison camps in St. Helena and Ceylon. On each of these islands were thousands of prisoners and a score of Christian Endeavor societies had been established in each of the two great cantonments. Daily meetings had been held, full of spirit and power. Conventions had also been held among the Endeavorers, and a little paper called *De Strever* had been published.

The prisoners had amused themselves by making Christian

Endeavor pins of bone, and also sleeve links with the Christian Endeavor monogram upon them. Most wonderful of all, 250 prisoners from St. Helena alone had volunteered, before they left their prison, to go as missionaries to the heart of Africa. From these prison camps many of the young men in that audience had recently been released, while others who sat by their side had worn the British khaki, and had been their strenuous foes only a few months before. The memory of this moving scene often cheered me afterwards as I remembered in those dreadful days of the World War, that the impelling love of Christ might bring together even those who were fighting in the hostile camps into which the whole world was divided.

The voyage on the " Armadale Castle " from Capetown to Southampton was memorable only for its smoothness and lack of adventure. As Captain Robinson said to me one day, " One can usually drive a hansom cab from Capetown to the Isle of Wight, and you would not get wet if you kept the door shut, unless possibly in the Bay of Biscay," — such a delightful reputation for smooth water did this journey deserve.

This Captain Robinson was the most remarkable captain I have ever sailed with. For forty years he had been in the service of the Union Castle Line, most of the time as commander of one of its great ships. He was at this time the commodore of the fleet, always having the largest ship for his command, and never having had an accident even to the scraping of the paint on the ship's bow during all these years. He ascribed this, not to good fortune, but to the good providence of God, for he was the most religious of men.

Every morning he used to summon the passengers to prayers on the after-deck, calling out as he breezily swung along to his post: " Come along, come along to prayers! " He was followed usually by two or three hundred passengers, including diamond kings from Kimberley, barmaids from Johannesburg, and the mixed crowd which a South African steamer carries.

These devotions he usually conducted himself, and always held services on Sunday in the first and second cabins, and the steerage, besides having a Sunday school for the children, in his own spacious and beautifully fitted up room.

In this cabin I spent many hours with him, and I noticed that frequently when we heard the watchman in the crow's nest cry out, " Four bells and all's well," or " Eight bells and all's well," he would raise his hand and looking up to heaven would say reverently, " All's well, thank God! " ·

After sixteen days we sailed into the Solent, landing again in Southampton where we said good-bye to our good captain, heartily repeating with him after this happy voyage, " All's well, thank God! "

CHAPTER XXVII

YEARS 1904–1905

HOME AGAIN AND OFF AGAIN

HOME BY WAY OF FRANCE, ENGLAND, SCOTLAND, GERMANY —
MY FATHER'S GRAVE — A CALL ON PRESIDENT ROOSEVELT
— CROSSING THE SEAS ONCE MORE — A HISTORY OF
CHRISTIAN ENDEAVOR — OBER-AMMERGAU — NORWAY
AND KING HAAKON.

HRISTIAN ENDEAVOR had now become such a world-wide movement that there was little rest for any one who might be considered its exponent at whatever port he might land, and both at Southampton, where we arrived from South Africa, and London, my daughter and I found scores of friends to welcome us, and a large programme outlined for Great Britain, which took us to almost every part of the United Kingdom.

My time on shipboard had not been altogether wasted, and I found on reaching dry land that during the sixteen days on the " Armadale Castle," I had written sixteen articles of considerable length, seven for my own paper, *The Christian Endeavor World*, four for a syndicate of newspapers, two for *The Independent*, and three articles for other papers, whose destination my note book does not record.

I am sorry for the man who has nothing to keep him busy on a long voyage. It is apt to be most wearisome, and perhaps demoralizing if the bar, the smoking-room, and the card-tables take up most of his time. But with a fountain pen and a pad of paper and plenty of time left for exercise and deck games of all sorts, a voyage, however long, can scarcely be weari-some. Moreover, the articles thus written, and which number many hundreds all told, have in large part enabled me to pay the expenses of these many journeys, without drawing upon the benevolent funds of the Christian Endeavor society, or burdening the organizations which I have gone to address with a large expense account.

Immediately on landing, however, visions of leisure for literary work always disappear, and one has a feeling of being owned by the committees that at once take him in charge. It is not, however, a disagreeable slavery, for the friends are always kindness itself, though one sometimes longs for relief from being " entertained " by comparative strangers, and my wife and I must confess, that occasionally, on some journeys, we have " played hooky " from meetings and entertainers, and taken refuge for a short time in some obscure resort in Swit-zerland or Holland or Italy, where Endeavorers are few and far between.

Sometimes the hospitality of our friends, after a long and exhausting day of meetings, would keep us up until the small hours of the next morning, their generous kindness leading them to forget that strenuous duties awaited us on the next day. Lest these remarks may seem ungracious, let me hasten to add that this kindly hospitality has never found us ungrateful or unappreciative, but has often filled us with wonder that it should be lavished upon those who felt themselves so unworthy of it. Of course we never forgot that it was the cause which we represented that chiefly commended us to friends and ac-quaintances.

The first series of meetings that demanded my attention on this journey was the British National Endeavor Convention of 1904, held in London, one of the most important ever held in Great Britain. Its size will be understood when I note that it crowded with simultaneous meetings the City Temple, Exeter Hall, the Metropolitan Tabernacle (Spurgeon's great church), and Westminster Chapel, where Campbell Morgan was so long a pastor, and to which Dr. J. H. Jowett afterwards ministered. Albert Hall, seating 8,000 people, was used for an enormous praise meeting.

My duties in connection with the convention called for addresses in most of these places, as well as in Christ Church, Regent's Park Chapel, and Paddington Chapel. My diary records the fact that twenty-three delegates were present from Germany, and that an " International Brotherhood of Christian Endeavor " was organized. Alas! that the ties then formed, and cemented on future similar occasions, should have been so rudely torn asunder by the Great War.

It would be wearisome to record in more than a line or two the other places visited in Great Britain, like Sunderland, Edinburgh, Glasgow, Belfast, Cork, Dublin, Chester, Shef-field, Batley, Dartmouth, Exeter, Bristol, Liverpool, Swansea, and Southampton, in all of which places important meetings had been arranged and were well carried out.

While I was in Scotland, an invitation out of the ordinary came to me to address the General Assembly of the United Free Church which was meeting in Edinburgh. The grave and reverend fathers of this greatest branch of the Scotch Presbyterians received my short message very kindly, and the solemn decorum of the body in the historic Free Assembly Hall deeply impressed me with the staunch character and high intellectual standards of the leaders of this very important branch of the church universal.

A short journey to the continent of Europe followed these meetings in Great Britain, and I have records of important gatherings in Paris, Geneva, Lausanne, Karlsruhe, Stuttgart, Strassburg, and again in Liverpool, before sailing from the latter city for home on the last day of June, 1904. One brief holiday which I enjoyed with my daughter in the midst of these many meetings will not easily be forgotten. We sailed from Southampton on a channel steamer, and after stopping for a few hours in the Island of Guernsey, where the wharves were crowded with new potatoes, onions, and early " garden-truck," we landed at the French port of St. Malo for a visit to the wonderful rock fortress, castle, and church of San Michel, which stands up on the coast of France like a natural beacon for every passing ship.

It must be seen to be appreciated. No description unaccompanied by a photograph could do it justice. Rising sheer out of the water, at high tide almost surrounded by the lapping waves, it would of itself be a striking world landmark. But the little town also which climbs the steep sides of the rock, the quaint inhabitants who seem to have retained their old-fashioned customs as none others of their countrymen have, the striking castle, and historic church, all lend a unique pleasure to a visit to Mount San Michel. Even the closet bedrooms in the primitive hotel, where one's bed is shoved into an alcove barely wide enough to receive it, and the rival Mesdames Poulet, all of whom serve the only original " Poulet omelet," furnish memories that long abide.

Before the strenuous meetings on the continent began, which often, as in England, involved five or six addresses in a day, we also paid a little visit to Argentan, where one may see the descendants of his Norman ancestors in their old home, still retaining many of their primitive manners and costumes.

Returning to America in mid-July, we all spent a happy family summer in our little cottage at Pine Point, on the coast of Maine. The rest of the year 1904 need not be dwelt upon at length, though my journal records an almost continuous series of meetings in America, east and west and north and south, including addresses at the original Chautauqua Assembly, the National Congregational Council in Des Moines, and other important meetings besides Christian Endeavor conventions, as well as a delightful August fortnight with my eldest son and a little party of congenial friends, among our favorite trout-streams and lakes in northern Maine.

A mid-winter trip to Canada early in 1905 is worthy of mention, for then, for the first time, I saw my father's grave, at Three Rivers, in the peaceful little Protestant cemetery where for more than fifty years his body had lain. I was glad to find it marked with a comely stone containing his name and age, and the appropriate verse, " The memory of the just is blessed." Near to his was the grave of his older brother, Henry, and several members of this brother's family who had made their residence in Three Rivers for many years.

The spring of 1904 was saddened by the death of my adopted father, Rev. Edward W. Clark, and the next year by the passing of Mrs. Clark's mother, Mrs. Sarah F. Abbott. They both lived to the good old age of eighty-four, and were gathered to their fathers and mothers like shocks of corn, fully ripe for the great Reaper. In an earlier chapter I have spoken of my adopted father, and I need only add that his later years were passed in quiet and comfort at his home in Westboro, Mass., and that I was glad to do what I could to repay in his old age his early care and kindness to me. Soon after his death my adopted mother came to live with us in Auburndale, where she spent five happy years in " Sunny Corner," as she called the pleasant southwest room at " Hillcrest," which overlooked the tree-embowered Charles and the lovely Weston Hills. Here she lived until her peaceful translation in 1908.

Mrs. Abbott, who was the daughter and granddaughter of ministers, who married a minister, and trained three of her daughters to be ministers' wives, left a fragrant memory behind her in Andover, where she had lived during the many years of her widowhood. Many " theologues " and Academy boys whom she had nursed in illness, or cared for in times of financial distress, bore grateful testimony to her kindness of heart.

A visit to Washington about this time I remember with considerable interest because of a call on President Roosevelt, whom I tried to induce to come to the next International

Christian Endeavor convention, which was to be held at Balti-more. The pastor of the German Reformed Church, which the President attended, went with me, and we enjoyed a pleas-ant half hour's chat with the nation's strenuous chief. He was most unconventional, sitting on the corner of his desk, often slapping his knee by way of emphasis, and frequently punc-tuating his remarks with a " By George," or some other like expletive. " I set under him," he remarked, pointing to his pastor, and using the old settlers' expression of the days when the pulpits were high, and the square pews below compelled an almost literal interpretation of the phrase.

He took my plea under consideration, declaring that he would like to attend the convention, for he believed that the Christian Endeavor movement was one of the greatest moral forces in the country, but was finally obliged to decline the invitation on account of pressing duties in other places, which he explained in a long and courteous letter.

I recall another brief interview with President Roosevelt which I think must have occurred before this visit. I wanted his endorsement for a good citizenship constitution and pledge which I was proposing for the adoption of Christian En-deavorers generally. He received me, as was then his custom, in a large room opening out of the room where cabinet meetings were held. Here were probably twenty applicants for favors of various kinds anxiously waiting their turns. His plan evidently was to avoid prolonged interviews, and to talk so that all could hear, that there might be no private interpreta-tion of what he had or had not said. A distinguished senator was one of the waiting company, and, as he knew the door through which the President would emerge from another room, he stationed himself near by, to " nab " him as he entered. I did not hear the senator's request, but every one in the room could hear the President's reply, " Can't do it, Mr. Depew, can't possibly do it," and with a word or two more he passed on to the next visitor.

In the interview I have previously alluded to in the executive office of the White House, he spoke with the utmost freedom of national and international affairs, and the waiting reporters, as we came out, were, as usual, very anxious to learn his views. In his very frankness and exuberant outspokenness lay his safety from ill-natured interviewers, for few would take advantage of such a friendly conversation, in which there was no trace of " secret diplomacy."

The many and varied duties at which I have hinted were in part responsible, I suppose, for a collapse in health in the spring of 1905. Like the woman in the Gospels, I suffered much from many physicians, and was "nothing bettered, but rather grew worse." However, it was no fault of theirs, for my old enemy, nervous exhaustion, induced in this case, as it had been before, not only by overwork, but by an attack of influenza, laid me low, and for this the best physicians in the world can do little. Dr. Rest is about the only one who can help, but I did not give up without a prolonged struggle, during which I visited the excellent sanitarium at Clifton Springs, took a short sea trip to Norfolk, and tried other remedies. Most reluctantly I was obliged at last to cancel a long series of conventions in the west, and, greatly to my sorrow, was unable to go to the International Convention at Baltimore. This gathering, however, suffered little from my absence, and was one of the best of the long series. Here was started the plan for a central headquarters for the Christian Endeavor movement. These plans after more than a dozen years took shape in the substantial and dignified office building on the corner of Mt. Vernon and Joy Streets, Boston.

To it something over two hundred thousand dollars were contributed by more than a hundred thousand Endeavorers in all parts of the world. More than fifty countries in Europe, Asia, Africa, the Americas, and Australasia, have part in this unique building. I was told that it was started as a memorial to myself, a kindly thought, prompted, doubtless, by the illness which prevented me from going to Baltimore, but as I recovered, and was not in need of a post mortem memorial, I preferred that it should be called the World's Christian Endeavor Building.

My health improved somewhat in the summer, aided by abundant doses of Maine air and sunshine, taken in liberal quantities at our cottage at Grand Beach, in the pine woods, and on the trout ponds of the Moosehead Lake region.

However this prescription did not seem to bring back complete health and strength, and in October, with Mrs. Clark and my youngest son I sailed for Europe with four objects in view, namely, to complete if possible, my restoration to health; to write the history of the first twenty-five years of Christian Endeavor; to do what I could for the cause of the young people on the continent of Europe; and to help prepare for the world's convention, which was scheduled to be held in Geneva, Switzerland, in the summer of 1906.

In some good measure I was able to carry out these purposes. My health continued to improve, and after some weeks of travel in Italy, during which we again visited Genoa, Pisa, Florence and Bologna, Padua and Verona, spending also some days in Venice, we went *via* Switzerland to Munich, where we made headquarters for some three months, while writing the history to which I have alluded.

In this I was greatly assisted by Mrs. Clark and her busy typewriter which she always carries in her trunk, for she wrote from dictation the 630 large pages of this volume, besides assisting me with many suggestions which I was glad to incorporate in it. The book was profusely illustrated with nearly two hundred half-tone engravings, portraits, and etchings, and is the only complete history of the first quarter century of the movement.

We found Munich a comfortable and hospitable place of residence, and especially suited to our needs just at that time because, being a Roman Catholic city, the absence, for the most part, of Endeavor societies gave us the leisure for writing that we could not otherwise have had. The American Church under the leadership of Rev. Mr. McCracken, was a pleasant religious home for us and some scores of other Americans with whom we there became acquainted, though we had little time for social enjoyments.

The quarter-century history of Christian Endeavor being finished and despatched to the publishers, we indulged in a little holiday trip to Ober-Ammergau, which is only a few hours' ride from Munich. It was mid-winter, and the next decennial production of the Passion Play was some years in the future, yet in some respects the visit was more enjoyable on this account. There were naturally no crowds of gaping tourists. Indeed we were the only guests in the principal hotel of the village. For this reason we could better judge of the ordinary life of the little town and of the character of the actors who have made so deep an impression upon the religious world.

The judgment we formed of their sincerity and genuine religious purpose was altogether favorable. They live in the humblest style, working at their trades, with no halo around their heads, and evidently unspoiled by the fame they have achieved throughout the world. Moreover they are unambitious for the wealth their great play might bring them. It is truly remarkable that these peasant actors, when the excitement of the ten-year epoch is over, an epoch that brings thousands of visitors from all lands to their little village, can settle down so quietly to their daily tasks, with no consciousness apparently of the fact that for a time they were the observed of all observers, and that their fame had been trumpeted throughout the world.

The World War and its disastrous aftermath necessarily prevented the production of the Passion Play in 1920, but I am glad to know that it was revived in 1922, for I think its moral and religious influence is wholly good.

We called on several of the actors, among them Anton Lang,

who took the part of the Christ, and Peter Rendl, the St. John of the play, and also on Andreas Lang, who was the King David of another play given in the five-year interval. Of him we bought some wood carvings representing "The Good Shepherd with the Lost Sheep," and also one of "The Last Supper," in which the figures of the apostles are copied from the people who represented them in the play, though the pose is that of Da Vinci's famous "Last Supper." So perfect and accurate are these little figures that one can recognize the faces of the actors in each one.

The little church with its crowded cemetery is evidently the heart of the village, and I was convinced that the peasant actors not only preserved their simple piety, but performed their parts in the great tragedy from a sincerely religious motive. The weather was very cold and deliciously bracing, and the crisp snow lay on every hill, and in the valley through which the little Ammer winds its way, while the glorious hills and plains, and the dark pine trees, were even more impressive under their glistening mantle of snow than they could be in summer.

On returning from Ober-Ammergau I was again called to Scandinavia to attend meetings in Christiania, Gothenburg, and Stockholm.

My visit to Norway on this journey was of peculiar interest because I was permitted to see some fruit of the Christian Endeavor seed which I had been allowed to sow on a previous visit. Some years before I had spoken at the university, but somehow received the impression that my audience, though exceedingly polite and friendly, thought I was talking about some strange and rather *bizarre* American organization, of which little use could be made in Norway. But on this visit I found that a number of Endeavor societies had been formed, and that some very warm friends of the movement were advocating it throughout the length and breadth of Norway. Pre-eminent among them were two Lutheran pastors of Christiania, — Pastor Meyer and Pastor Klaeboe.

Pastor Klaeboe has since been especially energetic in the Christian Endeavor propaganda, sparing neither effort, nor time, nor money to tell of its value in training the youth of Norway for Christian service. He has travelled with me for hundreds of miles in the Scandinavian countries. He has been my guide, interpreter, and friend, to whom I owe a much larger tribute of thanks than I can condense in these paragraphs. He is president of the Norwegian Christian Endeavor Union, and at last accounts had no less than eighteen societies in his own great church in Christiania.

Rev. Horace Dutton, my neighbor in Auburndale, was for five years an unpaid pioneer Christian Endeavor worker in Scandinavia and near-by countries, and left a memory which I found twenty years later was held in fond remembrance in half a dozen countries.

On this visit I first became acquainted with Rev. Robert P. Anderson, then a missionary of the Disciples Church in Christiania. He was a cultured Scotchman who had lived in America. He has a real gift for authorship, and is of untiring industry. We soon persuaded him to come to Boston to be an associate editor of *The Christian Endeavor World*, a position he has honored ever since. He afterwards became editorial secretary of The United Society of Christian Endeavor and has contributed more to the literature of the society than any other man unless it be Dr. Wells.

While I was in Christiania I had the pleasure of an interview with King Haakon VII., the young sailor king of Norway, who in his person and name had revived the long line of the Haakons which began in the early Norse history of his kingdom. He is a grandson of old King Christian of Denmark, and married a granddaughter of Queen Victoria, so that there is plenty of royal blood in the family to maintain the dignity of the ancient Haakons. He impressed me as a wide-awake, alert, democratic young man, who puts on few kingly airs. On this occasion he wore not a single decoration.

Around the walls of the room in the palace where I was received were many pictures of ships, sailing vessels, if I remember rightly, and yachts, thus testifying to his right to be called " The Sailor Prince."

Another call that I remember with interest was on Bishop Bang, one of the most beloved and influential men who has ever held that high office. His nephew, Pastor Klaeboe, who had become the leader of the Christian Endeavor forces in Norway, called with me, which secured me a double welcome.

At the great service in the cathedral of Christiania, my friend, Stiftprovst Meyer, was my interpreter. I have rarely seen a church more crowded, and the scene in these northern cathedrals is often inspiring, because the people gather around the pulpit with seeming eagerness, many of them standing, while the audience stretches out into dim aisles beyond. The black-clad interpreter by my side in the high ruffed collar of the state church of Norway, also added another touch of picturesqueness.

After some large Christian Endeavor meetings in Berlin, Leipsic, and Augsburg, I returned to Munich, where my wife and son had remained while I journeyed to the north, and we soon started in the opposite direction for a southerly journey down the Dalmatian coast, which took us to Montenegro, Corfu, Greece, and Turkey. We went by way of Innsbruck, Botzen, and Riva, thence to Verona and Venice, across to Trieste, and down the beautiful island-sheltered coast of Dalmatia, which is well worth more detailed description in another chapter.

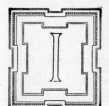 WOULD advise any of my friends who desire a picturesque and somewhat unusual trip to take the same journey down the coast of Dalmatia which we enjoyed as we travelled to Montenegro. The Austrian Lloyd steamers at that time made frequent trips along the whole Dalmatian coast, keeping almost entirely behind the barrier of islands which, on that side of the Adriatic, guard the shore, so that it is largely a land-locked voyage on waters as smooth as an inland river.

Pola was one of the first stops after leaving Trieste, and here the Austro-Hungarian navy had its chief port. During the years of the great war she sent out from here her submarines to prey upon the commerce of her enemies in the Adriatic and the Mediterranean.

But we were much more interested in the wonderful antiquities on the shore than in the gray and menacing iron-clads. Here is a vast colosseum, almost as large as its more famous brother in Rome, and in a far better state of preservation, at least so far as the outside of the tremendous arena is concerned. Here, too, are an exquisite Roman temple, and other antiquities of scarcely less interest.

Spalato, farther down the coast, contains the mighty palace

A Roman Temple of Pola

Built shortly before the Christian Era. Still in perfect preservation.

of the persecuting Emperor, Diocletian, who built his most magnificent residence, not in Rome, but in this, his birthplace, on the Adriatic. This, too, is well preserved, after all these centuries, and is large enough to contain within its walls a very considerable town. In fact most of the inhabitants of modern Spalato seem to live within the precincts of the old palace.

Still farther down the coast are the interesting towns of Zara and Ragusa. The latter is a town which has a memorable history as the capital of a little republic that maintained its independence for many centuries. Ragusa is now a somewhat popular summer resort, and boasts a fashionable and expensive hotel. At several other towns the steamer stops for a few hours, giving us a glimpse of ancient ruins and primitive modern inhabitants, until at last it winds by many a tortuous curve through the Gulf of Cattaro to the seaport of Cattaro, the last stop on the Dalmatian coast.

I would also advise my readers, if they ever take this journey, to go by one of the slow freight steamers which stop at every port. These steamers have sufficiently comfortable accommodations and afford one far more intimate glimpses of the country and the people than the more popular express line of boats.

The town of Cattaro was and probably is an ill-conditioned, dirty, run-down little place, inhabited by a mixture of many races who found here no " melting-pot," for Dalmatians and Albanians, Austrians and Hungarians, Croats, Slavonians, and Montenegrins, though they frequently touched elbows on the street, had no love one for another.

A score of horses whose gaunt ribs proclaimed the parsimony or poverty of their masters, were hitched to ramshackle victorias near the wharf when we arrived, while their drivers were all clamoring to take us up the Black Mountains to Cetinje, then the little capital of Montenegro.

We chose the most promising of them, but many times, as

we surmounted the steep mountain side, the harness gave way, and had to be mended with the rope and strings with which the driver had provided himself, evidently counting on such catastrophes.

But poor as was our vehicle and uncomfortable as was the journey in some respects, we were well repaid by the magnificent scenery which every turn of the road presented to our enraptured view. As one looks up the mountain from the streets of Cattaro, it seems impossible for horse or man to climb it. A multitude of narrow zigzags, looking like so many chalk marks on a black slate, show us from below the windings of the road.

I cannot speak for conditions at the present time, but the road had been well built with much labor and engineering skill, and was kept in excellent repair, at least as far as the Montenegrin border. There, however, it degenerated, for the little kingdom of the Black Mountain had precious few dollars to spend on road-making. The many zigzags added to the joy of the ride, for they afforded us every minute new glimpses of the panorama stretching out below; the windings of the silvery Gulf of Cattaro, the islands that stud the channel, and the further shores as well as the fortifications that defend the Gulf and harbor upon which we could almost seem to drop a stone from the heights that we were climbing.

At last the top of the first mountain was reached, the line between Austria and Montenegro was crossed, and we zigzagged down on the other side into a considerable valley where is situated the half-way town of Niegosh, where the then Czar of Montenegro was born and where he had a very modest little summer home. The houses of the people, for the most part, are exceedingly primitive, built of stone, often with no windows, and boasting little and rude furniture.

One such house that we visited, however, rejoiced in a Singer sewing-machine, of which the good mother seemed inordinately proud. Mr. Singer and his sewing-machine have been among the great civilizing factors of the world, for there is no remotest corner of Europe, or any other land, which I have visited, where the music of his humble but useful instrument is not heard.

The sterility of all this country is almost beyond belief. In every little crevice of the rocks to which soil can be carried, something green is planted. A tract of arable soil as big as a sheet forms quite a garden. Everywhere the rugged, broken chaos of rocks fills one with a sense of awe, and at the same time admiration for the plucky mountaineers who somehow manage to wring a living from inhospitable nature.

The men and women are fine specimens of humanity; the men especially are stalwart, tall and handsome, their good looks being set off by their picturesque embroidered vests and their little round hats. On the top of each was woven an H, the equivalent for N in their language, which showed their allegiance to their beloved Prince Nicholas, as he was called when we were there. He afterwards proclaimed himself Czar of the Montenegrins, and he died while an exile, under the protection of his son-in-law, King Emanuel of Italy. I regret that history does not seem to give him so high a place, as a man or a patriot, as I supposed he deserved, when I visited his little kingdom.

It grew dark before we had surmounted another range of hills and began to descend toward the plain, said to be the bed of an old lake, on which stands Cetinje, the capital. As we descended the dark mountain, made blacker still by a starless night, we could see the twinkling lights of Cetinje, and were glad enough to arrive at its one hotel, whose prices alone substantiated its claim to being " Grand " and " first-class."

Nearly opposite the hotel stands the by-no-means palatial palace of the Czar, and though I did not see him holding court, I was told that he often sat under a spreading oak in true patriarchal fashion and dispensed justice to his faithful subjects, who brought their disputes before him for adjudication.

There was little to detain us in Cetinje, for it is simply a large, straggling village, whose most spacious and ornate building was that of the Russian embassy.

Alas for the little kingdom of Montenegro! Overrun by its stronger neighbors, blotted off the face of the earth as an independent kingdom after its long struggle of a thousand years to maintain its independence against Turk and Christian alike, it is now unwillingly incorporated in the kingdom of the Serbs, Croats, and Slovenes.

On our further journey, while waiting for our steamer to sail from Cattaro for Corfu, a curious phenomenon occurred. As I was writing on the steamer's deck, I noticed that my paper became covered with an impalpable white grit. I would brush it off, and in a few moments more, the same fine white ash covered the paper again. I could not account for it, until I learned, several days afterwards, of the tremendous eruption of Mt. Vesuvius, from whose crater this fine dust had been blown for hundreds of miles, until it dropped on the deck of the little steamer in the harbor of Cattaro, and perhaps was carried still farther over the black mountains of Montenegro.

Corfu is another tropical Paradise where brilliant flowers and delicious fruits abound, and where many Europeans spend their holidays. It so happened that the English fleet, while we were on the island, made its rendezvous at Corfu's principal harbor. On one of the ships were King Edward and Queen Alexandra, who had come thus far to meet their son, the Prince of Wales, and his wife, on their return from India. King George of Greece had come to Corfu to meet their Majesties, and a great reception was given them.

All the royalties rode by our hotel in state, close under our windows, and one could not help thinking how easy it would be, were any one so ill disposed, to drop a bomb into the royal carriages, or to conceal an infernal machine in one of the many bouquets which were thrown at the distinguished guests as they drove through the streets. The King of Greece looked very apprehensive as he scanned the throng on either side of the roadway, and I imagine that the same thought was in his mind, and that he was exceedingly glad when he had convoyed his regal visitors back to their ship and seen them safely aboard a British iron-clad. Such is one of the penalties of royalty! "To be a king is a dangerous job," as one of them recently remarked, a remark which the late war underscored many times over.

At night all the ships of the fleet were brilliantly illuminated with electric lights stretched around the decks, and up the masts and spars to the topmost peak, a truly magnificent spectacle.

We did not delay long in Athens though it was a most interesting time to visit the ancient capital, for half the royalties of Europe had assembled to witness the Olympic Games, about to take place in the historic stadium, which had lately been re-seated and embellished in pure white marble by M. Averoff, a wealthy Greek philanthropist. Athletes as well as princes were gathering from all parts of the world, and every day we could see the contestants in the games practising in this truly magnificent stadium. More than two millenniums ago this stadium was built by the orator and statesman Lycurgus. Two hundred years later it was renewed in solid marble from Mt. Pentelicus, " almost exhausting its quarries," we are told; then for centuries it was unused, covered with debris, its site almost forgotten until recently rebuilt, as I have said, in more than its original glory.

Ninety thousand people can gather on those glistening marble seats. Afterwards, when spending some months in Athens, while writing a book about the cities of St. Paul, I was interested to remember that the great apostle doubtless visited this stadium, perhaps frequently, and that here was suggested to him many of the athletic similes of which he was so fond; the runners in the race, the boxers who did not beat the air, the discus throwers, and the athletes who " kept under " the body.

Unfortunately my engagements compelled me to leave

Athens the very day before the games began, but it was most satisfactory to learn afterwards that the American athletes acquitted themselves so well in every respect, winning a large number of the events.

"Good luck to you, boys," I said to a group of them as I was about to leave, "I hope you'll win!"

"Oh, we wish you could stay and root for us," answered the spokesman; "there are so few Americans here." I, too, wished I could stay and "root" for them, but other duties called us on, and we sailed for Smyrna.

Here, as in many other places in the Near East, Americans have made themselves felt most beneficently by their educational institutions. Here is the International Institute, a great college, ably presided over by Dr. McLachlan. Here, too, is a well-equipped Girls' College, under the care of the Women's Board of Missions, and here are two or three Protestant churches under the care of American missionaries.

The colleges are of a character similar to Robert College in Constantinople, the College for Girls in the same city, and the American University in Beirut. There are others in the interior of Turkey of a grade almost as high. No institutions in the world are more useful, and of none have Americans greater reason to be proud. It has always been a great pleasure to address the students of these colleges, as I have on several occasions, for one feels that, if he ever should speak a word "in season," it is then, since he has before him the future leaders of half a dozen races of the Near East. As I correct the proofs of these pages I have to record that the Girls' Institute of Smyrna has been burned, the International Institute threatened, and the theological, and other schools of the interior suspended, because of the hostility of the ruthless Turk, after his victory over the Greeks in September, 1922.

The return journey to western Europe has been of much interest in retrospect, as it took us again through the Balkan states and Hungary, countries on which the eyes of the world have been centred since the great war for the freedom of the small nations began.

Philippopolis in Bulgaria is an interesting old Bulgarian town with a long history. Its quaint buildings lean over to shake hands with one another across narrow streets. It was then a centre of a flourishing American mission.

Sofia, the raw capital of Bulgaria, was a straggling country city. I remember a pathetic attempt at an art gallery which I visited, where a few specimens of Bulgarian pictures and statuary were exhibited. Nevertheless such a gallery showed the aspirations of a people that had just thrown off the Turkish yoke, and whose hopes were all for a national life of their own. Alas, that they were misled by crafty King Ferdinand in the World War, and cast in their lot against their own kinsfolk, the Slavs.

After the meetings in Sofia and Philippopolis we next spent a few days in Hungary, visiting Budapest and Pecs, a large number of Endeavorers greeting us in each city. Pecs is of peculiar interest because it was long on the border-line between Mohammedanism and Christianity. Indeed the Moslems possessed the city for centuries, as two or three mosques, now converted into Christian churches, testify, the tall minarets taking the place of the conventional steeple.

However we may feel about the acts of Hungary in the great war, we must remember that for years and years she was the chief bulwark of Christianity, and rolled back over and over again, at the cost of vast numbers of men and vast treasure, the hordes of Moslems.

Budapest, which I think I have before characterized as, in my opinion, one of the two or three most beautiful cities in Europe, had long been a centre of Christian Endeavor activity. Here the Endeavorers supported with the help of other friends, a well-equipped hospital, situated in beautiful grounds, and conducted on distinctly Christian principles.

Soon after the meetings in Hungary, Mrs. Clark, with our

youngest son and the daughter of a missionary who had come with us from Smyrna, sailed for America from Genoa, while I remained behind for three months to attend various meetings in Europe, and especially to prepare for the third World's Christian Endeavor Convention which was scheduled to be held in Geneva in the early days of August.

Before that event my diary records some great meetings, among them one in the City Temple of London, presided over by that delightful but erratic theological comet, Rev. R. J. Campbell, also a very successful British National Convention in Leeds, and many other meetings, in Nottingham, Swindon, Leicester, Wisbech, Huddersfield, Sheffield, Manchester, Oxford, etc.

At this time I had become much interested in Esperanto, and had large hopes that it might become a long-hoped-for universal language. I advocated it on the platform and in print, and for many months an Esperanto department was conducted in *The Christian Endeavor World*. In Liverpool I attended a meeting of a hundred Endeavorers who were studying Esperanto, and became proficient enough in the language to write an occasional home letter in it.

I still believe that it might be a great unifying force of immense value to the world, but unless it is taught in the public schools in every land, and practically made compulsory as the one secondary language, while all must, of course, know their own, I now see little hope of great usefulness from it. It is exceedingly easy to learn, especially if one has a rudimentary knowledge of Latin, but unfortunately it is quite as easy to forget.

Much of my time during the early summer of 1906 was spent in preparing the programme, and obtaining speakers for the World's Endeavor convention in Geneva. My part in these preparations I accomplished largely while staying at Scheveningen, Bonn, Interlaken, and Geneva.

Some of the difficulties attending such a gathering can be

A Christian Endeavor Convention Picnic

Of English, Irish, and Scotch Endeavorers, Loch Fyne, Scotland.

imagined from the fact that people speaking in their native tongues thirty different languages participated in the meetings. One part of the programme was printed in no less than twelve languages, namely French, German, English, Swedish, Norwegian, Finnish, Lettish, Italian, Spanish, Hungarian, Marathi, and Esperanto.

However the task was at last accomplished, and the convention was carried through successfully and with great blessing to the thousands who were in attendance. The three principal languages spoken were French, German, and English, large halls being assigned to each language. A great united praise service, and a united consecration meeting were held, and it is thrilling even in memory to recall the responses of those who spoke a score and a half of languages, each group telling in their own tongue of their purpose to serve the one Lord and Master, Jesus Christ.

No less moving was it to hear the twenty-third Psalm repeated in unison, the thirty languages blending in one, and again the prayer, " Our Father," to the one God who hears and answers His children whatever tongue they speak.

In the historic cathedral of St. Pierre where Calvin thundered and pleaded in days of yore, I was asked to preach on convention Sunday, taking the life of the great reformer for my subject. I was later honored by a request for a copy of this sermon for one of the documents to be placed in the corner stone of a monument erected at the quadri-centennial of the birth of the great Genevan.

The convention being over, nothing detained me from the speediest possible return to America via Liverpool.

Thus ended a busy and exceedingly varied eleven months, spent in a score of the countries of Europe and nearer Asia.

FROM PEACEFUL LAKE MOHONK TO DIS-TRACTED JAMAICA

THE SMILEY BROTHERS — CORNELL UNIVERSITY — ANDREW
D. WHITE — A TERRIBLE EARTHQUAKE — A RUINED CITY
— THE CANAL ZONE — COLONEL GORGAS — THE PRES-
IDENT OF PANAMA.

FTER returning from Europe, the later months of 1906 and the earlier weeks of 1907 were spent in America, with nominal headquarters at our home in Auburndale, though many engagements east and west made the home-life somewhat fragmentary. Among these engagements was one at Lake Mohonk where for a number of seasons Mrs. Clark and I were guests of the Smiley brothers, either at the so-called " peace conference " in the spring, or the " Conference for Indians and Other Dependent Races," in the fall.

These were notable meetings, which were interrupted by the great war, but which admirably fulfilled their purpose, that of calling the attention of leading men, and through them of the whole country, to these great subjects. In those days we fondly hoped that the last great war had been fought, and that kings and politicians could never be so insensate as to plunge their people into such a hellish struggle as that which began in 1914. Plans for a " United States of the World," for a " World Court," and all the attendant blessings that would flow from universal peace were discussed. Let us not say that they were discussed in vain, for we may still hope that the brightest visions ever cherished at Lake Mohonk will yet be realized.

The autumn conference was equally valuable in stirring the consciences of the people to the wrongs that have been done to the Indians, and the need for practising the teachings of Christianity toward all the " dependent races," the Filipinos figuring largely under that euphemism.

All the surroundings of Lake Mohonk tended to make these conferences memorable; the glorious scenery from the mountain top where the hotel is built; the charming intellectual and social atmosphere which the guests found there and also brought with them; the distinctively religious thought with which each day began in the public devotions of the great hotel family; and above all the personality of the Smiley brothers, those wonderful " Cheeryble Twins," who radiated serenity and peace wherever they went. Their hand-grasp as the guests arrived was a benediction, and whenever the waters of discussion were liable to become troubled, as sometimes they were, for free discussion was allowed and opinions sometimes sharply clashed, their words of Quaker wisdom were always the healing oil of controversy. When the older brothers were translated to the eternal haven of perfect peace, the meetings were carried on by the younger brother, Daniel and his gracious wife, in the same spirit and with the same success.

I remember that on this or some similar occasion I wrote a magazine article claiming that Lake Mohonk was the most beautiful spot in the world. Opinions of course may differ, but as I think of the natural beauties of the place, and the indefinable spirit of hospitality and moral and spiritual elevation, I am still unwilling to recede from the superlatives of that article.

A week at Cornell University, a week of eight days, by the way (for preaching in Sage Chapel on two Sundays was always included in the engagement), was also one of the events of this fall of which I am writing, as it was every year either in the fall or spring for fifteen or twenty consecutive years. With each visit I found that the university had expanded in numbers and in equipment, and I regard it as one of the greatest democratic institutions of America.

Ezra Cornell founded the university on the theory that no branch of human learning was inferior to any other; that to study mechanics and the composition of the soil and the diseases of cattle was as important, as honorable, and as necessary as to study the Greek Dative, or the Differential Calculus. That spirit still pervades the university, and the students of the agricultural college are not looked down upon as " Bucolics " or " Boeotians " by the classical students, because they give their attention more to the composition of fertilizers than to the composition of Latin poems.

Andrew D. White, who was one of the greatest educators and diplomats whom America has ever produced, started the university on its shining way, and was a resident on the college hill during most of the years that I served as a university preacher. He was always in the chapel for the Sunday services. His fund of rich experiences as ambassador to Russia and Germany, as well as his earlier struggles with New York politicians when the university was being founded, made a call upon him an event of one's life. I know of no American autobiography more charming for its simple recital of the experiences of a rich, varied, and useful life than his.

Dr. Jacob J. Schurman, who succeeded him, and for many years administered the university, was a worthy successor, one of the great college presidents of the country who thoroughly believed in and carried out the principles of Ezra Cornell, and who has served his country in important positions as president of the first Philippine Commission, and as ambassador to Greece, where I had the pleasure of meeting him on one of my visits to Athens.

On a bitterly cold January night in 1907, with my daughter,

Maude Williston, I left Auburndale for a six months' journey to the South American republics, and incidentally to Jamaica and the Canal Zone on the way thither, and to Europe on the way home. In those days the quickest and most comfortable route from South America to North America was by way of Lisbon and Liverpool, a waste of time and money, which like many other things the World War has already corrected.

On account of the age and illness of my adopted mother, Mrs. Clark was unable to accompany me on this journey as so often before, and I was fortunate to have a daughter to be my delightful guardian, travelling companion, and secretary.

Three days before we left America, we heard that Kingston, Jamaica, which was to be our first port of call, was destroyed by an earthquake. Our ship carried provisions and hospital supplies for the wounded, and I was bidden to carry the affectionate greetings and sympathy of American Christians.

We found the conditions in Kingston, where we arrived five days after sailing from New York, even worse than we had expected. Scarcely one stone, or to speak more accurately, one brick, was left upon another. Many bodies were still buried under the ruins among which relatives and friends were frantically searching, hoping they might find some spark of life among those who were caught in these death traps. Walls were still tottering, and occasionally, because of earth tremors, were toppling over. A large cornice of the Constant Springs Hotel, where we took refuge, though it was five miles out of the city, fell the first night we were there. Every now and then we felt the earth quake, and it can be imagined that those were anxious days for visitors, as well as dreadful days for the people of Kingston, many of whom had lost dear friends and relatives, as well as all their property. There was comparatively little insurance, and it was uncertain whether even that could be collected. Archdeacon Nuttall of the Church of England was the general of the occasion, and received with gratitude the assurance of America's sympathy and support.

The English Governor of the island, whose name I have forgotten, had treated in a very gruff and discourteous way the commander of the American man-of-war who had immedi-

A CHURCH IN DEVASTED KINGSTON

ately rushed his ship to the scene of the disaster with what provisions and surgical appliances he could command. He was snubbed by the Governor, and was forbidden to send a relief party ashore, an act which created great indignation both in Jamaica and America.

News had come of this action on the day we sailed from New York, and I remember the hot indignation of Dr. Grenfell, the saint of Labrador, whom I met in the private office of the publisher, Mr. Fleming H. Revell. Grenfell seemed to want to take not a whip of small cords, but a good strong horsewhip and lash some sense into the thick head of his stupid and self-important compatriot, the Governor of Jamaica. Needless to say, the said Governor was soon relieved of the cares of office.

Long, long rows of white cots had been set up in the improvised hospitals in Kingston and vicinity, and everything possible was done by the doctors, white and colored, and by the surgeons from the United States men-of-war, to relieve the dreadful suffering. Thousands of people were encamped in the open spaces, some under shelters of boughs and fragments of canvas, where tents could not be obtained. No church had escaped the earthquake, and I preached to a large congregation on the lawn of the Congregational Church, which of course had been wrecked, as well as the manse near by, though one or two rooms in the pastor's house were still habitable.

The ruin extended far and wide for many miles around Kingston, but in most parts of the island comparatively little damage had been done, and I was able to hold the scheduled Christian Endeavor meetings which had been planned in other towns, like Brownstown, Montego Bay, Port Antonio, Spanishtown, and others. Indeed in some respects the meetings were more successful than they might have been ordinarily, for the colored people had been greatly frightened by the earthquake, and were in an unusually religious mood.

A jeweller told me that his business had been greatly increased by the earthquake. It may seem a singular statement, until it is explained that wedding rings had come to be in great demand by conscience-stricken couples who had lived together for many years without the rites of holy matrimony. The earthquake convinced them of their sins, and the whole stock of wedding rings in the island, I am told, was cleaned out in a few days.

When the schedule of meetings in Jamaica had been finished we sailed for the Canal Zone with a great crowd of dusky deck passengers who were going to work on the Canal, for Jamaica, with its 600,000 black and colored people (there is a fine distinction in these terms), furnished almost unlimited man power for the digging of the big ditch.

A cordial welcome awaited us in Colon from Presbyterians, Congregationalists, and Church of England people. Several meetings had been arranged in Colon, Panama, and one or two other points along the Canal. One of these was in Christ Church in Colon at which Colonel Gorgas, America's great sanitary engineer, presided. No man in the whole Zone was so beloved as the colonel-doctor. He had just cleaned up Cuba, banishing the " Yellow Jack " forever from that fair island, and had already accomplished the same result for the Canal Zone. Moreover he had attacked the still more insidious though less fatal disease, malaria, and had nearly conquered this pest too, and had thus made the building of the Canal possible.

The French had been conquered in their previous efforts to build the Canal, not by the difficulties of the Culebra Cut, or by their insufficient machinery, but by the insignificant and pestiferous mosquito. Colonel Gorgas had found that the mosquito must be routed, or the United States government would be. By an extensive system of drainage; by screening every house and public building in the Zone; by a liberal use of kerosene on all stagnant water; by carrying out a thorough inspection of every private house to see that not even a cupful of water was left in the open in which a mosquito might breed, the work was accomplished, the Canal was made possible, and Colon was changed from a pest hole to a health resort.

Colonel Gorgas was not only a great physician and administrator but a thorough-going Christian and a kindly gentleman, and his cordial words added much to the interest of the meetings I have mentioned.

" How did the Panamanians stand this interference with their natural and vested rights in bad drainage, bad water, and mosquitoes? " I asked. " Oh, they were just indifferent," he replied, " they didn't care so long as we paid for the so-called improvements." So well loved was the good Colonel that all the people were delighted when President Roosevelt on his famous visit to the Canal actually hugged him openly on his arrival.

Another man of special interest whom I remember meeting during our week in Panama was President Manuel Amador Guerrero, then the President of the tiny republic. He was a doctor of medicine by profession, a man of education and refinement, with a piercing black eye, and an eager cordial way of grasping your hand that made you feel at home at once in his modest establishment.

Another man, whom I was especially glad to meet was Hon. H. G. Squiers, the American Minister to Panama, a position just then of great importance. I had before met him when he was Secretary of Legation in Peking, just before the Boxer troubles. During the siege of Peking he won golden laurels, though he modestly claimed, as I have before related, that some of the missionaries whom I knew, especially Dr. Ament and Dr. Gamewell, were the real captains in that siege. Such praise was all the more remarkable because Mr. Squiers was a Roman Catholic and would not be supposed to be prejudiced in favor of Protestant missionaries.

He told me a story which illustrates the Roman Catholic point of view as well as any I ever heard. He said that he and Dr. Ament were much thrown together during the siege, and became quite intimate, so that on one occasion Dr. Ament said to him, " I can't understand, Squiers, how a man of your intelligence can believe in some of your doctrines, the infallibility of the Pope, for instance." " I replied to him," said Mr. Squiers, " I do not see how a man of *your* intelligence can believe in some of your Protestant doctrines, but as for the infallibility of the Pope, my belief in that is the same as your belief in the Supreme Court of the United States; — not that the Pope can never do wrong or make a mistake, but that he is the highest authority we have in religion, and since there is no higher, we bow to that when once the decision has been made."

I do not vouch for Mr. Squiers' interpretation as being the usual Catholic view, but it is of interest to know how an intelligent Romanist looks at this question.

THE WEST COAST OF SOUTH AMERICA

PANAMA CANAL IN THE MAKING — PECULIARITIES OF THE
WEST COAST — LIMA, THE PARIS OF SOUTH AMERICA —
HARVARD UNIVERSITY IN AREQUIPA — A PERILOUS JOUR-
NEY — LAKE TITICACA — BEAUTIFUL SANTIAGO — THE
CHRIST OF THE ANDES.

 UR visit to the Canal Zone happened to come
at a most interesting time, when the great
water-way which divided the two Americas,
and united them more closely to the rest of
the world, was in the making; 4,000 car-
penters and builders, 3,000 diggers, and tens
of thousands of workmen of all descriptions and from almost
every nation and tribe and tongue in the world, were employed
to accomplish this monumental scheme, which the dense captain
of the British steamer that took us from Jamaica to Colon even
then told us with a sneer would never be accomplished.

The " Guatemala," on which we sailed from Panama on the
west coast, put off her sailing date in an exasperating manner
from day to day, but at last got under way, and we were off
for the long voyage of twenty-three days, down the sterile
west coast of South America to Valparaiso. The first few
days of the journey, however, showed us a coast that was anything but sterile. It luxuriates in a wonderful growth of
tropical vegetation.

So curious are the indentations of the Panama Coast that
when sailing from Panama on the west coast, we were actually

farther east than when we arrived at Colon on the east coast.
But soon the points of the compass became natural again,
and straight away south by west we sailed along the coast of
Colombia.

We cast anchor for the first time on this voyage sixty miles
up the Guayas River, just far enough from Ecuador's chief
port, Guayaquil, to escape the Yellow Fever which was then
raging and carrying off its victims by the thousand every month.

CULEBRA CUT WHEN THE PANAMA CANAL WAS BUILT

We could not go ashore on this account, but, as we did not go
to them, the mosquitoes came down the river, in swarms
billions strong, to visit us. So thick were they on the bulwarks
of the vessel that in some places they painted black the white
woodwork of the upper deck. We screened our cabin doors
and windows as best we could, but passed one or two most uncomfortable nights while lying at anchor in the stream waiting
for our cargo, since no one was allowed to go ashore or come
aboard for fear of quarantine regulations further on.

Fortunately the mosquitoes that can fly three miles are not of the virulent variety. Though they caused much discomfort they brought no disease with them. The Guayas is a magnificent stream, many miles wide as it approaches the ocean, and great islands of tropical vegetation, sometimes bearing large bushes and trees which had broken off from the shores, floated by our ship back and forth as the tide ebbed and flowed.

Every day of the voyage our steamer stopped at some port on the route to take on or discharge cargo, and thus the monotony of the voyage was much relieved as we sailed chiefly in the night time.

Our ship was a regular menagerie of domestic animals, cows and pigs, ducks and chickens. Great quantities of tropical fruits formed part of the cargo. Besides the domestic animals and fowls, other varieties of the feathered tribe were represented in great variety on our ship. Parrots and paroquets were in the majority. They are found everywhere along these shores, and are brought for sale to the ships in large numbers. Besides, we carried other birds like canaries from Chili, redbirds from Peru, and an occasional long-legged bird somewhat like a crane, that hopped solemnly along the deck inviting the passengers to scratch its neck, for which attention it seemed genuinely grateful.

At first I could not imagine for whom the tons of oranges, mangoes, and green vegetables which took up most of the space on the after deck were intended, but soon after leaving Guayaquil I found that we had come to the dry zone of South America, where it never rains, and where fresh fruits and green vegetables are in keen demand at every port.

At noon of one day the ship will steam out of the port of Guayaquil in a pouring tropical shower, during which perhaps an inch of rain will fall in an hour. At midnight of the same day it passes the point on the Peruvian shore, close to the Ecuadorian border, where we were told it had not rained for sixteen years, and might not rain for sixteen years to come.

A remarkable change in the temperature of the morning bath takes place between sunset and sunrise. One day it is hot and unrefreshing, the bath thermometer standing at about eighty degrees; the next, one shivers with the cold as he steps into the bath and finds that there is a difference of thirty degrees by the thermometer. The Antarctic current which sweeps up the west coast of South America performs the same beneficent task for these hot and arid regions that the Gulf Stream performs for the northern countries of Europe. The Antarctic current brings coolness and health to the tropics, the Gulf Stream brings warmth and life even to the Arctic regions of northern Scandinavia.

Our first long stop on the west coast was at Callao, the port of Lima, the capital of Peru, a busy, thriving seaport, and the gateway to a very interesting capital that prides itself on being the "Paris of South America." We were accused by some friends who met us at Callao with buying lottery tickets as soon as we got ashore. Mildly resenting the charge we found that it was nevertheless true, for the tickets on the tram-car which took us to Lima, were also good for an infinitesimal chance in the national lottery which was soon to be drawn. The purpose of this lottery, it was said, was to provide a special inducement to Peruvians not only to buy tram-car tickets, but also to preserve them. Thus a check was placed on the rapacity of conductors, who otherwise might steal them when once used and sell them again to the next passenger.

Lima is a bright and interesting city with a charming river, the Rimac, dashing and splashing through it at a great rate. The city is also exceedingly interesting historically, for it has been besieged and sacked; has seen revolution and counter revolution; has conquered and been conquered, and has come out of every tribulation still vigorous, and often stronger, richer and more prosperous than ever.

Bright and beautiful as it is in its many colors, it is largely a city of mud, or sun-dried adobe bricks, which would melt away in a good Yankee northeast storm. Yet it is wonderful what fine effects can be obtained from such material, and an abundance of vari-colored pigments. The cathedral in the central square is a truly imposing and beautiful building, but the most interesting relic it contained for my eyes, was a glass coffin in which are exposed the bones of the infamous Pizarro, the heartless conqueror of Peru. I was glad to see him in a place where he could make no more trouble, and could commit no more barbarities.

While in Lima I had the pleasure of an interview with His Excellency Don José Pardo, President of the Republic. Though we knew no language in common, my kind inter-preters, Hon. R. I. Neill, United States Chargé d'Affaires, and Rev. J. S. Watson, a well known missionary, supplied my lack of Spanish.

Mr. Watson explained the object and extent of the Christian Endeavor movement, whereupon President Pardo asked, " Is it a Catholic organization? " " No," answered Mr. Watson diplomatically, " It is just Christian." " Then," said the Presi-dent to me, with a twinkle in his eye, " we shall have to apply Section IV. of the constitution to you." At which the others smiled audibly for they understood, as I did not, that Section IV. was the article of the constitution which forbids the propa-gation of any religion except the Roman Catholic. However we all saw that the President was not very serious, and he went on to say to me: " The spirit of the people of Peru is very tolerant, though the constitution is very intolerant." President Pardo was a young man with a pleasant face, modestly dressed in civilian clothes, and is the son of D. Manuel Pardo, Peru's first civilian president, who came into power in the early seven-ties, and whose memory is greatly honored throughout the Republic.

Before leaving Peru an excursion in the high Andes came near preventing the writing of this biography or the perform-ance of any other labors on our part on this mundane sphere.

This was the journey on the Oroya Railway which climbs the Andes to a height of nearly fifteen thousand feet, toled thither by the rich copper mines on the summit. In a little bob-tailed car, used especially for such ascents, together with other fellow passengers, we mounted, one by one, the incredible zigzags. This railway is considered one of the engineering marvels of the world, ranking with the Suez Canal, the St. Gothard Tunnel, and the Culebra Cut.

Of course we never thought of taking umbrellas or water-proofs in a country where it had not rained for a hundred years, so we all started gaily up the mighty mountain, enchanted by the grand and rugged scenery which in this respect is unsur-passed in all the world. I was deeply interested in the signs of the past civilization as we beheld the terraces built far up the mountain slopes in Atahualpa's time. To these terraces, built with infinite toil for three thousand feet above the plain, earth had been carried on the backs of men, and gardens and vineyards planted by the patient Incas of a thousand years ago.

The climate of the mountains is not the climate of the low-lands, as we soon found, and a drenching rain began before we reached the end of our journey. This storm, unusually severe even for the mountain region, loosened vast quantities of soil and rock, and on the return, coming around a sharp bend in the road on the edge of a frightful precipice, a sheer drop of thousands of feet, our little engine ran into a small mountain of earth and stuck fast, for some twenty-four hours.

Fortunately the car did not go over the precipice. With the other passengers, summoning what good nature we could com-mand, we trudged through the driving rain for five miles down the track, constantly menaced by small avalanches of mud and stone which rattled down the steep mountain side, until we came to the next station, where, after a wait of some hours, another train took us back to Lima.

A visit to the fine Harvard observatory near Arequipa was another memorable event of our journey in Peru. In order to reach Arequipa, one must disembark at Mollendo, a port which vies with Antifogasta as being the worst landing place in the known world. Indeed there is no port or harbor in any sense of the word, but simply an anchorage ground on the storm-beaten coast. Even when no storm is raging the mighty swell of the South Pacific seems to heave the little boats in which we land up to the stars, and again to drop them down toward the bottomless pit. The landing may not be as danger-

OUR LITTLE TRAIN IN A LANDSLIDE ON THE HIGH PERUVIAN ANDES

ous as it seems, for accidents are comparatively rare, though only in good weather is a landing possible.

Six hours of steady climbing by rail from Mollendo brought us to Arequipa, beautiful for situation, and of special interest to Americans because of the Harvard observatory, which here seeks to view the stars through the pure air of the Andes, 8,000 feet above the sea. The city of Arequipa itself is a bigoted, priest-ridden city with a big cathedral and interminable streets of dirty adobe houses. But the fresh, clean, sweet, flower-decked home of the American astronomers seems like a little paradise, after passing through the purgatory of Arequipa's slums.

The observatory is used solely for photographing the stars, and we saw a single negative 17 x 14 inches in size which had caught the pictures of no less than 400,000 stars, and were told that it would take two thousand plates of this size to photograph the whole southern heavens as seen from this observatory.

" What is man, that thou art mindful of him, and the son of man, that Thou visitest him! "

There are few places in the world that enjoy such magnificent scenery as does this observatory. Mighty Misti, and Chachani, tower more than two miles above us, though we are a mile and a half above the sea, while the rushing Chili River cuts a deep gorge at the foot of the observatory hill. What view in all the world combines such mountains and such a valley, with roaring river and busy city to give life to the superb scene?

But Arequipa was less than half way to our destination, which was La Paz, the capital of Bolivia. Up, up, ever up, the railway climbs. At last after some twenty hours of steady ascent from Mollendo, the highest pass, 14,666 feet above the sea, is reached. This is almost the same height as the top of Mt. Blanc, but so near the Equator are we that the snow line is 2,000 feet higher still. Many of our fellow passengers suffered from " mountain sickness," which in its visible effects does not differ from sea-sickness. On this occasion the two Americans suffered far less than the native Peruvians.

Lake Titicaca is some thousand feet or more below the highest point of the railroad pass, and we crossed it in the night in a little boat whose bullet holes were reminiscent of one of Bolivia's frequent revolutions. Then another sixty miles of railway, and we looked down into what seemed like a vast crater, and, behold! in the lowest depths of this crater was a city of 80,000 inhabitants, La Paz, the capital of the mountain republic of Bolivia.

Here, so far removed from what we are pleased to term " civilization," we found people buying and selling and getting gain, marrying and giving in marriage, living and dying like the rest of us, and believing all the time that their capital is the very centre of the earth, on which all eyes should be fixed. The immediate surroundings are barren and desolate, yet it is a city of flowers and fruits, for a few miles down the mountain side, in an opposite direction from that in which we came, rich tropical vegetation abounds and is brought up on the patient backs of llamas, and no less patient Bolivian peasants.

The llama is a most interesting little beast of burden, timid as a hare, but docile as a pet dog if he is not overloaded. He will take a hundred pounds on his back without complaint, and toil on day after day, asking for little food or water; but add another five pounds to his load, and he will lie down, as obstinate as a mule, until relieved of his extra weight. Long lines of these creatures, their small ears constantly pricked in fright, continually toil up the Andes and are driven through the streets of La Paz in great numbers.

Only one meeting detained us in La Paz, and the sight-seeing did not take many hours. There are several large Catholic churches, out of one of which my daughter was hustled rather unceremoniously, because, not knowing their customs, she wore a hat in church. The Methodists have a mission here, and we made some pleasant acquaintances among them. The American Minister, a very chatty gentleman, had just learned from a young man who travelled with us that his yearly salary had been raised to $10,000. We felt, as I have no doubt he did, that to spend his life in La Paz, however light his duties, was well worth the money.

Returning to Mollendo we took another steamer for the rest of the journey to Valparaiso, a steamer whose machinery was out of order, whose valves leaked, which could make but five miles an hour during part of the journey, and would inevitably have been wrecked had a storm arisen. Nevertheless, with all these drawbacks and the further disadvantage that the steamer was crowded almost beyond belief before we reached Valparaiso, so that some of the passengers slept in the companionways and, it was said, in the bath-tubs, it was a thoroughly interesting journey.

As we passed the guano islands, off the coast, vast swarms of water-birds darkened the sun, and seals and walruses, porpoises and acres of writhing water-snakes filled the sea. In no part of the known world is nature so lavish with her fauna. Huge flocks of pelicans would drop down hundreds of feet into the water with a splash that could be heard a mile away, fill their great pouches with the abundant fish, and struggle into the air again, soon to take another dive for prey which they could never miss, so abundant was the sea life.

At many ports, especially Antofagasta, nitrate was being loaded into waiting ships that gave these little ports a semblance of great activity. More valuable than the richest gold mine have these nitrates been to Chili, and we do not wonder that Peru was extremely sore that they were taken away from her in the last war between these two republics.

So bitter is the feeling that even the children share it, and it is scarcely to be wondered at that a little boy, when asked by the missionary if Christ died for all men, insisted on making an exception of the Chilians.

Arriving in the harbor of Valparaiso, a veritable Spanish Armada of small boats came out to meet our steamer, each one manned by pirates as it seemed, who swarmed aboard our ship, fought for our baggage, and demanded almost at the point of a gun that we should hire them to take us ashore at a price at least five times the legal fare. When we were almost ready to yield to their demands, a friend came aboard and rescued us from the bandits, who knew that they could not impose with impunity upon a resident of Valparaiso.

Viewed from the sea one does not wonder that this great Chilian port is called the "Vale of Paradise," though our mental vision of Paradise receded as we approached the city, and was entirely blotted out when we entered the busiest section of the city and found only blackened ruins, where, until within a very few weeks, fire had been smouldering for months. Less than a year before, Valparaiso, like Kingston, had been wrecked in a terrible earthquake, and the authorities were very slow about rebuilding the city, showing nothing of the enterprise of San Francisco, which, to a like extent, had been wrecked by earthquake and fire. We found some good friends and had some most interesting meetings in Valparaiso and Santiago, whither we journeyed a few days after landing.

Santiago, "Jamestown" when translated into English, is indeed the gem of the Pacific Coast of South America. No city has a more beautiful park than Santa Lucia. It is a tremendous isolated rock rising five hundred feet in the very heart of the city. Man has supplemented nature in making Santa Lucia the most beautiful city breathing-place in all the Americas. Strings of many colored electric lights at night take the place of the flowers by day; fountains and marble statues appear at unexpected corners; cool grottoes invite one to linger in their shade on the upward climb, and a gurgling brook that comes leaping down the hillside adds its music to the songs of the birds in the trees, while far off on the horizon great snow-clad giants of the Andes rise 20,000 feet and more above the sea, seeming to hem in the city on all sides.

Here the Presbyterians have a splendid work, and we found it a most delightful missionary centre. President Montt, then Chief Magistrate of the Republic, received us very cordially. He is the son of one of Chili's greatest presidents, and looked not unlike President Diaz of Mexico. His swarthy face, like that of Mexico's former president, declares his partial Indian descent. His official residence was the large and stately palace at Santiago, yet it has about it a certain republican simplicity, characteristic of the one who was then its official resident, who gave his people an honest and on the whole most successful administration.

Our visit to Santiago fell in Holy Week. On Thursday of Passion Week it was indeed a strange and funereal sight that we gazed upon. The whole city was in mourning. Every woman was clothed in black, and a foreign woman with a picture hat would have been as much out of place as a wedding wreath at a burial. Indeed very few foreigners even ventured out without the black mantilla over their heads, otherwise they might have been in danger of mob violence.

On Good Friday all business was suspended. The people flocked by the tens of thousands to see the images brought out for their annual procession, a dozen great floats representing our Lord in Gethsemane, betrayed, scourged, and finally nailed to the cross. They were each borne on the backs of groaning, perspiring men, who could carry them only a few feet before they set them down to rest, while the assembled thousands that lined the sidewalks stood with uncovered heads in reverent silence as they looked upon these crude representations of our Lord's last sufferings. The scene seemed to me solemn and impressive.

An American young lady in our party was made faint for a moment by the stifling crowd and heat and odors, and had to retire to the shelter of a neighboring doorway. " A judgment on the heretic," some women in the crowd were heard to say. " She could not endure the presence of the Lord."

In 1907 the tunnel through the Andes, which connects the republics of Chili and Argentina, had not been completed, and the journey across the continent was a far more formidable matter than it is to-day, and involved a long and hazardous stage-ride journey from Juncal to Las Cuevas in Argentina. In those days this was indeed a hair-raising trip. Twenty or more little coaches, each holding half a dozen people, met the passengers at Juncal. These coaches belonged to two rival lines, one of which painted its cabs yellow, and the other black. The drivers indulged in frequent races to get ahead of their deadly rivals, and often in most inopportune places. Our own driver of a black coach attempted a short cut over a small hill to get ahead of a yellow coach. The horses floundered among the rocks, and we all saved ourselves from a serious smash-up by jumping out and righting the vehicle. Another carriage in the procession tipped entirely over.

Going up the mountain, however, on the Chilian side was not extra hazardous, as the horses were obliged to walk. But after reaching the Argentine boundary the descent is very rapid, and the zigzags are as numerous as the curves are sharp. The driver whipped up his horses, and at break-neck speed we dashed along, four horses abreast. The outer ones edged away from the precipice, and crowded the inner steed against the bank. There is no wall and no stone posts, as on the Swiss roads, to guard the sides, and each side is either a precipitous mountain or a fathomless precipice. Around every curve the coach slewed with only two wheels on the ground, and the precipice only six inches, as it seemed, from the outside wheel.

On the height of the pass, on the exact boundary between the two countries, stands the most marvellous statue in the world, the Christ of the Andes, erected by the joint republics in gratitude to Almighty God for their escape from a war which had seemed inevitable, when wise arbitration and conciliation took the place of shot and shell. Their cannon were melted down to form the most benignant statue of the Prince of Peace.

Upon the base of the pedestal are inscribed the words from Ephesians " He is our peace, who hath made both one." The statue has been described so often that I will not dwell upon it, but will only add that in the majestic loneliness of its situation, surrounded by the mighty Andes, it is the most impressive statue on the face of the earth. No longer do most travellers see it, for the new tunnel passes directly under the statue.

I was fortunate in this respect in making the journey when I did. During the World War the memory of this majestic

THE CHRIST OF THE ANDES
On the boundary between Chile and Argentina.

figure, standing among the towering Andes, often seemed to bring a message of peace, as I told my audiences in both hemispheres its story and its meaning for us.   In later days the treaty of peace, and for the limitation of armaments between Chili and Argentina, has often been referred to as prophetic of what the Washington Conference may by its example accomplish for the whole world.

CHAPTER XXXI

YEAR 1907

THE EAST COAST OF SOUTH AMERICA

THE WONDERFUL CITY OF " GOOD AIR " — AN AUDIENCE WITH
PRESIDENT ALCORTA — RICH LITTLE URUGUAY — RIO DE
JANEIRO — THE PRINCE OF CITIES — A UNIQUE PRAYER
MEETING — SAO PAULO — THE COFFEE REGION —
HOME VIA EUROPE.

FTER reaching Las Cuevas the journey to
Buenos Ayres afforded no unusual thrills.
In the Andes region the scenery is surpass-
ingly beautiful, but the last five hundred
miles before reaching the capital is over the
interminable flat prairies, as fertile as our
own best Kansas soil, where is raised a large portion of the
world's wheat and live-stock.

Here the wealthy nabobs of Buenos Ayres have their great
haciendas, enormous farms tilled by Italian or Spanish peons,
who often live in wretched little huts while the owners of these
vast estates luxuriate in the palaces of Buenos Ayres. This
" City of Good Air " seemed to me more remarkable for many
other things than for the purity of its atmosphere, for it is
a low-lying city in the delta of the great River de la Plata.
But it is truly a glorious capital, surpassed by few in any part
of the world for its public buildings, its palatial homes, and its
general air of wealth and prosperity. There are slums, it is
true, but they are not greatly in evidence, for they are shut
away from the passers-by in huge buildings surrounding an
inner courtyard or patio.

We found here, as elsewhere, some warm friends who welcomed us to their churches and their homes. Prices were, and probably still are, excessively high in Buenos Ayres, and one wonders how any one but a millionaire can live there. An ordinary Derby hat cost $12, while $19 or $20 was not an unusual price. Collars were $2.50 a dozen. For lawn neckties such as I could then buy for ten cents at home, the dealer unblushingly asked seventy-five cents, and kindly told me I could get three for $2. Nineteen dollars would pay for a pair of boots which then cost three and a half at home, and a good suit of clothes cost $200. It is true that these prices must be divided by two to find the cost in gold, but even then the price was excessive, though since the war North American prices have not been far behind.

In the large hotels $12 a day was the minimum rate, and from that the prices mounted to $50. The problem of the existence of poor people is solved by the *conventilla,* great tenement houses built around a courtyard, every house containing, perhaps, hundreds of rooms, in each of which lives a whole family; five or six sleeping in one bed, I was told, and the cooking being done over charcoal braziers in the courtyard. Consequently, if provisions are not abnormally high, the *conventilla* solves the problem of existence for the very poor.

The palace which contains the government offices of Argentina is an imposing building fronting on the beantiful Plaza de Mayo. Here I was received in state by Senor Alcorta, the President of the Republic. He was a great stickler for etiquette, and I came near committing *lèse majesté* by being three minutes late at the appointed interview, for I had been tendered a reception by the Protestant ministers of Buenos Ayres only an hour before my appointment with the President. However by persuading the cab driver to whip up his horses, we reached the palace just in season. I was accompanied by Hon. A. M. Beaupré, our American minister, and by the presiding elder of the Methodist Church, as my interpreter,

a gentleman who had the reputation of being the best interpreter in Argentina. The president spoke no English, but Dr.
Brees put my questions and remarks into such elegant and
courtly Spanish that, however much a stickler for the proprie-
ties the President may have been, he could have found no fault
with the interview.

The visits to the Presidents of the four republics that I have
mentioned, and the other high dignitaries whom I met at various times, left with me the impression that, however much
the subordinate officials of the South American republics may
deserve their reputation for graft and dishonesty, this rotten-
ness did not reach at this time to the higher places in the
government, and that those in the highest positions in the leading republics of South America were at least honest men and
true patriots.

"I see a mountain," cried Ferdinand Magellan, on January
15, A.D. 1520, as he sailed by the South American coast on his
momentous voyage round the world. "I see a mountain,
Monte video!" His exclamation has given a name to the
capital of the little republic of Uruguay, where we lingered
for a day or two on our journey up the coast to Rio de Janeiro.
It was our fortune to reach Montevideo on April 19, an anniversary familiar to Massachusetts people.

We found the banks and shops closed, and the city wearing
a general holiday air. It could not be, I thought, that six
thousand miles away they were celebrating the Concord fight
and the Battle of Lexington, and I was soon informed that
it was the anniversary of the "Landing of the Thirty-Three,"
a day as religiously observed in Uruguay as the landing of the
Pilgrims in New England. The Thirty-Three were a band
of adventurers who on April 19, 1825, landed on the shores
of Uruguay, then under the domination of Brazil, rallied the
people to their standard, and soon, in spite of desperate efforts
on the part of Brazil, Uruguay was free and independent.

I was told a curious story of the miscarriage of justice in

the former annals of Uruguay, which I think has rarely been matched. In 1897 President Borda was assassinated in the streets of Montevideo. While he was marching at the head of a religious procession a grocer's clerk was seen to walk deliberately up to him, press a pistol against his white shirt front, and fire point blank. Of course the President fell. He was buried without a *post mortem* examination, which seemed unnecessary. When the grocer's clerk, who was arrested red-handed, came to be tried for his life, his lawyer pleaded that according to Uruguayan law a *post mortem* examination was necessary, to prove whether the President died from fright, heart disease, or a pistol shot. So his client could not be convicted. The jury, strange to say, took the lawyer's view of the case, and condemned the assassin to three years' imprisonment for " insulting " the President — an insult with a vengeance, indeed.

Montevideo strikes the tourist, fresh from the stir and bustle of mighty Buenos Ayres, as rather a sleepy old town, and as somewhat commonplace, if he comes from the north, with the glories of beautiful Rio de Janeiro in his mind's eye. But its inhabitants are never tired of praising the city for its situation, its climate, and its sedate business ways, which I was assured more than once are far superior to the greed for the almighty dollar evinced in Buenos Ayres, Rio de Janeiro, and pre-eminently in the United States.

The potential wealth of Uruguay is no doubt enormous, for though the smallest republic in South America, it is as large as England and is practically one vast pasture, which now feeds hundreds of thousands of cattle, and which might as well feed millions, on its rich native grasses.

No two shores can present greater contrasts than the east and west coasts of South America. The barren, sterile, forbidding mountains of Chili and Peru give place on the opposite side of the continent to softly rounded hills clothed to their summits in living green, vast savannas, and interminable forests. The few rivers on the west coast are short and rapid, while on the east coast some of the mightiest streams in the world, the La Plata, the Amazon, and the Orinoco, pour their muddy tides into the Atlantic.

No country has made greater progress since the twentieth century was born than the Republic of Brazil. Then its great ports, Santos, Rio de Janeiro, and Bahia, were the favorite haunts of yellow fever and every tropical disease. Captains avoided them as far as possible, and made as short a stay as business requirements allowed, and then often paid a large toll in the death of half their crew. Early in the century the authorities of Brazil woke up to the desperateness of the situation and began house-cleaning in good earnest, until now few ports are safer than Santos, which was formerly the worst of all pest-holes, and none is so beautiful as Rio de Janeiro.

As our steamer from Buenos Ayres sailed into the magnificent harbor of Rio, between the towering mountains that shut it in, we saw to our surprise two steam launches coming out to meet the steamer, and still more to our surprise, on the launches a large number of Endeavorers, who greeted us with true Brazilian enthusiasm.

The mystery of the government launches being used on such an occasion was soon explained. It seemed that the rabid Catholic papers of the city had spread abroad the news that I was an emissary of the government and a special agent of President Roosevelt's to spy out the land, an innocent letter of introduction from the President being the cause of this last absurd rumor. Moreover, the papers went on to apply various uncomplimentary adjectives to myself and to the Christian Endeavor movement, which they called the latest spawn of Protestantism. The government, however, took no stock in this puerile propaganda, but recognized its source and animus, and, by offering the Endeavorers the free use of the government launches, thus showed their disapproval and contempt of the priests and their stories. Moreover the government

BOTOFOGO BAY, RIO DE JANEIRO

An avenue of wonderful beauty skirts the magnificent harbor.

gave the Endeavorers free transportation on the government railway to São Paulo, some two hundred miles from Rio de Janeiro, where the chief Brazilian convention was held.

Delightful but busy days awaited us in this charming capital, which I have no hesitation in saying, both for situation, and for the improvements made by man, is in most respects the most beautiful city in all the world. Its natural attractions cannot be surpassed. The great harbor, which could hold the navies of the world, with plenty of room to spare, the striking mountains hemming it in, have always been there, but only a very few years before my visit the people of the city, under intelligent and enterprising leaders, resolved to make their capital worthy of its natural beauties.

They had a serious job before them for in order to construct the *Avenida Centrale* alone, the chief thoroughfare through the heart of the city, five hundred houses and stores of all descriptions had to be bought, condemned and destroyed. They were taken at their assessed value, and many a tax-dodger, who had for years paid far less than his property was worth, found that it sometimes pays to be honest.

This street alone shows something of the enterprise and thoroughness with which this work was done. It is a mile and an eighth long, over a hundred feet wide, and lined on either side with artistic and often truly imposing and magnificent buildings. Forty-five little ovals of flowers and foliage plants, with one Brazil tree springing from the middle of each oval, add a touch of natural beauty to the great thoroughfare, while at night the ornamental pillars bearing three arc lights in each oval, make the street almost as light as day. The broad sidewalks, on which ten people can walk abreast, are mosaics of black and white flint made by workmen brought from Portugal for the purpose, and laid after the Lisbon fashion.

But this is only one of the beautiful streets. The roadway around Gloria Hill to Botofogo is equally charming, and the

Monroe Palace of pure white marble, where the Pan-American Congress has held its meetings, is a worthy jewel in this ring of exquisite avenues.

A sunrise prayer meeting in connection with the meetings in Rio de Janeiro greatly impressed me. We gathered in the early morning on top of Corcovado, for this unique service.

MT. CORCOVADO WHICH RISES FROM THE CITY OF RIO DE JANEIRO
On the top of this pointed peak the Endeavorers of Rio held a sunrise prayer meeting.
From photograph by Mrs. W. F. Chase *née* Maude Williston Clark

This mountain springs almost from the heart of the city, and is connected by a trolley line with all sections.

From the harbor side Corcovado looks as though it terminated in a needle point, but when we reached the top I found that there was a little plateau on which perhaps a hundred people could stand. The view was magnificent in every direction. The great Organ Mountains, and the striking peak called in the Portuguese language, "The Finger of God," which seemed to stretch up to the clouds, enclosed the beautiful bay on the farther side, while the great city of a million inhabitants lying at our feet and waking in the early dawn to the labors of a new day added a touch of cosmopolitan life to the scene.

The meeting was as impressive as the view, as one after another took part in the simple, unstereotyped way that Endeavorers have. Suddenly the sun, which had just risen, peered around the elbow of one of the eastern mountains, and, quite spontaneously, the whole congregation joined in singing in the Portuguese tongue the old hymn with which in English we are so familiar,

> " The morning light is breaking,
> The darkness disappears."

It was indeed a scene and a meeting long to be remembered.

Rio de Janerio, like Buenos Ayres, draws much of the wealth of the great republic to itself. This is unfortunate for both Brazil and Argentina and tends to make these cities more and more the only centres of the business and social life of the republics. It seemed to me that both cities were revelling in new-found wealth. The streets of Rio had just been made possible for automobiles, and there was a constant procession of cars through the well-paved thoroughfare of the capital, the throttles of the horns constantly open, as they dashed along, making a pandemonium of noise which the Brazilians must have enjoyed better than did their visitors.

São Paulo is a populous and thriving city, and seemed more American, or, I should say United Statesian, than any other that I saw in South America. It is an educational centre, and one of the finest normal schools in the world is located there, admittedly built on models furnished by our own country, which sent one of our most eminent teachers, a Miss Brown, to establish it. Her memory is revered throughout Brazil.

The most interesting journey which we made was to the

heart of the coffee district, some five hundred miles from Rio. My kind friend, Colonel Feraz, had invited me and a dozen mutual friends to visit his fazenda, or coffee plantation a few miles from Jahu. The soil is the color of brick dust, and the roads and sidewalks, and the houses where the water of the frequent rains had splashed upon them, were all red. Even one's linen, one's face and hair, take on a reddish hue, after a short ride or walk, on a dusty day.

As the forty-niners in California talked nothing but gold, and as in Kimberley in South Africa, you hear of nothing but diamonds, so in Jahu and vicinity they not only raise coffee and sell coffee, but drink coffee several times a day, talk coffee, and for what I know, dream coffee at night. The Presbyterian pastor's wife in Jahu told me that she frequently served fifty cups a day to friends and neighbors and passers-by. It must be added, however, that the cups are like large thimbles.

When within about a mile of his house, our host modestly remarked, " These are my trees." We were driving through an avenue of glossy-leaved, coffee saplings, the size of a small apple tree. " How many trees have you? " we asked. And he almost took away our breath by replying, " 430,000."

The full-grown tree is about twelve feet in height, of bushy and rather dense growth, and the coffee berries grow on the twigs and small branches close to the wood. In May they are at their handsomest, and the red berries, looking for all the world like Cape Cod cranberries, contrast beautifully with the glossy leaves, and glow like rubies in their dark setting.

I am tempted to linger longer on the many novel delights of this South American journey, but other equally interesting travels that are to follow, remind me that I must not give disproportionate space to this one. The conventions being over, and our duties accomplished so far as possible, we naturally had to struggle with the question of how to get back to Boston.

A line of small American steamers which carried a few

passengers, sailed once a month, but not being able to wait
for the next steamer, we found that our only alternative was
to take an English steamer for Liverpool, via Lisbon, Portugal,
and Coruña, Spain, and thence across the Atlantic to our home
port. Since the war, as I have said before, communication between North and South America has been vastly improved.

One bright afternoon we bade good-bye to Rev. Eleazer dos
Sanctos Saraiva, the energetic secretary of the Brazilian as well
as the South American Union, and our many other Endeavor
friends, and took passage on a British steamer for the other
side of the Atlantic. Our steamer, like others plying between
America and Europe at this time of the year was crowded to
the limit with hundreds of Spanish and Italian workmen returning to their native lands. They were crowded together
in a shameful way and the steerage accommodations were most
wretched and dirty. Hearing that there was a man dying in
the steerage, I found him in the very peak of the ship, where
the motion was excessive. He was lying on a miserable cot,
with nothing but a piece of bocking between him and the
slats, and nobody to look after him except his kindly fellow
passengers of the wretched steerage. He had been put aboard
the ship at Valparaiso by heartless relatives, who, knowing
that he was dying of consumption, wished to get rid of him,
and he had already been at sea several weeks in these dreadful
conditions. I at once found the captain, persuaded him to
detail a steward to look after him and give him a little more
comfort, which he ought to have done without any persuasion.
The poor fellow died the next day.

We stayed in Liverpool just long enough to catch a steamer
which sailed the following day. This voyage I remember in
part because of the churlishness of the captain, who took special delight at the table in saying uncomplimentary things about
America and Americans, and who often monopolized the
shuffle-board equipment when the passengers wished to play.
However he must be forgiven now I suppose, because his good

ship, the "Devonian," was one of the many in which I have sailed, including the "Lusitania," which succumbed at last to a German submarine, and the captain, I understand, bore himself heroically in the disaster.

During these long voyages I had written a book of considerable size about South America, entitled " The Continent of Opportunity." It was fully illustrated, and was received with some favor, going through five editions in the next ten years. I have been pleased to see the title of the book applied to South America by many writers since it was published. In missionary circles it had been the fashion to call it " The Neglected Continent." To my mind the later term is by far the better one, for among all the continents, east and west and north and south, I know of none that presents vaster opportunities for the coming centuries, to the business man, the welfare worker, or the Christian missionary.

CHAPTER XXXII

YEAR 1908

A VARIED YEAR

AN OLD ENEMY — AN OLD FRIEND — HORACE FLETCHER —
FIFTY-ONE PHOTOGRAPHS IN TWENTY-ONE DAYS —
ENGLAND, SPAIN, FRANCE, SCANDINAVIA, HOLLAND — A
CHURCH SERVICE IN GRÖNINGEN — CARRIE NATION'S
HATCHET.

O MAN that is born of woman no more dis-
tressing affliction can come than one that
centres in the nerves. The heavens above
grow black, the grasshopper becomes a
burden, and all desires fail, yet the sufferer
receives little sympathy. " Only a matter of
nerves," his friends are likely to say, yet a serious trouble of
the heart or the lungs, or a broken leg, would be much easier
to bear. This affliction has been mine several times owing to
overwork, as the doctors have always assured me; perhaps it
was over-worry. Whatever the cause my old enemy overcame me again in 1908, and once more, following an attack
of influenza, I was the victim of that horrible monster,
Neurasthenia.

The first six or seven months of the year were spent in the
illusive pursuit of health at Clifton Springs and elsewhere,
but in September I had recovered sufficiently to go abroad, and
to address meetings in several countries, but especially in the
British Christian Endeavor Increase Campaign.

An interesting friend whom I met for the first time on this
voyage was Horace Fletcher, the dietitian, who has the some-

what unique honor of having his name made into a common English noun, verb, and participle, for people speak of Fletcherism, to Fletcherize, and Fletcherizing. He was a most entertaining mortal and we had many a long steamer-deck talk about his speciality, which may be summed up in a single phrase, "Don't eat so much, but eat it more."

He told me the story of his life; how, at fifty years of age, he was completely broken down because of over-indulgence, like many another hail fellow, in the so-called "good things" of life, which often turn out to be the worst things. Not that he was especially dissipated, but he had neglected his health, and expected a premature end.

Then he began seriously to study the situation and his own habits, and to learn that he was eating too much and not eating it enough; so, being a man of resolution, he reduced his allowance, began to masticate his food instead of bolting it and soon not only regained his health, but was able to rival the strong men of the colleges, testing himself with men who were thirty years his junior.

He took incredible bicycle rides before breakfast. He reduced his weight by seventy pounds and began to enjoy life so much that he was able to write some "best sellers" on "Happiness" and "Menticulture," and other books having to do with what he called "Dietetic Righteousness."

I remember that I saw him afterwards at Chautauqua when he was well over sixty years of age, and he could then turn a double somersault from a spring-board into the lake, and come up as fresh and smiling as a boy who had not known a third of his years.

I found out afterwards that he was in Dartmouth College for a few weeks during his freshman year, but was soon lured away by his adventurous spirit to China and Japan, where he became a crack rifle shot, and taught some of the future eminent generals of Japan how to shoot from the shoulder, an art on which he wrote a standard treatise. On account of his early connection with Dartmouth, and his subsequent interesting and adventurous life, the trustees accepted a suggestion from me, and conferred upon him, greatly to his joy, the degree of A.M. more than forty years after he had unceremoniously left the college halls.

The Christian Endeavor World took up his propaganda with enthusiasm and he became a regular contributor, and many of my friends, as well as myself, can testify to the value of Fletcherism. His theories, good as I believe they are, did not greatly prolong his own life, for he died at the age of sixty-nine, in Europe, in war time, while telling the half-starved people how to make a little food go a long way. Perhaps the war if not a bullet killed him as it did so many millions of others.

We landed in Italy, and, after a brief holiday there and in Switzerland, I engaged in a six weeks' Increase Campaign in the United Kingdom, a campaign which was modeled after the successful effort of the same sort which had so largely increased the number of American societies.

Grimsby, Cleveland, Bristol, Sheffield, Manchester, Wrexham, Worcester, London, Norwich, Glasgow, and Edinburgh were among the score or more of cities reached on this my tenth visit to Great Britain.

During my tour through the United Kingdom Mrs. Clark stayed in London, near the British Museum, whither I was able occasionally to return for a day or two. She was engaged in writing a book entitled " The Gospel in Latin Lands " for the Central Committee for the United Study of Missions. To this book I contributed some chapters on South America.

Synchronously with the campaign in Great Britain *The British Weekly* printed a bitter attack on Christian Endeavor from the pen of an anonymous Congregational minister, and then opened its columns to the experiences of ministers *pro* and *con*, evidently, from its editorials, desiring the *con* rather than the *pro*.

The editor soon confessed that enough ministers had responded to fill several numbers of that large paper. Page after page of comments appeared for five or six weeks, but only six or seven of them were adverse criticisms, and as someone said, " in every instance of adverse criticism, the author preferred to blush unseen behind the prudent veil of anonymity." The great majority of replies, however, were favorable, and none who wrote thus were unwilling to sign their names, many of which were known in America as well as in Europe. Thus the first attack turned out to be a boomerang.

Photographers were busy on this trip as usual, and my notebook records fifty-one group pictures in twenty-one places, in six weeks.

Our visit to Spain in this year was of interest because it was just ten years after the Spanish-American War, and I took special pains to learn whether any feeling of enmity still existed among the people against the Republic which had so speedily vanquished the Spanish fleet and army. I could find no signs of rancor or animosity among the people whom I met, and I was assured that the Spaniards generally had settled down to the opinion that few better things had ever happened to their country than the Spanish-American war.

The Endeavor convention in Barcelona was an immense success. From Madrid and Saragoza, from Seville and Bilbao, from San Sebastian and the Balearic Isles, came the Endeavorers with their banners, many of them of exceeding beauty, and the whole convention was full of life and color.

Other meetings I attended in Holland, France, and Scandinavia, I recall particularly a church service in Gröningen, Holland, where I went to address the students of the university. The visit seemed to take us back into the past centuries. Here and there in the great church was a *grande dame* of the old *régime*, who wore the gold or silver headdress of ancient times, a close-fitting skull-cap of gold for the back of the head, and above the ears, ornaments which looked like small mirrors.

After the Scripture-reading and prayer the minister began his sermon. The text was pointed out to us in a huge Dutch Bible as big as a Webster's dictionary, a Bible which had been printed more than a century before. All of my seatmates in the pews near-by followed the reading of the preacher in equally large and ancient tomes, printed in the old German characters which have not been commonly used in Holland for many years.

After the minister had been speaking for about ten minutes he stopped and gave out another Psalm. During the singing a boy took down two very long handled collection bags, and held them up, solemnly, while the collectors first deposited their offerings, thus setting a good example to the rest of the congregation. Then they went their rounds, each one clad in an immaculate dress suit, swallow-tail coat, white necktie, and black gloves, for it is no ordinary function to take up a collection in a Dutch church.

In fact there was not one collection but three, with no intermission between them. The Psalm was finished and the minister began what seemed to be the second part of his sermon, but still the collections went on. For fully half an hour the collectors quietly went their rounds, taking up one offering for the poor, then one for church expenses, and still another for missions, and every man, woman and child within the range of my vision put in something every time.

After the collection the minister gave out another Psalm, and then seemed to continue his sermon for ten or fifteen minutes more. During the sermon one man after another put on his hat, but did not go out. One particularly tall, shiny hat in front of me unpleasantly challenged my attention. Then one and another would stand up and stretch his legs, and after standing for perhaps ten or fifteen minutes, would quietly resume his seat. Yet in spite of these distractions, and in spite of the fact that I could only understand an occasional word of the sermon, I felt the solemnity and sincerity of the service and, doubtless, could I have understood the preacher and known more of the customs of the church, some of the oddities that I observed would have seemed less striking.

On my return to America I was able to enter heartily into a great evangelistic campaign in Boston under the leadership of Dr. J. Wilbur Chapman, whom I regarded as one of the two greatest evangelists; Gypsy Smith, in my opinion, being one of the few to compare with him for ability, real eloquence, and in securing lasting results.

The National Endeavor convention in St. Paul in the summer of 1909 kept up the high reputation of its predecessors. On one of the convention days a stand had been erected on the State-House grounds for an open-air meeting with addresses by Hon. W. J. Bryan and Governor Johnson, then very popular in Minnesota, who died not long after, mourned by all who knew him.

An amusing incident occurred while the speaking was going on. When I went to the temporary platform to introduce the speakers, I had handed to Mrs. Clark the gavel of Minnesota pipestone, ornamented with Minnesota copper, which had been given me by the convention committee. It was in the shape of a miniature tomahawk, and while she was holding it a lady standing near-by said to her, " Excuse me, Madam, but are you Carrie Nation? " The redoubtable " Carrie " was then at the height of her fame as a saloon-smashing temperance propagandist, famous for her " hatchet," and the mistake was perhaps not unnatural as the woman looked at the gavel, but it afforded material for much family fun in after days. It was all the more amusing as Mrs. Clark is by no means an Amazon, nor a woman of belligerent manners.

At this convention another most successful " Increase Campaign " was launched which brought in the course of two years a million young people into the Endeavor movement. Never did the young people take up more enthusiastically any suggestion I ever made than this one. Their eager willingness to respond to any appeal that commends itself to their common-sense, however much labor it involves, has always been a peculiar joy to me. Indeed the harder the work proposed, the more eagerly they take it up. Young Christians do not seek soft seats or easy tasks. I fear I have made such a remark before, but I have been tempted to make it still oftener. No one knows how much I have had to blot. By this time another journey around the world began to loom large upon the horizon, but this unusually interesting journey must be the theme of another chapter.

AROUND THE WORLD IN FOUR MONTHS

PART I

AGRA 1909 — " 600 AMERICAN MILLIONAIRES " — TRAVEL
TALKS AND LECTURES — THE TAJ MAHAL — THE
PRAISES OF THE NATIONS — A CONSECRATION SERVICE
BY LANGUAGES — OUR " ROUND-TOP " MEETING.

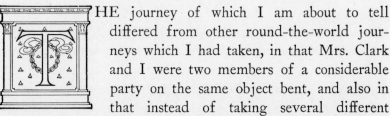 HE journey of which I am about to tell differed from other round-the-world journeys which I had taken, in that Mrs. Clark and I were two members of a considerable party on the same object bent, and also in that instead of taking several different steamers from country to country, as on other journeys, one ship, the Hamburg-American Liner, " Cleveland," carried us all the way from New York to San Francisco, thus entirely encircling the globe with the exception of the width of the American continent. This was the first of the famous round-the-world-tours inaugurated by the company, and was under the charge of the well-known American excursion-manager, Frank G. Clark.

The big steamer was crowded from stem to stern with 650 passengers. Even the steerage department had been made over into " first-class " rooms for the occasion. All were first-class passengers and shared the same fare in the common dining-rooms, and the price of tickets varied according to the accommodations. The trip was widely advertised, and the number of American passengers travelling together, all of whom were reputed to be "millionaires," created much interest and excitement at every port where we landed. The excursion on this huge scale was considered a great success, though, because of the war, it was not many times repeated in after days.

The reason that our particular party joined the excursion was that it afforded a comfortable and moderately economical method of attending the fourth World's Christian Endeavor Convention, which was held in Agra, India. It also enabled all who wished to go, not only to attend the convention, but to encompass the globe at an expense scarcely more than the journey to India alone would have cost. As a consequence, nearly fifty Endeavorers and their friends sailed one bright October day from New York.

In our especial party were General-Secretary Shaw of the United Society, Treasurer Lathrop and his wife, two or three ministers, and a number of veterans of the Christian Endeavor army. Not many young people, however, could afford the expense of the trip. We found many sympathetic friends among the other passengers and formed many pleasant acquaintances.

Several other Endeavorers bound for Agra joined us in Egypt. At least half a dozen books of greater or less merit afterward recorded our adventures; most of them first saw the light in the country papers to which our fellow-passengers contributed.

There were both advantages and disadvantages in this wholesale method of seeing the world. The chief disadvantage was that everybody on board wished to see the same things at the same time, and there was consequently a great congestion as the gang planks were thrown out at different ports, and also at certain points of interest in the various scheduled excursions on land.

However, on the whole, the plans were carefully laid and

admirably carried out, and there were positive advantages in the fact that special pains were taken to open all places of interest to the tourists, and every city visited was in its best clothes and on its best behaviour, to attract as many dollars as possible from the pockets of the " American millionaires." Many cities were gaily decorated with banners and emblems and triumphal arches of welcome. The shops were filled with the largest assortment of the most costly goods, and prices had soared to a dizzy height in anticipation of the expected harvest. When we visited the shops in Yokohama, Tokyo, and Kyoto a few years later, we found a far smaller variety of goods to tempt the foreigner and prices considerably more moderate.

The journey was also made of much educational value to many by frequent lectures and "travel talks" by those of us who had studied up particular countries, or had been over the route before.

We touched briefly at Funchal, Madeira, at Gibraltar, Naples, and had a few days in Cairo on our way to Bombay. At nearly every port from New York to San Francisco, Christian Endeavor meetings were held, often attended by large numbers, while the Sunday services on the steamer crowded the large dining-hall saloon, and were apparently thoroughly enjoyed by all. Most of the passengers, including the Christian Endeavor party, left the steamer at Bombay, and made their way overland to Calcutta, while the " Cleveland " went around the great peninsula and picked up its living freight of Americans on the eastern shore of India.

It may be of interest to relate that the Cleveland being the largest ship that up to that time had gone through the Suez Canal, the passage was a somewhat precarious one. Once the big ship touched bottom, but as all the passengers had gone ashore at Port Said and did not go on board again until she reached Suez, her burden had been lightened enough for her to barely pull through. The toll extorted by the Canal management for this little trip of a few miles was $25,000.

OUR ARRIVAL AT THE CONVENTION CITY, AGRA, 1909

General Secretary Halliwell between Dr. and Mrs. Clark. Dr. Herbert Anderson lifting his hat.
Mr. Hiram N. Lathrop, Excursion Manager, at right with garland.

THE VICEREGAL ENCAMPMENT

Furnished by the British Government for the World's Christian Endeavor Convention in Agra. More than 400 tents all told.

It would be interesting, did space allow, to dwell on the cordial welcome-meeting in Bombay, and to tell of other meetings and receptions, and the visits to Jeypore and Delhi, to Cawnpore and Lucknow and Benares, but the great gatherings in Agra overshadow in my memory the lesser meetings and receptions.

The Agra convention was undoubtedly in many respects the most remarkable gathering of any kind ever held on foreign missionary soil; — remarkable for its numbers, its enthusiasm, and the perfection of its arrangements in all details. The viceregal government of India contributed its whole encampment, consisting of several hundred tents, besides two great audience tents, holding two thousand people each, an immense restaurant-tent, and another large one for the sale of literature. Not only was this enormous encampment contributed by the government free of charge, but it was freely transported from Calcutta to Agra, nearly a thousand miles. Moreover the viceregal government put us under further obligation by contributing the use of Macdonald Park, a little outside of the native city of Agra, and within a quarter of a mile of the Taj Mahal, which all artists admit is the most absolutely perfect specimen of architecture on the face of the globe.

On the morning of our arrival at the grounds we were met by a throng of native Endeavorers who hung garlands of flowers around our necks and greeted us with songs and addresses of welcome. Some of these natives had come long distances at large expense, like the delegation of more than a hundred from Burma, who had travelled some 1,500 miles by land and sea. Others who could not afford railway fare had walked, some for a week, to get to the convention, bringing their scanty outfit and cooking their chupratties on the way in a hole in the ground in lieu of a kitchen range.

Some of these parties of young native Christians made a genuine evangelistic tour of their journey to the convention and return, holding meetings in different towns and villages on the way, and coming to the convention, as can be imagined, in the full glow of religious ardor. Not less than 4,000 native delegates and four hundred missionaries attended the meetings, and at least a dozen foreign countries were represented by missionaries or other delegates.

Many of the meetings were peculiarly inspiring. I recall with special emotion the great song service, where the " Praises of the Nations " were rendered in a most elaborate and appropriate programme. The praises of Europe and America, of Asia and Africa, of ancient and modern times as they were sung, led us to understand as never before the Psalmist's command, " Let *everything* that hath breath praise the Lord."

On account of the difficulties of language, two simultaneous meetings were usually held, one tent accommodating those who understood English, while in the other Hindostani was spoken. There were representatives of more than thirty languages in that cosmopolitan throng, and when the consecration meeting was held all united in one great audience to renew their vows of allegiance and reaffirm their pledge of service.

There was only one way in which the roll-call in such a consecration meeting could be conducted, and that was by calling the list of languages. As it fell to my lot to conduct this meeting, I asked each group giving its testimony in song or word to speak in the tongue in which its members were born, however many other languages they might have acquired. So in Hindi and Hindostani, in Bengali and Marathi, in Tamil and Telugu, in Burmese and Karen, and in twenty other languages the responses came. Sometimes a great company would stand together when the language happened to be the native tongue of many. At other times only two or three or a half dozen stood together while, when the Thibetan tongue was called, only one solitary individual arose to tell of his devotion to the Master. Of course the Euro-

WORLD'S CHRISTIAN ENDEAVOR CONVENTION IN AGRA

A few of the delegates and some of the tents furnished by the Viceregal Government of India. Literature pavilion, one audience tent to the extreme right, others are sleeping-tents for native delegates. 400 tents in all composed the White City of Agra, 1909.

pean languages were not omitted, and responses came in French and English, Spanish and Swedish, in German and Norwegian, from this wonderful cosmopolitan throng.

There were many scenes of exceeding picturesqueness. One Endeavorer had come on his camel, still another had come on a borrowed elephant, and though most of the native converts were poor and from the humbler castes, some fair-skinned high-caste Brahmins were in the throng, and at least one high native official with his wife and daughters who were bespangled with gold and jewels to a surprising extent.

The marvellous attractions of the Taj Mahal, the Pearl Mosque, and the vast Sandstone Fort in which ten thousand soldiers might get lost were not neglected, yet the delegates stuck with wonderful persistence to the convention during all the sessions. Many of the most eminent missionaries of India were present, like William Carey the third, of whom I have before spoken, Dr. Herbert Anderson of Calcutta, Dr. Robert Hume of Ahmednager, Bishop Warne of the Methodist Episcopal Church, Mr. Bandy and Mr. McGaw of the Presbyterian Mission, and nearly a score of well-known missionaries from Burma. Indeed it is useless to attempt to mention all who helped make this meeting what it was, lest my pages become a mere catalogue of names. This was my third view of the Taj, and each visit has impressed me more than the last with its unique majesty and beauty. Whether seen in blazing mid-day sunlight, in the dusk of twilight, or under the full Indian moon, no flaws can be detected in this marvellous piece of human handicraft. One day the delegates to the convention went in procession to have their pictures taken in the beautiful garden which fronts the main entrance to the Taj, and thither Mrs. Clark and I were borne at the request of the Endeavorer who boasted an elephant, on the back of his huge beast. There was no ladder by which to climb to our seats, and no howdah to which to hold, and it was a most precarious journey, though fortunately a short one, from the park to the entrance of the great Tomb. We succeeded in scrambling up the mountainous elephant and in holding on to each other and to one or two other members of the party, who essayed the slippery bareback trip with us.

One of the most impressive meetings of the convention was not scheduled on the programme. In fact it did not take place until the convention had formally adjourned. It was hours before the tents could all be struck, and the thousands of pieces of furniture be carried out on the backs of coolies, so that many were detained for a whole day after the meetings closed. Early in the morning of that supplementary day, several hundreds of us found our way to a little rise of ground just outside of the encampment, which we called our "Round Top," for a closing sunrise service. It was in the delicious cool of the Indian morning before the burning sun appeared.

Dr. Shaw had discovered on the top of the hill a rude cross made of two straws, which a native Christian had evidently placed there at his morning devotions. Dr. William Carey, who had charge of this meeting, turned this to good account. With all the wisdom and fervor of his great grandfather, he held this little cross in his hand, and pointing to the magnificent Taj which loomed up in all its glory, apparently but a few rods away, he spoke somewhat as follows: "Yonder is the noblest memorial of human love, the love of man for woman, of the Great Mogul for his beloved Empress, but here in my hand I hold the supreme symbol of Divine Love; no vast mausoleum of marble and precious stones, but a simple cross, reminding us that He died for mankind, and that 'The way of the Cross leads home.'"

Thus ended this memorable convention, but I should not be doing justice to those who made it such a success did I not pay a brief word of tribute to Rev. Herbert Halliwell, General Secretary of the Indian Christian Endeavor Union, and

THE TAJ MAHAL

Visit of some of the delegates at the Agra Convention to the Taj Mahal, the most wonderful tomb in the world.

the committee who labored untiringly with him for the success of the meetings.

All went away feeling not only that a genuine inspiration had been received, but that a permanent impression had been made by the Christian forces of India, a view borne out by the rapid growth of the Christian Endeavor societies in the Empire in the years after "Agra 1909."

AROUND THE WORLD IN FOUR MONTHS

PART II

JAVA — THE WILD MEN OF BORNEO — OPEN HOUSE IN
THE PHILIPPINES — TROUBLOUS CHINA — HOSPITABLE
JAPAN — BEAUTIFUL HONOLULU — HOME AGAIN.

HEN the serious business of the convention
was over the delegates felt at liberty to take
as many excursions as the time at their disposal would permit. One of the most interesting of these was to the deserted city
of Fatehpur-Sikri, about twenty miles from
Agra. It seems marvellous that a splendid city should be
deserted for hundreds of years and yet show so few signs
of decay, but in the marvellous climate of India the tooth of
time does not seem to gnaw stone and mortar as in other
lands. For this reason, the Taj, though built four hundred
years ago, is as perfect and untarnished as when it came from
the hands of its great architect.

It is still more wonderful that Fatehpur-Sikri should have
been deserted at all while its forts and its palaces, its sultana
houses and even its mint and its splendid mosque were still
intact. The chief mosque is still in a wonderful state of
preservation, and is said to be a copy of the famous mosque
at Mecca. Fatehpur-Sikri was built by the great Emperor
Akbar, at the behest of a Mohammedan hermit-saint who
lived in a cave near-by. Upon obeying the saint, the great

desire of his life was granted, and a son and heir was born, who afterwards became the Emperor Jehangir, who surpassed Akbar himself in fame and glory.

Jeypore, Delhi, Cawnpore, each had their own points of special interest. The physical and moral filth of Benares and its hundreds of pilgrims bathing in the germ-laden waters of the Ganges, and the dead pilgrims sizzling on the burning ghats on its banks seemed to afford a weird fascination for some of our fellow travellers.

Reaching Burma we did not go far " on the road to Mandalay," but lingered for a few days in Rangoon and Insein, where the Christian Endeavor meetings were only second in importance to those in Agra. Here the Baptists have a remarkably fruitful work which extends far into the interior of Burma and to the borders of Siam. An audience of 2,000 people was easily gathered in one of their great halls, for no mission has been more hospitable to Christian Endeavor than this. The success of missionaries had stirred up the Buddhists to new activities, and to enthusiastic worship. The great Shwe Dagon Pagoda, the real world centre of Buddhism, seemed most popular, and the Buddhist propaganda was remarkably active. The colporteurs of the " Buddhist Tract Society " distributed literature in English to us, deriding Christianity and praising Buddhism, and I was told that a Buddhist Endeavor society had also been started to counteract the influence of Christian Endeavor.

Our excursion-manager had provided for us as many breaks in the long journey from India to China as could be managed, and we made interesting stops at such seldom-visited places as Batavia in Java and Labuan in British North Borneo.

In the beautiful city of Batavia the excursionists were welcomed by hundreds of pleasant-faced Javanese, who all seemed as jolly as sand-boys. A large number of odd little carriages drawn by diminutive ponies came to the station to transport the passengers to the sights of the city. The early drivers very carefully picked for the lean and hungry Cassius-like people of the party, leaving the well-fed and rotund for the cabbies who came later. We understood the reason for this partiality when a very stout lady, climbing into the back of the little chaise, almost lifted the pony from his feet as she weighed down the back end, much to the amusement of her fellow-passengers.

The neat, well-trimmed gardens of Batavia, the charming country residences, the canals by the roadside all reminded us of Holland, for the rulers of Java had evidently brought their Dutch ideas of order and cleanliness with them, greatly to the benefit of the native race.

At Labuan " the wild men of Borneo " had been imported, from nobody knew where, for the delectation of the tourists. I suspect that their bushy hair and beards had been allowed to grow long for the occasion; that they were dressed in a garb that looked as fantastic to them as to us, and that they were instructed to roar in a wild and passionate way as they performed the Dance of the Head-Hunters. No doubt in private life we should have found these actors very tame and peaceable individuals, and possibly excellent citizens, but they did their best to live up to the expectations of the tourists, and to our boyhood traditions of the wild men of Borneo.

At Manila we found the town wide open, not in the offensive bibulous sense, though doubtless plenty of booze could have been found, but wide open in its hospitality to the greatest crowd of fellow-Americans who had ever visited its hospitable shores since our occupation of the island.

The street-car conductors would take no fares from the tourists, the restaurants furnished free lunches on certain occasions, and I am almost inclined to remember that the waiters would take no tips, though at this distance of time that seems quite improbable.

I was much impressed with the progress that the island had made during the few short years they had been under the care of our government. The splendid roads, the good schools taught by teachers who are thoroughly interested in their work, and the swarms of bright-eyed little Filipino pupils showed what could be done for backward races in a very short time. However I am glad to know that the benevolent despotism of that period has gradually given way to a larger and larger participation of the native peoples in the government of their own country, and I trust that before long it will be wise and possible for us to redeem our early promises and make the islands a free and independent nation.

In these islands, as well as in all other parts of the uncivilized or half-civilized parts of the globe that I have visited, the missionaries have had the largest share in the uplift of the people. Some of the brightest pages of American history have been written by the missionaries who have gone to the Philippines, and in many parts of them they are still the one great leavening and uplifting force.

China, though the biggest country of all which we visited on this journey, received for various reasons the scantiest attention. The periodical political troubles which have racked China for the last half-century were then acute. Not, to be sure, as serious as on our last visit in 1900, at the time of the Boxer uprising, but still sufficiently troublesome to make any extended tour unadvisable. In fact our excursion-manager was warned not to take his party up the Pearl River from Hong Kong to Canton lest the presence of so large a number of Americans would be misunderstood, and would cause offensive riots and perhaps bloodshed.

However on consultation it was decided to risk it, and when we reached Canton great crowds of scowling Chinese crowded the wharves and lined the roadside as we walked up to the city. Some of the good ladies in the party were mortally afraid of these black looks and evidently thought that their last hour had come. But great precautions were taken by the authorities, a large force of police was called out, and one policeman detailed for every eight foreigners. Our chairs and jinrikishas were carefully guarded, and nothing untoward happened throughout the day, while the merchants in jade, ginger, and Chinese kickshaws did a " land-office business."

The contrast between the police arrangements which I saw on this occasion and my memories of my first visit to Canton eighteen years before, was decidedly in favor of the new China. The ragged, dirty guardians of the law whom I remembered had been replaced by well-clad " coppers " in handsome uniforms, who thoroughly understood their business. The city seemed more thriving and prosperous, the open sewers less obnoxious, and the more than " seventy smells of Cologne " which I remembered had been reduced by at least a score.

Two weeks were spent in Japan, and the visit of the " Cleveland's " excursionists was a triumphal welcome all the way from Nagasaki to Tokyo. The streets were dressed in their gayest bunting; beautiful arches erected for the occasion bore emblems of cordial greetings; elaborate functions with flowery addresses of good will from municipal authorities had been arranged, and though doubtless the Japanese had an eye to the main chance and expected that a good many American dollars would be left behind by the " millionaires," the welcome, I believe, was entirely genuine. In all the visits to that country that I have made, I have found a sincere liking for Americans and things American. The common people regard us as their best friends among all foreign nations. Commodore Perry is one of their patron saints, and, in spite of the abominable way in which the Japanese have at times been treated in this country, and their national pride wounded by unfair discriminations, the genuine friendship that exists between the two nations has, though menaced, never been destroyed. We will have only ourselves to blame if this most progressive nation of the Orient ever becomes our enemy.

I was surprised to learn from one source and another that

I was being very seriously criticised by some missionaries and in some Christian Japanese papers, because I was " promoting

TRIUMPHAL ARCH IN NAGASAKI
Welcoming the American tourists.

the open desecration of the Lord's day," " providing Geisha dances for the delectation of the passengers," and doing other things of a like nature inconsistent with my profession and professions. So during some days of my stay in Japan I was kept busy writing to the papers, telling them that I was not Frank C. Clark, the excursion-manager, but Francis E. Clark, who had nothing to do with the arrangements, and had indeed protested against the desecration of the Sabbath, which in a measure had been forced upon the passengers because the steamer had been scheduled to make its stops largely on Sunday at the different ports. A protest meeting of some of the leading passengers, held about this time, had a good effect, and the manager, who was not altogether to blame in the matter, was able to change the rest of the schedule more to the satisfaction of most of us.

The most memorable reception to the passengers of the "Cleveland" was given by Count Okuma at his delightful villa in the suburbs of Tokyo. To this he generously invited all the hundreds of Americans. In a beautifully decorated marquee, pitched in his spacious grounds, refreshments, and especially ices, so dear to the American palate, were served in great abundance. Japanese jugglers performed their wonderful sleight-of-hand tricks, to our heart's content, and a moving-picture camera made a permanent record of the gay scene.

In his very cordial address of welcome the Count spoke highly of the Christian Endeavor movement, and referred to my former visit, which I was surprised to have him remember. On this and many other occasions on the voyage, since the number of public speakers in our party was limited, it fell to my lot most frequently to reply to these kindly addresses, though the Rev. Mr. Vittum, an eloquent preacher from Iowa, Dr. Shaw, and others, shared these pleasant duties.

It was said that the straw mattings in the section of the villa furnished in Japanese style, suffered not a little from the rude footwear of the American guests, but if so, the Count showed no sign of irritation at any unconscious vandalism, but, together with the Countess, moved about among his guests in the most genuine, friendly, and democratic way.

An event of much interest to me occurred on the very day of our sailing from Yokohama, — an audience with his Majesty, Mutsuhito, the Emperor of Japan. This unusual honor was conferred for no personal merit, but because the missionaries felt that it would be a recognition of the Christian forces at work in Japan.

The arrangements for the audience had been made in part before I reached Japan, engineered largely by Dr. J. H. DeForest, the statesman-missionary, who had much influence in government circles. Hon. J. T. O'Brien, our American ambassador, entered heartily into the plan, and had made the final arrangements.

Some Japanese authorities, however, doubtless did not see any necessity for breaking precedents and allowing a religious worker from America, of whom probably they knew little, personally to meet the "All-Highest" of Japan, who was regarded by most of his subjects as clothed with divine functions. So one excuse after another put off the audience until, as Mr. O'Brien told me, the "embassy chose to be offended," and forthwith, on the last day of the "Cleveland's" visit, the hour was fixed for the audience.

In regulation court regalia, though it was only eleven o'clock in the morning, — dress suit, white gloves, white necktie, and tall hat, — accompanied by Mr. O'Brien, similarly arrayed, we drove in state in the embassy carriage, to the marvellous old palace. Crossing the wide moat we came to the door of the palace, and were ushered by various flunkeys and court officers through interminable corridors, all decorated with the royal emblem, the chrysanthemum, until we came to the waiting-room, where we were entertained by the Emperor's chamberlain. After a few minutes a messenger appeared to tell us that His Majesty was ready to receive us. Crossing the corridor we bowed low three times

before reaching the Emperor, according to the court requirements. He cordially shook hands, and through an interpreter who stood by, asked several very easily answered
questions, like, "When did you arrive in Japan?" "Did
you have a good passage?" "When do you expect to sail?"
etc.

Ambassador O'Brien had told me in advance that the Emperor would ask "a few fool questions" and that as it was
not proper for us to initiate any conversation, or make any
original remarks, my part of the interview would be very
simple. He also told me that the only person who has been
able to break through the court barriers was former Vice-
President Fairbanks, the last person he had taken to the
palace, some six months previous to my visit. Mr. Fairbanks
ventured some remarks and questions of his own which the
Emperor did not resent, doubtless owing to the official rank
of his visitor, nor did he object to the absence of Mr. Fairbanks' white gloves, which, at the last moment, the genial
vice-president had forgotten.

In spite of the formality of the interview, it was a most
interesting occasion to me, not only because of the personality
of the Emperor, but because of the line that he represented.
He was then fifty-eight years old, tall for his race, dignified
and courtly, with a sharp but kindly eye.

He shook hands with a good firm grip, and one felt in his
presence that he was speaking to no princely puppet, or merely
titular ruler, but one who had kingly qualities within himself.
For forty-three years he had been Emperor of Japan, and
marvellous changes had occurred during his reign. He was
the 121st Emperor in the same imperial line, and in respect
to the antiquity of his royal house no other ruler in the world
could compare with him. The Hohenzollerns and the Hapsburgs were mere infants of days as compared with Japan's
rulers, for the Japanese trace their royal line back to Jimmu
Teno and to the year 660 B.C. If we deal only with authen-

tic history we can go back to the year 500 A.D. and find the
ancestors of his Majesty's forbears on the throne fourteen
hundred years ago, and there has been no break in the succession since.

The reverence of the people of Japan for their Emperor
is almost pathetic. Some of my Japanese friends, who were
much impressed by the fact that I had had audience with their
Emperor, asked me if I had to go into his presence on my
hands and knees, and when I told them that I walked in on
my two feet, and actually shook hands with his majesty they
were quite amazed. Such extreme reverence, though it may
have its weaknesses, seems to me better than the irreverence
of the American small boy for his ruler, who would speak
of " Teddy Roosevelt," or " Woody Wilson " or " Hardy
Harding," as though they were his chums in the old swim-
ming-hole.

Mutsuhito was almost the last connecting link between old
Japan and new. He had seen his country shake off the
shackles of two thousand years of Chinese and Korean civilization, and adopt western methods of business, government, and
dress, the last a very doubtful blessing. It is safe to say that
no ruler in the history of the world had seen more marvellous
changes in his domain during his reign, and few have borne
themselves more wisely than " Mutsuhito, the Great."

The same day of the audience with the Emperor the
" Cleveland " sailed on almost the last lap of its journey to
San Francisco, charming Honolulu being the only other
stopping-place. Here, too, we had a great welcome, not only
from the hundreds of Endeavorers, but from the inhabitants
generally, and receptions, luaus, rides to the Pali, and public
meetings were the order of the day during our brief stay.
My second son, Harold, was then teaching in Oahu College,
so that Mrs. Clark and I had reason for unusual joy in this
last halting-place.

The steamer anchored for quarantine inspection some miles

out of the harbor, an inspection which took an unconscionably long time. In the meantime several small harbor boats with many friends on board had come out to meet our steamer. Unhappily for them the wind rose, and the waves mounted high, but our gruff and surly captain, who had often showed himself unaccommodating, would not take them on board, as he easily might have done, but, deathly seasick and drenched to the skin by the waves, they had to bear it as well as they could, until it pleased him to make the harbor.

No further incidents of importance occurred after leaving Honolulu, and in five days the friends of a four months' cruise separated at San Francisco, to pursue many different paths for their life's journey. Warm and enduring friendships had been formed, and many indelible mental pictures had been painted. Three or four books in my library, presented by as many fellow-passengers, give their impressions of this memorable journey.

While Mrs. Clark went straight home to her children with some travelling-companions who were going in the same direction, Dr. Shaw and I fulfilled many engagements on the Pacific Coast and in Canada. In these meetings we tried to make the Occidental Endeavorers better acquainted with, and more sympathetic towards, their Oriental brethren whom we had seen in these months of travel. One result of all such journeys is that they tend to bring the East and the West nearer together, not diplomatically, nor by trade relations, but in human sympathy, and by a realization of the common ties that bind Christ's followers in all lands.

IN THE GOOD OLD SUMMER TIME

FROM THE MAINE COAST TO CAPE COD — A HOUSE FOR $550.
— THE CHARMING MAINE COAST — WHY WE CHOSE
SAGAMORE — REFORMING AN ABANDONED FARM — RE-
JUVENATING AN OLD HOUSE.

URING the later years of my pastorate in
Portland, and throughout all the summers
of my Boston pastorate, and for nearly a
score of years afterwards, whenever we were
in America, we had spent our summers in
a little pine cottage on the coast of Maine,
where a colony of Portland people had established themselves some two miles on the Portland side of Old Orchard.

Not without reason, the colony voted to call the place
" Grand Beach," for it is certainly one of the finest beaches
in the world. Smooth as a floor, the hard sand gradually
slopes out into the ocean for six hundred feet at low tide,
affording safe bathing ground, while the surf rolls in end-
lessly on majestic waves.

Our first little pine cottage, painted a cheerful red, cost all
of $550. It seems incredible in these days of high prices,
that a two-story cottage with seven rooms could be built for
that very moderate sum, but so it was, and it afforded a happy
summer refuge for us for many years. Afterwards, a growing family made it imperative to build a larger cottage,
though still a very unpretentious one, at what would now be
considered a very unpretentious price.

More than most people I have prized my summer homes, for of late years they have given me almost my only chance for family life, which most men with a more stable habitation can enjoy the year round. Now that my grandchildren have come, we look forward to their visits with their fathers and mothers as among the green oases in life's journey.

Early in the new century the Christian Endeavor leaders began to feel that a summer home would be desirable, not only for themselves individually, but for the movement at large, where we might gather socially, and for occasional conferences. At the instance of Mr. George B. Graff, who was then the publication manager of the United Society, a number of us went to look at Sagamore Beach, some two miles from the village of Sagamore. Here Cape Cod begins to stretch out its long curved arm into the sea. The doubled-up fist, or according to the conceit of somebody, the beckoning finger, at Provincetown, is sixty miles from Sagamore by land, but only twenty-eight by sea across Cape Cod Bay. We found the shore and hinterland a rough and inhospitable place in those days, but we saw rare possibilities. The Bay stretched out its broad waters invitingly; a very fair beach made bathing and water sports practicable, and the rising ground behind, covered with scrub pines, in a kind of terrace-like formation, afforded ample building lots for a large colony.

The land near the shore, however, was covered with a dense growth of tangled, thorny shrubs, and, as I remember my first visit, it seems incredible that in so short a time a flourishing colony with some sixty cottages, two hotels, water-works, and electric lights, should have been built up.

The original colonists were Christian Endeavorers, who desired a quiet summer home amid good moral and religious surroundings for themselves and their children. After a time many other colonists arrived and Sagamore Beach largely lost its early distinctive quality, though it still remained a community of pleasant, friendly people. Many of us were greatly disappointed that our original plans could not be fully carried out, but we had to accept the inevitable when bankruptcy stared the colony in the face, on account of the high cost of roads, water-works, etc.

Yet the social, friendly atmosphere of the place is still very delightful. Each year " Colony Day " is observed, and on that day most of the colonists dress in Puritan costume in memory of the fact that the " Mayflower " passengers sailed around our Sagamore coast from Provincetown, where they first landed, to Plymouth their final abode, which is only a few miles from Sagamore as the gulls fly.

A Christian Endeavor conference was held every summer for several years, until its growing numbers compelled its removal to Northfield, where more ample accommodations can be secured.

A sociological conference was also held yearly for some time, under the leadership of Mr. George W. Coleman, who was so long identified with the Christian Endeavor movement as advertising manager of its newspaper organ, and who is now a trustee of the United Society. I have already spoken of the many honors which have been his.

It is no wonder that I was early drawn to cast in my lot with this new colony, though it was something of a wrench for my family and myself to tear ourselves away from the long-time, happy associations with the coast of Maine. In 1908, having disposed of my Grand Beach property to my oldest son, I built a cottage on one of Sagamore's sand hills, — a home which we called " The Dunes," and to which we transferred our affections as well as our summer " Lares and Penates."

For many years farm hunger had been growing upon me, and, the appetite increasing with age, we had made many excursions into the country, hoping to find an ideal abiding-place for our declining years, which we might also occasionally visit before the grasshopper should become altogether a burden. None of these excursions had been very fruitful, however, but soon after the Sagamore colony was organized, we discovered an abandoned farm lying on the very edge of the colony, with which we both fell in love at first sight. One bright November day we made an excursion to look the old place over more thoroughly before deciding to purchase, and a few hours spent in the Sunken Orchard, under the old apple

THE ABANDONED OLD FARM HOUSE AT SAGAMORE BEACH
Partially Reformed.

trees, whose red-cheeked fruit lay all around us, to be had for the picking up, completed the conquest of the farm.

As soon as possible I bought the old house with several acres of land that surrounded it, for a few hundred dollars. Various additions to the first purchase have been made from time to time, until now, I have, all told, some twenty-five acres of woodland and tillage, old orchards and new orchards, pine tree hills and sunken valleys, so peculiar to the topography of Cape Cod. This is the joy of my heart, and when in America, we spend many happy weeks in the spring and fall in the old farmhouse, often going to the cottage on the shore during the summer's hottest months. Hither come the children and grandchildren, and here we have established the home of our sunset years.

"My word!" as our English friends would say, but the farm was an abandoned one, when first we became acquainted with it! Indeed, it seemed as though it could never be re-formed. The old house, built in 1690, had apparently enjoyed no repairs for a century. A horse was contentedly munching his hay in the kitchen, when we first saw it. A slack and disorderly family had occupied a room or two which were only partially rain-proof. The land had been starved for as many years as the house had been neglected, and had to be well "fed up" before it would produce any worth-while crops. Yet the frame of the house was still there and capable of repair. Better than all, the cypress and pine trees, and the old apple trees, the Sunken Orchard, and Pine-Tree Knoll and a lovely view of the sea and the Cape Cod canal were there. In the course of years, by the steady work of excellent Portuguese laborers from the Cape Verde Islands, with whom Cape Cod abounds, the abandoned farm has taken on a large degree of respectability. The woods have been cleared of decaying brush and useless trees, young orchards have been planted, the spring in the old sink-hole has been cleared out, and has spread itself into a lovely little duck pond, surrounded by black alders, willows and tangled grape vines and covered with water-lilies. The old house, with the help of a skilful architect, after a few years was remodeled without destroying or injuring the old lines.

The house has the advantage of having even harbored a ghost; for what ancient house in New England would be without this attraction? I have been solemnly informed by an old man who lived there, that he has often seen the wraith of Father Crowell, one of the earlier inhabitants, lying in the little bedroom off the great living-room, and has smelled the synthetic coffee and doughnuts which Mother Crowell would prepare every morning before daylight for her ghostly family. However my own eyes and nostrils are not sufficiently acute to detect the presence of these disembodied spirits, and our occupancy of the farmhouse has never been disputed by any former resident. I shall take occasion in a later chapter to tell about the more thorough reformation of the old home which I have come to love so much.

THE LILY POND IN THE "SUNKEN ORCHARD"
Sagamore Beach.

As has happened to many another family when the children become old enough to leave the home-nest, our house in Auburndale became too large for the sole occupancy of Mrs. Clark and myself, and as our duties frequently called us to spend much time in other countries than our own, " Hillcrest " was vacant much of the time for several years after the death of my adopted mother, and the departure of our children for

college or for homes of their own. At length, though very
much to our regret, it seemed best to sell our much-loved
home overlooking the Charles River and the Weston Hills,
and thus save the money which might be applied to better uses
than maintaining the claims of sentiment and pleasant
memories. It was with sincere regret that we left our friends
in Auburndale, the beautiful village, which, at two widely
separated intervals in my life, had been my happy home.

THE CLARK FAMILY TO-DAY

Dr. and Mrs. Clark, their daughter, three sons, two daughters-in-law, and
seven grandchildren. The son-in-law was absent when the picture was taken.

As can be imagined, there are not a few real disadvantages
in a life broken by long journeys as mine has been for so
many years. One misses the companionship of old and tried
friends, loses touch with church, denominational, town, and
village interests, to some extent; becomes of less use in
narrower circles of religious and community life, as he is
obliged to spread himself more thinly over a larger area.

I have often wished that I might allow my roots to run more deeply into the soil, instead of transplanting them temporarily so often. Yet there are compensations and privileges which one must not forget. As I think of the tens of thousands of worthy and interesting people whom I have met in many lands, of their kindly greetings and affectionate remembrances; as I receive their letters from every land, full of genuine interest; as every daily paper becomes of more interest because it tells of the places we have seen, and recalls the friends who live in them, I feel that even a word of complaint concerning the disadvantages of a wandering life is unworthy, and that I should not forget to say of these unusual and undeserved advantages, " the lines have fallen unto me in pleasant places; yea, I have a goodly heritage," even if it is chiefly a heritage of memories and friendships.

CHAPTER XXXVI

YEAR 1911

IN OLD HOMES OF NEW AMERICANS

A LONG ZIGZAG JOURNEY — ITS PURPOSE, TO ACQUAINT AMERI-
CANS WITH AUSTRO-HUNGARIAN IMMIGRANTS — POLAND
— RUSSIA — PETTY PROHIBITIONS — CRACOW — CZER-
NOVITZ — WHERE A CAMERA IS A NOVELTY — ROUMANIA
— CROATIA.

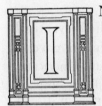

I N THE fall of 1911 again the call seemed to come to visit the "regions beyond," where Christian Endeavor was gaining a struggling foothold, and where I felt that I might perhaps help it to a larger life. Our chief objective was Russian Poland, Galicia, and the smaller countries then under the sway of the Austro-Hungarian monarchy from which so many immigrants had come to our own land during the preceding quarter-century.

Our plans expanded as we journeyed, and, before we reached home again we had visited each one of the seven cities of Asia to which the messages in the Book of Revelation were sent, and also as many of the cities which St. Paul made memorable as we could in the time at our disposal.

But that is another story, and this chapter deals chiefly with the various nationalities of the country then called Austro-Hungary and its neighbors on the east. I had long felt that there was a woeful ignorance in America of the immigrants who have come to us by the million from this part of Europe; an ignorance which breeds not only indifference, but the contempt that is well set forth in Robert Haven Schauffler's poem,

" The Scum of the Earth," and in Bishop McIntyre's verses
which begin:

> " Dago and Sheeny and Chink,
> Greaser and Nigger and Jap.
> The devil invented these terms I think,
> To hurl at each hopeful chap
> Who comes so far o'er the foam
> To this land of his heart's desire,
> To rear his brood, to build his home,
> And to kindle his hearthstone fire.
> While the eyes with joy are blurred,
> Lo! we make the strong man shrink,
> And stab his soul with the hateful words,
> Dago and Sheeny and Chink."

The double purpose of this journey resulted eventually
in the publication of three books, to one of which I gave the
title that heads this chapter, " Old Homes of New Americans,"
published in 1913 by Houghton and Mifflin Company;
another, entitled, " The Holy Land of Asia Minor," describing the present appearance of the Seven Cities of Revelation,
which was published by Scribners in 1914.

The third and largest book of the three, published by
Putnams in 1917, was entitled, " In the Footsteps of St. Paul,"
and was the result in part of a later journey, in which we
finished the round of more than thirty cities which the great
Apostle had dwelt in for a longer or shorter time in his early
life, or in the course of his great missionary journeys.

These books were written partly during a somewhat prolonged stay in Athens, partly on steamer journeys, and partly
after reaching America again, and owe not a little of what
merit they may have to my wife's urgency and ever-ready
typewriter, which together with her busy fingers, were often
at my disposal, as well as her valued criticisms and suggestions.

The 1911 journey, begun in the early fall, took us first to
Rotterdam. A few days in Holland gave us an opportunity

to go to the tip end of the Great Dyke, the Helder, which *holds* in the furious North Sea from overwhelming the polders of the low country. Here we found a Christian Endeavor enthusiast who hoped to make the movement a power in Holland, an ambition which now seems likely to be realized, but which, like many other good projects, was interrupted by the cruel war of the nations.

Then came some memorable days in Germany, with a great convention in Cassel, which so crowded the halls where it was held that standing-room was often at a premium. As I think of the dear friends whom I met on that and during longer sojourns in Germany, I cannot believe that the heart of the German people is as callous and blood-thirsty as the literature of England and America in war-time would have us believe.

I think that President Wilson was far more nearly right than the militarists and penny-a-liners who lost no opportunity to berate the German people, when he declared that it is the militarism of the leaders that we are fighting, and that the true spirit of Germany is the spirit of its poets, and its devout Christians, of its early philosophers and reformers, rather than that of its Nietzsches and its Prussian war-lords, who did so much to bring about the world-wide catastrophe.

We took advantage of our brief stay in Cassel to hunt up (with some difficulty) the home where the Brothers Grimm wrote their household stories which were the delight of my boyhood more than any other books save perhaps " The Swiss Family Robinson." It is an unpretentious gable-roofed house, with a tobacconist's shop underneath, and a tablet marking the place where the famous masters of the fairy story wrote their tales. It was while we were there that we heard an amusing little story of the brothers. In one of their fairy tales is an account of a tailor who ended by marrying a princess, and the story closes with these words, " Whoever does not believe this story must give me a mark." It is told that a little girl one day knocked at the door of the Brothers Grimm, and said,

"I have read your story of a tailor, and I cannot believe it. I don't believe that a tailor ever married a princess. I haven't as much money as a mark, but here is a ten pfennig piece, and I will bring the rest as soon as I can." I do not vouch for the truth of this story, but it seems to me not improbable, so realistic is the impression made by many of these tales.

After attending a number of conventions and rallies in Germany we made our first essay into Poland, where I had been invited by the Lutheran pastor of Pabianice, to attend an Endeavor convention for Russian Poland. It was no easy matter, even in those days, to cross the border between Germany and Russia, and my passport though it was duly signed by Elihu Root, Secretary of State, and bore the great gold seal of the United States, had to be viséd seemingly at every crossroad after leaving Germany.

Moreover the Russian authorities at the border, disregarding the divine command, "What God hath joined together, let not man put asunder," tried long and earnestly to prevent Mrs. Clark from following me through the wicket-gate that led from Germany into Russia, because the passport did not give her name, but simply said that I was accompanied by my wife, and how did they know that this little woman was my wife rather than some bloodthirsty anarchist with a bomb for the Czar concealed about her person? However, after much argument and consultation, and the untying of numerous bundles of red tape, they decided to make her a present of a name, and christened her "Mary" upon the passport, so that she had to remember that while in Russia her name was Mary and not Harriet.

Pabianice we found to be a thriving manufacturing town in the suburbs of the great industrial city of Lödz. When we reached the railway station we saw a lady eagerly scanning the cars as they passed, and when she saw us looking out of the window, she frantically beckoned to us to get out, though we had been told to go on to Lödz, the next station.

In the meantime she had begged the station master to delay the train one minute and had sent a porter to one end of the train, and a gentleman she had found in the station to the other end, showing them each a photograph of myself, while

POLISH PEASANTS
A remote village in Russian Poland.

she anxiously looked at each car from the platform. It was a very long train and she had only three minutes in which to find some strangers who were not expecting to get off there, and whom neither she nor either of her messengers had ever seen. But she did it, and triumphantly escorted us to the pleasant, comfortable parsonage in due time. With such an example of executive ability we had no doubt that the convention which she and her husband had arranged would be a success, as proved to be the case.

Young people had come from many parts of Russian Poland, some from a distance of 250 miles, with an intelligent zeal and devotion that spoke well for the training of their churches and societies. As on so many other occasions it was found difficult to obtain a good intepreter for my addresses. At last the problem was solved by impressing into the service the wealthiest man in town, the owner of great cotton and woolen mills. I understood afterwards that he was anything but a religious man, and I fear that he was greatly bored in having to translate a gospel sermon, which I had been asked to give, as well as an address upon the principles and practice of Christian Endeavor. However, he was polite enough not to express such feelings, if he had them.

I was much impressed with the splendid manufacturing plants of this vicinity. Here I saw the best American machinery and the latest improvements in sanitation and hygiene, which we do not usually expect to find in a country which we have always considered backward and unenterprising. But this part of what was then Russian Poland manufactured goods for all of Russia, and had grown rich on its almost unlimited clientele.

Though the Jews were not then allowed to work in the mills the streets were full of frowsy long-bearded Hebrews in skull caps and gaberdines that reached to their heels. They were the shop-keepers of the neighborhood, the peddlers and the petty tradesmen, and were heartily disliked by the Poles for their sharp practices. To these practices, however, they had been driven by years of persecution. Foxes and weasels can live only because they are sly, and are able to take an intellectual advantage of their stronger and more stupid enemies.

Warsaw, as we expected, we found to be a great and thriving city worthy of its ancient lineage and history. Some months before starting on this journey I had been asked to address an Endeavor meeting in Riga, on the Baltic Sea, where lived some very earnest advocates of the movement. So, knowing the difficulties that would undoubtedly be put in the way of any humble American preacher who wanted to speak on a religious subject within the territory controlled by the holy Orthodox Church and his Majesty the Czar, I had asked Ambassador Guild, a personal friend, who had been the Governor of Massachusetts, to get permission for me to speak. He had written me concerning the matter two or three times, that he had been able to get no satisfactory reply from the court authorities. However, we went to Riga hoping to find the permit there, but it had not arrived.

Up to the last minute our suspense was maintained, when, as the Endeavorers were upon their knees, praying that the authorities might relent, a telegram was handed in, the purport of which was that though no official permission would be given me to address the meeting, I might take a chance and do it, without permission, if the police of Riga did not object. They apparently did not, for the meeting went on successfully, and nothing was done to me when shortly afterwards we went on to St. Petersburg, as it was then called, and I was allowed to speak, not only in the English American Church but in Baron Nicolay's mission and at the Y.M.C.A.

All these petty regulations and hindrances in the way of free speech showed the stupidly minute particularity to which the repressive powers of an autocracy will descend, and were slight indications of the foolish tyranny which, little by little, was preparing the way for the great catastrophe which overwhelmed the bureaucracy, sent the Czar into exile and to death, and involved the whole empire in years of chaos and anarchy. My difficulty in getting permission to speak was of course a most trivial circumstance, but it was indicative of a stupid, mediaeval rule which in the twentieth century was bound sooner or later to be overthrown.

I found Ambassador Curtis Guild as genial, friendly, and companionable as he had been as the Governor of Massachusetts, and no man has ever been more popular either at home or abroad. His ambassadorial flunkies clad in scarlet livery, one of whom stood behind each of our chairs at the dinner table, did not spoil his sturdy American democracy or common sense, and Boston did well to honor him by dedicating to his memory the fine granite steps that stand at the head of the Oliver Wendell Holmes' "Long Walk" across Boston Common.

As a matter of contrast between old Russia and new Russia in the matter of vodka drinking, I recollect that the droschky driver who took us from the hotel to the station when we left St. Petersburg was more than "half seas over." In an insane and reckless manner he drove through the crowded streets, whipping up his poor horses, which fortunately had more sense and sobriety than their driver. When I remonstrated with him in as forcible terms as I could command, he simply turned round and leered at me, letting his steeds take their own course through the thronging thoroughfare. Who could have dreamed that in a few short years Russia even while the Czar still reigned would become the soberest nation in Europe, instead of the most drunken. Its present degree of sobriety I cannot vouch for.

Our next journey was to Austrian Poland, and embraced the interesting cities of Cracow, Lemburg, as well as Czernovitz, the capital of the Bukowina. Of all the cities of eastern Europe Cracow was to us decidedly the most worthy of a visit, not only because of its unrivalled history and its memorials of the past, but because of its present-day beauty and interest. It is delightfully situated on the left bank of the Vistula, at the junction of the Rodowa.

The ancient Gothic Tuch-Haus (Cloth-House) is of special renown, and there is no quainter spot in Europe than these old booths dedicated to the drapers' trade for centuries past. The Stanislaus Cathedral is the Westminster Abbey of Poland. Here are the tombs of the great Polish emperors, and here lie the mortal remains of the Sigismunds, of John Sobieski, who withstood the might of the Saracens with his little army, when the cowardly King Leopold had fled in terror from Vienna. Had it not been for Sobieski and his brave Poles doubtless all Europe would have been overrun by the Moslems who were thundering at the very gates of Vienna, then almost the last stronghold of the Christians.

Here, too, lies Kosciusko, who fought side by side with Washington at the battle of Saratoga, and was afterwards the governor of West Point Military Academy. No Polish hero is more honored in his own country or in ours. When I was a school-boy a favorite declamation was Campbell's stirring lines whose climax seemed to me — the *ne plus ultra* of heroic verse:

"Freedom shrieked when Kosciusko fell."

It was "Goose-market Day" while we were in Cracow, and every other person we met had a great white goose in his arms, either taking it to market, or carrying it home in triumph after a half-hour's haggling in the open square. These thousands of geese were interned in little huts, or lay helpless on the ground with their legs tied together. Occasionally we saw a peasant woman with a goose stuffed into the loose waist of her dress, only its head sticking out, and looking with amused interest apparently at the busy scene around.

The art of Cracow is by no means negligible. The churches are adorned with some masterpieces by Thorwaldsen, and by Peter Vischer, while the carved wooden altar of the fifteenth century by Veit Stoss, a native of Cracow, is greatly admired by connoisseurs. Most interesting to us, however, was it to remember that here Copernicus received his education in the ancient university, and here the beautiful statue of the astronomer stands sentinel-like in the ancient cloister.

The Poles have been as distinguished in literature as in military science. In front of the Cracow Tuch-Haus is a statue of the great poet Mickiewicz who is considered by critics the equal of Wordsworth or Shelley as a nature-poet. One sees his statue everywhere throughout Poland, but Cracow possesses the noblest one of all. Here too, Lelewel, who has been called the Polish Tolstoy, and Anton Malczewski, another immensely popular poet, are honored, while the modern Sienkiewicz, who is as well known in America as in Poland because of his great story "Quo Vadis," and other historical novels, is also a name to conjure by in Cracow.

Lemburg, then the capital of Austrian Poland, though a larger and more bustling city than Cracow, is by no means as interesting historically, or from the standpoint of art and architecture. Here I remember with pleasure, my interpreter, a Jew who was especially gifted linguistically. He was on his wedding tour, and so everjoyed was he with his good fortune that whenever we congratulated him upon his marriage, or spoke appreciatively of his "dear wife," the water welled up into his eyes, and once he actually burst into tears. He was the only man in my acquaintance whose connubial bliss was exhibited in this extraordinary manner.

However, he was a most excellent interpreter, as I had occasion to know not only in Lemburg, but in Leipsic where he had previously translated one of my addresses.

Great numbers of Ruthenians, or "Little Russians," live in the vicinity of Lemburg, and though looked down upon as inferiors by the Poles, they hold their heads very high and will not take any "back talk" from their neighbors, as the boys would say. On one patriotic occasion, I was told, a procession of Ruthenians marched into Lemburg, or Lwow as the city is called in Polish, the women arrayed in their best finery, all the men wearing stove-pipe hats, and many of both sexes sporting eye-glasses or lorgnettes to show that they were as well educated and as literary as the Poles. The most interesting, if not the finest, building in Lemburg that I recollect is the headquarters of the Ruthenian Life Insurance Company, which in the tiles on the outside bears specimens of Ruthenian handicrafts, representing the colored embroidery and art needle-work of Ruthenian women, a standing monument visible to every visitor, of the artistic dexterity of this people.

All this country, as we know, has been ravaged time and again by the hostile armies in the mighty conflict which began in 1914, yet how peaceful was the scene in 1911! the shepherds in their great sheepskin coats, each of which made a sort of tent for its wearer, watched their flocks on the hillsides. The goose girls in every valley and meadow, industriously knitting as they walked along, led their white and noisy flocks to new pastures beside still waters. The farmers ploughed the soil with their primitive instruments, little realizing that this same soil would soon be ploughed by the shrieking shells of opposing armies.

Through Przemysl and Stanislaus, that figured in our papers for months as the great centres of death and destruction, we passed on our way to Czernovitz, the capital of the Bukowina, which the fortunes of war twice gave into the hands of the Russians, and then passed over once more to their temporary Austrian victors.

We found Czernovitz interesting because of its comparative aloofness from the rest of the world. It is a very considerable city, where a Kodak camera was still a great curiosity, and when Mrs. Clark went out into the market place to snap some rare Bukowino costumes she was almost mobbed by a crowd of men and boys and market women who wanted to look into the eye of the camera to see the picture that she had taken, and who were also extremely eager to be " took " themselves.

Indeed so close did the eager crowd press around her that I had to sally out from the hotel, which overlooked the market place, and by physical force rescue her from their friendly curiosity.

Yet Czernovitz does by no means consider itself a primitive back number. Here is an arch-episcopal residence of the Greek Church, a cathedral, and a university with a considerable number of students, who swaggered around in their different colored corps caps, leading a big corps-hound on a chain, in humble imitation of Heidelburg and Bonn.

Our journey from Czernovitz to Bucharest was a hard all-night ride in a second-class car with no " lying down accommodations," and we were thoroughly wearied when early the next morning we reached the bright little Parisian capital of Roumania.

Whether Bucharest is always as crowded as on that bright, cold morning in November I know not, but we tried hotel after hotel in vain for accommodations. The polite landlord at one hostelry would commend us to the hotel across the street, declaring that every room in his house was occupied. Mr. Proprietor across the street would commend us to the Boniface around the corner, and Mr. Round-the-Corner would assure us that we could find splendid accommodations at Mr. Down-the-Street's, while Mr. Down-the-Street turned us back on our tracks towards the station, where at last, in the ninth story of a very unpretentious hotel, with a very pretentious name, the " Hotel Splendid," we found accommodations for a day or two.

There were few gayer cities in the world in those pre-war days than Bucharest, and she had good reason to be proud of her palace, her splendid public buildings, and her fine shops. I do not recall a more beautiful post-office building than that which Bucharest boasts. The substantial post-office buildings in New York and Boston are quite put to the blush by this artistic creation.

There was evidently no premonitory cloud of coming disaster in the sky in those days. As in Belgium's capital, before Waterloo, "there was a sound of revelry by night," the people prided themselves on being considered as gay, if not quite as wicked, as Paris. Gorgeous, high-powered automobiles raced through the streets, most of them blowing musical horns which are so much more melodious than the "honk, honk," of our Cadillacs and Fords. The people thoroughly believed that their invincible army could defend them from all foes. How little any of us knew of the disastrous days which the fates were even then weaving in their mysterious loom!

It was indeed a zigzag journey which we had undertaken, and its next lap took us to Cronstadt in Transylvania (Brasso in Hungarian) the chief town of Transylvania. This is a bright and enterprising little city, with fine mountains to the east, and the interminable rich plains of Hungary, stretching to the west as far as Budapest. Here, too, the Endeavor movement had found a foothold, and we made some delightful friends in this heart of the Carpathians.

The fortunes of war and the evil fortunes of the unjust treaty of Versailles, have transferred all this region from Hungary to Roumania, a disastrous transfer so far as Hungary is concerned, and especially disastrous to the Protestant churches of that ravaged state.

Another zigzag of our journey took us into Croatia, and to its charming little capital of Zagreb, or Agram, as the German name then appeared upon the map. I was surprised to find here a city whose name I am ashamed to say I had never heard six months before, a thriving little metropolis with a university of its own, some beautiful parks and historic monuments of which the people are quite as proud as are we of Bunker Hill monument or the Minute Man of Concord.

To be sure the Croatians had not enjoyed even nominal independence for nearly a thousand years, having been under the heel of the Hapsburg monarchy for centuries, but they hark back to the great days of King Jellacic and they show us proudly the holes in the stones in front of St. Mark's church, where were the five iron bars to which their last king was bound when he was burned at the stake by his cruel captors. Then ended the Golden Age of Croatian independence, but their natural love of freedom and hatred of their overlords made the Croats firm friends of the Entente Allies even though they could not help them to win the war. They have since obtained their independence as part of the new Kingdom of the Serbs, Croats, and Slovenes.

Here in Agram I made the acquaintance of my good friend Samuel Schumacher, a teacher in the Lutheran school, who gave all his vacation time to the propagation of Christian Endeavor, not only in Croatia, but in Servia, Slavonia, Roumania, and Herzegovina. He was a most devoted and unselfish man, and I shall not forget his pathetic letter which he wrote just after the war broke out, saying that now at the call of his Emperor he must join the colors and carry the sword and the rifle to the very people to whom he had just been telling of the gospel of the Prince of Peace. I shall have more to tell about this good man in a later chapter.

Late one evening as we returned from a meeting in Agram, I saw a throng of several hundred men, women and children marching along the streets, loaded with bundles and bags of all shapes and sizes from feather beds to tin kerosene cans. These I was told were emigrants about to start for America, a thousand of whom gathered there every week from the country round about, for Croatia is one of the old homes of the millions of new Americans who during the last quarter of a century have left Austro-Hungary for the New World, — an unprecedented immigration which only the Great War of the Nations and our new laws have partially stopped.

The next day we found many of these same would-be-Americans on the train that bore us to Trieste from which place, with them, we were to sail, stopping short however at Patras, while they kept on, bound for the land of boundless hope. They were a rough, sturdy, but good-natured, patient, and cheerful crowd, making their fourth-class cars ring with their native songs, and taking with them to America brawny arms, stout hearts, and cheerful courage which I believe will in time make them worthy citizens of our Republic.

A WINTER IN ATHENS

CORINTH ON THE GULF — FISHERMEN AND TURKEY-WOMEN — PHOEBE'S OLD HOME IN CENCHREA — THE GLORIES OF ATHENS — INTERESTING SIGHTS FROM OUR WINDOW — AN INTERVIEW WITH KING GEORGE.

E BADE good-by to our fellow-Americans-of-the-future at Patras, and immediately boarded the little train which once a day crawled slowly along the shores of the Gulf of Corinth to Athens. Its leisureliness is much to the advantage of the unhurried traveller, for it gives him the opportunity of getting many long views of delightful scenery and more than passing glimpses of many Greek villages which the train never seemed in a hurry to leave. At length we came in sight of a symmetrical truncate sugar-loaf mountain and remembered from previous visits that it was none other than Acro-Corinth the famous citadel of Old Corinth. In a few minutes the conductor called out " Corinthos," and we disembarked for a few days' stay in the modern village which is so unworthy of its ancient name and fame.

However dilapidated and forlorn modern Corinth may be, no traveller with a spark of imagination can fail to be impressed with the events of mighty moment which have taken place on the shores of its blue gulf.

Though modern Corinth does not stand upon the site of the great city of Greek and Roman times, which was some three miles away under protecting hills, yet this whole region is saturated with the memories of heroic deeds of old. At two different periods, once under the Greeks, and once under the Romans, Corinth was in many respects the most important city in the world. It controlled the trade routes between the East and the West. It was the seat of learning as well as of wealth and political supremacy. It was the city where Paul spent many months with his friends Aquila and Priscilla, from which he wrote his earliest epistle, the one to the Thessalonians, and to which he wrote important letters.

The present town has little to detain the traveller except as he is interested in the life of modern Greece. Yet with the thought of the past in mind even homely, commonplace events are gilded with the radiance of the past centuries. We were interested in the fishermen who every morning rowed far out into the Gulf of Corinth, and, when a mile or more from the shore, threw out their drag-net which twenty brawny companions on the shore began to draw in, hand over hand.

It would often take a couple of hours to make a single haul, and then the loot was frequently of small account, being, perhaps, half a bushel of tiny fish of the sardine family. But the great joy of fishing in the Gulf of Corinth, as well as in the Maine woods, or the Adirondacks, is the *uncertainty* of the haul. It is the gambler's chance that makes the patient fisherman. The next cast of the fly, the next haul of the net, may bring the prize of the day, so that one's interest is always kept on the *qui vive,* and though fishermen have been dragging the waters of the Gulf of Corinth for thousands of years, they still manage to draw their little crowd of interested spectators to the shore every morning as in St. Paul's time.

The turkey-women were another source of mild interest. With a long wand they would drive their errant flock every morning through the streets of Corinth, keeping them surprisingly well in hand. The Corinthians who desired a turkey dinner would meet the flock somewhere on the long street, and with the help of the driver would pick out a promising specimen which, after much chasing and vociferous gobbling on the part of the victim, was caught and ignominiously felt of by the prospective buyer. If he was satisfied with the plumpness and tenderness of the fowl a bargain was struck after much haggling, and he would bear away his prize in triumph.

For the second time within a few years we made a most interesting visit to the ruins of ancient Corinth, which to a considerable extent has been unearthed by the American School of Archaeology, though much yet remains to be discovered. However here are some of the marble streets laid bare, which must have been trodden by the feet of statesmen and kings, apostles and martyrs. We took pleasure in imagining that one of the circular shops whose ruins are exposed was the very one owned by Aquila and Priscilla, where St. Paul wrought with his tent-needle, and we were especially interested in a fragment of a marble tablet preserved in the little museum bearing in Greek letters the word *Synagogue* which undoubtedly was placed over the door of the one synagogue in Corinth, where, according to St. Luke, " St. Paul reasoned every Sabbath and persuaded the Jews and the Greeks."

As we were anxious, upon this and a succeeding journey to visit every possible place made famous by the great Apostle, we took special pains to visit Cenchrea, which few travellers in these days think it worth while to attempt. Baedeker gives it scarcely a line, yet this proved to be to us one of the most interesting of all our excursions.

The road thither was exceedingly rough and barely passable for the antiquated hack which we engaged. So deep were the ruts that the driver had to throw himself dexterously from one side of his seat to the other, a gymnastic performance in which we also assisted, to prevent the carriage from overturning at certain critical points. Indeed the road came to an abrupt end when we were within half a mile of Cenchrea. And yet this was once one of the magnificent highways of the

world, connecting the two ports of Corinth, the one on the
Gulf, and the other on the Aegean Sea. Over this road passed
the wealth of the world. It is said to have been enclosed at
one time by high walls stretching the whole distance between
the seas, — about eight miles.

When we reached the site of ancient Cenchrea, in whose
port once rode the navies of the nations, we found it absolutely desolate. Not even a ruin on the shore showed where
the busy seaport once was, though a few great blocks of stone,
half under the water, indicated the site of the wharves. It
was a most peaceful and lovely scene. The bright waters of
the Aegean, dotted with many islands and surrounded on all
sides by lofty, verdure-clad hills indicated one of the most
charming spots for a summer resort that could be imagined,
and we said to ourselves, " If this were only in Switzerland,
how the tourist hotels and funicular railways would spring up
almost over night! "

We rejoiced that the tourist had not discovered this little
Paradise, but that here we could dream of the ancient days
whose glories have forever passed away; of the great apostle
to the Gentiles coming here from Corinth to " fulfil his vow,"
and from here sailing for Ephesus on his way to Jerusalem
on one of the missionary journeys which did so much to make
over the old heathen world.

In all the wide landscape we saw but two living creatures,
a man and a horse ploughing a distant hillside. No house is
visible from the shore, but a little distance back is the humblest
and smallest of Greek churches which it was ever my lot to
enter. A rude painting of the Christ stood upon the floor. A
cheap icon was in one corner; a rough altar and some candle
spikes covered with the drippings of years were all the furniture that the little church contained. We naturally thought of
" the church that was in Cenchrea " of which Paul spoke in
his letter to the Romans, and of the faithful Phoebe, a member of this church, whom he honored by committing to her

this noble epistle that she might carry it to the Christians in Rome.

Nearly three months on this occasion we spent in historic Athens, which we found was an unexpectedly enjoyable place for a winter residence. The hotels were comfortable, and, with one or two exceptions, by no means extravagant in their charges. I am speaking of their normal condition before the great war. The sun shines much of the time, giving ample heat on a bright day for the fireless rooms, and though occasional frosty days and snow-squalls varied the monotony of

RUINS OF TEMPLE OF JUPITER IN ATHENS
The Acropolis in the distance on the left.

the climate, we were able to endure them without too much discomfort by the aid of a small " spirit-of-wine stove " and plenty of wraps.

Every morning we worked busily over the volumes I had in preparation " Old Homes of New Americans," the homes which I had just visited in Austria-Hungary, and " In the Foot-steps of St. Paul," whose steps we had been following on this journey, and were tracing almost every day during our stay in Athens. The great delight of a residence in Athens is in its innumerable interesting walks and its incomparable views. In these we indulged every pleasant afternoon. Of course we followed St. Paul many times to Mars Hill, and journeyed with him from the Piraeus where he disembarked, through the long walk once enclosed between high walls and crowded with statues, to the Agora or market-place.

Frequently we watched from the Acropolis the sun setting in a blaze of glory; or sat on the marble seats of the stadium and recalled the athletic triumphs of the past; or viewed from the top of Lycabettus the most magnificent historic panorama in the world. All these joys far more than made up for the small discomforts of hotel life in the city of Timon and Pericles.

Even without the supreme attraction of her antiquities, Athens is to-day a peculiarly interesting city, and when we remember that scarcely more than seventy years ago she was an unkempt, dilapidated town, ravaged by centuries of Turkish misrule, we wondered the more at her bright, clean streets, her well-kept shops, filled with the products of many climes, her beautiful university, her wonderful museum and her public buildings, well worthy of any prosperous nation of twice her size. I am speaking of Athens before the World War in which Greece played a foolish part. What she looks like now, I cannot say.

There was always something of interest to be seen from our windows which faced on Constitution Square and the Rue du Stade. The Greeks are an excitable people, and every Greek is a potential politician or general of the army. If New York had as many daily papers in proportion to her population as has Athens, they would be numbered by hundreds. A crisis was impending every day, even in those peaceful times, while the crowds of excited gesticulating people at the street corners and in the cafés confirmed the impression that Athenians are still " eager to hear or to see some new thing."

Gala days are numerous in Athens, and troops of soldiers were constantly marching through the streets; the royal guards seeming particularly effeminate in their pleated skirts or fustanellas. Though they looked like ballet girls, they could fight like heroes, as they proved on more than one occasion in the World War.

Sad processions often followed the gay through the busy streets, for almost every day a corpse was borne past our windows to its last resting-place in the beautiful cemetery on the outskirts of the town. The officiating priests were always clad in gorgeous raiment and marched at the head of the funeral procession. Then came two men bearing the coffin lid held upright, then many carriages loaded with flowers, and then the coffin, borne on the shoulders of several bearers, with the face exposed to every passer-by.

To wander through the shopping streets revived classic memories, for each one has some name that takes one back to his schooldays of Greek mythology or history.

In one of Poe's stories a reluctant father promises his daughter to a suitor when two Sundays come together in one week. Nothing daunted, the suitor accepts the challenge and in going around the world gains an extra Sunday in the week that he returns to his out-witted father-in-law. If we did not have two Sundays in a week we at least had in Athens two Christmas days and two New Year's days in one year, for the Greeks follow the old Julian calendar, which puts their year thirteen days later than ours.

Christmas day is not observed with unusual festivities, but New Year's eve was a time of wild hilarity. The streets were so crowded as to be almost impassable. They were carpeted with confetti, and the hats and shoulders of every passer-by were powdered with the little flying discs of colored paper. Miles of narrow paper ribbon, called in Germany *Schlangen*, were thrown from every balcony, festooning the streets from side to side, and entangling the feet of the passers-by in a cobweb net.

Men and boys and girls alike blew horns vociferously throughout the evening and late into the night. On New

Year's day came a solemn procession and service in the cathedral, attended by the royalties and diplomats, and every
" Who's Who " individual in Athens. From our window we
could see the great white palace of the king, which a few years
before had been partially burned down, and was very slowly
being repaired, while the approaches to it, and even the entrance to the royal chapel, were in a most shockingly unkempt
condition.

The average Greek whom we met had very little use for
royalty. One of them told us that King George was a good
man who did no harm, a good deal like " a fly on the wall,"
as he expressed it.

Through the kindness of United States Minister Moses,
now Senator Moses, I had an interesting interview with King
George, who soon afterwards was foully assassinated in the
streets of Salonica. He was a genial and friendly potentate,
who owed his long and peaceful reign to his kinship with half
the rulers of Europe. He was the son of the King of Denmark, a brother-in-law of the late King Edward of Great
Britain, and uncle of the Czar Nicholas of Russia, uncle
of the King of Norway, and he was related to Kaiser William
of Germany. Few could boast more royal relatives.

I respected him particularly for sticking to his religion, the
religion of his ancestors. He was one of the very few
Protestants in his domains, where the religion of the Greek
Church is almost synonymous with patriotism and loyalty.
Yet he retained his allegiance to the Lutheran church to the
end of his life, and built a chapel within the palace where
Lutheran services were held every Sunday, which anyone was
free to attend. When he asked about my faith, he replied
to my avowal of Protestantism, " I, too, am a Protestant.
Don't you think we have a fine little chapel and a good minis-
ter to preach to us every Sunday? "

One of the conditions, however, to which he agreed when
he ascended the throne was that his children should be brought

up in the Greek faith, the faith of their mother, who was a Russian princess. King Constantine, who was often seen upon the streets, then the Crown Prince, is a devout member of the Orthodox Greek Church, as are all the members of his family. He afterwards figured largely in the eyes of the world, and by the Entente Powers was considered a perfidious monarch, playing into the hands of their enemies.

Greece, being overwhelmingly, indeed almost unanimously devoted to the Greek Church, there is little room for Protestantism, and consequently none for Christian Endeavor societies, so that calls for public addresses were fewer than in almost any city we could visit.

There is, it is true, one small church of the reformed faith in Athens, founded by the late Dr. Kalopothakes, eminent in the brief and scanty history of Protestantism in Greece. Here we occasionally attended the services, but as they were in the Greek tongue we more often went to the Church of England, or to the German service in the palace.

The pastor of the Greek Protestant Church was a worthy man whose hands were stayed up by the son and daughter of Dr. Kalopothakes and a small congregation of believers. On one occasion he asked me to baptize his little son, a sturdy infant of two years of age. The parents had been waiting for two years for the arrival of a Protestant minister who might perform the ceremony, but they desired that it should be according to the Greek custom of triune immersion.

The parlor of the pastor's house was filled with friends and parishioners to witness the ceremony. A large, deep tub was brought into the room and filled with tepid water. Then the infant, who was old enough to be frightened by these preparations, and doubly enraged at being handed over to a stranger, was given to me for the ceremony, which proved to be a serious and trying one.

Had he been but a few weeks old the rite of immersing him three times, in the name of the Father, the Son, and the

Holy Ghost, would have been a comparatively easy one, as I had found it on another occasion when baptizing the son of a Greek parishioner in Boston. But this lusty boy had no notion of being immersed. He braced his little feet against the sides of the tub, screaming with all his might, and absolutely refused to allow his head to be put under, doubtless thinking that he was about to be drowned. I did the best I could, but it was far from being a satisfactory service to either the parents or the officiating minister. Had it not been for

MARS HILL, ATHENS
On which Paul preached his great sermon to the Athenians.

the solemnity of the occasion my struggles with the child would have seemed supremely ridiculous. But the parents and friends realized that I had done the best I could under the circumstances, and the ceremony was concluded with the usual congratulations, and the passing around of abundant sweetmeats and confections.

Whether it is true or not that " man wants but little here below," Mrs. Clark and I were obliged to be contented for several months during our stay in Athens with a very meagre amount of wearing apparel, — nothing more indeed than we could carry in our suit-cases. The two trunks which we had sent from Rotterdam to Athens failed to make their appearance. Day after day we haunted the office of " THOMAS COOK "ετ ὑιος," but we could get no word from our wandering trunks. Letters and cablegrams were dispatched but brought no satisfactory answers. At length we received word that they were traced to Vienna and Budapest. After about three months word came that they had arrived at Salonica, but would be sent no further, as they were billed to go through by rail, and there was no rail communication between Salonica and Athens.

Evidently the shippers in Rotterdam had small knowledge of geography, or the routes of travel. There was nothing for it but to follow our trunks to Salonica. The mountain had to go to Mahomet, and after a three days' journey by sea we found them in the custom house, none the worse for their long tour, but of little value to us for the time being, since we could not take them on our journey to Asia Minor. So we sent them home to America where they arrived in due time, having scarcely been unlocked from the time we left Boston. Such are some of the joys of journeying, but " travellers must be content."

IN THE FOOTSTEPS OF ST. PAUL

PART I

OLD THESSALONICA — PRISON OF THE GREAT ASSASSIN —
SEVENTY BURIED CHURCHES OF BEREA — WHERE PAUL
FIRST SET FOOT IN EUROPE — PHILIPPI, ITS DRAMATIC
HISTORY.

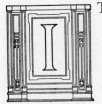

T HAD long been our ambition since visiting some of the cities made famous by St. Paul to complete the circuit, and if possible see every one of the places which he made famous by his residence, or even by a passing visit, in his many missionary journeys. The opportunity was too good to be lost, and, having a few weeks at our disposal before other duties called us home, we resolved to visit as many of St. Paul's cities in Asia Minor as possible.

Salonica was our starting-point. To the church in this ancient capital Paul wrote his first extant epistle. Here he lived for some months, plying his tentmaker's trade before he was driven out by the persecutions of the rabid Jews. Even were it not for these historic associations, Salonica would still be well worthy of a visit. It was the third largest port in the Turkish Empire. It was then (1911) in the hands of the Turks, though their dominion was near its end. The Young Turks were in power, and Abdul Hamid II, the " Great Assassin," was imprisoned in a villa in the outskirts of the city. It was a genuine satisfaction to see his prison house, strongly guarded by a thousand soldiers, whose camps encircled it, and to know that the astute ruler who had played his cards so shrewdly and so infamously, and had so long kept alive " the sick man of Europe," was now put where he could do little more harm. I had seen him go to mosque in regal splendor in 1893, guarded by 10,000 soldiers, and now he was a prisoner execrated by all.

In Salonica, as in almost every considerable town of the Near East the American missionaries have made themselves felt, and Dr. J. H. House has here established an excellent industrial school for boys of all nationalities. He has built a typical American home and schoolhouse in a sightly location overlooking the Thermaic Gulf, with magnificent Mt. Olympus, the home of the gods, in the not-distant background.

In a memorable excursion from Salonica we visited the ancient city of Berea, to which the apostle was driven by Jewish persecutions, and whose people he found " more noble than those of Thessalonica." To-day the city is especially interesting because of its " hidden churches," of which there are no less than seventy, belonging to the Greek Catholic faith. Though when we visited them it was no longer necessary to hide them from the wrath of the Mohammedans, yet it had been necessary in earlier days.

To use a modern term, they were " camouflaged " much as ships and trenches were during the war. Indeed, so well concealed are they that it would be impossible for a stranger to find them. Fortunately we had for our guide a Greek gentleman, a native of the town, who had made the study of these churches a specialty. He took us to eight of them, hidden in the most obscure and out-of-the-way nooks. We would enter a courtyard, where perhaps a woman was doing her washing, or cooking the noon meal, and, after passing through two or three doorways, we would see another inconspicuous door, on which a rude cross was chalked. This would prove to be the entrance to a little room with its rude

icons, its altars, and its candle spikes, where, on certain Sab-
baths of the year, services are still held. Many of these
hidden churches had a double exit, or perhaps an underground
passage, so that if the Turks attacked the front door, the
congregation could easily escape from the rear.

In 1911 Macedonia was in a very excited state politically,
and deeds of violence were exceedingly common. Indeed they
have been common ever since. Special passports for travel
had to be obtained for every station, and almost at the
moment that we entered Berea a Turkish policeman was shot
by an Albanian, who was allowed to get away without even
an attempt at his arrest. The poor policeman was taken back
to Salonica on the train by which we returned in the afternoon,
and he died on the way.

There are no undoubtedly genuine relics of St. Paul's
residence in Berea, though a high modern, wooden pulpit in an
open, grass-grown square is called by his name. It is possible
that the tradition may have some foundation in fact, that he
there preached to the " honorable " Bereans. We liked to
imagine that the immense cypress trees which flanked the
square, dated back to St. Paul's time. At least they were of
great antiquity, and one which had been cut down, seemed
to show nearly rings enough to carry its infancy back to the
beginning of the Christian Era.

Several interesting communities find their homes in
Berea; the Wallachians, for instance, who live in a great
compound within the confines of the city during the winter
months, spending the summer season with their flocks on the
hills. The Gypsies have a whole street to themselves and
are for the most part tinkers and blacksmiths.

The chief charm of modern Berea is its running water and
its many fountains, an ancient characteristic from which it derived its name.

Our next excursion in the footsteps of St. Paul took us
with Dr. House for our interpreter and guide to Kavalla and

Philippi. The railway which connects Salonica with Constantinople carried us as far as Drama, whose name at one time figured extensively in the records of the great war. Here in its early months a horrible drama indeed was enacted. We found there a Protestant Bulgarian church, under the care of the American missionaries, with a native pastor, and a flourishing Endeavor society. But we could not linger long with our Bulgarian friends, for we had to push on the same night with the aid of an ancient hack, drawn by equally aged horses, to Kavalla, where we arrived long after dark. The ancient name of Kavalla was Neapolis, as we read in the Book of Acts. It is a town of peculiar interest to modern European Christians, for here Paul and his associates, Silas, Timothy, and Luke, first set foot on European soil, called thither by the vision of the man of Macedonia.

Kavalla is now one of the most flourishing seaports of the East, having been built up by an immense trade in Turkish tobacco. The great stone tobacco warehouses and the palaces of its tobacco magnates give evidence of the chief industry of the place. But indeed, Kavalla, or Neapolis, has always been a place of importance. It could hardly be otherwise, with its fine harbor and its proximity to Troas on the Asian coast. Here Mohammed Ali was born, and the very cradle in which he was rocked, hung from the low roof of his birthchamber, is shown to the traveller to-day.

A splendid Roman aqueduct, borne on arches sixty feet high, is still in good preservation, and until recently it brought water to the thirsty Neapolitans. It is singular how popular the ancient name of this city is in every land. Italy has its Naples, America has innumerable Newtowns and Newtons, and many cities of the name of Neapolis are scattered through the ancient world. Nablous in Syria is only another form of the same word. Sometime in the remote past all of these places were new towns, or new cities, however ancient they may seem to-day.

The most interesting place we saw in Kavalla was the soup-kitchen endowed by Mohammed Ali, where once a week every one in the city, be he resident or passing visitor, be he Mohammedan, Christian, Jew, or Gentile, can obtain a square meal, free of charge. When we saw it, four-foot logs were blazing under the huge pots which contained the savory mess for the next day's meal, though we did not have a chance to test Mohammedan hospitality. Since that day Kavalla has passed through the vicissitudes of war. The Turks had to yield the city to the Greeks, and the Greeks, under the pusillanimous rule of Constantine, practically made a present of it, with its forts and its garrison, to the Bulgarians, who captured it without a struggle. Now, in the strange shuffle of the nations made at Versailles, it has become again a part of the kingdom of Greece.

Bright and early the next morning we left Kavalla for Philippi. Rattling by the homes of the tobacco-trust millionaires, up a steep hill and down its long slope, we came at length to the historic plain where the great battle between the Republicans and Monarchists of Rome was fought. Here Cassius and Brutus led their troops, brought over the hills from their camp in Sardis, against the Imperialists, led by Octavius and Mark Antony. The monarchists won the day, and the doom of republican Rome was sealed.

Hither came, with his three companions, the unknown Jew who had just set foot for the first time in Europe, perhaps the very day before, for we do not know that St. Paul made any stop in Neapolis. But in Philippi he found some congenial spirits holding a prayer service by the water-side. Among them was Lydia of Thyatira. Here he founded a church, and here persecution followed him as in every other city. He was thrown into prison, and was marvellously released by an earthquake, according to the Scripture narrative. To this city, as we all know, he afterwards wrote a letter which the world will not willingly let die.

There is little indeed left in Philippi for the modern traveller to see. The ancient marble-paved Roman road which connected the city with Kavalla, and which was part of the famous Ignatian Way, is still to be seen in some short sections, and we made a point of leaving our carriage literally to walk in the footsteps of St. Paul, for this is the highway he must have trodden in this first journey on European soil, a journey destined to be so momentous in the history of the Christian church.

Nothing at all of ancient Philippi is left above ground, save a few ruins, of which the only conspicuous one is thought by some to be the palace of the Governor of Philippi. It at least was once a building of considerable importance, for some of the stones that I measured were twelve feet in length and four feet thick. Here also are several great springing arches, with fine ornamentation visible in many places.

Behind these ruins rises the Acropolis of Philippi, crowned with a rude and useless Turkish fort. We speak of *the* Acropolis as though there were but one and that at Athens, whereas, as a matter of fact, every important Greek and Roman city of ancient times had its acropolis or mountain of defense.

Up this acropolis in ancient times, especially after Octavius had made Philippi a Roman colony, streets and houses of the city crowded, from the plain to the top of the hill, which was crowned by a huge, dark castle, while stone walls of great thickness were built all around to protect the city from attack. Curious knobs of dark rock here and there were cut into the shape of Greek idols, and the seats of the open-air theatre (for every Greek city has its theatre) and the remains of the temple of Silvanus can still be traced on the hillside.

As we stood among the ruins with our backs to the Acropolis, in front stretched the great plain where the Battle of Philippi to which I have alluded was fought. There, on that field, according to the Bard of Stratford, Brutus soliloquized:

> " Oh, that a man might know
> The end of this day's business ere it come!
> But it sufficeth that the day will end,
> And then the end is known. Come, ho! away! "

There, on that field, Cassius ran upon his own sword, which was held by his slave Pindarus, while he exclaimed:

> " Caesar, thou art revenged
> Even with the sword that killed thee."

In order that the army might not be overwhelmed by the news of the death of their great leader, his body was secretly sent off to the island of Thasos in the bay of Kavalla, while the battle was still raging. On that same field of Philippi Brutus killed himself by running upon his sword.

> " Brutus, the noblest Roman of them all! "

When the news of the disastrous battle of Philippi reached Portia, the wife of Brutus, in her island home at Nisida, near Naples, where afterwards Paul landed on his way to Rome, she is said to have killed herself by the most horrible of all suicidal methods, swallowing live coals of fire. Such were some of the tragedies connected with the bloody field of Philippi.

More than any other of the St. Paul cities that we visited Philippi seemed the city of the dead. Distressingly dilapidated Turkish cemeteries abound in all directions, four or five lying close to the site of the ancient city. Nothing more forlorn can be conceived than a Turkish graveyard with its decaying and broken stones leaning to every point of the compass. The graveyards in the neighborhood of Philippi have not even the natural ornament of a cypress grove, which redeem many Turkish burying places from utter desolation. Still the Plain of Philippi was green and beautiful in the spring-time, and the little river beside which Paul found the praying women, flows between low banks bright with flowers. Here we saw two women upon their knees, but alas, unlike their sisters of ancient times, they were not praying, but washing their soiled linen, an equally praiseworthy operation, perhaps, if only the prayers were not omitted in their proper season.

Returning to the railway at Drama, we boarded the train for Constantinople, and, after a very short stay, again took the train on the famous Bagdad Railway (which has figured so largely as among the provocations of the Great War) for Konieh, the ancient Iconium of St. Paul's day.

THE RIVERSIDE
Where prayer was wont to be made.

This journey then subjected the traveller to no hardships, for the railway is well built, and the first and second-class cars were very comfortable. At Eski Shehir, where we took the train on our wagon journey across Turkey, going in the opposite direction nearly a score of years before, we spent the night, as the trains ran only by daylight. We did not find that hotel accommodations had improved much in the last twenty years, but did find a greatly increased trade in Meerschaum clay, for which the place is famous, since it contains the best deposits in the world. Dealers in pipes and cigarette-holders, and strings of beads and curious ornaments of various kinds, besought our patronage. The beads are peculiarly in favor among the Turks, for every man in Asia Minor, be he Moslem or Christian seems to carry a string of beads of some kind in his pocket, which he fingers, not as an act of religious devotion, but apparently simply to keep his hands busy, while he talks with his neighbors, or plays one of his interminable games of dominoes.

We had hoped to be able to visit Antioch in Pisidia, where the Apostle preached his first recorded sermon, and which is some miles from the station of Ak Shehr, but found that the roads were still impassable on account of the winter snows and washouts, and that no one would think of the possibility of making the journey until settled weather came again. So we pushed on to Konieh, where we arrived on the evening of the second day from Constantinople, and found our good friends of former days, Dr. and Mrs. Dodd, whom we had known in Cesarea, ready to receive us with open hospitality.

CHAPTER XXXIX

YEAR 1912

IN THE FOOTSTEPS OF ST. PAUL

PART II

ICONIUM — THE OLDEST CITY IN THE WORLD — SELJUKIAN
TURKS AND THEIR WONDERFUL MOSQUES — WHY THE
DERVISHES WHIRL — FINDING THE SITE OF LYSTRA —
HOW " CHRISTIAN DOGS " FOUND FAVOR — FROM STONES
TO MELONS — A NOBLE MISSIONARY DOCTOR.

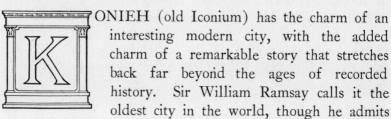ONIEH (old Iconium) has the charm of an interesting modern city, with the added charm of a remarkable story that stretches back far beyond the ages of recorded history. Sir William Ramsay calls it the oldest city in the world, though he admits that Damascus may dispute its supremacy. Like Damascus, a city here was made inevitable by the springs and rivulets which flow down from the Lystrian hills and make it a perpetual oasis in the great Anatolian plain, so much of which is uninhabited and uninhabitable for lack of water.

Like our own Colorado and Montana uplands, and like the veldt of South Africa, the Anatolian plains are thousands of feet above the sea, and though naturally fertile, need the vivifying influence of the rare springs and water-courses to make them productive. These Konieh has in abundance, and in consequence, the city is surrounded by a fringe of gardens and orchards several miles wide, which always have made, and doubtless always will make it a place of importance.

440

I know of no city in all Asia Minor which has left a more abiding impression on my mind than Konieh. Many of the objects that greeted St. Paul's eyes are seen by travellers to-day. Then, as now, the twin peaks of St. Philip and St. Thekla, which rise straight out of the plain, kept guard over the city to the westward. Then, as now, the soft-footed camels plodded their way slowly and majestically through the narrow streets, and knelt in the wood-market to have their heavy burdens of logs and fagots from the mountains unloaded. Then, as now, the traders in the little booths under the brown awnings in the bazaar sat cross-legged before their small stock of wares, inviting passers-by to stop and purchase. Few of the notable features of street life have much changed, for in the slow-moving East customs and costumes and manners remain the same from generation to generation.

The golden age of Iconium, however, was not in St. Paul's day, but in the years from the twelfth to the fifteenth century, when the Seljukian Turks, the best of their race, made Konieh the capital of the splendid Empire of Roum. " The city was then so magnificent," it has been said, " with beautiful buildings, palaces, mosques, and mausolea, that the proverb arose, ' See all the world, see Konieh.' "

Many a traveller to Constantinople or Smyrna looks on with supercilious curiosity at the whirling dervishes in their daily devotions, but if he would view them with an eye to their ancient history he would remember that to them it is a religious service as solemn as a prayer meeting. The founder of the sect, who lived in Konieh, read the story of David " dancing before the Lord " and concluded that there was a spiritual significance and virtue in the act. Thus the whirling to solemn and sacred music became one of the characteristics of their worship, which has been carried to such an extreme in some places that the dervishes lose themselves in dizzy ecstasy, and even gash themselves with knives as a part of the ceremony.

For the most part, however, the whirling is done with solemn propriety, each dervish dodging his whirling neighbor with great expertness, and then retiring to the back of the room, and standing upright to recover an equilibrium which one would think would be greatly upset.

The chief mosque of this sect in Konieh is one of the most beautiful in the world. The tiles with which it is plentifully decorated are of Christian blue rather than Mohammedan green, and it is thought by many who have investigated the

THE WHIRLING DERVISHES OF ICONIUM

subject that the Mevlevi dervishes have more in common with Christians than any other sect of the Moslems.

There are many ruins of extreme beauty in Konieh, and the carving around the doorway of an old Seljukian college is equal to the finest stone tracery of the Indian mosques and palaces in Delhi and Agra.

Especially in the "Great Mosque" is the mosaic work of marvellous intricacy and beauty. It is hung with magnificent rugs, and scores of beautiful lamps in silver and brass, while the tomb of Hazret Mevalana, the founder of the order, is especially dazzling in its magnificence. It is covered with shining cloth which looks like a pall of solid gold, and as

Hazret is buried standing up, it is of peculiar shape for a sarcophagus.

But one is tempted to linger too long in Konieh. Scarcely less interesting was our excursion in search of the ruins of Lystra. It was a cold February day when with Dr. and Mrs. Dodd we started in two large Turkish *arabas,* our horses decorated with thousands of blue " evil-eye beads " braided into their manes and tails and various parts of the harness. If any caravan could thus be guarded from evil, ours was

Courtyard of the Mosque of the Whirling Dervishes in Iconium

surely safe from harm. One of our *Araba-jis,* or drivers, was a Greek with a long brown scarf wound around his head; the other was a Turk, dressed like a kavass, with much gay embroidery about his person, and some murderous-looking but harmless pistols tucked into his girdle.

Soon after we started the snow began to whirl around our wagons, and a blizzard such as is not uncommon on the wind-swept Anatolian plain threatened our further progress. But we pressed on through mud and snow and slush for some eight hours, until we came to a small river crossed by a fine Roman bridge sadly out of repair, so that we had to cross the stream by a ford and drive our horses through the belly-deep water. Just beyond lay the wretched little Turkish village of Khatun Serai, the modern Lystra. The ruins of the famous city of old lie less than a mile away.

Lystra in Paul's time was largely inhabited by a rude and barbarous people, and its inhabitants are no different in character to-day, though of a different race. Indeed we found the inhabitants even less hospitable than they were in Paul's time. Prying faces were thrust behind the curtains of our

THE GUEST HOUSE OF LYSTRA
From photograph by Mrs. Clark.

araba to look at the strange women of America with their unveiled faces.

The *Mudir*, or headman of the village was among the first arrivals in the motley throng that surrounded the wagons. In reply to a polite request that we might visit the ruins of the ancient city he gave a prompt and surly refusal.

The boys and young men, taking their cue from the headman, began to revile us as "Giaours" Christian dogs, and, when we started out to try to find the ruins without assistance, the boys pelted us with snowballs and stones, and then gathered on a neighboring hilltop to hoot and yell at the hated Chris-

tians. A kodak pointed at them by one of our party soon
dispersed them, and they scuttled down the hillside in great
haste, lest the evil eye of the camera should blight their lives.

It might be supposed that it would be an easy thing to find
the ruins of a once important, populous city of Roman times,
when we knew that we were within a mile of them, but such
was not the case, for scarcely a relic of ancient Lystra appears
above ground, and in every direction are found more or less
of the remains of ancient dwellings, half buried in the ground.

Indeed the site of Lystra was long and vainly sought by
archaeologists. Sir William Ramsay passed within a few
yards of the site of the city for which he was searching without finding it, and it was only the discovery of a Lystrian coin
and a single monumental inscription by Professor Sterrett of
Cornell University that settled forever the site of the ancient
city.

Fortunately we had with us Sir William's latest book with
invaluable descriptions and pictures of the site of Lystra.
From this we were enabled to determine the particular hillside and plain on which the ancient city was situated. It was
too late however to inspect it closely that evening, and slowly
and toilsomely we made our way through the mud and snow
back to the little village.

In the meantime a wonderful change had come over the
hearts of the modern Lystrians, for they had learned that one
of our company was a missionary doctor, whose fame had
penetrated to their remote village. Now it seemed they could
not do enough for us. They turned out of the only guest-
room in the village two Turkish loafers, and gave it to us for
the night, selling us eggs and other provisions, and presenting
to us some delicious winter melons, which keep in good condition until spring. Some seeds from these melons I afterwards planted and found that they yielded as good fruit from
the soil of Cape Cod as from that of the uplands of Asia
Minor.

A constant procession of lame, halt, and half-blind invaded our hut which was shared by our four horses and our two *araba-jis*. All were helped and comforted by our good missionary doctor, some receiving medicine and slight treatments then and there, and others were invited to visit the hospital in Konieh, where they could be cared for.

In St. Paul's time the Lystrians were noted for their fickleness of disposition. First they treated him and his companion as gods; then they stoned Paul and left him for dead. The humble modern travellers who followed in St. Paul's footsteps were treated in a reverse fashion by the modern Lystrians; first they stoned and reviled us, and then, in hope of favors to come from the missionary doctor, they treated us as their most honored guests.

The next morning, without any opposition from the *Mudir*, we inspected more narrowly the site of Lystra, but found little of interest except some broken pieces of marble and other building stones, some on the plain and some on the slopes and crest of a hill about three hundred feet above the plain, which was once the citadel or acropolis of Lystra.

It required something of a scramble to reach the top of the steep hill, but the glorious view well repaid us for the exertion. Lystra's citadel was situated in the centre of a valley with a wide reach of fertile, well-watered country stretching out beyond, for the two streams which flow near the town bring life and beauty to this favored spot in the Lycaonian upland. No wonder that some magnificent Sultana from Konieh in the time of the Seljukian Turks made the village her country residence as the name of Khatun Serai, or the "Lady's Mansion," indicates.

Lystra like most of the ancient cities of Asia Minor has served as a quarry for the neighboring villages, and for nearly two thousand years past, when any of the inhabitants wished to build a house or a mosque, a retaining wall or a sheep-pen, they have hastened to the almost inexhaustible treasures which were built up with so much pains and expense into the beautiful cities of old. Magnificent marble columns, ornate capitals, memorial stones covered with inscriptions, and even the tombs of the dead have served the vandals of later generations, and provided them with abundance of material.

The most interesting site in all Lystra is that of the temple where Paul and Barnabas were hailed as gods. Just before the land begins to rise to the hill on which the chief buildings were situated on the south-east side of the citadel, stands a

A VERY OLD FOUNTAIN IN LYSTRA

Famous in ancient times. Where Paul doubtless drank. Dr. and Mrs. Dodd, missionaries in Iconium (modern Konieh), and their son and Dr. Clark. From photograph by Mrs. Clark.

pedestal on which is an inscription showing that it was dedicated to Augustus whose worship was connected with the chief temple. Here undoubtedly was the temple of Jupiter " before-the-city," where the people brought oxen and garlands to do honor to the Christians who so peremptorily refused their worship.

After spending a few hours among the ruins we bade adieu to the birthplace of Timothy, the residence of the godly

Eunice and the pious Lois, and the city to which Paul alluded in the pathetic story of his adventures and his persecutions which he endured for his Master's sake. " Once ,was I stoned," and that once was on the plain just outside of the walls of Lystra.

Returning to Konieh, we spent another day or two with our missionary friends whose pioneer work in this intensely Mohammedan city we greatly admired. We were interested in the way in which the good missionary physicians had started their evangelistic work. Though there had long been in Konieh and is now an excellent school of high grade for boys, called the " Apostolic Institute," presided over by an Armenian graduate of Yale, there had been little distinctively evangelistic work carried on there until the arrival of Dr. Dodd and Dr. Post a few years before to establish there a Christian hospital.

The Turks were practically inaccessible, but there are a multitude of Greeks in Iconium, whom our friends wished to reach. So at family prayers in a room opening upon the main street they sang various Christian melodies which at first attracted a few Greek young men who wished to come in and enjoy the singing. They would not have responded to any invitation to a Bible reading or preaching service, but gospel music hath charms not only to soothe the savage breast but to attract the young Greek rough-necks from the street, for such many of them proved to be.

When we were there quite a large congregation had been gathered each day and while some evidently came to scoff, others remained to pray, or at least to listen reverently to a prayer. Being asked to address them I tried to pave the way for my remarks by telling them that I had come from Boston to speak to them, and asked them how many had heard of Boston. What was my chagrin as a loyal Bostonian, proud of the Athens of America, to find that these young fellows had never heard of the city by the Charles. Going further in my search for geographical knowledge, I found that very few had heard of New York, but when I asked how many had heard of Chicago almost all the hands went up. My humiliation was then complete, and there was nothing for me to do except to go on with my address as best I could. During the World War which so soon followed this visit of ours, the heroic missionary doctors with their families and their associate, Miss Cushman, stuck to their posts, relieving thousands of the sick and wounded, caring for the dying, and bringing physical and spiritual comfort to multitudes in those distressing and dreadful years.

We soon left Konieh, going by rail across the Anatolian plain, and decided that, as we would be in the vicinity of several of the Seven Churches of Revelation, we would try to visit them all, a journey which added a fitting climax to one of the most interesting years of travel which we had ever spent.

THE SEVEN CITIES OF REVELATION

AN INTERESTING JOURNEY TO OLD PHILADELPHIA — SARDIS — THYATIRA — PERGAMUM — SMYRNA — EPHESUS — LAODICEA — A PERSIAN TOMB AT SARDIS — IMMENSE RUINS OF PERGAMUM — DESOLATE RUINS OF LAODICEA — SCRIPTURE ILLUSTRATED.

ROM my boyhood the messages from the Spirit through St. John as recorded in the Book of Revelation have had an unusual fascination for me. They are so striking in their figurative language, and yet, when studied carefully, have such significance for modern church life. On this account I was especially attracted by the possibility of making a visit to each of these cities on this journey. St. Paul had lured us to the vicinity of several of them and we resolved if possible to see them all.

Iconium is situated on the high Anatolian plain, and a day's journey brought us to Ushak on the edge of the great table-land. The next day we descended to the plains below. At the foot of the hills lies Philadelphia, the ancient city which commemorates the brotherly love of Attalus Philadelphus, and Eumenes. This is the only one of the seven cities, with the exception of Smyrna, that received unqualified praise from the "Spirit" who sent the messages through the Apostle John to the churches.

Here we met by appointment our friends Dr. and Mrs.

Edward Riggs, long-time missionaries in Turkey, whom we
had invited to go with us as our guests and also as our guides
and interpreters. Their companionship and knowledge of
the language and customs of the people made the journey far
more interesting and profitable than it could otherwise have
been.

Philadelphia, now called Alasheir, or the " Spotted City "
(why spotted we never learned), is one of the least interesting
of the seven because almost no excavation work has yet been
undertaken there. However, in a Greek school of some pretensions are displayed a few beautiful tablets and statues and
fragments of inscriptions which were discovered in digging the
foundation of the school building. Doubtless many rich finds
await the archaeologist who may have time and money to spend
in unburying the hidden treasures of ancient Philadelphia.

Going out into a vineyard in the outskirts of the city, we
saw a hole in the ground which had accidently caved in while
the vine dressers were at work, and there, but a few feet below
the surface, was an ancient wall covered with beautiful frescoes,
whose colors were still fresh after their entombment of a
millennium and a half.

Another reason why more interesting discoveries have not
yet been made here, is that there has always been a considerable
city on the site of Philadelphia, and many streets of houses
would have to be demolished to make a complete investigation
of the ruins beneath the surface.

Yet Philadelphia has interests of its own, and is still a place
of considerable importance. Lying as it does almost on the
foothills that lead to the vast plains beyond, it is now, as it
was in the days of the Seer of Patmos, the Open Gateway to
Anatolia, and the commendatory message to the church, " Behold I have set before thee an open door which no man can
shut," gains new emphasis as we remember how the great
Roman highway to Anatolia passed through this city, and that
the modern railway which connects the plains of Smyrna with

the " regions beyond," still makes it " an open door " of distinction and importance.

Here we spent the night in the home of a friendly Greek who, for a very considerable consideration, was willing to take us in, since, strange to say, there is no hotel in the city. We were much interested in the streams of water that flow through many of the principal streets, often making a temporary footbridge necessary in order to cross from one side to the other. It was the time of the irrigation of the vineyards, and water is turned on periodically from the reservoirs in the hills, and in order to reach the vineyards it must flow through several of the city streets.

Great water buffaloes frequently blocked our path, and we apparently had to choose between wet feet in the irrigated streets and being impaled on their formidable horns. However they are harmless as well as stupid beasts, and it was not difficult to avoid them.

The Greek church of chief interest in Philadelphia contains a curious old painting representing a litteral interpretation of Rev. I: 11–18. The Apostle John is " lying as if dead " at the feet of the figure of Christ who holds in His right hand " seven stars," and " out of whose mouth proceeds a sharp two-edged sword," while his countenance is " as the sun shining in his strength." He stands in the midst of the " seven golden candlesticks," his " head and hair as white as wool," his eyes are as " a flame of fire," and he is " girt about at the breasts with a golden girdle."

This crude and realistic picture was a fitting prelude to a journey among the cities which the Revelator has made supremely interesting to the Christian student.

About three hours' ride by rail from Alasheir, the ancient Philadelphia, lies Sardis, " Sart " in the Turkish tongue, and this proved to be in many respects the most interesting of the seven cities.

After a walk of a mile or more from the station, over a

broken country, we saw looming on the horizon two huge, fluted pillars of granite, standing some thirty feet above the soil, wonderful monuments of an ancient civilization in this now desert country. For centuries these mighty columns alone marked the site of old Sardis. For a time after we came in view of these pillars they were the only striking objects within our range, but as we drew nearer, we saw that there were a hundred men or more delving in the ground at their base, that a little gravity tramway was carrying away the dirt and stones; and, peering over the edge of the excavations, we saw the remains of two remote civilizations, which the Princeton Expedition of American Archaeologists was unearthing.

No richer finds have been discovered anywhere, for here the remains of the ancient Lydians have been unearthed, and the only marbles ever discovered that are inscribed in the Lydian tongue. Though the letters are as sharp and clear-cut as if engraved yesterday, they had not then been translated, as the value of some of the Lydian letters had not been discovered. We found, too, that the apparent height of the two great pillars, six feet in diameter, which seemed to sprout above the soil, was but half of their real height, and that thirty feet more of their height had been buried by the fall of the Acropolis of Sardis in the terrible earthquake of the year 17 of the Christian era.

These pillars and scores of their companions, equally huge, which lay prostrate and had been buried for nearly twenty centuries, belonged to the Temple of Artemis (Diana), which was built or perhaps rebuilt in the time of Alexander the Great, and which seems never to have been completely finished.

But more wonderful than the remains of this mighty structure were the remains of a still older sanctuary, part of which lay beneath the ruins of the great Greek temple. This temple was built by Croesus, the Lydian king, who was afterwards conquered by Cyrus the Great and dragged at the victor's chariot-wheels.

Nowhere in the world do we find more concentrated history than in Sardis. Croesus, whose name has become a synonym for wealth, reigned here. Here Solon, the wisest man of old, whose name in all languages stands for erudition as the name of Croesus stands for wealth, came to visit the king. Across these plains swept the victorious hosts of Cyrus the Persian, and Darius the Mede. From the plains of Sardis started the Republican army under Brutus and Cassius, on their ill-starred journey across the mountains to the plains of Philippi, as has already been recorded.

When we arrived at Sardis the head of the American expedition, Professor Butler, and Mr. La Rose, one of his assistants, with a number of workmen were unearthing a Persian tomb on a hill a half mile from the ruins, a hill tunneled with hundreds of graves, since for centuries it had been the necropolis of Sardis. Many of these tombs had been opened, and the one discovered on the day that we were there, a beautiful sarcophagus of Persian terra cotta, when opened, was found to contain the remains of a young girl. Her bones and her luxurious black hair were all that remained after more than two millenniums of entombment, though some trinkets and tear bottles and jewelry proved that she belonged probably to the Persian nobility.

On the opposite side of the excavations was the citadel of Sardis, a small mountain which had been half levelled in the terrible earthquake of which I have spoken. It still rises abruptly to a sharp peak from the plain, showing an almost perpendicular wall on the side toward Sardis, and was supposed in ancient days to be impregnable. But the sense of security which it gave to the ancient Sardians was their undoing, for during the centuries, on more than one occasion, the enemy stealthily stole around to the other side of the citadel which was less steep, surprised the garrison, captured the acropolis, and had Sardis at their mercy.

Nestling under the shadow of the acropolis was the temporary home of the archaeologists, and also the little museum of priceless treasures which they had collected, and which must later be turned over to the Turkish government. Our new-found friends were most hospitable, and invited us to share their noonday meal, which we were not loath to do after living for days on the meager fare of dirty Turkish or Greek eating-houses. The only people in the neighborhood besides the American archaeologists and their little army of workmen were some nomad Turks living in wretched fashion under squalid camel-hair tents, or under a thatch of straw.

The whole region swarms with historic memories. A few miles away, but in plain sight, are the *Ben Tepe,* or the "Tombs of a Thousand Kings." As a matter of fact there are only about six hundred of these tombs, and they were not all occupied by kings by any means. Some of them are doubtless the tombs of the high priests, or of the great nobility. They are all great round mounds of earth, some rising quite to the dignity of hills, and have long since been looted of any valuable treasures they might originally have contained.

The little River Pactolus still flows through the plains, close to the ruins of the great temples of Alexander and Croesus. We crossed it by a little footbridge on the way to the necropolis, and recalled how Croesus retrieved its golden sands, for its wealth was not altogether mythological by any means, coined the gold into tokens of wealth, and thus became the first great trader between the East and the West. Some traces of gold are still found in the Pactolus, though its largest wealth was exhausted thousands of years ago.

Leaving Sardis on the same afternoon we spent the night at Manisa, the ancient Magnesia, which has given us one or two important English words, magnetism and magnesium, which was here first discovered. There is little to be seen in Manisa, though its bazaar, as in all eastern towns, was interesting, and its copper bazaar was particularly noisy with the interminable tap, tap, tap, of a hundred coppersmiths, who laboriously pound out pans and pots and platters from the yellow metal.

Late on the afternoon of Washington's birthday, 1912, we reached Thyatira, now called Ak Chehir, which also lies on a branch of the French railway on which we had been travelling for many hours. Thyatira, like Philadelphia, is one of the less interesting of the seven cities, and for the same reason, because from the time of St. John, and probably for centuries before, a city has existed on this site, and there is little possibility at present of recovering its underground treasures. Nevertheless Thyatira has an interest for Biblical scholars, for not only was one of the messages of the book of Revelation sent to the Christian church here established, but it was the city of Lydia, the friend and hostess of St. Paul at Philippi, the wealthy woman who was " a seller of purple."

We bought some of Lydia's " purple," the madder root, which grows wild and in abundance in all this region. It yields a dye which, however, by no means corresponds to our idea of purple, and it is difficult to understand how Lydia could have made much money out of the muddy red dye stuff which the madder root we bought yielded.

We were much interested in a call on the Protestant Greek pastor of Ak Chehir. He lived in a modest, but pleasant home, and we were proud to have our pictures taken with his three little daughters, charming girls who rejoiced in the appropriate names of Lydia, Syntyche, and Chloe.

He went with us to visit the great man of the town, the Turkish Bey, who lived in a fine house in the outskirts of the city, which overlooked his humbler neighbors, and the great fields of wheat which he cultivated. In his ample grounds we saw a beautiful carved sarcophagus, now used as a fountain and watering-trough, as are many other sarcophagi in Asia Minor. The great unknown, who once occupied this tomb, and whose virtues are inscribed in elegant Greek upon the outside, little knew to what purpose his grave would be put.

Ak Chehir is a city of some 20,000 people, and the hotel at which we stopped was a great rambling affair with an immense courtyard that harbored cows and buffaloes, hens and geese, and also afforded ample accommodations for the few guests which the railway brings to Thyatira.

The next day we reached Soma, on the way to Pergamum, and a lady's *Line-a-Day Book,* to which I have access, abounds in the adjective " horrid " for that day. " It was a horrid road to a horrid hotel where we spent a horrid night," while the

PERGAMUM, ONE OF THE SEVEN CITIES OF REVELATION
The ancient city, famous as the most magnificent city of its day, was built
on the hill to the left.   Photographed by Mrs. Clark.

eating-house where we tried to stay the pangs of hunger was more " horrid " still, but when necessity drives, needs must.

There was fortunately nothing of interest to detain us in Soma, and, as the branch railway makes this its terminus, early the next morning we set off for Pergamum, the only one of the seven cities which lies far from a railway. We packed ourselves into an araba, and rode forty-two kilometers over a rough road, with much " jouncing and bouncing," according to the aforesaid *Line-a-Day Book.* Commendable efforts had been made to mend the road, or at least good intentions were shown, for piles of broken stone lined the roadside, and here and there for a mile or two at a stretch the stones had been pitched into the middle of the highway, and had been left there for the few passing arabas or foot passengers to tread down into a decent thoroughfare, — a quite impossible task.

The beautiful scenery, however, well repaid us for the discomforts of the journey. We seemed to be travelling on the rim of a great bowl which dipped below us, while the hills on the farther horizon constituted the outer rim of the bowl.

The soil in this region is fertile, and the vegetation luxurious. Many little streams, crossed by rude bridges, bring life-giving water to the thirsty earth.

After about six hours of bouncing and jouncing, the noble citadel of Pergamum came in view, the one imposing landmark in all this region. At the base lies the modern city of Bergama, reminiscent, even in its spelling, of the magnificent ancient capital, which at one period of the history of Asia Minor, was almost, if not quite, the greatest city in the world.

It was the glorious capital of the Province of Asia, to which flowed the wealth not only of that great province, but of the regions far away. The modern town is confined within narrow limits at the base of the old citadel, but the ancient city climbed clear to its top, and planted its splendid temples and baths, gymnasia, libraries, and private palaces on all sides of the great hill, which was at once the fortress and the fashionable quarter of Pergamum.

Never have I been so impressed with the extent and the magnificence of ancient ruins. One can walk for hours and hours between broken marble columns, over tesselated pavements, climbing quarries of cut stone, finding everywhere inscriptions clear cut and indelible which tell of the mighty past. And yet these are only remnants, for the most beautiful of these marbles were long ago carried off to Berlin, and are now stored in the extensive Pergamenian Museum, where I afterwards saw them.

The ruins are now absolutely deserted of human kind, and

one can walk in solitude through the empty streets, and climb over the remains of a former glorious civilization with no one to molest or make one afraid. The modern Pergamenians, it is true, on a holiday, make the ruins a picnic resort, and it interested us to see a company of maidens among the ancient piles playing " Drop the handkerchief," " Ring-around-Rosy," and other games which seem as indigenous to Asia Minor as to America. Who knows that such games have not been played in the streets of Pergamum, before as well as since the days of its destruction, for the last two thousand years.

The weather was perfect, and we greatly enjoyed our two days amid the splendid relics of the past. On Sunday we made our way to the ruins of the " Temple of Rome and Augustus," and as we sat upon the doorstep, looking off upon the wide and peaceful prospect, we read the familiar passage in Revelation which must have been so comforting to the struggling and persecuted church in Pergamum:

" I know where thou dwellest, even where Satan's throne is."

We were actually seated on the base of Satan's throne, for the Temple of Rome and Augustus was " the throne " or " seat " to which St. John alluded. Here were brought Christians for trial, and here they were condemned either to abjure their faith in Christ or to suffer a horrible martyrdom. Many sculptured blocks of marble still remain in this ancient temple, though of course its best remains have been sent to Berlin.

There are few more beautiful views in the world than that from the Temple of Rome and Augustus. Green fields stretch out in every direction. The two chief rivers of the region, the ancient Selinus, and the Cetius, make the meadows green. Immediately in front are the three artificial hills which Pausanius nearly two thousand years ago told us were the tombs of Auge, the mother of Telephus, of Andromache and of Pergamus, while far off in the distance one can see on a clear day the shining water of the Aegean Sea.

In the modern town of Bergama are fifteen mosques, several khans, a respectable hotel called " The Alhambra," whose portly Greek proprietor was proud to be immortalized by our camera, and several interesting bazaars. Processions of ragged camels constantly edge their way through the narrow streets, their paniers bulging with cotton, wool, and leather, Bergama leather having a great reputation in these days.

In ancient times Pergamum was noted for its ointments, its pottery, and its parchment, the latter article, so vital to the records of civilization, receiving its name from this, the chief city of its manufacture. In the olden times, too, Pergamum was a notable seat of learning as well as of wealth and of marvellous architecture. Here was one of the most celebrated libraries of the world, containing 200,000 volumes, which were given by the prodigal and piratical Antony to his mistress Cleopatra, for which she probably cared little except as a sign of her conquest of the world-conqueror.

In one of the bazaars of Pergamum, which is also celebrated for its cutlery, we bought a two-edged carving knife, a reminder of the Revelator's message to the ancient church, " These things saith He that hath the sharp two-edged sword." It has proved to be an excellent knife, and the date inscribed on it, " 1912," frequently recalls to us our visit to the once mighty metropolis of Asia.

In these Bible lands one is constantly reminded of Biblical expressions. In the uncleanly Greek eating-house in Bergama where we obtained our meals, four polite Greeks kindly vacated the table at which they were seated, in order to give our party a chance to sit together. We found that our predecessors had thrown the bones from their mutton chops under the table and a couple of dogs were fighting at our feet through all the meal for these delicatessen. Now, as in the olden time, " even the dogs may eat of the crumbs which fall from their master's table."

After two delightful days in Pergamum our araba-ji drove

A STREET IN SMYRNA
Probably destroyed in late massacre.

us back to Soma, where we were obliged to spend another night in its filthy hotel, and thence we went on by rail to Smyrna, the second most important seaport in the whole Turkish Empire. This too, as we know, was one of the Seven Cities, and one of the two that received unstinted commendation from the Master. Here also we were reminded of the way in which the Revelator fitted his message to the church to which he wrote. " Be thou faithful unto death, and I will give thee the crown of life," he said to the faithful Christians of Smyrna. Alas! poor Smyrna! How much Smyrniot Christians of 1922 need the comfort of this passage.

This capital was called " the City of the Beautiful Crown," and as one looks up to the mighty acropolis which towers over the modern city he sees the ruins of the ancient crown of palaces and fortresses which seemed to encircle and diadem the hill. So familiar was this appellation that one of the greatest poets of Smyrna in noble verse had long ago told the people that " the true crown of the city was not a crown of noble buildings but of just and righteous citizens, who alone constituted the city's glory and treasure."

In going to Ephesus over the well-appointed English railway we passed through " Paradise," which, as compared with most Turkish railway towns, is a Paradise indeed, since there is established a splendid American " International Institute " to which I have before alluded, and which, since my last visit to Smyrna, had been moved to the suburb of Paradise.

After two and a half hours, some forty-eight miles from Smyrna, " Ayasolouk " is called by the guard with stentorian lungs, and we find that we have come to the railway station of the ruins of Ephesus where was the church that " lost its first love." Ayasolouk, which means Holy Theologian, referring to St. John, is the termination of the journey of many tourists who think they have been to Ephesus. Here, it is true, are the remains of the great temple of Diana, commonly

associated with Ephesus, and the ruins of the Church of St.
John of the Middle Ages. But the really important ruins
of Ephesus are three miles away, and can be reached only on
foot or on donkey back.

As the railway time-table allows a stop of only about two
hours, a time insufficient to visit the real Ephesus, many travellers see the exceedingly scanty relics in the neighborhood of
Ayasolouk, get a good dinner at the excellent tourist hotel,

AMONG THE RUINS OF EPHESUS
From photograph by Mrs. Clark.

and hurry back to Smyrna with the impression that they have
" done Ephesus."

There has, indeed, been more than one Ephesus, or at
least, according to the prophecy of St. John, "its candlestick
has been removed" more than once "out of its place." The
most ancient city was established near Ayasolouk. The Ephesus of St. John and St. Paul was three miles away, where the
chief ruins are to-day. The city was then on the seashore
with a splendid port, but the little river which brought down
mud and silt from the mountains, after some centuries made
the port impossible, and the candlestick of Ephesus was

moved back near the original site, where in the Middle Ages it was an important city ecclesiastically and politically. At this time the Church of St. John was almost as famous as the temple of Diana had ever been, its annual revenues amounting to $100,000 a year.

Then came the unspeakable Turks, who wherever they go destroy every vestige of ancient civilizations, and since then Ephesus has been little more than a dwelling-place for owls and bats and jackals. Still the glorious ruins remain. Though the excavations are not yet complete, the old city has been more thoroughly unearthed than any other of the Seven Cities, unless it be Pergamum. Here are long streets paved with marble, with the remains of marble colonnades on each side. Here are the ruins of great temples, a splendid library, a beautiful market place, a great gymnasium, and a stadium where the Grecian youths exercised themselves.

Perhaps the most interesting ruin is that of the enormous theatre, capable of seating 24,500 people. Though the marble slabs have been removed on which the people of Ephesus sat as they witnessed the games, it is not difficult to follow the outline of the seats, for as in all these old theatres (and every ancient city had one or more) the seats followed a semi-circular excavation in the hillside, and rose one above the other.

In the proscenium are heaped together in endless confusion, capitals and friezes, and drums of columns and architraves.

Though the temple of Diana was three miles away, it was in this theatre that the mob shouted the praises of Diana for two long hours. Here the common sense of the town clerk of Ephesus at last prevailed and quieted the people by telling them that every one knew that Ephesus was the temple-keeper of the great goddess Diana, and that Paul and his companions were neither robbers of temples nor blasphemers of the goddess. If my readers will again study the nineteenth chapter of Acts, they will refresh their minds on these stirring events in the life of the apostle. As we stood in the theatre we could hear in imagination the hoarse shouts of the angry mob, as they monotonously invoked the goddess; also the politic words of the town clerk, and could see Alexander, the Jew, vainly trying to gain a hearing from the people who would not listen to a despised Israelite.

So far had the bigotry and veneration for the poor little wooden goddess in her great temple gone, that the Ephesians of Paul's time were proud of having their city called Neocoros or " Temple Sweeper " of the goddess. This name was originally given to the lowest class of slaves who kept the temple clean, but the Ephesians put the name Neocoros upon their coins to show that the city desired no greater honor than to be known as the temple-sweeper of the goddess Diana.

The last of the Seven Cities whose message is recorded in Revelation is Laodicea, and it was the last city that we visited on this journey. It lies upon the same line of railway as Ephesus, some eighty miles beyond that city, on the well-managed English line that runs southeast from Smyrna. Throughout the whole distance from Ephesus to Laodicea the road follows the valley of the Meander, or its scarcely less celebrated tributary, the Lycus, which joins the Meander shortly before it gets to Laodicea.

Great orchards of fig trees fill the valley of the Meander, the most celebrated region in the world for the unequalled Smyrna figs, and throughout almost its whole length we saw the shapely trees with their smooth white bark, which have contributed so much to the wealth of the province. Visions of college classics and of the mythical stories of childhood were brought to our minds by every turn of the meandering Meander, and its banks on that spring day, bright with millions of gorgeous anemones, made it seem the fit abiding-place for the spirits with which mythology peopled its banks.

The modern Turkish names of many of the stations on the

way to Laodicea are most interesting. For instance *Balachik* means " Little Place Up Above," *Deirmanjak* means " Dear-Little-Mill "; while a station still further south called *Kuyukak* means " Dear-Little-Well." These affectionate diminutives show how dear even to the Turk are the " scenes of his childhood."

At length after nearly a whole day's journey, a journey long in time but short in distance, we reached Gonjeli, at the foot of the great hill which is covered with the ruins of Laodicea. Here once was a proud, rich city, and here was the church which received the most scathing rebuke spoken by the Spirit to any one of the seven churches of Asia. Laodicea was famous for its banking houses, its millionaires, its doctors, its eye-salve, and its wool, which was long and soft, glossy and black. The secret of raising the breed of sheep that produced this wool has now been lost, but in St. John's day this glossy, black wool which came from Laodicea and was then woven into beautiful and costly garments was famous throughout the world.

Remembering these sources of wealth, the banking houses, the eye-salve, and the black wool, we better understand the special point of the Spirit's exhortation: " I counsel thee to buy of me gold tried in the fire," and " white garments that thou mayest be clothed," and " eye-salve to anoint thine eyes that thou mayest see." The true gold of spiritual riches, the white garments of righteousness, and the medicine for spiritual blindness, were the things that this lukewarm church needed. Laodicea is the most desolate and God-forsaken of all the Seven Cities. Even Sardis, though quite as dead, is far more interesting to the traveller. The barren, utterly deserted hill on which Laodicea stood rises above the mean little Turkish village of Eski Hissar and contains not a single inhabitant. No wandering shepherd even pastures his flocks among the ruins. Wolves and foxes may, perhaps, occupy the artificial caves at night, but no living creature picks a scanty subsistence from between the rocks which strew the ground so thickly that scarcely a blade of grass can grow. The ruins cover hundreds of acres, and though they have been quarried for a thousand years by all the villages round about, yet there is enough good building material left to erect another city on the site of the ancient metropolis.

Some of the great stones of an ancient temple I measured and found them to be four feet long and three feet thick. A splendid aqueduct brought water from the hills miles away. But the most impressive ruins are those of two great theatres and a vast stadium. Each theatre is built into a natural hollow in the hillside, and I estimated that the theatres together would seat from fifty to seventy thousand people, and the stadium, nearly twice the size of that at Athens, would accommodate not less than 140,000. Evidently the Laodiceans were a pleasure-loving people.

If the ruins of Laodicea are depressing, the mighty mountains of God which surround it are inspiring. Snow-clad hills 8,000 and 10,000 feet high keep guard over the city to the south. Under the shadow of one of these hills lie the ruins of Colossae, while in the opposite direction lies Hierapolis, to which we journeyed on horseback on the day after our arrival at Laodicea.

The ruins of this city are far more interesting than those of Laodicea, for some of the buildings are still in a tolerable state of preservation. But most interesting are the enormous terraces of calcareous deposit which comes from the hot springs that rise in a deep pool beyond the ruins of the gymnasium. The deposits are of snowy whiteness, and from a little distance one thinks that he must climb an ice mountain to reach the site of the " holy city." A more accurate figure would be a frozen Niagara. The hot day on which we climbed it, however, had no suggestion of ice. A footpath enables one to make his way over these remarkable terraces and stalactite formations to the ruins of old Hierapolis.

All about were numberless little basins, the water of a lovely bluish tint, and quite warm to the touch. In one great hot pool I took a delicious bath in company with several brawny Turks, and afterwards our little party ate our lunch in the shadow of a triumphal arch. Altogether our visit to Hierapolis was one of the most interesting of all these months of travel.

The next day we returned to Smyrna and soon after took passage for Naples on the ill-fated " Senegal," afterwards torpedoed, like several other ships on which I have sailed. From Naples the good ship " Cedric " took us to New York, and this long and varied journey was over.

IN THE HOLY LAND ONCE MORE

A SIXTIETH BIRTHDAY — PALESTINE JUST BEFORE THE GREAT
WAR — JERUSALEM — NAZARETH — DAMASCUS — BAAL-
BEC — BEIRUT — TYRE — SIDON — CAIRO — ASSIOUT —
ALEXANDRIA — SYRACUSE — EARTHQUAKE-RUINED MES-
SINA — POZZUOLI — ROME.

T MAY seem somewhat strange that while I was still holding the office of president of the United Society, and of the World's Christian Endeavor Union, I could give so much time to foreign travel that was not altogether connected with Christian Endeavor meetings.

The truth is that at the convention of 1911, when I had almost concluded my sixtieth year, I had urgently striven to be released from my presidential duties, feeling that some younger man could carry the burden more easily and success-fully. But my resolution was received with a storm of protest from my colleagues and from the trustees who yearly elected me, and it seemed useless to press the matter. However, I made it plain that, as I received no salary, if I did not relinquish the office entirely, I must be free to spend my time where, in my own opinion, I could do most good, and that the responsi-bility for the promotion of the work in America must rest largely upon my colleagues. This responsibility they were both willing and able to accept, and I felt fully at liberty to spend as much or as little time in my Boston office as I deemed necessary.

If it would not seem egotistical, I would describe at some length, more than one very kind reception and dinner given me at this time in view of my thirty years of connection with the Endeavor movement, when various kind things were said, many of which I felt were undeserved, for my friends and the public generally have always given me much more credit for the initiation and success of the Christian Endeavor movement than I should have received.

One present received on my sixtieth birthday I particularly cherish; a gold watch-chain from the young people of America. Its thirteen four-sided links contain on each side the name of one State or Province of North America, not forgetting either Alaska or Hawaii. The idea originated with Karl Lehmann, then Secretary of Christian Endeavor for the Southern States. The money was collected, I understand, in very small sums, and really represented in a unique way the young people of North America.

Two loving-cups, one from the trustees of the United Society, another from my colleagues in the office, and still another received later from the people of Claremont, my boyhood home, where the town as well as the church a little later gave me a very unusual welcome, are also among my treasured possessions. One cannot have too many cups or other such tokens if they tell of the love of cherished friends.

It must be remembered also that all my journeys, whether to the Seven Cities of Asia, to the Cities of St. Paul, or elsewhere, were really only incidents in Christian Endeavor tours.

I have always gone abroad in response to invitations from various countries and have taken occasion to make these other journeys as tributary to them. Moreover the articles and books which these unusual journeys have made it possible for me to write, have also made it possible to undertake other Christian

Endeavor journeys in many lands without expense either to the United Society at home for salary or travelling expenses, or to the people whose conventions I attended.

With few exceptions I have spent six months out of every twelve in America, frequently a year or more at a time, and have been able in those months to keep in touch with my work at home, and to attend many conventions and union gatherings in the United States and Canada. No other man of the office force could then have visited the societies in other lands, because the treasury of the United Society could not afford it, and because no one could be spared from the special work he had to do. For this reason the journeying business naturally and almost inevitably fell to my lot.

During the summer of 1912, after our return home, my dear wife came near making a longer journey than any we had taken together; for a severe attack of appendicitis, and a serious operation were very disquieting events of that summer. However, in the end, she successfully joined the " No Appendix Club," to which many of her friends already belonged, and as soon as she was well enough to travel several circumstances induced us to go abroad again. Her own health I felt would be improved, as she would be free from household cares.

We had visited only about half the Cities of St. Paul, and were anxious to complete our self-imposed task. Our youngest son had just graduated from Dartmouth College, and had had a partial promise of a journey to the Holy Land if his college course should be creditable to himself and his parents. Urgent letters had come from the Endeavor unions of some sections of Great Britain and Europe; and especially from Scandinavian countries, asking that I visit them once more. The Christian Herald Publishing Company wished me to write a book about Palestine, which I did not feel competent to undertake until I should visit the Holy Land again. All these considerations together induced us to take another journey to the Near East.

On the third of October, 1912, my second son, Harold, celebrated the thirty-sixth anniversary of the wedding day of his father and mother, by marrying Harriet Scoles Adams, the daughter of Rev. Harry Adams, a Congregational minister then settled in Cliftondale. By a singular coincidence this was also the wedding anniversary of the bride's father and mother. It proved to be the same kind of a lovely third of October that his mother and I remembered in 1876, and which has been repeated every year since, almost without exception. Mr. Adams and I performed the ceremony and the young couple started on their brief honeymoon. This beloved pastor, not many years later, was killed in a sad automobile accident in Florida.

Two days later, on October 5, we sailed on the "Martha Washington" for Trieste. This too, was one of the steamers that figured in the early days of the Great War, being interned in New York harbor when the war broke out. The second Balkan war was just at its height, and something like a thousand patriotic and hilarious Greeks took passage in the steerage and the second class, determined to fight for their native land if opportunity should offer.

Nothing of moment signalized this voyage, though it gave us an opportunity to spend a few hours in Algiers, a city we had never before visited. The botanical garden, the Kasbah, the great mosque and palace were interesting, but our steamer did not allow very careful inspection.

Landing at Patras we took the rail, as on previous journeys, to Athens, and in two or three days sailed for Alexandria on the "Mount Athos," a small and dirty Russian steamer which only afforded us the accommodation of a small, dark, stuffy, inside stateroom. The decks were so piled with baskets of fruit that there was scarcely standing-room upon them, and we were glad enough that the voyage involved only two days of discomfort.

Arriving at Alexandria when the scare of some infectious

disease was prevalent, we all had to put out our tongues as we lined up in a row, and undergo a somewhat thorough and lengthly medical inspection. No occasion makes a line of people look more self conscious and foolish than such an exhibition, and none can seem more ridiculous to the looker-on, as he sees one long red tongue after another run out for the doctor's eye. This is a process which we have had to endure in other parts of the world. The compensation for such enforced ridiculousness is that these inspections have doubtless prevented the spread of many plagues which in former days carried devastation from country to country and to the ends of the earth.

The very next day we sailed on the Khedivial Line for Jaffa. I have rarely taken a more lovely journey. The soft air, the beautiful smooth sea, the line of the Egyptian shore sharply cut against the moonlit sky, all combined to make that evening sail a memorable one. We expected a terrifically hard landing at Jaffa, for, after leaving Port Said, a portentous thunder storm seemed to be following our ship and rapidly gaining on us. The landing was rough enough, as it usually is, but we were so fortunate as to get ashore before the storm actually broke.

For nearly a week the ships that followed were unable to make a landing, and some travellers whom we afterwards met were obliged to go on to Khaifa, and then, because of the heaviness of the road, were scarcely able to make their way to Jerusalem in order to get even a glimpse of the Holy City, which they had come so far to see!

One of these unfortunate travellers, whom we met in a hotel in Khaifa, started in a wagon with others for Jaffa and Jerusalem, but the roads were so bad that they only journeyed for a few miles before their wagon broke down. Some of them stopped in a little Turkish village for the night hoping to get on in some way the next day, but the woman of whom I have spoken and her husband appeared at the hotel again in the evening. She explained her return by saying that she could not make up her mind to stay in that village. " Why! " she explained, " they do not even speak your own language. The idea of staying or travelling with people who do not speak your own language! Why, I would not think of such a thing!" So she lost her visit to Jerusalem, though some of the others succeeded in making the journey safely in spite of the language.

This visit to Palestine was less than two years before the beginning of the Great War, and consequently one of the last of a thousand years of Turkish misrule over the Holy Land. The evidences of this misrule were everywhere seen in the Holy Land in those days. The difficult, and in some places almost impassable roads throughout Palestine, which in Roman times was girdled with fine highways, was another indication of the lack of public spirit of the Turk. The denuded, rain-washed hillsides, the miserable villages with houses unfit for a dog's kennel, which, with their rounded mud roofs looked from a little distance like rows of gigantic beehives; all these indications of poverty and shiftlessness show what the Turkish rule had done for the land of Jesus and His apostles.

Poor Palestine, once so rich and fertile, " the joy of the whole earth " as the Jews esteemed it, had indeed fallen upon lean and bitter years. Let us hope that her sorrows are over, and that under a just and wise government, supported by the League of Nations, it may again blossom as the rose. This journey may be considered of especial interest to some, as old things were soon to pass away. Let us hope that all things may become new.[1]

A great gap had been made in the wall of Jerusalem near Jaffa Gate, to provide for the entrance of William Hohen-zollern and his suite. On this famous visit to Jerusalem he tried to persuade himself and the people that he was their chief protector and defender, and a bosom friend of the Sultan. I

[1] As I correct the proof of this chapter I cannot speak so hopefully of the passing of Turkish misrule as I could when the chapter was written a few weeks earlier.

do not believe the story that he also proclaimed himself a Moslem, and the Defender of Mohammedanism; it seems hardly likely, since I noticed that he wrote in the royal visitors' book in the beautiful German Church which he had built in Jerusalem, his favorite Scripture verse, " There is no other name under heaven, given among men, whereby we must be saved."   This was written in a bold and supposedly royal hand, while underneath the Empress had inscribed her motto of similar import, " Other foundation can no man lay than that is laid, even Christ Jesus."

It has been a pleasure to remember, since the wonderful campaign of General Allenby redeemed Palestine from the rule of the Turk, that the city is being beautified and in part rebuilt, a symbol at least of the rebuilding of the spiritual Jerusalem.

It is most gratifying, also, to remember with what reverence the British army entered Jerusalem, quietly and on foot, without the blare of trumpets or the boom of the guns of victory.

The memory of our whole journey throughout Palestine, from Gaza to Jaffa, to Jerusalem, to Samaria, to Jenin, to Damascus, to Beirut, has had an added interest since the historic and triumphant march of the British troops throughout the whole length of this land of sacred memories.

Unfortunately our journey began at the time of the " former rains " and during much of the early part of it we were drenched by Pluvius. It seemed as though both the " former and the latter rains " were pouring down upon us at the same time.

Nablous, the ancient Shechem, was our first resting place after leaving Jerusalem, and, as we drove up to the door of the German hotel, the windows of heaven appeared to be opened, and all the watery contents of the firmament were poured upon us.

Every Bible student knows that near this spot was Jacob's Well, where Jesus talked with the woman of Samaria. The hill on whose slopes Nablous is situated is the ancient mountain where for more than two thousand years the Samaritans have worshipped. This was the mountain of which the Samaritan woman said in her conversation with the Master: " Our fathers worshipped in this mountain; and ye say that in Jerusalem is the place where men ought to worship." In this same mountain the sons and daughters of the Samaritan fathers have worshipped ever since. The sect is now reduced to about seventy souls, but they still have their high priest, their Samaritan book of the law, and their occasional service on the mountain top.

Here, too, opposite Mt. Gerizim, is Ebal, " the Mountain of Cursing," as Gerizim was " the Mountain of Blessing." They seem too far apart for the proclamations of blessing and cursing described in the book of Deuteronomy, yet travellers who have studied the situation have declared that, owing to their peculiar formation, it is possible to talk from one to the other without a modern megaphone.

Jenin was our next stopping place, a wretched Turkish town with one or two tumble-down mosques, the only building of any pretension and size being the Hamburg-American Hotel. The Germans had built almost the only decent hotels in all Palestine. In Shechem and Jenin, in Nazareth and Khaifa, in Tiberias and Damascus, as well as in Jerusalem their inns alone afforded decent food and clean lodging to the wayfarer.

We were so fortunate as to be able to spend a Sunday in Nazareth, and, instead of climbing the long zigzags which lead from the Plain of Esdraelon up to the mountain home of Jesus' boyhood, in the American wagon which was our means of conveyance on this journey, we chose to walk by the short cuts, that we might in imagination, at least, plant our feet in the footprints of the Master, and enjoy the splendid scenery which every turn in the mountain road revealed.

Nazareth, like Jerusalem and other holy places in those

days was a place of disillusionment to the traveller. Though some fine churches, hospitals, and schools had been built by foreign Christians in memory of the Master's boyhood and young manhood, yet the trail of the Turk was over it all. The rotten carcass of a dead horse befouled the air as we walked from our hotel to the " Well of the Virgin," and the strains of rag-time music from an American gramophone. grated upon our ears as we passed a Turkish inn.

THE FOUNTAIN OF THE VIRGIN, NAZARETH

Where Jesus and Mary undoubtedly drew water and carried it home as here represented. The only fountain in Nazareth.

The " Well of the Virgin " itself is one of the few places in Palestine that fulfills one's expectations and realizes one's dreams. Here to-day come the women of Nazareth, many of them noted for their beauty, with their water jars, to fill them at the one well of the city. Many of them were accompanied by small children, and it took little imagination to see the Virgin and the boy Christ carrying home the day's water-supply from this ever-gushing fountain.   Here we could feel, as scarcely anywhere else in Palestine, that Jesus and His mother must have come many a time, for wells like this are among the few unchangeable features of an eastern landscape, and the customs are almost equally unchangeable.

I have described in another volume the sacred sites of Nazareth and of other places in the Holy Land, and must hurry on lest my book, like too many other autobiographies, should become inordinately long.

From Nazareth we went to Khaifa and there discharged our grouchy and overreaching Turkish driver whom we had engaged, together with his outfit from the famous "American Colony" in Jerusalem.   I may pause here to say that we were much impressed with the kindness, courtesy, and fair dealing of this American Colony, about whom one hears so many contradictory reports.   Their intercourse among themselves seemed to us ideal in its gentle courtesy.   The men called each other Brother Joseph, Brother David, Brother John, etc.; and their speech and action showed that it was no brotherliness of the lip alone but of every-day life.

One day of our stay in Khaifa was devoted to a visit to Acca, or Acre, the old Ptolemais, where St. Paul landed, for we missed no opportunity to see the cities that St. Paul had seen, however brief his sojourn in them.

Acca is well worth seeing for itself, and for its historic interest.   The short three-mile journey thither from Khaifa was along a beautiful crescent beach of hard sand, much traversed by caravans of camels on their way to the seaport. Several of them we met, and could easily imagine ourselves back in the years of the great Apostle.   The useless walls of Acca have been bombarded by many fleets.   In more recent times Napoleon tried in vain to take the city, while about the middle of the nineteenth century the British and Austrians, then allies, captured it, and the crumbling walls still show evidence of these bombardments.

From the eastern wall of the city we could see the so-called prison of Abbas Effendi, the Baha, who so captured the hearts of many American women about this time. From the walls of Acre his prison looked like a beautiful villa in an oasis of its own, but to this oasis he was confined for more than thirty years, by Abdul Hamid, the Great Assassin. It so happened that the Baha, who died in 1912, was on the steamer which we later took from Liverpool, homeward bound. He was then surrounded by a coterie of worshipping women, and one or two men. Whenever he came to the table in the dining saloon they would all stand in reverent silence until he was seated.

One day he invited me to join him at afternoon tea in his stateroom, and he talked in excellent English of his principles of brotherhood and world fellowship, to all of which I could heartily agree. I imagine, however, that if he had told me of other Zoroastrian doctrines which he held I should have found it more difficult to subscribe to them. He was very complimentary concerning the influence of the Christian Endeavor movement in promoting good fellowship and unity. When I told him that I had recently seen the prison of his old enemy, Abdul Hamid, in Salonica, he said, " Yes, it is true; the Lord took the chains off of my neck and put them around his."

He was a very benevolent looking old patriarch, with a long white beard and a kindly, untroubled expression which I do not wonder won him friends and converts in America among those who, like the ancient Athenians, " found time for nothing else but either to tell or to hear some new thing."

Damascus, which was next on our route, we found the most interesting of all Syrian cities, except for its dearth of sacred associations. This dearth however is only comparative. Here we could follow Paul through the street that is called Straight to the home of Judas, where he lodged, and where he was visited by Ananias, through whose kindly hands he received again the sight which the vision on the Damascus Road had temporarily darkened.

Here, too, we could recall the far earlier days of Abraham, and remember that his steward Eliezer was a Damascene. The Abana and Pharpar still flow by the ancient city, the rivers which Naaman considered, with some apparent justice, so much better than the muddy Jordan for his cleansing bath. The former is now called the Barada, and flows through the very heart of the city, rising in a wonderful spring, some twenty or thirty miles east of the city of Damascus. The railroad to Baalbec follows the Barada in all its windings to its source, and there are few more picturesque journeys than this, made charming as it is by rugged hills and the leaping, sparkling river, which seems to hurry onward in order that it may bring life and beauty to the ancient city.

Around the city are miles and miles of beautiful orchards of semi-tropical growth, and it is said that the trimmings and waste woods from these forests of fruit trees provide the populous city with all its necessary firewood. The oasis which these rivers have made possible in the midst of the desert, also made it inevitable that a great city, perhaps the oldest in the world, should here be established, and we do not cavil at the truth of the old legend that Mohammed, when he saw the city, surrounded by its vast greenery, declared that he would not enter it, because man could have but one Paradise, and he preferred the heavenly home to Damascus.

In some respects 1912 was a particularly interesting time to visit Damascus, because of the excitement which prevailed in regard to the Libyan War in which Italy was then engaged. A " Holy War " had been proclaimed against Italy, and some hundreds of Moslems had come from India to arouse the people against the foes of Mohammedanism. They made a great noise and clatter, as they paraded through the narrow streets of Damascus, shouting their war cry and waving their banners in a belligerent manner.

We crowded ourselves into the sheltering nook of a friendly bazaar as they rushed by, but noticed that they received very little attention from the populace, and that the business of the bazaars was scarcely interrupted for a moment. Evidently the arousing Jehad did not arouse.

It is worth while recording some impressions of Damascus as it was at that time, since so many changes have since taken place. In 1912 the East and the West seemed to be fighting for the mastery of Damascus; civilization and barbarism struggling for supremacy. The swift trolley cars, rushing at break-neck speed through the tortuous streets, jostled the slow-moving camels.

The telegraph wires and the great monument to celebrate the completion of telegraphic communication with Mecca were indications of modern haste and the annihilation of space, while business was still carried on in the bazaars in the same leisurely way, over innumerable cups of coffee, as it had been for a thousand years past.

Instead of having an asylum for the insane with fine buildings and spacious grounds as in Western lands, the poor, demented creatures were chained to staples in the wall of houses or shops while they were covered from the burning rays of the sun only with a piece of ragged burlap. Other lunatics who were less dangerous, ran freely through the streets, some of them with small trees over their shoulders, with which in a terrifying, though really harmless way they would attack the passers-by, demanding backshish, which I, at least, thought best to give them as the guide books advised without any unnecessary parleying.

Many cook-shops lined the streets in some parts of the city, where grinning calves' heads were displayed. Savory pieces of lean meat interlarded with pieces of fat from the large, flat tails of the sheep, were broiling on spits over open fires, and almost on the sidewalk itself. The savory odors doubtless attracted many customers to these open-air cook-shops, in spite of the fact that the flat cakes of bread were laid out on the open side-walk, exposed to all the dust and microbes of the streets.

Yet there were some really good hotels of modern character and often under German control, which catered to wealthier customers, side by side with ancient cook-shops.

Damascus has been an important city during all the years of recorded history, and perhaps for centuries before recorded time, and it gives promise of being a metropolis for thousands of years to come should the world survive so long. It is a railroad centre of considerable importance, having communication with Mecca on the south, Aleppo on the north, and Beirut on the west.

We took the latter direction, but determined to spend at least a few hours in Baalbec that we might view its mighty stones. Baalbec is a city of mystery. Little seems to be known of its history or its rulers, but they must have been Titans if we may judge from the enormous stones which they heaved into place in building their mighty temples and palaces. It is a standing wonder that I have never seen satisfactorily explained, how in those early days, with the primitive tools that must have been used, such gigantic blocks could have been hewn out of the quarries, transported over miles of hilly territory, and hoisted into their places in the enormous walls which there towered to the sky.

We visited the quarry from which many of the largest stones have been hewn. One of them still lies near its original home, and, as one looks at it from a little distance and sees, as I did, a man stretched out upon it at full length, one gets the impression of an insect on a small hill. And yet it was such men, such creatures as are represented by that outstretched peasant, who hewed out these enormous blocks of stone and lifted them into their permanent abiding-place.

The journey over the Lebanon mountains to Beirut is one of the most charming in all the world. For miles magnificent views greet the eye as the train climbs the summit of the mountains and goes down to the Mediterranean shore in many zigzags on the farther side.

Dr. Howard Bliss, President of the Syrian Protestant College, kindly met us at the station, and insisted upon our being his guests. The college had been greatly enlarged and improved since we were there twenty years before. Something like a score of fine stone buildings dot the ample campus, while the view from the college grounds, over the city and harbor of Beirut and the open Mediterranean, is entrancing. The buildings and equipment of this college are equal to those of almost any of our American colleges. Neither Dartmouth nor Amherst, Williams nor Princeton, can boast of better dormitories or class-rooms, and the administration of the two Doctors Bliss, father and son, has been extraordinarily successful. Dr. Daniel Bliss was then still alive, though he died shortly afterwards, and I have seen few more beautiful sights than the handsome old President Emeritus, then nearly ninety years old, and his fine-looking son, jointly leading the morning prayers, with hundreds of attentive Syrian youths before them in the commodious college chapel. Alas! the son, too, has since joined the great majority, mourned by multitudes of the many races whom he inspired to a better life.

My friend, Dr. Charles E. Jefferson, of Broadway Tabernacle, New York City, happened to be in Beirut during part of our stay, and we heard him preach one of his admirable sermons to the college boys and their friends. He seldom or never " strikes anything but twelve " when he speaks, and I regard him as one of the very best preachers in America, simple in his style, quiet in his delivery, but most effective in the limpid logic of his thoughts, and the beauty of his illustrations.

One of the most interesting side-trips of all this journey was our visit to Sidon and Tyre, whither we went led by the memories of St. Paul and also by the historic and Biblical lore connected with these ancient cities. We were accompanied by Dr. and Mrs. Ford, Presbyterian missionaries of Beirut, and the thirty-mile carriage ride along the Mediterranean shore was a memorable one.

First we drove through an immense olive orchard, miles in extent, while many mulberrry groves which feed the silk-worm, grew at intervals all along the route. Near the water courses which we occasionally crossed, great clumps of olean-ders made the landscape gay. Scarcely ever, during all the journey, were we out of sight or sound of the sea. Sometimes great rocky cliffs and huge boulders against which the white surf perpetually dashed, hid the water for a few moments, but much of the way hard beaches of yellow sand stretched be-side the carriage road. On one of these beaches, we were gravely assured, Jonah was cast up, after his adventurous ride in the whale, and here is his tomb beside the very spot! The ancient care-taker let us look into the vault, and there, wonder-ful to relate, was not only the place where he had lain, but the very wooden coffin which contained his bones. To show that the coffin was no fake, we were actually allowed to touch it, and get so near to the illustrious mariner.

Another interesting incident of this ride was a call on a Druse prince, with whom our missionary guide was acquainted. He lives in a modest little castle on the very shore of the Mediterranean, and while the ladies of the party went into the inner room to converse with the princess, upon whom the profane eyes of strange men could never gaze, the prince entertained Dr. Ford and myself with cups of Turkish coffee, and the offer, which we declined, of Turkish cigarettes.

Several silk mills were passed on this journey, into one of which we went, and saw the boiling cocoons, and the filaments of silk unwound from them by the dexterous hands of Syrian maidens.

Sidon, though stripped of its ancient glory, is still an inter-esting city with a number of large mosques, from which we could hear the call of the muezzin five times a day, and fre-quently see the lonely dervish, pacing around the little balcony near the top of the minaret as he proclaimed that prayer was better than sleep and better than food. The Presbyterians are doing a fine work in Sidon, and their schools as well as their churches reach a large number of modern Sidonians.

Tyre and Sidon are always coupled together in Scripture phrase and in history. The next day we went on to Tyre, thirty miles south, which is a much more disreputable and woe-begone city than Sidon, even though very little can be said for the cleanliness of the latter in these modern days. It seems as though the terrible prophecies concerning Tyre had been entirely fulfilled. It is now but a wretched hamlet, with intolerably filthy streets, and with only one oasis, the mission house and premises of the English Woman's Missionary Society.

But how many memories the very name of Tyre brings back! The glorious ancient metropolis, "the Joyous City," whose destruction Isaiah predicted, the city which resisted the all-conquering might of Alexander the Great for many months, until at last he built, with incredible labor and loss of life, a causeway to the island on which it was then situated. This causeway is now a part of the mainland, half a mile broad, for the sea has washed in the sand on either side, and enormously increased its original proportions. Here are the remains of a Crusader's church, and some great pillars of ancient Tyre, mostly submerged, give a hint of her former glory.

As we looked at this squalid town, at the ragged fishermen drying their nets on the rocks that were once covered with palaces, the words of Isaiah seemed full of prophetic irony: " Is this your joyous city, whose antiquity is of ancient days . . . the crowning city whose merchants are princes, whose traffickers are the honorable of the earth? The Lord of hosts hath purposed it, to stain the pride of all glory, and to bring into contempt all the honorable of the earth."

We drove back to Sidon the same day, stopping for a short time to visit Zarephath in memory of Elijah, though there is nothing now to be seen but a hill, with a few small ruins. We visited what we were assured was the tomb of Elijah, a small

Moslem building with a little dome, a sad place with which
to associate the bold leader who did not hesitate to defy all
the prophets of Baal.

On reaching Sidon we visited both the Castle of the Sea,
and the Land Castle. The former is a striking landmark,
or rather sea-mark, for it is connected with the land by the
narrowest causeway, and one has to jump from one great
hewn stone to another to reach the ruins of the old castle.
At times these ruins are silhouetted against the sky, when the
sun is right, in a remarkable way.

But what interested me most in Sidon was the great hill
composed entirely of shells of the curious convoluted cockle
from which the famous Tyrian dye was made. Though Sidon
furnished most of the shells, Tyre gave its name to the royal
purple with which the robes of kings and conquerors were
dyed. One of these hills, as I remember it, is still something
like 150 feet long, and 50 feet high, and vast portions of it
very likely have been washed away during the last twenty
centuries. A few live Tyrian dye shells are still found, but
the mollusc seems to be practically extinct when compared
with the vast number of its ancestors. However, he is little
missed, since the aniline dyes have made him superfluous.

After spending two or three more busy days, crowded with
meetings and with calls among our kind missionary friends,
we took a ship of the Messageries Line, which by good
fortune proved to be a very comfortable one, to Port Said.
Here a most trying quarantine inspection, four hours long,
awaited us, before we could take the train for Cairo, where
we installed ourselves in the Khedivial Hotel. But our missionary friends would not allow us to stay long in the seclusion
of our inn, but insisted that we should take up our quarters
with them during the few days of our stay in this most interesting city.

The Christian Endeavor movement has long flourished in
the splendid mission of the United Presbyterian Church, and

we were kept busy with meetings of various kinds in churches and schools, and with sight-seeing, of which this wonderful city provides a superabundance.

An interesting trip up the Nile to Assiout occupied a couple of days. We could not afford the time to go by river, and so took a fast train each way. Our brief stay gave us a chance to see this interesting and ancient city of the fruitful Nile, with its palms and its abundant flowers. Many fine residences of the Egyptian nobles and bourgeoisie, some of whom have made great sums of money since the British occupation, are found here, as well as the slums where the proletariat live, and the Egyptian of this type is about the lowest in the world.

The United Presbyterians here have a fine college with half a thousand pupils, and the hospital, when we saw it, was besieged with a motley throng of afflicted humanity. Since our visit I have kept up a sporadic correspondence with some of the students, as I had with some of the missionaries for many years previously. One letter from an ardent Christian Endeavorer in the college tells of a " love committee " in the society, whose purpose is not to make matches, as its name might indicate, but to relieve the homesickness of the new students, and to make all feel at home in college circles. The college itself is called by many of the outsiders, " the Good Factory," because it has transformed the lives of so many of the boys, who have come from desperately unwholesome surroundings.

Our further engagements allowed us to spend but one night in Cairo on our return, after which we hurried on to Alexandria to take the steamer for Catania on the Sicilian shore. Nevertheless, before leaving Cairo, we had an hour or two for a visit to New Heliopolis, the wonderful, brand-new, spick and span suburb of Cairo, built on the yellow desert sands that have been made fruitful by abundant water. Here in the really palatial hotels and apartment houses the rich inhabitants of Cairo foregather when they wish to get out of the noise and bustle of the great city. New Heliopolis is brilliant with splendid flower gardens, fine avenues of trees, and all the charms which the fertile soil, when irrigated, can produce under Egypt's tropical skies.

I should have said, too, that we did not omit the Pyramids and the Sphinx. However many times one sees Cairo, conscience and inclination will not allow one to omit the Pyramids, the first of the Seven Wonders of the World. Our visit this time was made toward sunset, and a glorious crimson and golden sky added their greater glories to the stupendous impressions of these marvellous works of man.

In Alexandria we were the guests of Dr. and Mrs. Phinney of the Missionary Board, and though it was Thanksgiving Day, and abundant good cheer had been provided, not forgetting a turkey of Egyptian breed, we could not wait for dinner, and part at least of the lunch kindly prepared for us before we sailed had to be consigned to the Mediterranean.

Three days later, we reached Catania on the Sicilian shore. It did not detain us long though it is a city of historic interest, lying under the shadow of Mt. Aetna, which has more than once overwhelmed it, with frightful loss of life, so that the points of modern interest are not many.

The next day found us in Syracuse, a place vastly more attractive to the traveller. Few cities in all the world have seen and made so much human history as Syracuse. Carthaginians and Greeks and Romans, Normans, British and Bourbons, French and Italians, have battled for the island of which it was once the great metropolis. Here St. Paul stayed for seven days after escaping from the perils of the sea and the perils of the land on the island of Malta. Here Demosthenes and his Athenian army were defeated and overwhelmed by the Syracusans, and here Archimedes invented the screw and the lever with which he declared he could move the world, could he only find a *pou sto*. Here, too, he was killed while bravely defending his native city.

The most interesting statue in Syracuse is one of this same philosopher. It is situated in a beautiful little park near the sea, and close to the bubbling fountain of Arethusa, in whose limpid waters great fish go darting in and out among the rocks and water grasses. One might write a book about Syracuse, if one attempted to tell of its interesting historic sights, and I can merely catalogue a few of them, like Diana's temple and St. Paul's Church, the Greek theatre, the great amphitheatre, and the vast caves hewn out of the solid rock, called the "Ear of Dionysius."

Here it is said that the Tyrant could sit near the entrance and hear the plots of all the prisoners confined within the cave, even though they spoke in whispers, and it is perfectly true that at a certain point in the cave a distant whisper can be heard, and the slamming of a door sounds like a reverberating clap of thunder.

In the midst of the crooked, narrow lanes and dirty hovels of the modern city is a little church, on which is a recent tablet declaring that " here Paul once preached," a statement founded on facts as verifiable as the tomb of Jonah on the Mediterranean coast.

After leaving Syracuse, our next night was spent in ruined Messina. Although this was several years after the great earthquake the city had scarcely begun to recover from that terrible disaster. We reached there after dark, and as we walked through the deserted streets the great stone business blocks and warehouses seemed substantial and untouched as they loomed above us in the semi-darkness. But the next morning we saw that they were tenantless and that there was no light in the eyeless sockets of the windows, for they were mere shells. Everything within them was but dust and ashes, and there had been no attempt to rebuild these splendid blocks. The citizens, evidently discouraged by repeated earthquakes, were living for the most part in the *Campo Americana,* so called, the settlement of small wooden houses which had been transported ready made from benevolent America at the time of the earthquake. A little business was being done in temporary shacks, and the hotels were of the most primitive character imaginable. One night and part of a day were more than enough for Messina, but the discomfort of the dirty hotel was wiped from memory's slate by the charm of the next day's ride along the shore of southern Italy, always within sight of the sounding sea on one side and glorious, green-clad hills on the other.

In Naples we felt that we were back in the world again, and in a very familiar world to us. Here we stayed long enough to visit with considerable care Pozzuoli, the ancient Puteoli, drawn thither as to so many other places by the fact that here St. Paul landed, and took up his weary march, as a chained prisoner, on to Rome; for we were still following in his footsteps.

Pozzuoli is a filthy and degenerate city, in a most lovely situation. Every distant prospect pleases, but man and the immediate surroundings are vile enough. I do not dwell on these towns that we visited on this journey since I have described them at length in " The Footsteps of St. Paul," for that book was largely written in the cities that we visited, and the chapters appeared first as articles in *The Christian Herald*.

From Naples we made a somewhat zigzag journey to Montreux in Switzerland, visiting Rome for a few days, where we took especial pains again to see the Appian Way, and the Church of St. Paul without the Walls, the *Tre Fontane*, the House of Pudens, the Church of St. Pudentiana, the dungeon of the Mammertine Prison, and other places either of historic or traditional interest in St. Paul's life.

To Florence and Bologna, and Turin and Spallanza, we again gave a day each, and attended several Christian Endeavor rallies, thus hoping to do something for the cause which however has in Italy small chance to grow in the somewhat thin soil of Italian Protestantism.

To Montreux came our oldest son Eugene who was taking his college Sabbatical in Freiburg, his wife and their dear little son, and here the six of us enjoyed a most happy Christmas day and a holiday week together which we shall all long remember.

Chapter XLII

Year 1913

THE LAND OF THE MID–DAY MOON

FAR BEYOND THE ARCTIC CIRCLE — THE GREAT MAGNET — A DAY WITHOUT A SUNRISE — FARTHEST NORTH — A CHRISTIAN ENDEAVOR MEETING IN NORWAY'S NATIONAL CATHEDRAL — THE ROMANCE OF THE LITTLE NUT-SELLER — FINLAND'S BEAUTIFUL CHURCHES — MEET-INGS IN GERMANY, FRANCE, AND ITALY.

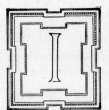 HAVE already described one visit to Scandinavia, but the journey of 1913 had so many interesting features, taking me to the farthest point north that I have ever touched, that I will devote to it a few pages.

On the very first day of 1913 I started with my youngest son, Sydney, for the Land of the Mid-day Moon. It is not necessary in these days to go by reindeer sledge or the light-footed skis, as in Bayard Taylor's time, for warm and comfortably upholstered railway trains run far beyond the Arctic Circle, lured thither by the great iron mines in Gellivara and Kiruna where Swedish iron, the best in the world, is mined.

On and on this adventurous railway runs, across the mountains that divide Sweden and Norway, to Narvik, a port on one of the splendid Norwegian fjords, which is kept open all the year round in spite of its latitude, by the beneficent Gulf Stream.

The place where we first found ourselves beyond the sunrise was Gellivara, where we spent a day and a night. We

went out on the snow-covered hills, anxiously watching the
eastern sky as it glowed and reddened from ten o'clock to
eleven, to twelve, and then gradually faded into a sunset
without a sunrise, until, by two o'clock, the chickens decided
that it was time to go to roost again. We had feared that
we might not have reached the latitude of a sunless day and
a mid-day moon, but were glad to see that the orb of day
rolled along just beneath the horizon and did not show his
face.

A little farther south we should have seen him touching
the eastern plain like a huge ball of fire, just skimming the
snowy uplands, or perhaps only half visible before he dipped
below the horizon again. I have read in the books of other
travellers that there is a weird and uncanny feeling about this
experience in these latitudes of the sunless winter days, but I
must say that I did not realize any unusual emotions. A
glorious dawn sank into a no less glorious evening and that
was all, while men went about their tasks with unconcern as
though it were broad daylight.

By two o'clock the electric lights began to twinkle all over
Gellivara and the iron mines near by, and working hours were
not curtailed by lack of sunlight. At intervals throughout
the day we heard tremendous explosions like the booming of
cannon in a great battle, but it was the peaceful battle of
workmen loosening the deeply imbedded ore. Hours would
be spent in drilling the holes in the mountain, with the latest
machinery. Dynamite would be inserted, and then, while the
workmen made themselves safe, fifty or a hundred detona-
tions would tell us that the mountain was being rent and the
precious ore loosened from its bed.

The iron mountain at Gellivara is only one of several in
this vicinity. A larger and richer hill is at Kiruna near by.
Several others were also being worked, and a still larger
number of iron mountains are known to exist which are waiting for future generations to exploit them.

The Reindeer Market is one of the most interesting features of these towns. The Laplanders often drive in with a team of half a dozen reindeer which, when they reach town, contentedly lie down in the snow and chew the scanty fodder provided for them.

The hotel accommodations in these northern towns are often found in connection with the railway stations, and are clean and comfortable, while the fare at the railway restaurants would make even George Harvey extend himself if he wished to equal it. As to price, the sum we paid seemed ridiculously small to one even casually acquainted with New York hotels, where a cup of coffee and a slice of toast would cost at least twice as much as a square meal of soup, fish, meat, salad, and desert, in a Swedish railway restaurant. It must be confessed, however, that these were before-the-war prices. They are now much higher in Sweden as elsewhere.

Strange as it may seem, the farther north we went the warmer it grew. On the Swedish side of the mountains the weather was intensely cold. We happened to experience nothing on this journey in Sweden colder than twenty below zero, though the mercury often goes to forty or fifty below. Push steadily north, cross the mountains, which in one or two places are tunneled, and you come into a comparatively balmy atmosphere even in mid-winter though you are 150 miles beyond the Arctic circle. When we reached Narvik in Norway it was raining instead of snowing. There was no sign of ice on the fjord, and we took a long ride in and out of its many bays on a little steamer, and scarcely felt the need of an overcoat. Yet, if I remember rightly, the sun had not risen upon the evil and the good of Narvik for a month, and would not rise upon them for another month. On the placid waters of this splendid harbor many ships loaded with iron were riding. One of them I noticed was bound for Philadelphia, showing that Pennsylvania in spite of her own mines, could not get along without the richer products of Sweden.

On our return from the far north we spent a night in Luleo, at the very topmost point of the Gulf of Bothnia. The whole gulf seemed to be frozen solid, and many vessels were in terned by a power mightier than either the Germans or the Allies exercised a year later. Luleo is a quaint old fishing town, not far from the Arctic Circle. It boasts a great summer hotel and a large and imposing Lutheran Church of brick. We had now come into zero weather again, and the rain which had fallen the day before was congealed on every twig and

ANCIENT NORWEGIAN CHURCH

branchlet, while the big church looked as though it was en-cased in glass from the foundation to the topmost spire.

Near Luleo is a high hill where St. John's Day, the day on which the sun reaches its highest point in the zenith, is always celebrated with glad rejoicing by these ice-bound people who, for weeks, have to live in a dim Arctic twilight.

Cutting across Sweden into Norway again, we came to Trondjhem where a large Christian Endeavor meeting had been arranged in the old Cathedral, famous throughout Nor-way as the Coronation Church of kings for centuries past, and their mausoleum as well. Here King Haakon, the present king, was crowned after the many years interregnum of purely Norwegian kings, while good King Oscar of Sweden reigned over both kingdoms.

It was interesting to me as I stood in the high pulpit with my kind interpreter, Rev. H. B. Klaeboe, to watch the faces of the people, several hundreds of whom were standing, throughout the service, around the pulpit in the dim religious light. One could not help thinking at the same time of all the high ceremonies connected with royalty and the commoner folks, ceremonies of life and death, baptisms and burials, which had taken place in that old sanctuary.

This cathedral is considered the finest piece of architecture in Scandinavia, and one of the few perfect Gothic buildings in the world.

My friend, Mr. Klaeboe, of whom I have before spoken, accompanied us in much of our further journey in Scandinavia, and rendered great service to the Christian Endeavor cause in obtaining a hearing for it from all classes of people, from King Haakon himself to the humblest peasant whom he found in the third-class cars. In Christiania and Bergen in Norway, in Gothenburg and Stockholm in Sweden, in Åbo, Tamerfors, and Helsingfors in Finland, I found the largest churches and cathedrals open to my message.

The cathedrals and churches of Finland were quite as interesting as those of the other Scandinavian kingdoms, especially the ancient cathedral of Åbo, some eight hundred years of age. Here, too, I felt the same sensation as in Trondjhem, for these stones also tell us the history of much of Scandinavia. In this cathedral is buried the pretty peasant girl, the little nut-seller who afterwards became the queen of Sweden; and I was reminded of the story that they tell of King Eric and Karin Mänsdotter, the beautiful peasant.

All kinds of objections were raised by the king's nobles and his relatives, and accusations of witchcraft were made against Karin. But the Swedish monarch, who had already been re-

fused as a husband by Queen Elizabeth, by Mary Queen of
Scots, and by two German princesses, would not be thwarted
in this genuine love-match, and married Karin in spite of his
nobles and relatives. " Then a brother prince, who felt
deeply the disgrace that had been brought upon the royal order
by this unseemly match, sent Eric a present of a handsome
royal cloak, in the back of which was sewed a patch of rough
homespun cloth. Eric accepted the gift, had the patch of
homespun embroidered with gold and studded with jewels,
until it was the most brilliant and valuable part of the garment, and then returned it to the donor." Karin's great black
marble sarcophagus, on which I gazed from the high pulpit,
reminded me of the little nut-seller, who became a queen, and
who showed her queenly qualities in adversity and exile. A
stained-glass window in the cathedral shows her dressed in
white robes, with a crown upon her head, stepping down from
her throne upon the arm of a Finnish page.

The churches in which our meetings were held in Tamerfors
and Helsingfors were more modern, but almost as large and
imposing as the Cathedral in Åbo. One is surprised to find
in this little country which we often consider remote and ice-
bound, such splendid churches.

In Tamerfors for instance, an important manufacturing
centre (whose name might be translated into our familiar
" Grand Rapids," since it refers to the deep and impetuous
stream that tumbles through the heart of the city), are great
churches of cut stone that would do credit to London or New
York. It is evident that the Finns are a thoroughly religious
people, and, though comparatively poor, do not begrudge the
money that is lavished on their churches.

I have always been struck, too, with the high grade of
civilization which these people of a stock strange to the rest
of Europe, and allied to the Turks, have reached. Universal education is no mere name in Finland. The people are
in many ways the best educated in the world. The school-

master is highly honored. The schoolhouses in the larger centres are models in the way of comfort and convenience. Ample light and ventilation are considered of special importance, and so particular are the authorities in regard to cleanliness that the modern schoolrooms are built with rounded corners, that unwholesome dust may not settle in them.

In Helsingfors, the capital, our meetings were held in the Church of St. Nicholas, a handsome building of the Greek style of architecture. It stands on a sightly eminence near the centre of the city which it dominates. Here state functions are observed, and the legislature meets for certain religious ceremonies.

I was much interested in the literature of Finland, especially in Kalevala, the great epic poem which is considered by scholars as one of the few that may rank with Homer's Iliad. From this poem, in his study of Scandinavian literature, Longfellow learned the metre of his Hiawatha. That many of the expressions and turns of thought in his poem were evidently suggested by the ancient Kalevala, is made plain by the following quotation from among many that might be given,

> " Pleasant 'tis in boat on water
> Swaying as the boat glides onward,
> Gliding o'er the sparkling water,
> Driving o'er its shiny surface,
> While the wind the boat is rocking,
> And the waves drive on the vessel,
> While the west wind rocks it gently,
> And the south wind drives it onward."

The Endeavor movement has taken a strong hold of the Finnish people belonging to the Free Churches, and we enjoyed many pleasant conferences and receptions in addition to the large public meetings. How little we realized, as we mingled with our kind hosts and hostesses, and saw the alert and eager young men and maidens, that soon this land was to be drenched in blood. Then, as on my previous visit, I was told sad tales of the ruthless oppression of the Czar and his ministers, who had taken away almost the last symbol of Finnish nationality, had forbidden the enforcement of the Prohibition law, which had been overwhelmingly voted, and had prevented the Finns from building the beautiful houses of parliament for which money in abundance had been voted and collected.

Soon the outraged feelings of this oppressed people were to assert themselves, and they were among the first to join in the revolution which overthrew Russian autocracy in 1917. But despotism had done its fearful work of repression only too well. Soon the proletariat rose against the bourgeoisie, the Red Guards against the White. The Bolshevists came down from Russia. Blood flowed everywhere. Thousands of the best citizens, including many of the Lutheran clergy, were killed by the Reds, and panic, hunger, and distress reigned everywhere. At length the Whites triumphed, law and order reasserted themselves, and a stable, popular government was established.

The literary output of this journey to the home of the Vikings was a substantial volume entitled " The Charm of Scandinavia," written jointly by my son Sydney and myself in the form of letters to " Judicia " at home, whose identity my readers can perhaps guess. My son wrote of the superior beauty and historic interest of Norway and Denmark, while I claimed that Sweden and Finland were superior in these respects, each trying to make out the best case possible for the countries he undertook to eulogize, leaving it for Judicia to decide which of us had won his case. Her decision was practically the same as President Lincoln's concerning the rival claims of two hatters who had each presented him with a tile, namely, that " they mutually surpassed each other."

After the meetings in the four Scandinavias (for Finland, geologically at least, is a part of Scandinavia) were over, we

hurried to Freiburg in Baden where Mrs. Clark and our oldest
son and his family awaited us. There we all spent a happy
month together, and enjoyed many delightful walks in the
vicinity of this beautiful university city of the Black Forest.
No hint of war was in the air. The people seemed as peaceful, not to say humdrum, as any in the world. The only
suggestion of militarism was the number of soldiers upon the
streets and the extensive barracks in the city and others a mile
or two from the university. A little more than a year later
Freiburg was experiencing many of the horrors of war. She
was bombed by the Allies over and over again. Thirty people
were killed, many buildings wrecked, and the people kept in
constant terror by the hostile war planes. Of course many who
escaped instant death were wounded.

During our stay in Freiburg "Judicia" plied her busy
typewriter at my dictation, and my part of the "Charm of
Scandinavia" was largely written there, though a number of
chapters of the book had already been penned while travelling
in the northern countries, for American periodicals.

A favorite morning walk before we settled down to our
writing was to the splendid old cathedral and the market
square which surrounded it. Every day more or less hucksters
were found in this square, but on the regular market days it
was filled from curb to curb. The cathedral itself is one of
the most interesting in all Europe, the Gothic doorway, often
crowded with children playing hide and seek, was particularly
interesting, for here much of the history of Germany can be
read in its statues and tablets. The old gargoyles, too, are
many and curious, some of them decidedly humorous, serving
the purpose, it is said, in the ancient days, of the modern
cartoonist. An old woman is represented in one of the niches,
with her mouth open, and showing a single tooth. The
legend connected with it is that during the Lutheran reformation the Protestants promised a husband to every maiden
lady who had as much as one tooth left in her head.

After leaving Freiburg we made our way to Lugano in Italian Switzerland, a beautiful little city with its lovely green-clad mountains, which all dip their feet in the lake. It has been more than once a favorite Swiss resort when we could allow ourselves a few days off from our strenuous duties. During the ten days that my family spent in Lugano I took a brief journey to southern France to attend a convention of the Methodist Endeavorers who live in the vicinity of the Cevennes Mountains. They are largely of Huguenot stock, and a splendid lot of young folks they seemed to be. Their leader, Rev. Edmond Gounelle, has no superior among the Christian leaders of France.

The most interesting incident of this convention to me was the excursion that we all took to Aigues Mortes, the seaport, now largely abandoned, from which St. Louis sailed on his crusade to the Holy Land. Here the Huguenots suffered many of their worst tortures, and we all went with reverent interest to the historic Tower of Constance, built on the enormous wall that surrounds the city. Here in the upper story we traced with our fingers the word " resistez," scratched with a needle in the stone floor by a woman who was imprisoned in this dark dungeon for thirty-four years, from her early girlhood, because her brother was a Protestant minister. It was a dismal, cold, and rainy day when we visited the tower, but our hearts were warmed by the memories of such devotion and heroism.

Immediately after the convention I joined my wife and son at Genoa and we sailed the next day for home on our old friend the " Canopic."

Chapter XLIII

Year 1914

A RECORD OF PROVIDENTIAL DELIVERANCES

HOW A POEM GLORIFIED A CITY — PLANS FOR A NEW ST. BARTHOLOMEW'S DAY — HOW THE BARCELONA POLICE FRUSTRATED PLANS — A BOOMERANG — A RUNAWAY AUTOMOBILE IN LONDON — ALMOST SHIPWRECKED.

 WILL not weary my readers with a detailed story of the year that intervened between the spring days of 1913 and those of that momentous year in the world's history, 1914. It was filled as all my later years have been with many journeys; — a trip to California to attend the fine National Endeavor Convention of 1913 in Los Angeles, many other journeys to smaller conventions, and in the autumn and early winter some weeks in Italy, where leisure was obtained to write a book about " Our Italian Fellow Citizens," after learning what I could on the spot during this and previous visits, about their homes, their hopes, and their prospects in America. This book, like the one entitled " Old Homes of New Americans," was written in the hope that I might in some measure throw light upon the immigration question, which was then as now looming large in America, and that I might, if possible, soften the antipathy with which the " Dago " is met in some quarters.

At length we found ourselves on the way to Barcelona to attend the Spanish Christian Endeavor convention, and there occurred the first of the three adventures to be recorded in this chapter.

503

On our way we visited Carcassonne, a place which has probably inspired more poems than any city of modern times. It is interesting to note how a touch of pathos in a single poem will make a city famous and attract to it tens of thousands of visitors. Most of my readers probably remember Nadaud's poem, which has been the inspirer of many others, and which has itself had several different translations.

A poor peasant who lived within sight of Carcassonne had desired all his life to visit the city and to see the archbishop and the generals who walked its streets, but his daily toil had made even that short journey impossible. His plaint was,

> " My wife, our little boy Aignan
> Have travelled even to Narbonne,
> My grandchild has seen Perpignan,
> But I have not seen Carcassonne!
> I never have seen Carcassonne! "

A stranger going by heard his sorrowful wail and told the old man that he would take him the next day to Carcassonne:

> " We left next morning his abode,
> But (Heaven forgive him!) half way on
> The old man died upon the road.
> He never did see Carcassonne.
> Each mortal has his Carcassonne."

Many translations of this poem have been made, and other poets have tried their hand at telling the same story. But though the poem has made the city famous, it scarcely needed such literary embellishment, for it is the most perfect specimen of a city of feudal times to be found in all Europe. Two massive walls surround it, numerous towers stand at the angles of the walls, from which splendid views of the surrounding country can be obtained. A modern hotel, made over from the old castle, and an ancient church stand at the angles of the walls, but the narrow hilly streets and mighty ramparts have not been altered in any essential particular since the Middle Ages.

Every post card of Carcassonne, and every scroll and banner and piece of china, which in all the shops are sold as souvenirs, bear the legend,

" J'ai vu Carcassonne! "

The modern town of Carcassonne lies two or three miles from the city on the hill, and derives its chief importance from its ancient mother.

From Carcassonne we went as quickly as possible to Barcelona, for neither " gay Narbonne," nor Perpignan, through which we passed, detained us more than a few hours. Crossing the Spanish border we soon came to Barcelona, the republican city of Spain, which always seems to be seething with new ideas, and always on the edge of revolt from the rule of the more conservative Dons. Perhaps on this account the soil of Barcelona has proved especially fruitful for Protestant ideas, and hence for the establishment of the Christian Endeavor movement.

Here the English Wesleyans have long had a strong hold, and the American Congregationalists have established a fine school for girls. Rev. Franklyn Smith of the Methodist Mission was then (in 1914) the president of the Spanish Christian Endeavor Union, and he had resolved, taking the occasion of our visit, that there should be a great demonstration to let the Catholics know that Protestantism was a live issue and could no longer keep its light under a bushel.

He engaged the Palace of Fine Arts, the largest and most beautiful hall in the city, for a Christian Endeavor rally. His contract for the hall was securely made before the priests woke up to the significance of the event, and Mr. Smith soon found that he had stirred up a hornet's nest. The Catholic bishop appealed to the mayor of the city to annul the contract, but he would not do it, declaring that the Protestants had as good a right to the hall as any one. Then the archbishop of the diocese took a hand, and told the governor of Catalonia that he must not allow a great Protestant meeting in the hall, but he took the same ground as the mayor of the city.

When no legal means of preventing the meeting could be discovered some " lewd fellows of the baser sort " banded themselves together to teach the Protestants such a lesson that they would never again attempt to hold a great demonstration in Spain. These all, so far as I know, belonged to the Carlist party, who are intensely bigoted Catholics, and ready to go to any length for their church, even to promoting another St. Bartholomew's Day. Their plan was to gain entrance to the hall with revolvers and other weapons, scatter themselves among the audience, and, at a given signal, shoot promiscuously right and left, perhaps taking especially good aim at the leaders of the movement and the speakers on the platform. In the mêlée and panic which would inevitably ensue, they expected to make their escape.

But they reckoned without their host, and the host in this case proved to be an astute chief of police and a faithful police force. The chief got wind of the plot and took every precaution to foil it. For some days before the meeting the excitement was great throughout the city. Some particulars of the proposed outrage had leaked out, and it was known at least that there would probably be a riot and promiscuous shooting.

Early in the afternoon of that May Sunday in 1914, Mrs. Clark and I left the Girls' School at Sarria, one of the suburbs, where we were staying, about five miles from the centre of the city. A serious question arose whether the girls, many of whom belonged to an Endeavor society, should be allowed to go with the pending prospect of a possible riot. At last however it was decided to take the risk, and several trolley cars were filled with the teachers and the young ladies.

As we approached we saw a great array of policemen and

gendarmes, nearly five hundred in all, drawn up along the streets. Every cross street within half a mile of the hall was specially guarded. Several policemen stood at the door of the hall, and searched every suspicious looking man who sought entrance, running their hands over their persons to see if they harbored any concealed " guns." Forty-eight murderous weapons, chiefly pistols, were taken away from these men, who were herded together in a little park surrounded by a high iron-spiked fence. Some twenty however, who were also suspected of being trouble-makers and who were known as Carlists, got within the doors. To each of these a policeman was assigned to sit by his side until the meeting was over. As a result of these precautions everything passed off smoothly. The publicity given to the meeting by the previous excitement attracted a tremendous audience, and the hall was crowded. Reporters from the leading papers of Spain were present, and several illustrated magazines sent photographers to take flash-light pictures of the audience. There was not a hitch in the programme. A choir of nearly six hundred Junior Endeav-orers led the congregational singing in fine style, and the hall was ablaze with beautiful banners brought in by the different societies of the neighborhood. Some eloquent addresses were made by Spanish pastors and by the missionaries while Don Carlos Araujo admirably translated what I had to say.

The meeting lasted two hours or more, and at the close the chief of police waited at the doors to see that all was safe. He was a well-known character throughout Spain who had recently been transferred from Madrid to Barcelona, because of his success in keeping a somewhat turbulent populace in order. When we thanked him for the great care he had taken he modestly replied that it was his duty to protect any law-abiding citizens and secure to them their rights, and he was glad that he had been successful in this instance.

As we came out we saw the suspects, whose weapons had been taken away from them, still herded together in the little park under the broiling sun, the object of the jeers of the passers-by. We felt that in some measure poetic justice had been done, and though they had not fallen into the deepest part of the pit which they had digged, Nemesis had in a measure overtaken them, and that very speedily. The Chief sent a small guard of policemen to see us safely to the American school, our temporary home, and they would not leave us until we were safe behind the big iron gate which enclosed the school compound.

As we heard the nightingales singing that night after we retired we could imagine that they were adding their congratulations to the many good things which had been said concerning the value of the Christian Endeavor movement in Spain, and the remarkable success of the demonstration. It was said by those who had carefully studied the history of the country, that not since the days of the Visigoths, a thousand years or more in the past, had there been such a demonstration for evangelical religion in the Iberian Peninsula.

While the meeting was going on in the hall the Methodist church over which Mr. Smith presided was set on fire, kerosene having been poured over the woodwork, but the fire was put out by friendly hands and little damage was done.

The next morning the papers were full of the accounts of the meeting, not only the journals of Barcelona but of all of the leading cities. Most of them denounced the intended outrage and massacre in no measured terms, saying that it was a disgrace to Spain that such a thing could be even attempted, comparing the plot to that of St. Bartholomew's Day. The illustrated papers and magazines too played up the story in great shape, and the matter was afterwards taken up in the Diet and discussed there. Doubtless the Republicans and the supporters of the present dynasty were not altogether sorry to have something on the Carlists, or Jaimists, as they are now called, since the present Pretender is James, the son of the original claimant to the throne.

I would not have it understood that I believe that the Catholic church or the Catholic people in general had anything to do with hatching this heinous plot. It was only a rabid element in the church that was responsible.

When the story reached America, and was printed in many of our papers, I was roundly denounced by *The Pilot* and other Catholic papers, as a hysterical alarmist who told all sorts of lies to discredit the Catholic church. I could at least refer my critics to the chief of police of Barcelona and to the papers and magazines of Spain for confirmation of the story, which they evidently did not wish to believe.

By reason of this meeting and the excitement attending it Christian Endeavor was widely advertised as well as the Protestant faith at large, and the incident did not a little, I believe, towards promoting more liberal laws respecting alien faiths throughout the kingdom. Before this no Protestant church could have a steeple, or bear any such ecclesiastical sign. Such churches must be built in back streets and inconspicuous sections. I understand that these laws have now been largely abrogated.

We afterwards had meetings in Madrid, Zaragoza, Valencia, and Bilbao. In all of these places we expected more or less trouble, since the news of the exciting events in Barcelona had preceded us. Especially in Bilbao things looked serious for a while. Since the Protestant chapel there was in a congested slum of the city, our friends did not dare to open the front door of the chapel for fear that rioters might surge in and make trouble, but a good audience made their way in by a side door and a back entrance, and no disturbance followed.

In Madrid Bishop Cabrera, whose lamented death occurred not long afterwards, and his son and daughter, especially Miss Pepita Cabrera, were ardent advocates of the Endeavor movement, and a delightful meeting was held in the little cathedral of the Independent Episcopal Church. I venture to say that it will be a long time before the echoes of the Barcelona meeting, and the assassination plot will die away in Spain.

A few days in Paris in May, 1914, so shortly before the world storm broke out, were as peaceful and uneventful as any that I have ever spent in the world's fashion-capital. Who could have dreamed that in a few weeks French soil would drip with blood, and Paris itself would be threatened! Two or three meetings engaged our brief visit in the city, the most memorable of which was a Sabbath that we spent with Rev. Victor van der Beken and his family in a suburb of the city. Mr. van der Beken, who early in the war days, worn out by his work, died, greatly lamented, was the efficient and well-loved secretary of the Christian Endeavor movement in France. The society in his own church was the most important factor in the life of his young people. Everything indeed centred around it, and the members of the Boy Scout troop, according to their rules, must first be active or associate members of the society, thus linking the secular activity of the Scouts with the religious work of the society.

As we came up to the door of the church, a troop of Scouts saluted us and followed us in, taking their places with their fellow Endeavorers, to whom Mr. van der Beken's sermon was chiefly addressed, as many of them were to unite with the church that day. A number of girls dressed in white were confirmed and at the same time admitted to the society, to each of whom, at the pastor's request, and at the expense of the church, I presented a Christian Endeavor badge, which in France is a C. A. monogram, standing for *Activité Chretienne*. After the service with the young people of the society and their parents, we adjourned with the Endeavorers to the pastor's house, for lunch.

We were met at the door by the pastor's little four-year-old son, who greeted us with a smile and a short address in English, which he had learned for the occasion, which was as follows: " My dear friends, I am very glad to see you, and to eat with you, if you have appetite." These words were pronounced very slowly, and carefully, with several halts to refresh his memory, for this speech was a great effort for the little fellow. But he did his part well, and as we did " have appetite " we cheerfully ate with him a very nice lunch, which the Endeavorers helped to serve.

Soon after this we left for London by way of Havre and Southampton, which, because of the larger boats and the good night's rest which it insures, has become our favorite route. The magnet which drew us to London at this time was an earnest invitation to attend the British National Christian Endeavor Convention, which proved to be a distinguished success. Such well-known English preachers as Dr. John Clifford, and Rev. F. B. Meyer are warm advocates of the movement, and are always present at such meetings in London.

The second of our three providential escapes on this journey occurred one black foggy night, as we were returning to the Thackeray Hotel from a meeting in Dr. Meyer's church. The asphalt roads were as slippery as grease, and, while in the middle of a busy thoroughfare the driver of the taxi lost control of the brakes, and the auto spun around in a circle in the midst of congested traffic. Fortunately we hit neither the curb nor any other vehicle, and the driver, trembling with excitement at his narrow escape delivered us safely at the hotel, saying, " You have never been nearer death than you were then," while the conservative porter at the door of the hotel vowed that he would never enter one of those death-traps if he had to walk all the rest of his life.

Though the convention was strictly British, it had attracted Endeavorers from several countries of the Continent, France and Germany and Holland being chiefly represented. The largest foreign delegation came from Germany, and none apparently enjoyed it so heartily as the five or six stalwart young Teutons.

One of the most interesting scenes was at the consecration

meeting in Queen's Hall, at which Dr. Clifford preached the sermon. It was a stirring discourse on the consecration of life to the highest ideals and to the Master of us all. After the various delegations had spoken their word of purpose and consecration, the young Germans stood together, and, while each held above his head in one hand a Union Jack, and in the other the German flag, their spokesman, in accents broken by emotion, voiced the feelings of them all, and their joy in the hospitality they had received and the blessed fellowship which they had enjoyed.

None spoke so feelingly of this fellowship as they, and yet it was less than six weeks from that date, that war was declared between their native country and the nation of their hosts, and most if not all of these young men were called to the colors. I have never been able to believe that they cherished rancor or bitterness in their hearts, nor do I believe that they ever sang a hymn of hate against their English friends. During all the terrible years which followed, the memory of that scene kept alive my faith in Christian charity and genuine international brotherhood.

Very soon after the convention we sailed on the old steamer " New York " of the American Line, from Southampton.

The last third of the voyage was through dense and dripping fog. When about 400 miles from New York, at three o'clock in the morning, in the proverbially darkest hour before the dawn, we were awakened by the hoarse bellow of two distinct fog-horns, one on our own ship, and the other evidently on an approaching vessel. For fully twenty minutes the hoarse screamers answered one another in this alarming antiphonal service. Then our ship slowed down, stopped and began to back water. Surely, we said, these two monsters of the deep can escape each other. They have the whole wide Atlantic in which to pass. Each captain must know the position of the approaching ship. It cannot be that there will be a collision under these circumstances.

But the fog-horn of the other ship, which was much louder than our own, kept continually booming out more and more threateningly. At last we felt a shock, though a comparatively slight one, and knew that we had been struck, while the vast bulk of the other ship, twice as large as our own, a Hamburg American Liner, scraped and scrapped our bulwarks fore and aft. By this time I had managed to get on a few garments and rushed forth (our stateroom was on the upper deck) in time to see the whole length of the leviathan as she slowly steamed by, ripping everything as she went. I could easily have jumped aboard but preferred to go to America rather than back to Europe and so stuck to our own ship.

At first we thought that the damage must be trifling, but we soon found that a great hole, thirty feet long and fifteen feet deep had been stove in our bows; that some of the sailors' rooms had been scooped out entirely, though fortunately none of them were in their bunks, and that a huge anchor weighing five tons had been ripped off the German liner and dropped on our deck. At once the stewards went about among the passengers, telling them to put on their life preservers, though most of us needed no such admonition.

After an hour or so it was decided that we could probably get into New York under our own steam. The other ship went on her way and the " New York " slowly nosed her way through the dense fog towards her American port. Had she not been an old-fashioned ship, built like a yacht, curved in on the sides, and with an " overhang " which took the force of the blow she would doubtless have gone to the bottom almost instantly. As it was, a canvas was rigged over the great hole, which, however, did very little good. But a kind Providence kept the seas calm, and, though we had two anxious nights and a day, we reached port without further adventure.

A few hours after the accident the steward rapped at my door, and handed in a marconigram from *The New York*

American, which read, " Please wireless us three hundred words about the accident." Scarcely had I fulfilled this demand than another message was handed in from *The New York Herald,* "Wireless us five hundred words about accident." This kept me busy for the rest of the night. When we reached the shore I found that the papers after interviewing some of the passengers had greatly exaggerated the " heroism " of Dr. and Mrs. Clark in calming the fears of the passengers, a tribute, so far as it was true, due much more to my wife than myself.

The collision occurred Friday night. Sunday morning found us still at sea. Though the officers of this line had little use for Sunday services, I ventured to ask the captain if he would not like to have a brief thanksgiving service in the cabin. He replied, " You can have one if you want to, but nobody will come to it; they'll all be busy packing to go ashore."

However a service was announced, and was attended by nearly all the passengers, and as we sang hymns of thanksgiving and voiced our gratitude to God in prayer and a brief address, there were many moist eyes even among the stalwart men, and it was deemed a most impressive service. Thus, with thanksgiving, ended this chapter of accidents and narrow escapes from death.

CHAPTER XLIV

YEARS 1914–1922

ON OLD BEACON HILL

boston's most interesting section — massachusetts' state house — the authors' hill — pinckney street — the world's christian endeavor building — the authors' club — the city club — the monday club.

EACON HILL is by all odds the most interesting section of Boston. It is crowned by Massachusetts' stately State House, which still retains, as we hope it always will, its famous " Bulfinch Front." The streets from there on the western side slope downwards, sometimes abruptly, to the level of the Charles River. Every street is alive with memories of the great statesmen of the Revolution, or of the authors of more recent date. John Hancock, Harrison Gray Otis, Pinckney, and Derne of naval fame, are inseparably associated with this historic hill, which received its name from the great beacon which in Revolutionary times stood upon its summit, and from which warnings of the approach of the enemy might be flashed far and wide.

Especially has Beacon Hill been distinguished as the residence of many of Boston's foremost authors, among whom I might mention Jacob Abbott, Louisa M. Alcott, Thomas Bailey Aldrich, Celia Thaxter, George S. Hillard, Lowell Mason (the composer of sacred music), Edwin P. Whipple, Alice Brown (all on Pinckney Street), and on streets near by, Margaret

Deland, Julia Ward Howe, John D. Long, William Ellery Channing, Mrs. A. D. T. Whitney, William Dean Howells, John Lothrop Motley, Francis Parkman, James T. Fields, W. H. Prescott, and others equally distinguished. For these facts I am indebted to Dr. Amos R. Wells' entertaining book about the Christian Endeavor Building and its surroundings.

Since my boyhood the State House has spread itself out in every direction. I remember the comparatively modest building, with its beautiful façade, up whose long flight of steps I used sometimes to climb with my adopted father when he was chaplain of the Massachusetts Senate. An old-timer would not recognize it with its extended marble wings, one on either side, the four-fold development in the rear, near which sits Governor Banks clad all in gold. Here, too, General Devens stands erect and commanding on his pedestal, while in front stand Daniel Webster and Fighting Joe Hooker.

Even now there is not room enough for all the departments and commissions which a modern State requires, and the octopus is spreading its tentacles farther over the hill with every decade. It was thought at one time that, as a residence section, Beacon Hill was doomed, that all the old families that had given it distinction would move out to the Back Bay, and that business, or an undesirable foreign element would engulf the historic sites. But of late years an almost unparalleled event in the history of cities has occurred, and Beacon Hill is again becoming the choicest residence section of Boston, not the " swellest," or the richest, but in many respects the most desirable. Quiet Mount Vernon, Chestnut, and Cedar streets are more popular with a large class of Bostonians than the noisy, dusty automobile-ridden districts of newer Boston. Lovely Louisburg Square (pronounce the " s " if you please), guarded at either end by the queer little statues of Columbus and Aristides, has all the charm of an old-world residence section. Indeed this is old for America, for here one Blackstone built the first house in Boston.

Pinckney Street, another of the long thoroughfares running down to the Charles, does not hold up its head so high as its more aristocratic neighbors. Nevertheless it has been a famous street in its day, and has been honored as the residence of many authors of renown. Now it is the last street harboring Americans as you look toward the north. The descendants of Abraham, Isaac, and Jacob have established themselves on all the northern slope of Beacon Hill, and decided, if not very outspoken efforts are made to keep them from moving farther south, — so far successfully.

Pinckney Street is now largely given up to rooming-houses, and in one or another of these we have found comfortable winter quarters for several years past when in America, and since giving up our home in Auburndale.

Let me not give the impression that Pinckney Street is to be despised. Many delightful people find their homes here for a few weeks or months, and it is still the abode of at least one famous authoress, Miss Alice Brown, who a few years ago received a ten thousand dollar prize for a play called " The Children of Earth." The Authors' Club once offered a prize for the best topical poem, which, much to her surprise, was given to Mrs. Clark, who describes in fanciful terms the street which has been our home for parts of eight winters. I will reproduce it here:

ON PINCKNEY STREET

On little old Pinckney Street
The houses stand prim and straight;
   With hearts all a-quiver
    They gaze toward the river
Like spinsters awaiting their fate.

Like spinsters awaiting their fate,
Like spinsters prim and shy,
   They stand in long rows
    On their very tiptoes,
And look up into the sky.

On little old Pinckney Street,
Those spinsters so old and wise
   Wear brick-red dresses,
   With curtains for tresses
And windows for bright little eyes.

With windows for bright little eyes,
Each window a bright little eye;
   They look over the way,
   And sadly they say,
" Alas for the days gone by! "

For once on Pinckney Street
They saw writers of great renown;
   They sigh for the past,
   But they smile at last,
As they think of Alice Brown.

They think of Alice Brown,
And Alice Brown they greet;
   For " The Children of Earth "
   Right here had their birth,
On little old Pinckney Street.

But Beacon Hill has meant more to us than scant quarters in a rooming-house, for it has been the home of world-wide Christian Endeavor for some nine years past. Here both the United Society and the World's Union have their headquarters, and here *The Christian Endeavor World* is published. For a number of years the United Society migrated from pillar to post, beginning with a single desk in the Bible Society's rooms on Beacon Street. Thence it moved to 50 Bromfield Street, then to 646 Washington Street, for larger quarters, then to Tremont Temple, where we occupied nearly a whole floor, and then to 31 Mt. Vernon Street, under the wing of the State House. Here the society bought five old brick buildings on Mt. Vernon and Hancock Streets, which we expected to tear down, and to build anew upon this eligible site. It was decided, afterwards, however, that a near-by corner, the one on Mt. Vernon and Joy Streets, was more eligible, and in 1917 the corner stone of the substantial and appropriate six-story office building was laid, which proclaims by the monogram over the doorway, and the inscription on the corner stone, that it is the *World's Christian Endeavor Building*.

On this site stood a mansion once occupied by a descendant of Harrison Gray Otis, which had to be demolished, and in still earlier days it was a part of the garden and nursery belonging to John Hancock. Now an obvious remark is that it is "a nursery for young Christians." Together with the State House it occupies the very crest of Beacon Hill.

It was dedicated in 1918, with appropriate ceremonies, a part of which were held upon the balustraded roof, which gives a splendid view of the city in every direction, since the building is on the very peak of the hill. In the vestibule, in bronze, is the following inscription:

ERECTED

TO THE GLORY OF GOD

BY THE GIFTS OF MORE THAN

ONE HUNDRED THOUSAND

CHRISTIAN ENDEAVORERS

AND THEIR FRIENDS

IN EVERY LAND

AND DEDICATED

TO THE TRAINING

OF YOUNG PEOPLE

FOR THE SERVICE OF CHRIST

AND THEIR FELLOW MEN

On entering the handsome vestibule the Memorial Room, to which my colleagues have kindly given my name, is on the right-hand side. This is an unusually beautiful room, and its glass-covered alcoves are filled with banners and badges, addresses from many countries, gavels used at various conventions, some thirty walking-sticks given me in all parts of the world, and mementoes of various kinds, most of which I have collected during the last thirty-five years.

On the other side is the attractive book and salesroom, containing every kind of Christian literature. Above, on the next floor are the private offices of the president, secretaries, treasurer, and editors. The four upper stories are rented to substantial publishing and other firms, one of which for several years was *The Atlantic Monthly*, before that famous publication moved to a home of its own. The building cost some $200,000, considerably more than it would have cost if it could have been built before the war began, but only about half of what it would have cost to duplicate it three years later.

On the whole we have enjoyed our winter home in Boston, on Pinckney Street, though we have found it rather hard to be confined to one or two rooms, after having spread ourselves out over a large house. However, there have been compensations. For instance, we have been able to attend the Friday meetings of the Boston Authors' Club, where we meet many congenial spirits. My colleague Dr. Amos R. Wells has long been a leading spirit in this club. When I first joined it, Julia Ward Howe was president, though she died a few months later.

She was succeeded by Major T. W. Higginson, a contemporary of nearly the same age, and famous for his anti-slavery zeal and co-operation with John Brown before the Civil War, as well as for his rare literary gifts. Mrs. Howe lived to be ninety-two years old, if I am not mistaken, and, on almost the last day of her life, she wrote a letter to the managing editor of *The Christian Endeavor World*. Her hand was then as firm and unshaken as that of a young girl.

World's Christian Endeavor Building
Boston, Mass.

Major Higginson was succeeded as president of the Club by the former Governor of Massachusetts and Secretary of the Navy, John D. Long, a man greatly beloved and honored in his life and mourned in his death, and he by the eminent novelist, Basil King, and Mr. King by the present president, Miss Alice Brown.

Those authors are eligible to the club who have published at least one bound volume, are recommended by two present members with formal letters stating their qualifications, and who receive no adverse vote. A few years later, Mrs. Clark, on the strength of her authorship of " The Gospel in Latin Lands," and a volume on " Junior Endeavor," was invited to join the club. Since then she has published another little book called, " Bible Autobiographies," which has been well received. A " Daily Message " for Christian Endeavorers, a birthday book has had a steady sale for many years.

We have here enjoyed the acquaintance of several well-known writers, like Nixon Waterman, the late Mrs. Eleanor Porter, the beloved author of *Pollyanna,* and many other wonderfully popular stories, Mrs. Deland, Caroline Atwater Mason, Judge Grant, Dennis McCarthy, Abbie Farwell Brown, and others too numerous to mention.

Another worth-while club to which I have belonged for many years, and to which I have occasionally spoken, is the Twentieth Century Club, which deals with matters of national and international interest, and often secures brilliant speakers from outside of the city. Though the club maintains many departments, and cultivates interest in art and letters, the chief interest to many centres in the Saturday luncheon, when topics of the day are freely discussed, often with much vigor and spiciness.

The Boston City Club, to which I have also belonged for a number of years, is an interesting organization. It is exceedingly democratic, has a membership of many thousands, and brings together people of all races, religions, and occupations, for friendly discussions of national and other problems. The dining and lunch rooms are deservedly popular, and furnish good meals at reasonable prices. Since this great club house is near our Christian Endeavor Building, together with my colleagues I often avail myself of its gustatory opportunities.

While not a club man in the usual sense of the word (though I venture to hope a clubable man), I have belonged to several other organizations, like the Monday Club, and the Winthrop Club. The former is made up of a company of a score or more of Congregational ministers, now with the lapse of years mostly of a younger generation than mine, who meet every other Monday during nine months in the year, for the purposes of fellowship and the reading to each other of sermons on the Sunday-school lessons for the following year. These are afterwards published in a volume called " The Monday Club Sermons." During the last thirty-five years I have contributed in all fifty or sixty sermons to these volumes, but have found the special value of the club in the fellowship of such men as H. A. Bridgman, Albert E. Dunning, the late DeWitt Clark, G. Frederick Wright, W. R. Campbell, Edward N. Noyes, Charles R. Brown, and others well-known in Congregational circles.

The Winthrop Club meets less often, and considers more philosophical themes. It, too, is made up of ministers of the vicinity, and its papers are usually weighty and stimulating.

TYPHOID FEVER AND ITS COMPENSATIONS

SOME PEACE ORGANIZATIONS — A JOURNEY THAT WAS NEVER
TAKEN — SEVENTY-FIVE DAYS IN BED — AT DEATH'S
DOOR — PRESIDENT WILSON'S LETTERS — AN UNKNOWN
CATHOLIC FRIEND.

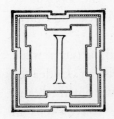 HAD long been especially interested in questions of peace and international friendship and good-will. One could scarcely be prominent in such an organization as Christian Endeavor without constantly bringing such matters to the fore, for ours is essentially a peace-and-fellowship society, based on loyalty to the Prince of Peace.

I had long been an honorary officer of the American Peace Society, of the Massachusetts Peace Society, and of one or two similar organizations. When war was threatened, we even formed a Christian Endeavor Peace Society which enrolled a multitude of members. Later it was submerged by the clamor and suspicion of the early days of the war.

The most important peace society with which I have been connected is the " Church Peace Union," of which I was one of the original trustees, and whose trustee meetings I always attend when in America. It was founded by Andrew Carnegie' in 1912 with a two million dollar endowment and enrolls among its officers and leaders many eminent men. Bishop Grier was its first president, and Dr. Merrill, pastor of the Brick Church, of New York, his worthy successor. Such men as Charles E. Jefferson, Robert E. Speer, John R. Mott, Secretary Brown, Hamilton Holt, and Bishop Wilson are among the leading members, while Messrs. Frederick Lynch, and H. A. Atkinson are its efficient secretaries.

Out of this organization has grown " The World Alliance for the Promotion of International Fellowship through the Churches," a long name, but one full of meaning. I am on the executive committee of this organization and am also one of its international committee.

In May, 1915, I attended two peace conferences, one of the " League to Enforce Peace," in Cleveland, in which I had been asked to make an address, and the other, the annual and last peace meeting at Lake Mohonk. Of the League to Enforce Peace former President Taft was the leading spirit, and for it he worked incessantly.

On my return to Sagamore I had planned, after a week of rest, to start on June 4 on a long Christian Endeavor journey to the Pacific Coast, and the schedule was outlined, and arrangements had long been made for large conventions in Missouri, Oklahoma, Texas, Kansas, Colorado, New Mexico, Arizona, and California.

The railroad tickets for much of the journey had been bought, and the reservations on the sleeping-cars made, when, on the first day of June, a peculiar lassitude accompanied with fever induced me to call in the doctor. I said to him, " Doctor, I have just four days to spare before I start on a convention trip to the Pacific Coast, and you must fix me up for it." He shook his head knowingly, but said nothing until the next day, when he announced that the trouble was typhoid fever, and peremptorily sent me to bed, engagements or no engagements, a bed from which I did not rise for seventy-five days, until on the fifteenth of September I was allowed to sit up for fifteen minutes. The illness was a painful one and for a long time my life hung in the balance. After the fever had dragged its weary length along for several weeks a little rashness of diet, prescribed by the head nurse, resulted in a relapse, which very nearly prevented the rest of this volume from being written. However the Lord was gracious and full of compassion, and after three or four months I began to feel like myself once more, and to accumulate some missing avoirdupois.

Yet there were many compensations, some of which at the time I was too near to death to appreciate. The care of my wife and my children who could be with me, was constant and unwearied. Many kind friends expressed their solicitude and in a way that quite amazed me. About a month after the illness began I was surprised to receive (unsolicited of course) the following letter from President Wilson, though when it came I was too weak to have it read to me:

" White House, (Cornish, N. H.)

July 4, 1915.

" Dear Dr. Clark,

" I have heard with the deepest distress of your illness. I hope that it will cheer you a little to think with what solicitous affection we are all hoping for your speedy recovery. The great work you have done in the world has made you a multitude of friends, and none wishes for your welfare and recovery more heartily than does your sincere friend,

WOODROW WILSON."

As soon as I was able I dictated a note of thanks for his kind remembrance of me, and at once received the following letter in reply:

" THE WHITE HOUSE
" WASHINGTON

September 2, 1915.

" My Dear Dr. Clark,

" Your letter of August 30 brought me very good news in telling me of your steady recovery, and I was very much touched that a letter to me should be one of the first things that you thought of when you were strong enough to write.

"May I not say how glad I am sure all Christian people will be that you should have gained your health again, and may I not wish for you a very complete return of health and strength and many years of continued great usefulness?

"Cordially and Sincerely Yours,

"WOODROW WILSON.

"Rev. Francis E. Clark,

"The Dunes,

"Sagamore Beach, Mass."

Many letters and telegrams from personal friends and others received during this illness I collected in a little scrapbook entitled "Rewards of Typhoid Fever," for I felt indeed that such kind, unexpected, and undeserved letters made up for much suffering and weakness. I find letters in this scrapbook from John Wanamaker, from a multitude of dear Christian Endeavor friends, from prisoners in Auburn, N. Y., State Prison, and the Kentucky penitentiary in Frankfort, the letter representing the "White Christian Endeavor and Good Government League of the Kentucky State Reformatory" as well as a colored society in the same institution.

One of the letters that touched me most deeply was from Dr. Albert J. Lyman, pastor of the South Congregational Church in Brooklyn, who was taken ill with the same disease on the very same day as myself. "From my sick bed," he wrote, "I send you my loving remembrance. You are weaker than I, but otherwise our cases are similar. Dear man of the people and of God, *you will pull through.* His smile is above you, His arm beneath you." His prophecy of my recovery proved true, but alas, he grew weaker as I grew stronger, and he died in the late summer. His widow is a long-time friend and former parishioner in South Boston, an eminent teacher, who carried on for many years in Philadelphia one of the most successful private schools in America.

Perhaps the letter that surprised me most was from an unknown friend, a Roman Catholic, who gave no address, so

THE GREAT CHICAGO CONVENTION IN 1915

that I never could thank him for his letter. It enclosed a little picture of the " Bleeding Heart of Jesus," and he wrote:

" Dear Sir,
" Enclosed please find a little heart, and won't you kindly pin it on your clothing somewhere to honor Him who loves men so much, and Who is so little loved in return. Please do not be displeased with me, but do as I ask you, and I can assure you that the sacred heart of Jesus will give you a speedy recovery. You are sharing in my prayers, Sir."

According to the wish of my Catholic friend the little token was pinned upon my nightdress, for though I had no superstitious belief in the charm, I felt a warm regard for this unknown friend whom I should never see, and a sincere faith in the efficacy of his prayers.

During the most critical days of my illness the conventions which I had hoped to attend on the long journey between the oceans were going on, and the most hopeless days of all were passed while many thousand Endeavorers were meeting for the World's Convention in Chicago, in the great colosseum, made famous by so many national political conventions. Telegrams came every day from the convention, asking for news and assuring my faithful watchers of the constant prayers of the convention, messages of which I could not even be told at the time.

I trust I shall be pardoned for quoting from the letters of these known and unknown friends, and for adding further an editorial note from *The Continent*, the leading national Presbyterian journal. It was published in October, 1916.

" An immediate personal mercy to themselves, multitudes in this and other countries will deem the good providence of God which has granted recovery to Dr. Francis E. Clark from the grievous siege of illness which he has undergone this summer. Typhoid fever in a man's sixty-fourth year is in the best circumstances a perilous episode, and anxiety was increased in Dr. Clark's case when the normal course of the disease was lengthened by relapse. But a constitution which no indulgence of appetite or recklessness of habit had ever vitiated was the solid foundation on which the good Lord was pleased to lift up His servant's life again, and so the world is still to have the light of Dr. Clark's example and teaching for added years to come. If the question were on identifying the best-loved man alive to-day in the universal church, Roman Catholics, of course, would feel obliged to vote for the pope; but among the free churches there's no film of doubt that the majority would go heavy for Christian Endeavor's admired founder and leader. And the happy thing for those to testify who know him individually is that in a beautiful harmony of Christlike gentleness and Christlike strength he thoroughly deserves all the love millions of young people and old have lavished on him."

It makes me blush to copy such undeserved praise, but, in after years, my children and perhaps some Endeavorers may like to read what one friendly editor found it in his heart to write.

CHOIR OF THE CHICAGO CONVENTION, 1915

A WINTER IN HONOLULU

"BEHIND THE VEIL" — BEAUTIFUL HONOLULU — OUR WEL-
COME — OUR HOSTS — A HAPPY WINTER — OFF FOR
JAPAN.

CONTINUED to improve throughout the early fall, but was still far from strong and was frequently warned of the insidious effects of typhoid fever, and that the after-math was often worse than the original disease, as indeed it afterwards proved to be in my own case. We resolved, therefore, to spend a few weeks in charming Honolulu and then, if health and strength should permit, to go on to the Orient to attend conventions in Japan and China, to which I had been invited.

There were more or less impromptu Christian Endeavor meetings in Sacramento and San Francisco, when Endeavorers learned that I was there, though I had meant to slip quietly out of the country without any engagements of any kind, as my health was far from established.

The Endeavorers of Oakland and San Francisco were most kind, arranging a banquet for us with the leaders of the movement, taking us to the great World's Fair, then in progress, where the Exposition grounds in the evening were such a blaze of light and color as the world had never seen before, but my health and my wife's solicitude prevented me from enjoying these glories for more than a few moments.

Soon we were upon the Pacific once more in a comfortable

stateroom of the "Matsonia" with five days of peaceful voyaging before us. Though I was up to very little physical exertion I could use my pen once more, and kept up my weekly articles for *The Christian Endeavor World,* and while on this steamer wrote my first and only story, entitled "Both Sides of the Veil," describing the supposed experiences of two members of a family of five who had been killed in an automobile accident and suddenly found themselves on the other side of the "great-divide." I attempted to show how they might influence for good the remaining members of the family, the father, son, and daughter, keeping them from evil ways, and suggesting good thoughts and deeds, though the earthly members of the family never realized their presence. It was meant as a counter blast to the crude spiritualism of the day, and to show that it was not necessary to consult mediums or to see ghosts in order to receive impressions from beloved ones who had "entered in behind the veil."

This short story of four chapters was published a year or two later in *The Christian Endeavor World,* and while I received enthusiastic commendations for it and assurances that it had helped many of my correspondents, a few others perceived in it dangerous spiritualistic tendencies. One good ministerial brother denounced its author as an emissary of Satan, who was leading the young people of the world astray, not perceiving that the object of the book was to counteract what both he and I regarded as the most insidious form of spiritualism. If we believe that there is a future life, and that our friends are somewhere on the farther shore, conscious of our trials and loving us still, why should it be thought a thing incredible that they should be allowed to influence us in conscious or sub-conscious ways? If that be heresy, dear brethren, make the most of it!

Early in November we reached Honolulu, where I had been several times before, but never for so long a stay. If there is one city in the world more inviting than Honolulu to a semi-

invalid, or to one tired in body and soul, I do not know where
it is.   The soft and balmy climate where the mercury climbs
to the eighty degree mark at noon almost every day winter
and summer, and seldom goes beyond it, the tempering breezes
always blowing from the all-embracing sea; the tropical vegetation, ever green from almost daily showers, and ever in
bloom; the hill resorts within a fifteen-minute ride by automobile when one is surfeited with the sea; the many races
living together in harmony, with their varied and colorful
costumes; and, above all, the extraordinary hospitality of the

A STREET IN HONOLULU

people, leave nothing to be desired.   Yet, less than a hundred
years ago, the site of Honolulu was a barren, wind-swept plain,
the red dust flew in clouds along the primitive paths lined with
the grass houses of the natives.   Where charming residences,
many of them palatial in size and architecture, stately churches,
public buildings, and splendid school and college buildings
now stand, were the rude dwellings and the crude agriculture
of the native Hawaiian.

Three generations of missionaries and their descendants
have changed all this and literally have made the island of
Oahu and the neighboring isles to blossom like the rose.   In-

stead of the thorn has come up the palm tree, and instead of the briar have come up the Poinsettias, and surely they are to the Lord for " a sign " of what faithful Christian men and women can do, for the material as well as the spiritual welfare of a country. Not one of the beautiful palms and flowering trees and glorious shrubs with possibly one or two exceptions, were natives of Hawaii. They have all been imported, and have flourished in their new habitat as never before. It is true that the native inhabitants of the island have dwindled, but that was inevitable, owing to their contact with the vices of civilization, rum and lust.

The Hawaiians have always lived on the best terms with the missionaries who came to uplift them. The condition of the remnant is far better than if it had not come under missionary influence. The native Hawaiian blood flows in the veins of some of the leading families.

The result of the mixture of the races has never been so completely demonstrated as in Hawaii. For the most part it seems to justify the claims that mixed races are sometimes the strongest. In Kawaihao Seminary for girls there are some twenty races and cross races represented. The Hawaiian-Chinese combination seems to be particularly happy; the children often retaining the best qualities of both races. The superintendent of Christian Endeavor societies of the Hawaiian Islands, Mr. Akana, is certainly one of the finest looking men to be found in Honolulu or any other city. His mother was Hawaiian and his father Chinese. Besides Chinese and Hawaiians, there are Japanese, nearly 100,000 of them, the leading element in the population, Portuguese, Koreans, Spanish, Italians, Filipinos, and a comparatively few full-blooded Americans, largely the descendants of the missionary families.

At the union meeting of the Christian Endeavor societies the groups are usually arranged according to races represented, and messages at the consecration meetings are given in the languages of all the countries mentioned, and all with equal fervor and sincerity.

To return to the day of our arrival in this earthly Paradise — we were met at the wharf by Mr. Theodore Richards, the treasurer of the Hawaiian missionary society, whose wife is a descendant of one of the earliest missionary families. He took us to his delightful home and insisted on our staying until we could establish ourselves, which we soon did, in the Royal Hawaiian Hotel, with a room and a Lanai looking out on a charming courtyard, while a big royal palm, towering over it, provided grateful shade. We took our meals at different restaurants and have seldom found an abiding-place away from home more entirely satisfactory. This was especially true of our rooms, which were large and airy, with many windows but no glass, for wire netting alone is necessary in this elysium.

We had enough writing to keep us moderately busy, for I cannot conceive of any enjoyment in a holiday with no employment. Even if Satan finds no mischief still for idle hands to do, idle hands are the most wearisome and unhappy of all. We had before this made a number of acquaintances in Honolulu, and our acquaintance with them ripened into friendship during our three months on the island. The Athertons, the Judds, the Dickeys, the Waterhouses, the Damons, the Gulicks, the Hitchcocks, and others, many of whom were descendants of the missionaries, always opened wide their hospitable doors. After a few weeks Mrs. J. B. Atherton insisted on our leaving our hotel and making her lovely home on College Hill our own. Her automobile with a little Japanese chauffeur whom American girls would have called " very cute " was at our disposal, and in our great breezy room some of the earlier chapters of this autobiography were written.

In order to enjoy the change to country life we spent a week or two at Kahala, five miles from the city, in the cottage of Mrs. Waterhouse, and though it rained almost incessantly, and a devastating " Kona " swept over the island while we were there, yet we enjoyed the outing, and especially the sea bathing, for the waters around Hawaii are as mild and delicious as the air. An outer reef keeps the sharks from Kahala Bay, and the only drawback to bathing is the sharp coral which covers the sand under the shallow water. In some places this has been dredged away. An interesting feature of

REPRESENTATIVES OF TWENTY-SIX RACES AND CROSS RACES
In the famous school in Honolulu.

Kahala was the native fishermen with their long spears, wading through the shallow water in search of their prey. Especially at night, the twinkling bobbing lights which they carried to attract the fish added an especially picturesque feature to the view from our cabin on the shore.

The great church of Honolulu is the Central Union Church, practically, though not nominally Congregational. This is one of the wealthiest and most generous churches in the denomination, and its leading members for the most part belong to the old missionary families. Its annual benevolences amount to some fifty thousand dollars and its activities for the many races of Honolulu and for the other islands of the group are numerous. The Episcopalians have a beautiful church and group of church buildings and a very considerable following, while the Methodists, Baptists, and Disciples of Christ also have good churches and congregations. The Portuguese, Chinese, Japanese, and of course the native Hawaiians have vigorous evangelical churches of their own, largely helped by the workers and the money of the Central Union Church.

A favorite excursion of mine after the day's writing was done, on these beautiful afternoons, was to the Waikiki Beach, three or four miles from the city, for a plunge in the mild but tonicky waters of the Pacific, or for a visit to the most wonderful aquarium in the world, where fishes of incredibly brilliant hues, dyed with far more colors and shades than any rainbow ever boasted, disport themselves in the glass tanks, and seem often to pose for the benefit of visitors. The far-famed aquarium at Naples, which every orthodox traveller who visits Italy is supposed to see, cannot for a moment compare with the exhibition fish of Honolulu, either in brilliancy of coloring, oddity of shape, or in the happy arrangement of the aquarium.

My health constantly, though slowly improved, and early in February I felt that I could again take up my life-work in the interests of the Christian Endeavor cause in other lands. Various meetings had been arranged for me in Japan, Korea, and China, and I especially hoped to be able to attend the All-China Convention, to be held in Hangchow in April. I realized afterwards how rash was this undertaking.

We bade goodby to our kind hostess, Mrs. Atherton, who has recently gone to her exceedingly great reward, to the Richards family, who had done so much for our comfort, and to many other friends, and boarded the " Shinyo Maru " of the Nippon Yusen Kaisha Line, a fine steamer of ten or twelve thousand tons. Except for the captain this steamer was thoroughly Japanese in its personnel, though built chiefly with an eye to the patronage of foreigners.

What awaited us on the other side of the Pacific must be reserved for another chapter.

Chapter XLVII

Year 1916

JAPAN IN 1916

POLITE REPORTERS — A LIGHT (?) SCHEDULE — EMINENT
EDITORS — A NOBLEMAN'S MEMORIES OF AMERICA —
COUNT OKUMA'S CORDIALITY — ASANA'S PALACE — A
PEACE BANQUET — THE LATE EMPEROR'S TOMB — OUR
JAPANESE "DAUGHTER."

FTER a dozen days and nights on the "Shinyo Maru," the snow-capped peak of beautiful Fuji loomed in sight and we soon found ourselves made fast to the pier at Yokohama. I did not know that I was expected except by the Endeavorers and some missionary friends, and was surprised to have six polite reporters from different daily papers, with notebook and camera, waiting on the dock for us. Indeed they scrambled aboard the steamer and insisted, though in a most polite way, on having an interview and some pictures before we could go ashore and greet our friends.

Be it understood, however, that they were no rough and ready wielders of the pen, or scribblers just out of high school, like some of the American reporters I have seen, but suave and courteous to the last degree, like all their countrymen. Bowing low, with many apologies, they prayed that the honorable passenger would retire with them to a quiet part of the deck, where his honorable face might be exposed to their worthless camera, and his gracious words be recorded in their poor notebooks.

Who could resist such cheerful and courteous pertinacity, and when the next day some of their reports were translated for me I mentally thanked the Lord that they were not as some other reporters whom I had known, or even as certain editors, for they gave the substance of what I had said accurately and dressed it up with generous sentiments of their own.

In contrast with this, I remember an American reporter who has more recently sought an interview. In this he told his readers very little of what I had said with accuracy, but devoted a column to my personal appearance, and in staring head-lines gave this information:

"DR. CLARK WEARS A GRAY SUIT. HE BUT—TONS HIS COLLAR IN FRONT. HE HAS A PLEASANT SMILE. HE IS SOMEWHAT BALD, BUT HAS GRAY HAIR."

The Japanese press doubtless has many faults and perhaps is no more accurate, and just as biassed as our own, but it does not often deal in such trivialities.

Not feeling over strong, I had urged the committee of arrangements for my meetings to give me a light schedule of work while in Japan, and I have no doubt they intended to do so, but one engagement led to another, and that often to a third which seemed inevitable, and my days in Japan were far more full of toil than they should have been, as the sequel of this visit will show.

The chief meetings were held in Tokyo, Kyoto, Kobe, Nagoya, Shimonozeki, and Moji, while the annual National Convention of the Endeavorers was held in Osaka. In each of these cities several addresses, receptions, etc., were expected and Mrs. Clark did her full share in talking to the women's meetings and to the Juniors, in audiences that were quite as large as those that brought the older young people together. I was particularly interested at one of the meetings, I think in Osaka, to see three Buddhist monks in the audience, who apparently listened with the greatest interest, and afterward came forward and asked some questions concerning the work of which I had been speaking.

My interpreter for most of these meetings was Rev. T. Sawaya, the able secretary of the Japanese Christian Endeavor Union. No one ever had a better interpreter, for he knew English as well as Japanese, and had picturesque ways of explaining what otherwise might be obscure to the audience.

CHRISTIAN ENDEAVOR SEAMAN'S HOME NAGASAKI, JAPAN
Now given over to local authorities.

I always felt that however dull I might be, my hearers would be instructed and entertained. Mr. Sawaya, too, is a born actor, and when telling a Bible story or an incident that had any dramatic possibilities, he would so act it out that even the youngest children would be spellbound by his address.

I had the privilege also of preaching or speaking to the missionaries in my own native American tongue in several of the cities of the empire. Not especially because of my visit, but because of the renewed activities and vigor of the leaders, the Endeavor movement took a new start from the convention at Osaka. The slogan of that meeting was "Double Your Numbers!" and within a year the doubling up process had actually been accomplished. Twice as many live societies were recorded as had previously existed, and the next year the gain in numbers was still further increased. It was a gratifying fact, too, that the societies in the American Methodist Mission predominated over all the others, showing that Christian Endeavor, if allowed to exist, is as good for the Methodist Episcopal Church as for any other.

While in Tokyo for nearly a week we were the guests of my friend and college classmate Dr. and Mrs. James H. Pettee, whose guests we had previously been when he was living in Okayama, and whose daughters had often lived in our family in Auburndale, almost as daughters of our own. Dr. Pettee had recently removed to Tokyo to be in a sense the Dean of the Congregational missionaries, and had charge in an unofficial way of their national interests, since he had been upon the field for nearly forty years. This gave him access to many of the leading men of the empire, and he kindly took occasion to introduce me to several of the makers of modern Japan, whom he knew. Among others we called on two or three of the leading editors of great daily papers, which had a circulation in the hundreds of thousands. One of these, Mr. Tokutomi, we afterwards met again in Seoul, where he is also the proprietor of a leading Japanese paper. He was a most agreeable man, talked freely about affairs in Japan and America, insisted on serving us tea and cakes, and on having our pictures taken with him and his managing editor around the tea table, a gustatory courtesy which has never been accorded to me by an American editor.

A well-known Japanese nobleman who received us most graciously, and who spoke English with fluency and precision, had been educated in part in the Rice Grammar School and the Latin High School of Boston, and had attended Harvard College. He told me of one thing that struck him as peculiar,

— namely, that every American household that he visited with his schoolmates had family prayers in the morning. He did not know how to behave at first, but when he saw that all dropped upon their knees and buried their faces in the seat of the chair, he did the same, and soon learned the significance of the religious ceremony. I wonder if his experience would be the same should he visit America to-day.

He also said that during all the years since his return to Japan he had been trying to interpret the American people to the Japanese, but found it a difficult task. They could not understand the inter-relation of our National and State governments; how California could be so bitterly hostile to the Japanese while the rest of the country was friendly; or how discrimination against his countrymen was allowed on the Pacific Coast and not upon the Atlantic. I do not wonder that he was puzzled to explain these matters.

We again called upon Count Okuma, and for the third time he received us in his beautiful villa as graciously as ever, and recalled several instances of our former visits. The Count was at this time the Premier of Japan, and had, when we called, just returned from a tussle with the opposition in Parliament, a struggle in which we learned, from the next morning's papers, he had come off victorious as usual. This was the closing session of parliament for the season, and he was in high feather, and full of good humor, keeping the conversation in his own hands, in a most voluble manner, as was his wont. Before we left he gave us a letter of introduction to Count Terauchi, the Governor-General of Korea, whither we were intending to go. Terauchi was destined within a few months to succeed Okuma as Premier of the Empire. Count Okuma was in European evening dress, and he received us as before in the European part of his beautiful home, where a bright fire blazed upon the hearth, and modern paintings hung upon the walls.

The Count was especially friendly in his allusions to

America, and in spite of certain utterances of which our jingo papers have made the most, I believe he was absolutely sincere in his frequent protestations of a desire for friendly relations between Japan and America. As we were leaving, he took a lovely bouquet of orchids from a vase upon the mantel-shelf, and sent them with his compliments to Mrs. Clark.

This visit occurred not long after the coronation of the young Emperor, and post cards and illustrated booklets and " furoshukis " all over the empire were emblazoned with pictures of Count Okuma toiling up the steps of the imperial palace in Kyoto upon his knees to do homage as premier, in the name of the people of Japan, to the new Emperor. It was said that the stump of his leg, which had been shot off at the knee by an assassin many years before, was raw and bloody before he reached the top of the stairs, but, old man though he was, well along in the seventies, he pluckily went through with the ceremony, while the people proclaimed him with cheers as second only to the Emperor himself.

Soon after our arrival in Tokyo, we were invited with our fellow-passengers of the " Shinyo Maru " to a reception at the palace of Mr. Asano, the chief owner of the Nippon Yusen Kaisha Line. I think in no other country have I seen such a lavish display of wealth and luxury. Mr. Asano is many times a millionaire, and his maritime ventures had poured untold wealth into his coffers because of the European war and the universal shortage of shipping which had raised freight and passenger rates enormously. He had expended his wealth with a lavish hand on his great house and magnificent grounds, and had the custom of entertaining the first-class passengers of his principal ships after every voyage.

He, too, like many wealthy Japanese, maintained both a European and a Japanese establishment, joined together by corridors, but as dissimilar in furnishing and appearance as two houses could well be. The European house was filled with the most expensive and modern furniture, bric-a-brac, candelabra, frescoes, and paintings. The huge drawing-room easily accommodated two or three hundred seated around small lacquer tables, on which refreshments were served, while a foreign prima donna sang to us, and Japanese jugglers performed wonderful feats of sleight of hand. There were immense treasures of all sorts of articles of *vertu,* under glass cases, for our inspection. In the Japanese part of the house, with its paper walls and sliding panels, only a very few decorations and " kakemonos," appropriate to the month of March, and some pigs in plaster and papier mâché (for it was " the year of the pig ") sparsely adorned the rooms.

As I was known to have some connection with various peace societies of America, the Church Peace Union, the American and the Massachusetts Peace Societies, and other similar organizations, a reception and banquet were kindly arranged for me by the Japanese Peace Society of Tokyo. Baron Shibusawa, a wealthy and noted nobleman, well-known for his earnest advocacy of peace, his son-in-law, another baron, and many other titled Japanese were present, together with the American consul, and several missionaries, for the society was an international one. Most earnest speeches in favor of peace and good-will among men, though the world was then in the throes of the most awful war of all history, were made, both by the Japanese and English-speaking guests, with especial emphasis on the necessity of America and Japan keeping on good terms. I attempted to tell them something of the efforts of the American peace societies to keep our country out of war, for it was then a year and more before we entered the conflict, and President Wilson had yet to be elected on the slogan, " He Kept Us Out of War." The *menu* was an elaborate one in foreign style, with no chopsticks, rice, or soy in evidence.

Another interesting excursion that I enjoyed when in Kyoto, the sacred ancient capital, where we spent a few days with our old missionary friends the Carys, was to the tomb of the late Emperor, to which Dr. Tasuku Harada, then the president of the Doshisha, invited us to go. The journey of eight or ten miles was accomplished in one of the few automobiles of Kyoto, and seemed full of peril, not so much to the occupants of the automobile as to the swarms of Japanese children and their elders, who stolidly clattered through the highways paying no regard seemingly to the honking horn that warned them of our approach. By the skin of their teeth they escaped destruction a thousand times, and at last we drew near to the sacred and solemn last resting-place of the great Emperor.

Thousands and thousands of pilgrims lined the roadway from the nearest railway station, and we were told that something like ten thousand mourners had visited the grave every day since the funeral of his majesty. Many came by train, many by jinrikishas, and many walked scores of miles to do homage to their late ruler. As we approached the grave the road widened out into a great boulevard beautifully kept, and lined on either side by tall pine trees, which had been transported full grown from a distance and which were swathed in cloth to make their life and growth more certain.

At last we came within sight of the tomb itself, but were separated from it by two rows of stone posts beautifully carved and set parallel to one another. Beyond the outer fence was a bubbling fountain with various bamboo dippers near-by. In this fountain the devout worshippers washed their hands and rinsed their mouths from all defilement before they ventured to do homage to the Emperor.

As I was about to approach a little nearer to the sacred tomb, Dr. Harada asked me if I had worn my dress coat, or at least a Prince Albert under my overcoat. I had to confess that I had not, but simply an ordinary business suit. He expressed his regret that I would not be allowed to approach the second line of carved posts and get a nearer view of the tomb, for that was the imperative law. Every one must lay aside his outer garment, and approach the grave in formal clothes or else stand far away. I remembered that a few years before, when I had an audience with the living Emperor, I was required to wear evening clothes, white tie and gloves, and a tall hat, as was to be expected, since this is the usual custom of courts, but I had not realized that after he was dead he would expect the same formalities.

However, we washed our hands at the fountain, and stood afar off gazing curiously, and with some reverence at the vast pile of pebbles painted white that covered his last resting-place. It was truly an impressive mausoleum. A hill clad in sombre evergreens rises directly behind the grave, which sets off the little mountain of white stones and gives the whole place an air of solemn grandeur. Just beyond is a magnificent view of the distant country, for the grave is upon a sightly elevation, and not far away, though out of sight from the Emperor's grave, is the mausoleum of the late Empress, a replica of the Emperor's tomb on a smaller scale.

On returning to Kyoto we had the pleasure of visiting the ancient palace, the former abode of the Mikadoes of Japan, where the impressive ceremonies of the inauguration of the new Emperor had recently taken place.

The palace, though enormous in size, and consisting of many different buildings, is marked by extreme simplicity, much more so than the palace in Tokyo, where I had had the interview with the old Emperor. An interesting building on the palace grounds had a small chamber where the new Emperor, after various washings and ceremonies, watched and prayed, clad in mediaeval armor, during the whole night before his inauguration, while many nobles in a little pavilion near-by, kept him company in his vigils and his prayers. The building on the palace grounds are all low, mostly of one story, and with no suggestion of the influence of foreign architecture.

While in Kyoto, too, we enjoyed a delightful reception given by the missionaries and the faculty of the Doshisha, and I had the privilege of speaking once more to several hundreds of the advanced students of this famous institution, as well as to the theological classes.

Another pleasant reception in the Girls' College at Kobe, which is now under the care of the eminent educator, Miss Charlotte DeForest, left a happy memory. These Japanese receptions mingle the formal and the informal, the jovial and the serious, in a very happy way, and are far less stiff than the line-up of the average American reception, where one must stand for an hour while his hand is squeezed and battered out of shape by some hundreds or thousands of stalwart shakers.

We sailed from Moji for Fusan in Korea, after a day spent in the Presbyterian Girls' School in Shimonozeki, a fine institution worthy of the great denomination that fosters it. The evening before we sailed, some kind friends tendered us a banquet in foreign style in a foreign hotel in Moji, after a large meeting in the Union Tabernacle, a church which is a triumph of interdenominational fellowship, bringing all the Christians of the city together for work and worship. The banquet was notable for its elaborateness and its distinctly foreign character, and for the many dishes to which a somewhat failing appetite on the part of both of us scarcely allowed us to do credit. A good Christian Japanese lady of means accompanied us to the steamer, declaring that she was our spiritual daughter, and would always bear us in mind in her thought and prayer. Thus with these good omens and kindly farewells we ended our fourth visit to lovely Nippon, and sailed across the rough strait that separates Japan from her new dependency, the Land of the Morning Calm.

CHAPTER XLVIII

YEAR 1916

IN THE LAND OF MORNING CALM

KOREA AFTER SIXTEEN YEARS — GREAT IMPROVEMENTS —
NATIONAL UNREST — TWELVE HUNDRED PEOPLE AT A
PRAYER MEETING — PNEUMONIA — BEST LAID PLANS
GANG AFT AGLEY — MUKDEN, THE BARBARIC.

OREA just at the time of which I write deserved the soubriquet which heads this chapter more than it had a few years earlier, or than it did a few years later. It was apparently a time of both morning and afternoon calm for this long peninsula and its eighteen millions of inhabitants. A few years before, when Japan first took over the control of the country and gave up its pretence of merely "peaceful penetration," riots were numerous, and harsh measures were resorted to, which the rest of the world loudly disapproved and did something to modify. Many of the insurgents were found among the Christians since they were among the more enlightened and freedom-loving portion of the people, and the missionaries were for a time in disfavor with the Japanese government.

Again, three years after the visit of which I write, the general uprising of the subject nations after the Great War (induced by world restlessness as well as by President Wilson's splendid idealism and his famous "fourteen points") was shared by the Koreans who demanded that the same freedom that had been given to the Poles and the Czechs should be

meted out to them.   Once more many Christians were among
the insurgents, and the incipient rebellion was put down with
savage cruelty by the militarists who were then in control of
Korea.   Fortunately, this phase of Japanese rule is now
ended, and, we may hope, for all time.

But there was an interval between 1910 and 1919 when this
ancient kingdom, now reduced to a satrapy of Japan, seemed
to deserve its ancient name, and apparent peace and good will
(perhaps only on the surface) reigned throughout the peninsula.   We were fortunate to visit Korea in one of these happier
years.   It was cold and raw enough on the March morning
when we stepped from the deck of the steamer after a stormy
night upon the Korean channel.   And yet, disagreeable as
was the weather, and dim as was the light of the early dawn,
we could not help noticing the great changes for the better
which had taken place in this leading seaport of Fusan since our
last visit.

Sixteen years before, Korea was under the rule of a decadent
and corrupt monarchy.   Its last and worst days as an independent nation had come.   China, Japan, and Russia had been
for centuries battling for the supremacy of this unhappy land.
Nominally Korea still gave tribute to China, though Japan
was even then by far the most important power, and Japanese
merchants and propagandists had penetrated to the far interior.

Fusan itself, in spite of its magnificent harbor, was a
wretched run-down little sea-port, but now we found it
equipped with splendid wharves and warehouses, and saw that
it was the terminal of a great railway system, that tapped not
only all Korea but far Manchuria, Mongolia, Siberia, and
China.   The white-robed "hicky-men" still carried their
enormous burdens on their backs, but the steam horse had
evidently come to share with them the heavy loads which previously they and the donkeys alone had carried.

As we travelled up the line toward the north we saw marvel-

lous material improvements everywhere. Fine public buildings had been erected in many places; agricultural schools had
been established in every province; automobile roads had been
built or projected, and the bare brown hillsides, which fifteen
years before had resembled an elevated desert of Sahara, were
now smiling with a young growth of pines, for the Japanese
had covered the waste places of Korea with hundreds of
millions of young trees.

These were some of the material gains from the Japanese
occupation. But such blessings do not compensate a people
for the loss of their national integrity and the absorption of
their national life in that of another, and, though the fires of
revolution did not break out in Korea for some years, they were
smouldering, as later events proved.

While waiting for a train to carry us northward we called
again on our friend Dr. Irvin, who, on a previous visit, had
accompanied us on the delightful trip to the Buddhist monastery in the mountains. He is no longer a missionary of the
Presbyterian Board, but has a large private practice of his own.

He told us of a terrible conflict that he had recently had
with three Korean thugs, who, on pretence of seeking medical
advice, had come in the middle of the night to murder him
and rob his house. He is a tremendously powerful man, and
was equal, single-handed, to the three ruffians, whom, after
a bloody struggle, in which much furniture was destroyed and
three heads were broken, he managed to put out of his house
just as relief came. These men were afterwards apprehended
and imprisoned for life. As told by Dr. Irvin it was one of
the most thrilling stories I ever listened to. It would make
the fortune of an O. Henry if he could work it up in all its
grim details.

Our first stop in Korea was at Taiku, where we were received
by a great company of uniformed boys from the Presbyterian
schools in true military fashion and by most of the Christians

of the city. The boys were drawn up in a hollow square, while we reviewed them and received their cheers, and then, in a long line of jinrikishas we rode off to an ancient park where the formal reception and the first Christian Endeavor meeting of the series was to be held. Our friends Dr. Pettee and Mr. Sawaya were with us and were also called upon for addresses.

Seoul, the capital, was our next stopping-place, and there we were the guests of the well-known Dr. Avison, whose splendid hospital with every modern appliance for advanced medicine and surgery is the pride of the Christians of Korea. On reaching Seoul we found an invitation to lunch from the Governor-General, Count Terauchi, which was accepted by the male members of the party, but declined by Mrs. Clark, as a sudden illness seemed to make it impossible for her to attend. Thereupon the Count cancelled his invitation to certain Japanese and other ladies who had been invited, and decided to make it a gentlemen's party. The next day, however, Mrs. Clark was much better, and the Governor-General, hearing of her improvement, again reversed his plans, once more invited the ladies to come, and carried out his original intention.

It proved to be an elaborate luncheon, with kindly speeches from the Governor-General, Chief-Justice Watanabe, the American consul, and the guests from America. The Count speaks only French and Japanese, and as Mrs. Clark was seated between the Count and the Chief-Justice, who also spoke only French and Japanese, she had to call up all her *lingua franca* which dated back to her school-girl days. My seatmate, fortunately, was a Japanese lady who spoke English most fluently, so that I had no difficulty with the social part of the entertainment. The luncheon, owing to the French *chef* of the palace, could not have been surpassed in any first-class hotel in Paris.

After the luncheon the Governor-General sent one of the members of his cabinet with us to visit some Korean schools, and also the museum, of which he is very proud, where were displayed products of the different enterprises which Japan was encouraging, and especially the revival of certain keramic arts, which had died out during Korea's decadent years. It is a well-known fact that Japan derived her knowledge of pottery and porcelain from Korea where these arts flourished when Japan was a barbarous country and looked across the channel for the beginnings of her civilization.

Another interesting visit made possible by Count Terauchi, was to the ancient palace of the deposed Emperor of Korea, who, by the way, had been given a consolation prize of several hundred thousand yen a year. Our party was conveyed in fine carriages drawn by pairs of spanking black horses. After driving through an enormous park filled with giant trees we drew up in front of a conservatory where tropical plants of all kinds and huge banana and palm trees flourished. It was a wintry day outside, and the change on entering the conservatory seemed like passing from the Arctic regions to the Tropics. Here tea and a certain kind of Kingly cake was served, and then we further explored the palace grounds which contained many royal residences, most of them of rather a humble character but built on the same general plan as the old palace of Kyoto, though with Korean peculiarities.

A generous reception at Dr. Avison's, and many meetings and preaching services filled to the brim our few days in Seoul, which we found in many ways a most interesting city. The superposition of modern Japanese civilization upon ancient Korea produces many striking contrasts. Side by side with some of the ancient hovels are splendid bank buildings, great government palaces and public offices, and the finest hotel in all the East. The signs over the doors are in Japanese and ill-spelled English, as is the custom at home of these progressive linguists of the Island Empire.

A supper and prayer meeting at Judge Watanabe's must not

be forgotten. His home is an evangelical oasis in an official Buddhist and Shinto desert. His earnest devotion to the little Christian church did not seem to weaken his influence with the Japanese officials, for indeed he ranked, as Chief Justice, among the highest of them.

It is a six hours' journey from Seoul to Pyeng Yang where some of our most important appointments in Korea were scheduled. This is one of the largest cities of inland Korea and for many years has been a great missionary centre both of the Presbyterians and the Methodists, especially of the Presbyterians. We were surprised to find that autos had penetrated so far into primitive Korea, and, as it was cold and raw, we were delighted that we were not obliged to take a breezy jinrikisha for several miles to the house of Rev. Mr. Holdcroft, who was to be our kindly host.

That same evening all the missionaries were invited to dine with us at Mr. Holdcroft's house, and we found them a splendid company of keenly intelligent, wide-awake, aggressive Christians, who had already accomplished great things for the civilization and evangelization of their part of Korea. The next day, March 21, was equally cold and disagreeable and reminded us of the worst March weather in New England. However we did not have much time to think of the weather, for six meetings of various kinds in Japanese and Korean churches and in missionary homes filled up the day, except for an automobile ride to different points of interest around this historic city where one of the great battles of the Chino-Japanese war had been fought.

The crowded native city was even more interesting to me than the battlefield, for here we could see where the Koreans for centuries had lived and died, bought and sold, and conducted their domestic functions, many of which as in all oriental countries are performed in the open air. I was particularly delighted with the evening congregation in the large Presbyterian Church which I was asked to address. It was the mid-week prayer-meeting evening of the church, and the congregation was little larger, I imagine, than at the regular mid-week service. At least 1,200 persons were present, the men on one side of the low partition, and the women on the other, squatting on the floor, on the platform steps, and in the far corners of the room, as thickly as human beings could crowd together. I stood with my interpreter directly behind the thin partition so that the male and female audiences on either side of it could see and hear. As can be imagined the singing was hearty and full-throated even if not absolutely perfect according to western musical standards.

This meeting and the strenuous days which preceded it must have been the last straws that broke the camel's back, for the next morning I rose at three o'clock with a raging fever, to take the train for Syen Chun. I managed to struggle down to the breakfast table but could not stay, and soon had to give up all thought of going on that day. A frightful chill which seemed to rattle all my bones in their sockets overtook me before I got back into bed once more, and Dr. Folwell, a medical missionary of the Methodist church, who was called at daylight, pronounced my trouble pneumonia, and ordered me peremptorily, to cancel all engagements for the next month.

This was a hard blow, for I had almost constant appointments to speak at meetings which had been arranged months in advance at Syen Chun, Mukden, Peking, Nanking, Shanghai, Suchau, and above all at the Christian Endeavor National Convention in Hangchow, in early April. However, for the present at least there was nothing for it but to stay in bed. It proved to be the beginning of many woes, even though a comparatively mild case of pneumonia. The fever kept up for days at a gradually decreasing rate. Our hosts, the Holdcrofts, were most kind, as were all the missionaries of the station. Even the governor of the province called, and Governor-

General Terauchi himself sent kindly inquiries concerning my health.

After ten days, hoping to save something out of the wreck of my plans for China, I decided to go on, though against the advice of all the missionaries, and with the very reluctant consent of the doctor. On the way to Mukden we spent one night in a delightful missionary home in Syen Chun. I was unable to hold meetings except with a missionary group who gathered in the home of two ladies who entertained us.

The next day a long ride in a cold car took us to Mukden, the capital of Manchuria, where we found a very comfortable Japanese hotel, built in modern style. This was characteristic of one of the many efforts of Japan in connection with their railway to tighten their grip on Manchuria and western Asia.

I must confess, as I look back upon it, that this whole journey from Honolulu on, was a most foolhardy undertaking. Much of it seems like a nightmare. I was not well enough to attempt such strenuous travelling and constant meetings as awaited me, but I did not realize how insidious had been the effects of the typhoid fever, or how little strength and vitality I had left. Still there seemed to be nothing left to do but to press on and take the attendant risks.

In Mukden we had great difficulty, owing to the stupidity of our Chinese driver, in finding the mission station where I was expected to make an address on Sunday afternoon. In spite of our protests he took us in an entirely wrong direction to a distant part of the city, miles from the mission house which was comparatively near our hotel. When we reached it we heard the leader of the meeting, which had been waiting an hour for us, pronouncing the benediction. However, the missionaries stayed together for another half hour to hear something about Christian Endeavor in other lands. The movement had already taken root in some parts of Manchuria in the missions of the Irish and Scotch Presbyterian churches.

A trifling incident over which we afterwards smiled occurred in the Irish Presbyterian Mission as we were introduced to a lady whom we understood to be " Miss Kelly." When, however, she soon afterwards introduced us to her husband, Rev. Mr. Miskelly, we learned our mistake and found that we had first been introduced to Mrs. Miskelly.

Our obtuse driver gave us a view of the city of Mukden which we should not have obtained had it not been for his stupidity, since we had to leave the city early the next morning. There are few cities in the world equal to Mukden for a sort of bizarre and barbaric picturesqueness. As we were driven slowly through its tortuous streets, crowded from curb to curb with human beings, through its gates, which dated back a thousand years, and which seemed to be continually opening before us, since the city has been surrounded in the course of centuries by several walls; as we saw the hideous but characteristic decorations, in which the old dragon of the Manchus was often reproduced in most grotesque forms, we wished that we might have a week to explore these fascinating but unsavory purlieus which seemed more typically characteristic of ancient China than anything we had before seen.

Peking had been wonderfully modernized since our first visit; Shanghai's large foreign element makes one sometimes forget that he is actually in China; Canton has been vastly changed and deodorized within the last quarter of a century, but Mukden is evidently the same old Mukden of a thousand years ago.

THE CHINA OF YUAN SHI KAI

UNWISE ECONOMY — BESIDE THE GREAT WALL — YUAN SHI
KAI'S PRETENSIONS — MEMORABLE SCENES IN PEKING —
HANGCHOW — TEN THOUSAND MILES OF TRAVEL FOR A
TEN-MINUTE SPEECH — IN A CHINESE REVOLUTION —
WEARY DAYS OF ILLNESS — CORMORANT FISHING —
HOME AGAIN.

HE next morning we left Mukden bright and early for Peking in a wretched second-class box car with tiny windows, for a cold and dreary two days' ride. As I was paying all our expenses and making personal contributions to the missions whose hospitality we enjoyed, and had no wealthy society at home to provide travel comfort, I felt that we must economize on these long journeys, an unwise decision very likely, considering my state of health.

This journey was a very uncomfortable one. The seats on the second-class cars were then either hard boards or made of slippery cane with a downward slant that made it impossible to sit upright unless one continuously braced himself against his impedimenta. Moreover the meals on these routes were then few and scanty, and the cold seemed to penetrate to our bones.

We spent the night at Shan-hai-kwan, on the shores of the sea, at the very foot of the Great Wall, which, after meandering for 1,200 miles across China, here comes to a full stop on

the picturesque and rock-bound coast. The foreign hotel had been closed for some reason, and we had to seek shelter in a wretched Chinese inn through which the cold March winds rioted in a way that was by no means good for a man who was just recovering from pneumonia.

However, the next day's journey was in a somewhat more comfortable car, and we reached Peking before nightfall and rejoiced to find ourselves in the warm and comfortable missionary home of Rev. Harry Martin after thirty-six hours of cold discomfort. Another disappointment awaited us here, for we found that many of our missionary friends whom we had expected to see had gone to the annual meeting of the mission at Pao-ting-fu, where sixteen years before we had seen the brave men and women just before their martyrdom in the Boxer uprising, as I have before related.

The disarrangement of my plans caused by the long delay in Pyeng Yang naturally prevented any large meetings in Peking, but we visited and addressed some of the schools of the American Board mission, and saw something of the marvellous changes which sixteen short years had wrought in China's capital. Legation Street which then had been a muddy, and at times, almost impassable thoroughfare, filled in places with filth and offal, was now a broad, wealthy avenue, lined with fine buildings of a diplomatic and commercial character. Department stores had been established, where goods from all parts of the world were offered for sale. The legation buildings themselves had been greatly improved and electric cars made access easy and possible to many parts of the city.

Our visit was toward the end of President Yuan Shi Kai's short and inglorious supremacy. He had been elected president because he was the " strong man " of China from the militarist's point of view, and at first he seemed to deserve the enconiums that were heaped upon him for his part in bringing order out of chaos after the fall of the Manchu dynasty. But the sense of power and authority went to his head and he yielded to unwise counsellors, and it is said also to the importunities of his wife, who like other women of history have exercised an unhappy influence over their lords. He resolved to make himself emperor and found a dynasty of his own to which his sons should succeed.

We happened to be there at the very time of the incubation of his ill-starred attempt. He had fixed the day when he should be proclaimed China's Caesar. The Forbidden City had been re-decorated in golden, glowing colors, and triumphal arches had been erected under which he expected to march with his conquering cohorts. He had even coined new silver dollars to take the place of the old " Mexicans," with his own face in bold relief upon one side.

Peking was in a ferment during our two days' visit, and rumors were abroad that several of the President's chief generals, who did not agree with his ambitious projects, had been beheaded on the day of our arrival. A counter-rebellion was expected to break out at any moment.

However things remained comparatively quiet except for these wild rumors and the natural excitement which they engendered. A little later Yuan actually proclaimed himself Emperor, and for a few days enjoyed his empty honors. But the best laid plans of kings as well as those of ordinary men gang aft agley. China would not brook another monarchy. Republican instincts were too powerful among the people for even a strong man to resist. Rival strong men appeared, and, however sinister their motives, they arrayed themselves on the side of the people against Yuan, and he was soon forced to abdicate and to denounce his previous pretensions in the most abject and humiliating manner.

The most interesting hours that I spent in Peking were with Dr. Ingram, an American missionary, who was one of the heroes of the siege of sixteen years before and who went with me over the battleground, showing the places on the wall where the fiercest conflicts occurred, as well as the places in the grounds of the British Legation where the Boxers were most stubbornly resisted. Here was placed by the besieged the one poor old gun that was fired with such tremendous effect. There we saw the exact spot where, by a sudden change of wind, the fire which the Boxers had relied upon to compel the capitulation of the besieged forces, was stayed. If any one can make the excursion to these ever-memorable spots and not believe in the divine protection given to God's followers he must indeed be a confirmed skeptic. The stores of hundreds of tons of rice, most unusual and providential, which the besieged were able to draw upon and thus prevent starvation, is another marvellous part of the story, but it would take volumes to describe it in all its details. I was especially interested because on our previous visit to Peking we had become acquainted with most of the missionaries and many of the native Christians who a few days later were involved in this memorable experience.

Sir John Jordan, who sixteen years before had charge of British interests in Korea, and with whom we became well acquainted in our long forty-day journey across Siberia, had now become British Ambassador to China, and had been knighted because of his diplomatic skill and wisdom. He received us most cordially and showed us the wonderful Chinese temple with its many treasures which had become the centre of the British Legation. It is a marvellous old building full of quaint and priceless carvings and decorations which had been made over into a delightful and comfortable residence for the ambassador. Lady Jordan, a charming hostess, urged us to stay to afternoon tea while Sir John and I recounted the incidents, both grim and humorous, of our long journey across Siberia in 1900, which journey she did not share, having been in Scotland at the time.

The next day the ambassador came to the train to see us off on our journey southward. This journey, too, by reason of the miserable second-class cars, the interminable waits at various stations, and my own ill health, was a most trying one, but after two days and a night we reached Shanghai and were made welcome by Judge Lobingier at his pleasant home in the outskirts of the city.

As we approached Shanghai we seemed to go from late winter into a late spring. Peach trees were in full bloom and the country was smiling and attractive in its blossoms and its greenery. But nowhere in China can you get away from the graves. It is no exaggeration to say that you cannot look out of the car window for five consecutive minutes without seeing a graveyard, sometimes a large and elaborate one with many mounds and horse-shoe enclosures of stone; sometimes only a single mound marked by a pathetic little memorial tag or a piece of mock money placed there in order that the deceased might have the wherewithal to pay his fare on the other shore. Graves, graves, graves! China seems to be a land of the dead rather than of the living, and yet when one enters the narrow, bustling streets of a Chinese city, or even of a considerable village, one wonders how there can be room enough in all China even to bury the teeming millions who are very thoroughly alive and most energetically active.

The same day in the afternoon we went on to Hangchow, our principal convention destination, but ill fortune seemed to pursue us all the way, for because of some delay in the train from Nanking, we lost the train on which we were expected to arrive in Hangchow, and we reached the national convention city after dark, and only just before the evening service of the convention. On the way, however, we had heard of the large and fine gathering of Endeavorers, and how the celebrated Dr. Main on his scarcely less famous white horse had led the long parade to an ancient pagoda on the hill-top for an afternoon outing. Dr. and Mrs. Judson, veteran Presbyterian missionaries, opened their hospitable doors to us for a couple of days, as we supposed, but for more than four weeks as it actually proved to be.

By the time we reached Hangchow I was feeling miserably ill, but determined to go to the meeting whatever it might cost. I was able to speak about ten minutes to the assembled Endeavorers, bring them greetings from America and from Japan and Korea, and then went back to the Judsons' home and to bed, where I stayed for nearly a month except for a few intervals of an hour or two between the days of fever and suffering.

My wife was able to attend and speak at some of the Endeavor meetings the next day, which was Sunday, the last day of the convention. Dr. Main, of whom I have spoken, is at the head of a famous hospital of the Church Missionary Society of England, himself a genial Scotchman, whose unfailing motto is, " Keep Smiling." He was most attentive, calling every day and sometimes twice or thrice a day, and doing his best to relieve my sufferings with calomel, Epsom salts, and other old-fashioned remedies, which were the only things that gave any relief.

Other friends, whose kindness we can never forget, were Rev. and Mrs. Edgar E. Strother, the joint field-secretaries of the Christian Endeavor movement in China, a most self-sacrificing and devoted couple. They stayed with us throughout those weary four weeks and were untiring in their efforts to relieve the monotony and the suffering of the sick-room. I was able to leave the financial arrangements for our board and our passage home with them. The steamer on which we expected to sail for Japan got away on schedule time, but, alas, we were not among her passengers, as we had fully expected to be, and steamer after steamer sailed without us, to our sore disappointment.

On the night of April 12, very early in the morning, we heard the firing of several heavy guns and said to each other, with little idea that we were stating a fact, that " a revolution must be on," though we knew that the Chekiang Province, of which Hangchow is the capital, had been threatening to revolt against the pretensions of Yuan Shi Kai, and the military party of the north.

When daylight came, and the good doctor made his daily call, we found that the revolution was no joke, that the independence of Chekiang had been proclaimed, the governor deposed, and a new republic set up. There were also rumors that the northern soldiers were marching against Hangchow from Shanghai, which was still loyal to the old régime. We learned that the railway had been torn up in places to prevent the approach of the northern troops, and that communication with Shanghai and the rest of the world was absolutely out of the question, except by a long and dangerous journey on the Grand Canal, which itself might be in the hands of the enemies of Chekiang for all we knew.

However there was nothing to do but to grin and bear it. I was too ill to go if there had been the best railway accommodations in the world, and it was impossible to leave Hangchow if I had been as strong as Samson. On the whole, it was the most orderly and peaceful revolution that ever took place. Except for the disturbance at the Governor's yamen there was no turmoil or looting, and no drop of blood was shed.

A hundred times more rioting and disturbance, to say nothing of the slaughter, occurred in the police strike in Boston in 1919 than in this revolution of a great province whose capital contains nearly a million souls. The police and gendarmes went about their business as though nothing had happened, and " business as usual " seemed to be the universal motto.

Unlike the Boxer Rebellion of sixteen years before, whose incipient threatenings we had seen, the revolution of 1916 was not directed against the foreigners. The missionaries were held in highest esteem. Dr. Main was consulted by the new officials, and many of them desired to send their superfluuos luggage for safe keeping to the missionary compounds, which in some places were piled high with trunks and impedimenta of all kinds. Many, in the early days of the revolution, took refuge in the compound of the missionary hospital, fearing the rioting and disorder which did not come.

My opinion of the self-restraint and good sense of the Chinese was increased a hundred per cent by these incidents, and contrary to what is often said that the mass of the Chinese care little under what government they live, I believe that the majority of the people wanted a democratic government and desired to defeat the machinations of the upstart emperor.

The weary days followed one another slowly enough, while steamer after steamer which we vainly hoped to take, sailed from the port of Shanghai, and I was too sick to be moved even if the rebellion had allowed free exit from the city. Fortunately the Endeavorers had all returned to their homes before rail communication was intercepted. That so many hundreds came to the convention in spite of the fact that they knew the rebellion had been scheduled for April 8, the day before the convention closed, was a testimony to the devotion and courage of these faithful Christians. Fortunately, whether or not the ringleaders desired to give the Endeavorers a chance to leave the city, the uprising was delayed for a couple of days beyond the appointed time which persistent rumor had set for it.

Occasionally, for a day or two, I would feel better, the fever would decrease, hope which " springs eternal " would revive, and it seemed as though we might get away if the rebels would allow it. Once I was able to take a short jinrikisha ride through the busy and attractive streets where are many stores of wealthy and prosperous merchants, and once I was allowed to get so far as to Dr. Main's summer home by the lakeside, two or three miles from the centre, for a social tea with a few missionary friends.

Hangchow is very proud of its West Lake, on which the city borders. It is indeed a beautiful sheet of water. Here are pleasure boats and little island resorts and suggestions that tell us that sometimes China plays as well as works, which foreign travellers are slow to believe. The convention delegates greatly enjoyed an excursion on the lake as well as to the pagoda which stands prominently on the hill above the lake. This pagoda had been given, I was told, to Dr. Main by the city in recognition of his valued services, but he had returned

WEST LAKE, HANGCHOW
Where the Christain Endeavor Convention of China in 1916 enjoyed a picnic.

it to the municipality for good and sufficient reasons. He was the only missionary, I believe, who ever owned a pagoda.

At last, on May 5, after a month in Hangchow, though feeling far from well, we started for Shanghai by the Grand Canal, a twenty-four-hour journey in a comfortable house-boat. An especially easy sedan chair was provided for me for the five-mile trip through the city to the Canal, and everything was done by my kind friends to make the journey as comfortable and safe as possible. Dr. Main seemed a sort of wizard, who could command boats and boatmen, and beds and bedding and provisions at a moment's notice.

There were six of us, including one young Chinese lady, in the little party on the canal journey, and the houseboat was pulled by a small steamer which had a convoy of one or two other boats besides our own. The houseboat in front of us was occupied by a Chinese family, whose performance of all their household duties and operations they did not seek to screen from the eyes of the public. A little slavey, who was perhaps the daughter-in-law of the old couple, and the wife

A COMMON MODE OF TRAVEL IN CHINA

of one of the strapping young men, seemed to have all the mean and dirty work put upon her, and she toiled for sixteen hours a day with apparently no interruption. Evidently the suggestion of servants' unions and strikes had not reached China.

The scenery was pleasing rather than grand. The rich shores on either side were teeming with a luxuriant growth of grains and vegetables. Huge water buffaloes came down to drink or wallow in the shallows of the Canal. Occasionally we passed teeming towns, multitudes crowding the narrow streets, which gave us some idea of the vast population which this wonderful Canal serves. The Grand Canal, well named indeed, connects Tientsin with Hangchow. It was open for traffic more than six hundred years ago, and was described with much accuracy by that hardy Venetian explorer, Marco Polo. At times it widens out into small lakes. Indeed in the hundreds of miles of its course it connects many lakes. The Erie canal is a pigmy beside it.

One of the most interesting sights was the fishing boats. Do not suppose, however, that they were equipped with nets

FISHING WITH CORMORANTS IN CHINA

and hooks and lines, or spears. Each boat held one or two fishermen, but chiefly a solemn row of cormorants on its edge, often a dozen or more of them. When the sharp eyes of these feathered fishermen spied their prey, they darted for it with unerring aim, and at once flew back to the boat bearing their trophies. A ring around their necks prevents them from swallowing, but it does not prevent their breathing apparatus from working. We hoped that these faithful birds were rewarded for their trouble, but probably only with the heads and tails and entrails of the fish they so patiently and loyally brought to their masters. For hundreds, perhaps thousands

of years, this odd practice has prevailed in China, and doubtless has afforded as much amusement as well as profit to many
generations of Orientals as did the trained hunting falcons to
our European ancestors of the Middle Ages.

About noon of the second day we reached Shanghai, a
hundred miles or so from Hangchow, and our boat was tied
up to a pier in the heart of the city, amid ten thousand other
craft of all kinds and sizes. We were made welcome by Dr.
Mary Fulton, a member of the celebrated Cantonese missionary
family, who was giving her time to the translation of certain
medical books into Chinese. At the same time she has helped
to establish a church for the Cantonese Christians, among
whom she was brought up. They abound in some parts of
Shanghai and still speak their own dialect.

China, like the rest of the world, was of course very much
excited by the European war, though she had troubles enough
of her own in all conscience. Feeling had in 1916 set strongly
against the numerous German residents of Shanghai. They
were boycotted, ostracised, and even turned out of the clubs of
which they had long been members. Official China, however,
was wavering as to whether she should cast in her lot with
Germany or the Allies, for it then looked as though the
Teutons would be victorious.

It was not until the United States decided to enter the war,
and politely asked China to join her that she decided to cast
in her lot with the Allies.

At last we sailed for Japan, hoping at least to get so far
on our homeward way, though a very ill turn on one night
of the voyage made our arrival even in Japan seem problem-
atical. However, the Yellow Sea was on the whole kind to
us, much kinder than on previous journeys, and after three
days we arrived in Kobe and took refuge in a small but comfortable hotel, not wishing to burden our hospitable missionary
friends with an invalid, though we were frequently upbraided
by them for not doing so.

Now our great anxiety was to get passage on some steamer for America. All, we were told, were overcrowded, and passages had to be engaged months in advance. Three or four steamers on which we had hoped to return and had tentatively engaged passage had come and gone without us, and we were almost in despair about getting away from Japan, where we should have been so glad to have had two weeks for the holiday for which we had planned if increasing illness had not prevented.

ANOTHER METHOD OF GOING TO A CONVENTION

We had almost given up hope of getting passage on any steamer, when some good angel intervened in our behalf and greatly to our joy we were offered a small cabin on the "Empress of Russia," one of the fine Canadian Pacific steamers plying between Japan and Vancouver. With some difficulty I was transferred from my bed to the steamer, and seemed somewhat better during the twelve days' voyage to America's shores. Even there our troubles did not end, for the round-trip tickets which we had bought before leaving home, obliged us to return over the Santa Fé Route, and compelled the long overland journey from Vancouver to Southern California before we could fairly start for home.

Many miserable days were passed on this long railway trip though there were short intervals of comparative physical comfort and we were glad enough when we reached Chicago. It was a question of some difficulty to decide whether I should go to a hospital or a hotel in Chicago, or should venture, ill as I was with a raging fever, to take the further journey to Boston. Finding it possible to get a stateroom on the Twentieth Century Limited, we finally decided to risk it, and as soon as the porter could make up my bed I was once more on my back for the twenty-six hours' journey to Massachusetts.

CLIMBING UP HILL DIFFICULTY TO HEALTHVILLE

A MONTH IN HOSPITAL — AMERICA IN THE WAR — ANXIOUS
DAYS FOR THE WORLD — IN FLOWERY FLORIDA — HOW
A PURITAN HOME RENEWED ITS YOUTH.

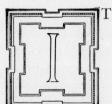IT CAN well be imagined that, after this long and distressing journey, I was glad to find myself at Sagamore at last, even though only half alive.

My youngest son, Sydney Aylmer, had been waiting impatiently for my return that I might perform the marriage ceremony which should unite him to Miss Margaret Elliott of Newton Centre. I arrived only a day or two before the appointed time, and rising from my bed was barely able to dress for the occasion and tie the hymeneal knot, I hope sure and fast, and then get me back to bed again.

Local doctors, as well as those across the seas, seemed to be much puzzled by my illness. One of them, knowing nothing better to do, suggested a long course of Vitalait as a possible help, but it proved to be as useless as all the other medicines which I had poured down a patient throat during the many previous months. When every known remedy had been exhausted I felt that it was time to consult a specialist, which I should have done long before. This specialist was a celebrated diagnostician, Dr. Josslyn of Boston, who, without hesitation, at once pronounced it to be a serious case of gall stones, frequently an aftermath of typhoid fever, and announced that I must at once have an operation.

The whole summer had been a long series of excruciating days of pain — coming about once a week, and leaving me dazed and exhausted for several days, until another attack was due. When September came, and with it Dr. Josslyn's advice, I was glad to undergo any operation which promised even a remote chance of life and health. On September 29, therefore, at Corey Hill Hospital in Brookline, the operation was performed by Dr. Fred B. Lund, a skilful surgeon who had given special attention to such troubles. For three or four days, I am told, my life hung on a hair, while on October 3, the fortieth anniversary of our wedding day, I almost passed over the river after a very severe chill accompanied by nausea and hours of distressing hiccoughs, followed by a sinking spell, from which I was with difficulty revived.

That seemed to be the crisis, for from that time on, step by step, I began to climb my Hill Difficulty back to health again. It was a great comfort that my dear wife could be with me almost all the time in the hospital, as she was allowed to occupy at night a room in the Nurses' Home near-by. Dr. Lund proved to be not only a skilful surgeon but a kindly and jovial friend, who relieved the weary hours with frequent visits. He was also a great lover of Horace, himself a poet withal, and frequently read to me translations of one of the Latin poet's odes, which he had achieved in the intervals of a very extensive practice.

Such an experience gives one a realizing sense of the value of friends and surprises one constantly with the thought that he has so many more than he suspected. The daily papers seemed to keep the people who were at all interested in the matter informed about my progress towards health, and flowers and fruit and letters of sympathy and later visits from my children and other friends made the slow days of recovery much brighter than they otherwise would have been.

I must not forget the kindness of Mr. Jacob J. Arakelyan, whose limousine was at my service in going to the hospital and returning to our home on Pinckney Street, and on many other occasions. Mr. Arakelyan is a remarkable example of a man who, amid the greatest difficulties, can by persistence, good judgment and fair dealing, make his way in America. Coming from Armenia, where he was born under the shadow of Mt. Ararat, as a lad of eighteen years, he sought at once the companionship of Christian people, and by industry and thrift accumulated a very comfortable fortune in the printing business, becoming, eventually, the proprietor of one of the largest printing establishments in Boston. He is as benevolent as he is prosperous, and gives largely to charities of all kinds, the Christian Endeavor movement being one of his especial interests. A conditional gift from him of ten thousand dollars was one of the larger sums which enabled us to complete the beautiful building, which now stands on the corner of Mt. Vernon and Joy Streets, and of which I shall speak later.

These trying experiences enabled me to realize more fully the goodness of my Father in Heaven, and also, I hope, to devote my life more unreservedly to His service.

In the early spring of 1917 came more and more exciting news concerning the war. I need not rehearse the political story of the sad years that followed.

The most important and practical thing seemed to be to encourage among the Christian Endeavorers food-production and conservation for a half-starved world. A Christian Endeavor Peace Union, which had been a popular organization in the early days of the war, like other peace societies naturally fell into abeyance, and the "Christian Endeavor Army of Universal Patriotic Service" took its place. I drew up the constitution of such an "Army," which was widely adopted by many unions, and the Endeavorers all over the country went to work with a will to plant war-gardens in the spring, and to preserve their fruits by canning and preserving and drying in the fall. Tens of thousands of such gardens were planted, it is believed, and warm commendations for these efforts were received, not only from the National War-Garden Commission in Washington, but from President Wilson, Mr. Herbert Hoover, and others.

I must not forget to state that in this work I was greatly encouraged by Mr. Charles Pack, the president of the War-Garden Commission of the Government, who gave me $500 to start the campaign. My college friend, Samuel W. McCall, who was then governor of Massachusetts, obtained from a special State fund which he administered, $1,000 for the same purpose. My youngest son, Sydney, who was in the United Society office for a few weeks at that time, also did his best to obtain funds for this purpose, and was chiefly successful among his own friends and mine, so that in all several thousands of dollars were obtained, which were expended for literature and correspondence in such a way that it is believed that millions of dollars worth of fruits and vegetables were raised and conserved by the Endeavorers for a needy world.

Strange as it may seem, in spite of the horrors of war, and the departure of multitudes of young men, the Christian Endeavor societies, as I afterwards learned, flourished continually in Germany. The five hundred societies increased to seven hundred, and at the close of the war many more field-secretaries were employed than at the beginning, and the many publications concerning the society were kept up and even increased.

To turn from the war to personal affairs — during the earlier weeks of 1917 with Mrs. Clark's help I revised for publication my book entitled "In the Footsteps of St. Paul," which G. P. Putnam had decided to issue. I shall have to confess that during my long illness I had become rather discouraged about the whole affair, but by the persistence and assistance of my wife, who copied on her typewriter the whole of the long manuscript, it was put into decent shape for the publishers, and was issued in the fall of that year, a comely volume of over four hundred pages, with many illustrations. It received unusually hearty commendations from the press, but those days of war excitement were fatal to any volume that did not deal directly or remotely with guns and aëroplanes. The sales were not large, but I hope it may have some permanent value.

My friends in the south decided that nothing could be so good for my health as a sojourn in Florida, and very kindly raised the necessary funds for the visit.

On the way we saw something of Washington in war times, or in times immediately previous to our declaration of war, which were scarcely less exciting than the days that followed. I remember nothing, however, of the debates in the Senate, which seemed to be taken up with inconsequential wrangling, and Washington sights being somewhat familiar, we pushed on to Florida. Daytona on the east coast has a lovely climate for a convalescent, and we enjoyed a few weeks there, and quite as much a little visit in charming Deland, where we were the guests of that good friend and ardent lover of Christian Endeavor, Mrs. Carrie Conrad.

Mrs. Clark had carried in her trunk her constant companion, a little Blickensderfer typewriter, which she had named in her quaintly humorous fashion, " Kezia," after one of the daughters of Job, because it was a patient creature always ready to do her bidding.

Many of her belongings, by the way, like trunks and suit-cases, as well as the animals and chickens upon the old farm, had names of her invention. " Darby and Joan " were the two steamer trunks that had faithfully accompanied us on many long journeys over many seas. An enormous accordion suit-case was appropriately called " Jumbo," while its smaller companions also had names of their own. The Jersey cow on the farm was known as " My Irene, the Village Queen," named by Mrs. Clark after the lady of a popular song of the day. Irene's calf rejoiced in the name of " Florence Nightin-gale," and another of her children is " Mary Lyon." The Angora goat which was Mary's affectionate and inseparable companion, was " Imogene." Most of the hens and chickens were named after the children and grandchildren of the family, and some for famous people, like the big rooster, " Christopher Columbus," and some for characters in books which we had lately read. The big pig was named " Onesima," being the feminine of Onesimus. Students of the Bible will under-stand the significance of the name when they remember the high price of pork in war times.

But to return to Florida, after this digression. Mr. Duncan Curry, the chairman of the All-South Christian Endeavor Committee, who was afterwards a lieutenant in the European war, had written to our friend Mrs. Conrad that Mrs. Clark would take with her a typewriter and hoped that " Kezia " would not be too noisy. Our good friend, not being acquainted with Mrs. Clark's *penchant* for naming all her belongings, prepared for Kezia a beautiful room with a fine outlook and comfortable sleeping-porch, and was greatly surprised and amused to find that Kezia did not appreciate the beautiful room, and was contented to sleep on a table.

This had been a hard winter for Florida. Much of the fruit had been killed by an untimely frost, and acres and acres of orange and grapefruit orchards were covered with a yellow carpet of decaying fruit which had to be removed at large expense, lest the ground be made sour and unfit for use.

Still the Florida people were by no means discouraged, for they had had many prosperous years since the last great frost, a hard winter when I also happened to be in Florida. Then an orange tree with any fruit upon it was in most parts of the State a rare sight indeed, and most of the trees were killed to their roots. During these twenty years since the " great freeze," Florida had wonderfully improved. Northern capital had built fine railroads and planted innumerable orchards.

Local enterprise had been stimulated, and some counties were spending millions on long stretches of the " Dixie Highway," a fine brick road, which made travelling a comfort and luxury. The early truck gardens, enormous strawberry beds, winter tourists, and the turpentine forests, vied with the orange groves in pouring wealth into the laps of the lucky Floridians.

I have already referred to our old farmhouse. During the fall of 1916 and the spring of 1917, this historic farmhouse near Sagamore Beach, originally built in 1690 by one of the

MRS. CLARK, HER TWIN GRANDCHILDREN, AND HER CHICKENS
At the Old Farmhouse at Sagamore Beach, Mass.

second generation of Pilgrims, was remodeled, greatly to our satisfaction, and thither we moved our furniture and many of our books from Auburndale and from the storage warehouse. At first it had seemed that it was impossible to repair the old house, so disreputable had it become through long years of neglect, but its bones were sound, and the broad beams and floor boards, hewed out of sturdy oak more than two centuries before, showed no signs of decay.

A skilful architect, Mr. Howland S. Chandler, of Boston, kept the original lines, but changed the location of the kitchen and living-room doors, found place for a bathroom, relaid one or two floors which were impossible to repair, designed trellises for roses and grapevines, painted all tastefully, and altogether made a charming residence out of the old Colonial house, which had seemed to have come to its last days.

To be sure, the ceilings are low, and some of the floors are uneven, but, with appropriate old-fashioned paper on the walls, abundant book-cases built in, and storage facilities for the curiosities and mementoes we had brought from foreign lands, the farmhouse has a charm for us that is all its own.

From several of our ancestors much old-fashioned furniture which well befits the house had come, some of it from my adopted mother's great-grandfather, General Artemas Ward, the first commander of the Revolutionary Army. Other relics that came from him, especially connected with the evacuation of Boston by the British when he was in command of the American troops, are also of much interest to many of our friends.

As I have said, I have not yet been able to learn the history of the old house, but in its earliest days it evidently belonged to a well-to-do family, for the east front room, apparently used as the best parlor, is ornamented with hand-carving of the rope pattern, which is the delight of architects and antiquaries. Our chief joy and comfort is an enormous fireplace, one of the six which the house contains, and is in the room which we use as living and dining-room. It is seven feet wide in front, and will take in, at the back, regulation four-foot logs which two men can scarcely carry in and place on the big fire-dogs. Here we sit in the spring and fall days, with a crackling fire roaring up the chimney, quite as comfortable, except in the coldest weather, as though the most modern heating apparatus warmed the old house.

The thought of the apples that must have been roasted, and the " roasting-ears " parched, and the corn popped in this old fireplace, add to the joys of the evenings at the farm, where books and magazines and an occasional game of dominoes or colorito, make the evenings pass all too quickly.

In front of the house is an enormous grapevine, which every year bears bushels of the old-fashioned Isabella grapes, and spreads over the pergola, which I fear is an architectural sin for a house of the early Georges. The great vine covers the whole front with an abundant shade. From the east windows we can view the sea and the entrance to the Cape Cod Canal, with ships and barges constantly going in and out.

For a better view, we built at the distance of a few rods from the house, a pretty and substantial Lookout, which our twin grandchildren after hearing read a missionary book on China named the " Place of Abiding Joy." Here, sheltered by the trees behind, we have a splendid panorama of marsh and sea, and distant Cape Cod shores, with the white spire of the church in Sandwich peeping through the trees, the great chimneys of the old glass-works mellowed by the distance, and the life-saving station and weather signals of Uncle Sam's brave life-guards in the far view. Alas! in one of the forest fires for which Cape Cod is unhappily famous, the Lookout was burned down in the spring of 1922, and three acres of pine trees went with it. The loss of the Lookout was made good, however, by the erection of a replica of an old Cape Cod windmill tower, which affords not only a fine Lookout, but two chambers for some of our numerous grandchildren.

THE OLD ABANDONED FARMHOUSE

Completely reformed and rejuvenated, with the tower which affords a splendid lookout over the Massachusetts Bay and the Cape Cod Canal. The farmhouse and tower, which is an exact replica of an old Cape Cod windmill, the wings omitted, furnishes ample room

CHAPTER LI

YEARS 1917–1919

THE LATER YEARS OF THE WORLD WAR

ORGANIZING CHRISTIAN ENDEAVOR ALUMNI — RECEPTION IN
MY BOYHOOD HOME — EFFECT OF THE WAR ON THE
CHRISTIAN ENDEAVOR MOVEMENT — THE SUDDEN END
OF THE WAR — A SALOONLESS NATION.

 N ACCOUNT of America's entrance into the war, and the restriction of ordinary traffic, it was deemed wise, almost at the last minute, to postpone the great biennial Christian Endeavor Convention which for two years we had been planning to hold in Madison Square Garden, New York City, in 1917. Naturally this was a great disappointment to the convention committee in New York, as well as to Endeavorers everywhere. But at the time there seemed no help for it. Partially to take the place of this meeting, a conference of trustees and field-secretaries was held at Winona Lake, Ind., and was productive of good results. In the biennial message which I am expected to give at these meetings, and in which the suggestions for the programme for the next two years are outlined, the most important new plan recommended was that of the Christian Endeavor Alumni Association.

These associations or fellowships were to be composed of the graduate Endeavorers of whom there are now many millions throughout the country, and were to stand in the same relation to the movement at large as the alumni of a college to their *alma mater*. I tried to work out the idea with considerable detail, and it was adopted with much enthusiasm, and with growing popularity throughout the country and in other lands as well. As I write it has already become a source of considerable revenue for the advancement of the Christian Endeavor cause throughout the world, and gives promise of increasing usefulness as the years go by, especially in bringing older and younger former members and present members together under the aegis of Christian Endeavor.

Two years later, Rev. Stanley B. Vandersall, field-secretary of the Ohio Union, was appointed to have charge of this work.

An event of special interest to me in September of that year was a visit to my boyhood home at Claremont, N. H. The new pastor of the church, Rev. Oscar Peterson, had learned of my early connection with the church, and invited me to come on to take part in his ordination, and for a special and personal " Old Home " celebration on the next day.

On reaching Claremont I was surprised to learn of the extent of the preparations for the occasion. The town was placarded with flaming posters about " Claremont's World-Famous Boy," who, by the way, had advanced a full half century beyond his boyhood, and whose modesty was shocked by the announcements that met him on every side. But it was well meant, and the meetings in the old church, of which my adopted father was once the pastor, as well as the public meeting for the citizens in the town hall, presided over by Honorable Hosea Parker, Claremont's " Grand Old Man," were more than could be asked for in the way of cordiality and kindly reminiscence of the past. Toasts were offered by various dignitaries of the town, and a beautiful illuminated address and a loving-cup are souvenirs of the happy occasion.

Beautiful Ascutney, " Bible Hill," " Flat Rock," and other well-remembered points of interest reminded me of happy boyhood days, and I was able to call on a few of the aged inhabitants who were my father's parishioners and the friends of my boyhood.

TRUSTEES AND FIELD-SECRETARIES OF CHRISTIAN ENDEAVOR AT BUFFALO, JULY, 1917

More than twenty denominations represented by their leaders in this picture.

In these days of course the World War occupied most of our waking thoughts and troubled our dreams as well. At times it seemed as though Germany would surely win, then again came bright days for the Allies, but all were days of anxiety and foreboding. Our oldest son Eugene went to Plattsburg to the Officers' Training Camp, graduated as a second lieutenant, and was assigned to Rochester University as personnel officer. All the colleges had been turned practically into war-camps, and military rule was supreme. Dr. Rush Rees, the president of Rochester University, told me that he was exceedingly glad to have a man of academic training and instincts assigned to his college, since some of the military men sent to certain institutions were arrogant and overbearing, and gave the presidents or professors, who were obliged to play second fiddle to them, a most uncomfortable time.

During these months, too, sad news came to me from across the water. In Great Britain the majority of Endeavorers of military age had gone to the front. The youngest son of Rev. John Pollock, the president of the European Union, who had twice visited us in America, was reported missing. His father has never been able to learn his fate. He was doubtless killed early in the war. Another son was an officer in the navy, and his daughter, now a missionary in Formosa, a Red Cross nurse. Mr. Pollock has told me that the dead boy never harbored any ill feelings against the German people, but as individuals liked them better than the French. Thousands of the leading families in Great Britain suffered like bereavements.

In America, too, the societies of Christian Endeavor suffered greatly from the loss of young men who responded to their country's call. Many societies and unions lost for a time practically all their active male members, but the young women came forward to do more than their share of the work. The young men below military age undertook a larger service, and the movement suffered far less than might have been expected, though here and there societies were disbanded and union meetings suspended. Not a few Endeavorers distinguished themselves for bravery on the field, and the first American to receive the Croix de Guerre was an Endeavorer from Indiana.

My colleague, Dr. Daniel A. Poling, Associate President of the United Society, went to France twice during the last year of the war, under the auspices of the Y.M.C.A., and did good service in the camps and the trenches, though necessarily absent from America for only a short time.

The winter of 1917 and 1918 will be remembered by all who survived it, as the most severe within the memory of the oldest inhabitant. Below-zero weather prevailed for weeks throughout the northern part of the country in late December and January. In New Hampshire the mercury ranged from thirty to forty degrees below zero, and even where the thermometer did not sink quite so low, the weather was just as trying, even as far south as Washington and Virginia.

During most of 1918 the war dragged its slow length along, and no one could believe that the end was so near. In March the Germans launched their fiercest offensive, and it looked as though they would soon break through to the English Channel, or perhaps attain their long-desired aim of entering Paris triumphantly. American troops were being sent across the water by the hundred thousand every month, but it was not until July that the tide seemed to turn in favor of the Allies.

In contrast with the fierce enmities and fightings which racked the world, our own spring and summer and early autumn were spent most quietly in Sagamore, with the exception of a journey to Memphis, Tenn., to the All-South Christian Endeavor convention, though of course we fully shared in the anxieties and terrors that made the world tremble. The chief economic effect upon us and our neighbors was the enormously increased cost of living, and our rationing by the government of certain articles, especially sugar and flour. Of sugar our ration amounted to an ounce a day for each person: Of this amount we limited ourselves to a half ounce a day on the table for each one, and the rest was reserved for cooking. We all had our little individual sugar-bowls and vied with each other to see whose half ounce would last the longest. The grandchildren enjoyed the game of the individual sugar-bowls more than their elders. The little twins made a special function of filling the sugar-bowls every morning, one of them uncovering the sugar-bowls, their grandmother measuring out the sugar, and the other twin putting the cover on again and watching to see who had eaten most of yesterday's sugar.

It was amazing to note with what good nature the people generally accepted these small privations, and how faithfully as a whole, they lived up to the government regulations. Until the war was over there seemed to be little profiteering and little hoarding, for great motives and a determined purpose had gripped the hearts of the people to see the war through. Of course America, when compared with other nations, had indeed little to complain of and few privations to bear. Our country was the granary of the world and no people suffered less than ours.

The generosity of the public during this year was almost beyond belief. Money was poured out by the millions for war relief, for Y.M.C.A., Salvation Army Community Camps, Red Cross and all sorts of good causes, while at the same time the missionary societies and churches did not lack funds or curtail their expenses.

The United Society of Christian Endeavor kept up its efforts for war-gardens, for production and conservation. Endeavorers did their utmost for the organization for the relief and entertainment of the soldiers in the camps at home and the trenches abroad.

Then, suddenly, early in November came the glad news

that the war was ended. The Armistice was signed. The nation went delirious with joy, and showed its delirium in the tooting of horns, blowing of whistles, rag-tag and bob-tail parades, and extravagances of all kinds which involved noise and shouting. However, I saw nothing in Boston that compared with the orgy on Mafeking Day in London where I then happened to be, when the news òf the tardy triumph of the British forces over the Boers reached that city. One reason, doubtless, was that hard liquor, which flowed freely in Great Britain, was banished from American saloons by the war-time prohibition.

At the same time there had been going on a wonderful temperance revolution throughout the whole country, not particularly connected with the war. In 1911, at the Christian Endeavor National Convention in Atlantic City, the slogan was adopted, "A Saloonless Nation by 1920, the 300th anniversary of the landing of the Pilgrims." It seemed to many an absurd war-cry, and, as a prediction, impossible of fulfilment. But the temperance sentiment had been gathering strength for many years. Congress at last authorized the States to vote on a Prohibition amendment to the Constitution. State after State in quick succession ratified the amendment, almost as much to the amazement of the temperance forces as to the liquor-dealers themselves. Such States as New York and Massachusetts and Pennsylvania with great foreign populations, which it was supposed would fight the amendment tooth and nail, went over, through their legislatures, to the temperance side, and New Jersey and Rhode Island were the only two States of the forty-eight that refused to ratify the amendment.

As I write it is too soon to tell of the results which will eventually flow from nation-wide prohibition, but already many jails are half empty, some of them closed up altogether, while the savings banks have received hundreds of millions of dollars that would otherwise have gone into the tills of the saloon keepers.

Strenuous efforts are constantly being made by some honest anti-prohibitionists, backed by all the evil forces of the old saloon days, boot-leggers and liquor-profiteers, to nullify or make ridiculous the law. But I believe practical prohibition has come to stay, and that the days of the unspeakably nefarious saloon are over forever.

An event that stirred Boston to much enthusiasm for that staid old town was the return of President Wilson from the Peace Conference in Paris. It was said that 30,000 people applied for tickets to Mechanics Building, where he was to make his first address after reaching America. I was one of the fortunate three or four thousand who obtained a ticket, and was much pleased with the modesty and self-restraint, but at the same time the undoubted strength, of the President's address. Feeling by this time had begun to run high. Some Republican Senators seemed to think that it was good politics to criticise and deride the President and abuse him for everything he did and said, either in America or France. From being the most popular man in the world during the days of the war, he became at length the most hated in some sections, and the most abused.

Yet party lines were not drawn altogether on this subject. A few members of his own party were violently opposed to the League of Nations, while some eminent Republicans like former President Taft, Attorney-General Wickersham, former Senator Crane, and others, supported the President and the League of Nations most courageously.

Though many of my friends were on the other side, I sided strongly with the President, and did all that I could, in a humble way, to promote his ideals. I was glad that my three sons agreed with me substantially in this matter, and that all my colleagues in the Christian Endeavor office also heartily supported the President in his fight for " The League of Nations " and for world peace.

While I am on this subject, I may as well refer to letters

I received from President Wilson in the summer of 1919. In reply to an earnest invitation to come to the biennial Christian Endeavor Conference at Buffalo in August of that year to speak on the League of Nations, he wrote as follows,

> " My dear Dr. Clark,
>
> " Your letter of July 23d gave me a great deal of pleasure and reassurance. I can assure you that your confidence and approval mean a vast deal to me.
>
> " I dare not hope to be present at the Biennial Meeting to which you so generously invite me, but you may be sure that my heart will go out to it, and that I know what I am missing in missing the opportunity to address so great and influential a body on a matter so near my heart.
> " Cordially and Sincerely Yours,
> " WOODROW WILSON."

The conference passed a strong resolution in favor of the League and there was also a spontaneous uprising for it at the close of the splendid address by Hon. Newton D. Baker, Secretary of War, in the latter part of which he earnestly advocated the League. As requested by the conference I sent word to President Wilson of this action, and though my letter required no reply he generously took the time in the midst of one of his busiest days, shortly before he started on his famous and fatal tour of the country in favor of the League, to write as follows:

> " My dear Dr. Clark,
>
> " You know how to cheer me, and the information brought me by your kind letter of August 12, has indeed done so. I thank you with all my heart.
> " Cordially and Sincerely Yours,
> " WOODROW WILSON."

I should have before mentioned the influenza scourge that afflicted the country, and indeed the world, in the autumn of 1918 and the winter following. As though war had not been enough to decimate the nations, pestilence was added, and terrible as the ravages of war had been, the deaths from influenza throughout the world were far more numerous. In many places coffins could not be obtained fast enough, in which to bury the dead, and in such a town as Sagamore, for instance, bodies had to be kept for a week, while coffins were sent from Chicago or other distant places.

Terrible reports from all parts of the world reached us concerning the disease. In China millions died of the plague, which seemed to be much like the old " Black Death," or pneumonic plague. In Samoa a quarter part of the inhabitants were carried off by it, while our troops in the cantonments at home and in the camps abroad, suffered more from influenza than from German bullets.

My health, by reason of the months I had spent on the old farm, seemed to be now quite re-established, and I was able to attend more meetings than for years past, and to take a tour as far west as the Missouri River in the early summer of 1919.

The chief Christian Endeavor event of that year was the Biennial Conference at Buffalo in August. On account of the high railroad fares and the dislocations caused by the war, we did not plan for a great convention as usual, but rather for a conference of leaders. The five hundred, however, who were first planned for, swelled to more than two thousand delegates, and the conference proved to be almost as influential and important as any of the greater conventions that had preceded it.

In the president's biennial message I proposed certain goals, among them a " fifty per cent increase during the next two years," " a society in every church or we will know the reason why," and " an Alumni Association in every local union."

These goals, and other suggestions looking to the reinforcement of Christian Endeavor on the old foundations of loyalty to Christ and the Church, to the Pledge, and to our underlying principles, were adopted unanimously and heartily, and a great Loyalty Campaign was at once started throughout the country.

CHAPTER LII

YEAR 1920

THE WORLD AFTER THE WAR

ALL of my contemporaries of these days will long remember the distracting and distracted years which followed the armistice and the impossible Peace of Versailles. While of course Europe suffered far more than America, our own troubles seemed serious enough. High prices, high taxes, and innumerable strikes were everyday affairs in all parts of the world. The most serious event of the kind in America was perhaps the police strike in Boston, when for some twenty-four hours the city was in the hands of the mob.

I happened to come back from New York on the morning after the strike began. All night the hoodlums, thieves, and thugs had ruled Boston. Passing up Summer Street to Washington Street, I was amazed to see scores of great plate-glass windows smashed, and their former contents looted. In the middle of the principal streets and on the Common groups of boys and young men were shooting craps and gambling with cards, unmolested. The crossings were unguarded by traffic · police, and the staid old city had the first taste of unrestricted license it had known in the nearly three hundred years of its existence. But within another twenty-four hours the forces of law and order had things well in hand.

Governor Coolidge's ringing slogan that " No man at any time, anywhere, has a right to strike against the public peace," Police Commissioner Curtis' prompt discharge of all the striking policemen, and Mayor Peters' cordial co-operation on the right side, put heart into every right-minded person, and hundreds of citizens volunteered to act as amateur police-men to save the city from further pillage. The example of the Boston authorities did much to settle forever the question of whether the servants of a State or of a municipality had a right deliberately to endanger the lives and property of their fellow-citizens.

My son Sydney, and my son-in-law, William Chase, were both among the police volunteers, and patrolled certain parts of the city night after night for three or four weeks. The substitute police force included many prominent people of Boston. Bankers and leading merchants, teachers and even ministers, gladly enlisted for this service.

A remarkable development of the war was the increase of Christian Endeavor societies in the countries that had suffered the most from mental and moral shell-shock. I have already mentioned that the societies in Germany had largely increased, though I expected that the war might make an end of all of them. The same was true of several other countries in the continental war zone, except France and Italy, where the overwhelming Catholic majority will never allow any large number of such Protestant organizations. The smaller coun-tries which were carved out of Russia and Austro-Hungary showed amazing vitality in this form of Christian service, and from Jugo-Slavia, and Hungary, from Poland, Latvia, Esthonia, and Finland, news began to come that the societies were rallying and multiplying, though in some places, especially in Hungary, the strong bands of Christian Endeavor of former days had been decimated so that they were numerically but a shadow of their former selves. However, they seemed to make up in self-sacrificing vigor for their lack of numbers, and soon, as is natural, the numbers also increased.

The World's Christian Endeavor Union was able to help all these countries to obtain field-secretaries of their own. Most of them on gaining their independence formed national Christian Endeavor Unions and many calls came from them for sympathy and fellowship as well as for cash.

I felt that this was the time, beyond all others when, if possible, I should carry this sympathy by word of mouth, and that perhaps more could be done in the way of reconciliation, and in creating a feeling of comradeship and good will among the young people of these societies in America and Europe just then, than could be accomplished later in a score of years.

Early in January, 1920, therefore, my wife and I sailed on the French liner "La Touraine" for Havre. The "La Touraine" is a so-called "cabin-passage steamer," meaning, in these days, second-class and steerage, and the rates are only about half as much as on the larger steamers that carry three classes of passengers. Our fellow voyagers were a very mixed company. French and Italians, Czechs and Slavs, Russians and Roumanians, Polanders and Finns, some Germans and a few German-American Mormons jostled each other on the decks. Doubtless many of these passengers had gone to America a few years before in the steerage, had made their ten, fifteen, and twenty dollars a day in wages during the war years when labor was scarce and muscle chiefly at a premium, and were going back in style with their newly acquired wealth, to visit their old homes, and to tell their neighbors of the wage-marvels of America. Many of them had never learned the use of a fork, and the napkins which the ship furnished were evidently to some unnecessary refinements.

However, we all got along well together, and it was interesting to see more of that side of life than one does on first-class steamers.

We made Paris our headquarters, as in those days was almost a necessity, considering the *visés* which one had to struggle for if one wished to set foot across any national boundary lines.

On the steamer we had made the acquaintance of a young Quaker who was returning to his blessed task of reconciliation and reconstruction in the devastated parts of France. We were glad to accept his invitation to visit him and his companions in Aubreville, not far from the Argonne Forest. It was indeed a scene of desolation which cannot be described or scarcely believed by those who have not witnessed similar sights.

Aubreville itself had not been entirely destroyed, but some of the villages in the vicinity had been actually wiped off the face of the earth. One could not have told that there had ever been a village upon their sites, except from some heaps of pulverized bricks. Great shell holes abounded. Some of them, where water had settled, looked like small ponds, miles of barbed wire entanglements and the indescribable *débris* which war leaves behind cumbered the roadsides. The hills in many places were honeycombed with dug-outs as though a swarm of elephantine swallows had made their homes in the banks. Some of them had been built by the Germans and some by the Allies, as this region had passed back and forth between the temporary conquerors and conquered several times in the course of the war.

The most elaborate dug-out that we visited was in the heart of the forest and was said to have been the abode of the Crown Prince. Though stripped of its furniture and much of its wood-work, it had evidently been a very swell affair as dug-outs go. A stove, a bath-room, tiled floors, and a separate servant's antechamber had been among its luxuries. But already the path to it was so grown up with weeds and bushes, and the plank walks had become so rotten that they were almost impassable, and the forest will soon reclaim it for its own.

I have not room to describe our visit to Clermont-en-

Argonne, La Grange, Chalons-sur-Marne, Varennes, all battered and bruised by war. On our way to the battlefields we stopped for a few hours at Chalons-sur-Marne, where the Quakers had established a fine maternity hospital. In the old building which they first used a thousand babies were born, many of whom will never know their fathers' names or nationalities. The babies were lying around, apparently promiscuously, wherever a ray of winter sunshine could fall upon them, but they were well wrapped up and cared for, though many of them were evidently poor, little diseased weaklings.

I could spend the rest of this volume in applauding the noble constructive work of these Quaker pacifists. Their consciences forbade them to fight, but they were no cowards, and they endured dangers and privations greater than most of the soldiers who did not absolutely get into the front trenches, and without even a soldier's poor pay.

We resolved that, if possible, we would on this journey to Europe accept the invitation of our friend Rev. Samuel Schumacher, of whom I have before spoken, who had survived the war and the terrible hardships which came to all the people of the Balkan nations, and was now the pastor of a promising church in Zemun, or Semlin, as it was formerly called, one of the chief cities of the new " Kingdom of the Serbs, Croats, and Slovenes," or Jugo-Slavia for short.

To visit this new kingdom with a long name was in those days easier said than done, and it took days to get the necessary *visés*. It involved innumerable hours of waiting in drafty passages before closed doors of out-of-the-way consulates in different part of Paris. Our own American consul-general very willingly extended my passport to include Jugo-Slavia, and the prefect of the Paris police gave me permission to leave the city. But Switzerland and Italy lie between France and

Serbia, and their consuls had to be hunted up and consulted and argued with and well paid for their stamps and signatures on our passports, though I assured them that I was not going to leave the train even for five minutes on my way through their domains.

Most difficult of all was it to find the Jugo-Slavian Consulate in a remote and dingy fourth story. But *perseverantia*, according to the old proverb, conquers all things, and at last my passport was decorated with a sufficient number of signatures of different consuls to allow us to start; (thirty-two of them in all before we reached home).

A fairly comfortable train, a post-war remnant of the famous Oriental Express, carried us to Belgrade without change, though with interminable delays in many places, and hours at every national border, where our passports were scrutinized microscopically, and where we frequently doubted if we should be allowed to go any further.

Through the lovely Rhone valley in Switzerland, through Milan and Venice and other famous cities our route took us, though of course we only obtained car-window glimpses of the wonders and glories, natural and architectural, past which we were borne.

In the neighborhood of Trieste we saw even more horrible destruction than in France, for the retreating and advancing armies of Italy and Austria had fought desperately for years over this ground, leaving nothing but desolate ruin behind them, though Trieste itself had been little injured.

Long before daylight of the second night we reached Belgrade. Though our friend Schumacher had come to Belgrade to meet us we missed him in the darkness and the confusion of the station, but at last we roused a sleepy droschky man, who took us to the Grand Hotel. It is always safe to say " Grand Hotel " to your driver in such an emergency. There is sure to be one of that name in every considerable or inconsiderable city in Europe.

The hotel was as " black as Pokonocket," and the air was icy cold, but at length after much rapping and ringing we roused a porter, who told us to our dismay that there was a general strike on in Belgrade, and that they had no cooks, no waiters, no chambermaids, no beds, no meals, no guests, and that they could not take us in. We reasoned with him, and after much persuasion, and still more material reminders of the duties of hospitality, he told us we might sit in the cold café until daylight. The chairs were piled up on the tables, and only a flickering light was burning, but it was better than nothing, and there we sat for four mortal hours, until it was bright enough to go out on the street.

We found that the strike extended to every minute form of service. There were no porters, no droschkys; the shops, cafés, and conditorei were all closed. At last we found a good lady, who ran a little establishment of her own with the aid of her daughter and no hired help, who gave us a cup of coffee apiece and a cookie.

Later we made our way, carrying our small hand luggage, to the steamer, and crossed the great river Save, which is here three miles wide, to Zemun or Semlin, on the farther side. In former days Zemun was in the province of Croatia in Austria. Here we were at the fountain-head of the World War. Here the very first gun was fired from the heights of Zemun into Belgrade the capital of Serbia. Of course Belgrade fired back upon Zemun, and for long years both cities knew the horrors of war, whose varying fortunes brought them first under one set of rulers and then under another.

We found indeed a cordial welcome from our friend Schumacher, who treated us throughout our stay like royal guests.

At this time Serbia was much in the eye of Americans as a famishing country, and lurid appeals were being made to send supplies to the starving children. As a matter of fact, however, the worst of Serbia's troubles were over. She had had two good harvests since the war. The richest farming lands of Hungary had been assigned to her as part of the spoils of victory. The very day before my daughter received a letter from us describing the abundant and delicious food which our friends had prepared for us, she had attended a lecture describing in harrowing terms the sufferings of the starving millions of Jugo-Slavia, and she feared that we also might be on the edge of dissolution from lack of nourishment. It would be well for philanthropists everywhere to fit their appeals more carefully to the facts, even if it sometimes means the abandonment of their special charity.

I do not mean to say that Serbia had recovered from the war. Though food was plentiful in most parts, yet everything else was extremely scarce and dear, save the things that could be produced at home. My ministerial friend there told me that he had to pay three thousand kronen for a suit of clothes, and six hundred for a pair of shoes. A krone, formerly worth twenty cents, had then come to be worth less than a fiftieth part of its former value.

Three important meetings were arranged for us to bring the right hand of America's fellowship to the Jugo-Slavians. The first was in the city hall of Zemun, where the mayor and counsellors had invited us to meet a select company of the leading citizens of the city, a hundred and fifty or so. English is almost an unknown tongue in that part of the world, and interpreters were very scarce and not too well fitted for their task. However, a priest of the Oriental Orthodox Church was found, who proved to have an admirable knowledge of both English and Serbian, and he gave eminent satisfaction to all who heard him. My greetings from America were received with great enthusiasm and applause.

Indeed just at that time America was by far the most popular country in the world with the Jugo-Slavians. President Wilson had righteously taken her part against Italy in the Fiume-D'Annunzio trouble, and he was, to these people, the chief of all the nations. In Belgrade we saw, and doubtless might now see, a " Wilson Park " and a " Wilson Avenue," a " Wilson Hotel " and a " Wilson Restaurant," and I do not know how many other things Wilsonian.

Just as the lecture and the concluding votes of thanks were ended, all the electric lights in the hall and in the city generally went out, but this was no unusual occurrence in those early days of the new kingdom, so, taking hold of hands, we groped our way down the black stairway and through the black streets until we reached the home of our friends.

Another meeting was held in the new Y. M. C. A. building in Belgrade, a barrack-like affair, whose secretary seemed rather discouraged at the outlook for his cause. Here my interpreter was a government official who professed himself to be an atheist, but he, too, had the very important virtue of being a good English scholar and an excellent interpreter, even though the views I expressed may not have been in accordance with his own. I think that his atheism was scarcely skin deep, for he had begun to go to the Y. M. C. A. meetings, and he expressed himself as greatly interested in the Christian Endeavor movement, and hoped some time to become a member of the society.

The most important meeting of this interesting series was held in the little country town of Novo Pasova, some thirty miles from the capital of the kingdom. Here came the Endeavorers, more than a hundred of them, from Serbia proper, and the provinces which the war had annexed to them, Croatia, Bosnia, and Herzegovina, to form their first national Christian Endeavor union. They were a sturdy lot of earnest, evangelical men and women, many of whom had suffered much for their faith, for, during the war and immediately afterwards, the low grade Serbians, who never loved the Lutherans and other Protestants, took much pleasure in breaking their windows, sometimes burning their houses and committing other depredations. We saw many windows boarded up because of these unbrotherly and unneighborly acts. Glass was then far too expensive to replace that which had been smashed in a wholesale way.

Novo Pasova had a large Lutheran element, and the leading families who were relatives of Mr. Schumacher, were strongly evangelical. But an unaccountable prejudice had been excited against the Christian Endeavor movement before our arrival by the rationalistic Lutheran minister, who would not allow the use of his church for the convention.

When we reached the hall where the meetings were held I was handed a formidable-looking document on foolscap, stamped with the town seal.

Of course I could not read it, since it was in Serbian, even worse than Greek to me. But my friend soon translated it as follows: *Rev. Mr. Clark of America is warned that he will be held personally responsible for any riots or bloodshed which may occur during his visit to Novo Pasova, and that none of his followers (the delegates) shall be allowed to carry firearms to the meetings.*" It can be imagined that I very willingly signed this document, and promised to abstain from bloodshed.

In order that they might know what it was all about and guard their peaceful town from bombs, or even incendiary language, four of the city fathers were the first to arrive, and took front seats, awaiting the opening session.

At this meeting it was most difficult of all to obtain an interpreter and the best we could do was to invite Frau Nigrovitch to come with us from Zemun. She had been a telephone operator in Chicago, and knew telephone English, though very little acquainted with the ecclesiastical variety. She had married a Serbian tailor and had gone back to live in her native town. We greatly appreciated her help, for she was obliged to bring with her, on a cold railway journey, little Paul Nigrovitch, her six-months-old baby, staying away from home for three days.

What idea the selectmen of Novo Pasova obtained of Christian Endeavor from my speech and her translation, it is difficult to tell. They listened in austere silence, but apparently were not displeased, for afterwards they came up to me, one after the other, and said that they believed it was all right and we might go on with our meetings. Naturally Mr. Schumacher was chosen president of the new union, and a list of other officers was chosen from different parts of the kingdom. The union now has an active field-secretary, giving his whole time to the work, and Mr. Schumacher is doing his best to raise money for a million-kronen ($40,000) Christian Endeavor church, which will stand one of these days on a prominent corner of a Zemun Street, with a big Christian Endeavor monogram on the tower.

One very interesting day I spent in Belgrade with my friend, who showed me the sights of this rather crude but important capital. The old palace from whose upper windows a few years ago the incensed people threw the worthless king, Alexander, and his worse than worthless wife, Draga, was pointed out. The city contains a new palace, some extensive fortifications, one fine hotel, not "The Grand," and some very creditable business blocks, as well as one or two city parks, which of course did not look their best in February.

King Peter was then alive, but feeble and blind. He was one of the very few popular kings that the war left in Europe, and his son Alexander, who lived in a very modest little house as royal houses go, was the real ruler.

The gaping wounds made by shot and shell were still evident in many places. The suffering in Belgrade had been intense during some phases of the war, and the scarcity of food almost unbelievable. The wife of an English professor in the National University told me that they had to burn every stick of their best furniture in order to keep the breath of life during one cold winter.

We called on some of the notables, but by far the most interesting call was on the beloved Bishop of Serbia, Nicolai Vel-

merovitch, or just Bishop Nicolai, as he is usually called. The Bishop's palace is a large and ornate building, the finest place in Belgrade except the king's palace, but its occupant is a most modest and unworldly man. He speaks English fluently, and we had a long talk about the affairs of the world, where order was just beginning to emerge out of chaos. His sentiments were all for peace, brotherly love, and the fellowship of the nations, and he has exerted a great influence, not only in the Balkans, but in other lands, for he is a traveller of distinction, and has visited Britain, as well as America, often preaching in the most distinguished Protestant pulpits.

If any man ever had a Christ-like face, I believe the good bishop has. A long black beard, regular features, and a beautiful kindly eye, tell of a character both strong and benignant. This gives but an imperfect impression of this remarkable man. We talked much about the estrangement of the churches, and he assured me of his warmest regard for the Protestant communion. " Our church has never had any quarrels with Protestantism," he said. " All our troubles in the past have been with the Roman Catholics." On leaving, he presented me with two or three little books of his in English, which expressed the same sentiments of world fellowship and Christian friendship, as his conversation.

Bidding goodby to our friend Mr. Schumacher, his most hospitable wife and fine family of children, after going through another series of passport agonies like the ones endured on our outward journey, we went back to Central Europe.

In Geneva one public meeting was held on a very stormy evening, and a delightful reception in the charming home of Rev. Ernest Sauvin, the most efficient secretary of the European Christian Endeavor Union, of whom I have before written. A conference with him and Miss Johanssen, who with great difficulty and much hardship had come from Finland across Germany to Geneva to meet us, was also of importance to the cause in some of the republics, for she put us in touch with friends in Esthonia and Latvia, who now, as well as those in Poland, have Endeavor field-secretaries of their own, by reason of the information I obtained at this conference, and the sympathy she aroused.

Crossing the channel to England we spent a few days among our friends in Edinburgh, Glasgow, Newcastle, London, and Liverpool. We were also able to attend the Scottish National Convention in Edinburgh which held its meetings in the sombre pile of the Free Church Assembly Hall. We were also present at the inauguration of one of the new holiday homes on the Clyde.

These holiday homes are a distinctly British contribution to the Christian Endeavor idea. There are eight or ten of them, all situated in the neighborhood of beautiful resorts, and they afford at a reasonable price, and in the midst of delightful surroundings, and with choice company, a vacation home for Endeavorers and their friends. They have been exceedingly popular and successful in every case. Though not money-making affairs, they pay five or six per cent on the money invested, and often turn a surplus back into the treasury for improvements and upkeep.

But their chief value is on the side of comradeship and spiritual and intellectual stimulus. They are not in the least pietistic, but are much given to songs, good cheer, and daily excursions to points of interest, yet a genuine religious atmosphere prevails, and the young people return to their homes refreshed in body, mind, and spirit, instead of weakened in soul by an idle vacation wasted, or worse than wasted, as is often the case in America. I wish we might follow their good example.

The meeting in London on Good Friday was, as always, an overwhelming affair, crowding the Metropolitan Tabernacle, morning, afternoon, and evening. Dr. F. B. Meyer was for the fourth time in twenty-five years elected president of the London federation of Endeavor societies, and declared that,

THE CHRISTIAN ENDEAVOR HOUSE IN LONDON
Here Endeavorers from all parts of England stay when in the city.

though he had just been chosen president of the Free Council, the highest honor these churches could give him, he considered this a greater opportunity and honor.

The societies of Great Britain had been hard hit, as was inevitable, by the war, and had lost thousands of their leaders, but this and other meetings showed conclusively that they were coming back to their old-time form and vigor.

A most interesting side trip which we took in connection with this visit to England was to the university and the parish church of my first ancestor in America, Rev. Zechariah Symmes, of whom I have spoken in the first chapter of this book. Cambridge was his university, and Emmanuel his college.

A visit to this famous university town would have been interesting in any event, but it was particularly delightful to imagine young Zechariah walking these streets, entering these hoary portals, and " sporting the oak " in one of the buildings of the great quadrangle of Emmanuel College. We imagined the young Puritan, who was destined to be driven from his native soil, in one particular room which we chose for him, whose window looked down into the quad, and we could almost see him with his serious face preparing there for his future work, rowing on the Cam, or, perhaps, strolling meditatively along its verdure-clad banks.

From this university went most of the educated Puritans who built up a new Cambridge, and a new Commonwealth across the sea.

Still more interesting was our visit to Dunstable where Mr. Symmes was the rector of the great priory church of this historic town. It is now the principal straw-hat town of Great Britain. Its narrow streets, quaint, old-fashioned houses and especially the great church were full of memories of him. Dunstable is an unspoiled English town and has scarcely been changed in its main outlines in three centuries. The names of the hotels reminded us of our Dickens, " The

Saracen's Head," the " White Horse," the " Red Lion," the " Blue Boar," and other similar names. As most characteristic of the great novelist we chose first the " Saracen's Head," but finding it full, we went to the " Red Lion " as next best, and found ourselves very comfortable there in a hotel as old-fashioned as its name.

The next morning, though it rained torrentially, we explored the town, and visited at length the old priory church. It is an unusually beautiful and spacious church, almost a cathedral in fact. Such were the great priory churches of old. But we found no traces of the Zechariah of old, and had no chance to search the records. He was doubtless anathema to the church authorities when he left there for America on account of his Puritanism, and they put up no monument to his memory as Charlestown in America afterwards did.

After a week for rest and writing in lovely Torquay by the sea, a most charming resort on the south coast, we sailed for home to take up again our suspended duties in the homeland.

Chapter LIII

Year 1921

MEXICO IN 1921

HOW ENGAGEMENTS MULTIPLY — A QUAKER CITY — MEXICAN
TRAINS THIRTY-SIX HOURS LATE — GOOD FRIDAY IN THE
CAPITAL — THOUSANDS OF CALLA LILIES — MEXICO'S
BEAUTIFUL PARK AND WONDERFUL MUSEUM — A RACE
TO MEET ENGAGEMENTS — GREAT CHURCHES IN TEXAS.

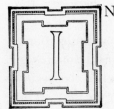N THE spring of 1921 I planned to accept
the invitation of the general-secretary of the
Southwest Federation of Endeavor societies,
Mr. W. Roy Breg, to address some conventions in Texas and Oklahoma, and we agreed
also to spend a week in Mexico together.
When this became known I was begged by Dr. Smolenske,
president of the Colorado union, and by Paul Brown of California, the much-loved Intermediate superintendent of our
national union, and, as I write, Pacific Coast Secretary of the
United Society, to extend my journey beyond the Rockies.
It seemed at first impossible to do so in the limited time at
my disposal, but, to the persistent and the enterprising all
things are possible, and at last these enterprising friends arranged a schedule which gave me one day in Denver, a day
and a half in California, a week in Mexico, and another in
Texas.

I mention this journey with more particularity than usual,
because it indicates how, over and over again, for nearly forty
years, these trips were filled to overflowing, by ardent friends,
so as to make the most of every moment.

At the crowded Denver gathering, Governor Shoup, an old-time Endeavorer, was one of the speakers. Years ago he had been the secretary of the Colorado State union, and had never lost his interest in it. Every year he attends the State convention and gives generously to the support of the State budget, declaring that it was the best investment he could possibly make, and he is an unusual investment expert.

Two of my college classmates, Judge Kerr of Colorado Springs, and Lucien Richardson of Denver, in a few hours of leisure that we had, took me into the heart of the mountains to Richardson's summer home. What a joy it is, after fifty years, to meet with the boys of the olden time, to recall the college jokes, to inquire after the welfare of never-forgotten classmates, and to compare notes concerning what has befallen us in half a century out of college. Truly there are few friendships like those of college days.

The convention in California was that of a single county only, — Los Angeles County, — but what a convention it was! Nearly three thousand young people journeyed to the beautiful Quaker town of Whittier, twenty miles from the City of Angels, to spend three days together in prayer and praise, in schools of methods, and Bible study, in hours of inspiration, and in genuine, jolly fellowship. There was no long-faced solemnity, but a hearty hilarity about these meetings, whenever hilarity was permissible, which told us that religion and joy should never be divorced.

Whittier is one vast orange, lemon, and grapefruit grove, with a comparatively small business centre, and the largest Quaker church, so it is said, in the world. In spite of its growth and prosperity it seems to retain the quiet, peaceful characteristics of its early founders. While there, it is not difficult to feel the " inner light " illuminating one's daily life.

I had travelled three thousand miles for the sake of less than two days with friends on the coast, but it was well worth while so far at least as I was concerned.

Coming back toward the East I met Mr. Breg at San Antonio for the journey into Mexico, where I had not been for twenty-five years. For the past ten years, indeed, Mexico had been in such an anarchical state, bandit-ridden and distracted in many ways, that an effective journey thither for religious purposes was scarcely to be thought of. Diaz, Madero, Carranza, had all made a mess of it in one way or another. But the Mexicans, like the rest of the world, were getting tired of the war and outlawry, and President Obregon was beginning to bring order out of chaos.

Though we knew that conditions were still very crude, the country much upset, and in some places dangerous for travel, we decided to risk it and try to visit our friends in Mexico City who had sent such earnest invitations.

A railroad strike, which had been slowly ruining the national railways for months, had thoroughly disorganized all the travel routes, but we did not realize how thoroughly until we crossed the border and found that trains were *expected* to be from twelve to twenty-four hours late in reaching the Capital from Loredo on the Texas border. The car shops had been particularly affected by the strike. Every engine was out of order, and had to be tinkered and set running again a dozen times in the course of an eight-hundred-mile journey.

Intolerable waits which we could not account for, and which no one would explain, delayed us at many stations; no less than twelve hours in one place, and seven in another, and our train was thirty-six hours late in reaching Mexico City. One meeting, arranged for at San Luis Obispo, had to be cancelled, yet we found that the welcome we received in Mexico City repaid us for the discomforts and exasperations of the journey. Dr. John Howland, president of the Union Theological Seminary, and his good wife were our kind hosts, and the intelligent earnestness of the Mexican Endeavorers and their thorough understanding of the principles of the movement, were evident at all the meetings. The largest Presbyterian church, made over from an old Catholic church, was the chief meeting-place. It was crowded as I have seldom seen a building packed. Since it was Easter Day, an almost unbelievable abundance of calla lilies reminded us everywhere of the resurrection of our Lord. In Mexico such lilies can be had for the picking. In another church which we visited no less than three thousand lilies were packed around the pulpit.

The City of Mexico at this time was bravely recovering from a decade of political confusion, assassination, and outrage. The bandit Villa had been bought off and was living peacefully on a great ranch of his own. Only one serious band of brigands was in the mountains, not far from Saltillo. President Obregon was giving our neighboring republic a just and on the whole popular administration, and Mexico's relations with the United States were visibly clearing up. Yet the scars of the past ten years of turmoil were evident enough. Great holes in many of the streets, made by incendiary bombs, could still be seen, and the Theological Seminary where we lodged was peppered with bullet wounds in many places.

The Mexicans made much of Easter time, and it was a lively scene that we beheld on the principal streets. Innumerable booths were filled with gimcracks of all kinds, especially with little devils in red and blue, made to be burned, while a big devil, as big as a man, and filled with some kind of powder, was exploded at ten o'clock on the Saturday before Easter, showing that the Prince of Peace was more than a match for his Satanic majesty. Never did I see a stranger or more lively scene than these Easter streets of the city of the Aztecs. Few cities have a grander park than Mexico City. Not that it is beautifully embellished with trim lawns and trained trees and statues and fountains as are many others, for nature has fortunately been left pretty much to herself. Enormous trees, that are supposed to be over a thousand years old, rivaling the Sequoias of California, are numerous. Giant twining vines and creepers and all kinds of tropical vegetation that can flourish a mile above the sea level gives this park a distinction all its own. It is crowned, too, by the magnificent Chapultepec Palace, where President Obregon holds his republican court. It was a disappointment to me not to meet the president as had been planned, but he was away from the city during the whole of our stay.

The National Museum is worth a visit of days rather than the hours which were all that our time permitted. Here are some of the noblest and rarest antiquities of Aztec civilization, the Sacrificial Stone, the wonderful stone calendar, and many rooms full of articles and mementoes that illustrate the ancient and modern history of the republic.

Our return journey to the States was more thrilling than the outward trip. If we should be more than six hours late in reaching Laredo on the border, it would upset the Texas programme and prevent us from attending the specially arranged and widely-advertised meetings in San Antonio and Houston. No train for weeks had been less than twelve hours late, and we could only trust to a good Providence to get us through on time. Every half hour's delay was a mental torture, but the train kept up to schedule time unusually well, and when within a hundred miles of the Texas line was only six and a half hours behind time.

If the engineer could make up half an hour we might still keep our appointments. So at three o'clock in the morning, in the coldest and darkest hour before the dawn, when some further engine trouble delayed us again, my friend went forward to the cab, and told the three men who occupied it, the engineer, fireman, and a sort of engine-nurse (a mechanic who always went along to help it when in trouble), that he would give each of them a five-dollar gold piece if they would make up just thirty minutes before reaching the border. Under this stimulus they did their best. The half hour was actually made up, and we reached the Mexican side of the Rio Grande, some twenty-five minutes before the train for San Antonio was due to start on the Texas side.

Still mountains of difficulty loomed before us. Our passports had to be *viséd* at the Mexican office to enable us to leave one republic, and at the United States office to enable us to enter another. Two custom-houses had to be visited, and our baggage examined, happily in a cursory manner. Then the emigration and immigration offices must be visited, for we were emigrants from Mexico and immigrants to the States. Finally came the sanitary office of the United States, where we were both vaccinated. Fortunately all these offices were near together. The officials kindly recognized our need of haste, and, incredible though it may seem, we passed them all in twenty-five minutes. The chauffeur opened his throttle, and we jumped into his machine. The conductor held the San Antonio train for four minutes, that we might get on board, and we reached the first appointment in San Antonio on the very hour appointed.

It had been some years since I was in Texas, and I was surprised at the growth of the cities and at the general prosperity of the State. Texas had "struck ile" and many "gushers" had been brought in. The State surely had little reason to complain of the hard times from which the rest of the country was suffering. Still, it is difficult to get altogether away from local disasters, and the onion growers in a great section of Texas near the Mexican line were in despair because the price of their crop, which largely feeds the United States with the "odorous bulb," had dropped from about ten cents a pound to one cent. Doubtless it was hard on them.

I was especially struck with the size and beauty of the churches in the leading centres like San Antonio, Houston, Dallas, and Forth Worth. Some of them, I was told, had an annual budget of $75,000 a year, and one of them, I heard, raised $150,000 yearly for home expenses and missionary

work. What a change this from the days of the Lone Star
Republic, when its few inhabitants fought with the wooden-
legged Santa Ana, and Sam Houston and his companions laid
the foundations for a great commonwealth!

Speaking of Santa Ana, I should have said that in the
splendid National Museum in Mexico City, of which I have
spoken, we saw his wooden leg, which has been preserved,
rather a grewsome memento of this national hero! Moreover,
in the same museum we saw several United States flags which
had been captured from our troops in the Mexican War, a
war of which we have no great reason to be proud. The
history books tell us nothing of the flags captured from *our*
troops, but much of our easy victories.

The Endeavor meetings in Texas, much as I expected, far
exceeded my anticipations. In almost every instance the
largest churches were crowded, as was also one in flourishing
Oklahoma City.

From Oklahoma I returned directly to Boston, after one of
the journeys longest in distance travelled (9,000 miles), and
shortest in time (three weeks), and most encouraging in results,
of my whole life.

Chapter LIV

Years 1920–1921

BEGINNINGS OF WORLD PEACE

A GLORIOUS VISION OF AMITY — THE ELECTION OF 1920 —
AN INTERESTING CEREMONY — PRESIDENT HARDING
BECOMES A CHRISTIAN ENDEAVOR ALUMNUS — THE
GRACIOUS LADY OF THE WHITE HOUSE — ENDEAVORERS
IN THE CABINET — THE GREAT WASHINGTON CON-
FERENCE — SOME PETITIONS AND THEIR ANSWERS.

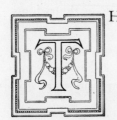HE years 1920 and 1921 were momentous for
America as for the rest of the world, for
then appeared for the first time for six long
years the dawn of a permanent world peace.
As I write (1922) it is still far from high
noon, but the promise for the coming years is
bright. The world has become sick of slaughter. It is no
longer considered unpatriotic for a mother to sing, " I did not
raise my boy to be a soldier." The Pacifists are coming into
their own, as was evident from the fact that Mr. Herbert
Hoover, the great philanthropist and saviour of starving
Europe, committed to the Quakers millions of dollars for their
relief and reconstruction work. Bitterness against Germany
had begun to subside, except in France, and the Versailles
Treaty was considered in many circles to be an impossible if
not an immoral one.

The Endeavorers generally were quick to take advantage
of this new turn of the tide against war, and in favor of
universal peace. How could it be otherwise, when their
brethren were found in every land, both among the former

622

allies and former enemies. In the countries most stricken by the flaming torch of war, the societies and Christian people generally, by their afflictions and distresses had been thrown back upon God as never before, and learned anew their true allegiance to the Prince of Peace.

I did my utmost to cultivate this spirit by articles and addresses, and found for the most part a ready response.

The political conventions and the election of 1920 presented problems of political conduct which were difficult for many people to solve. I was strongly in favor of the League of Nations as outlined in Paris, and felt that up to that time it presented the only hope for the peace of the world. I also felt that President Wilson was blocked in his purposes and his great aims were defeated by a group of " irreconcilable " Senators, who seemed to be influenced by personal animosity and partisan motives.

Undoubtedly the President's unwillingness to yield his point in any particular, and his dislike for a friendly conference with his opponents, prolonged the struggle, and in the end, for a time, at least, defeated his great purpose. But when he was stricken, like a soldier on the field of battle, the sympathies of many of us went out toward him even more strongly, and we felt that he was a martyr to the cause of his ideals. Whether to vote for Harding or Cox was a serious problem with many conscientious republicans.

I was much influenced just before election by the pronouncements of the " Committee of Thirty-one," which included such pro-League Republicans as Taft, Hughes, and Lowell, and others equally eminent, to the effect that under President Harding's administration we might get some kind of an association of nations or league with reservations, while there was no hope of the Democrats being able to control the Senate in such a way as to secure a ratification of the Paris league. Almost at the last moment I decided to vote for Mr. Harding, as I am sure did hundreds of thousands of wavering Republicans, and he was triumphantly elected, but not by any means on the issue of opposition to the League alone as many of Wilson's opponents declared. This was the first presidential election in which women had a part, and much interest and curiosity was excited as to how they would vote, and what influence they would have upon the political life of the nation.

It cannot be said that, as yet, their influence has been particularly marked one way or the other, but I think that they have made the polling places far more decent and orderly than in the old days, and I hope for great things in the future because of the influence of good women on matters of temperance and purity, and for the abatement of social evils.

Both Mrs. Clark and myself have been glad, of recent months, that at the eleventh hour we voted for the present administration. It has been growing in popularity and in wisdom, I believe, from the beginning, and the splendidly bold challenge to the world at the Washington Conference for the Limitation of Armaments has gone far to stamp it as one of the great administrations of American history. It is, of course, at present, too soon, in the autumn of 1922, to appraise it at its full value, but it certainly gives us reason to hope for the best.

Early in the summer of 1921, in compliance with the request of the Washington Endeavorers, President Harding consented to become an honorary member of the District of Columbia Christian Endeavor Alumni Association, and I was asked to go to Washington to conduct a little ceremony of initiation, and to give the President the Christian Endeavor badge.

On the day before this little event, so pleasing to the Endeavorers of the country, took place, I went with the leaders of the local union to Mount Vernon to plant a memorial tree. When we arrived, however, we found the tree which had been planted twenty-five years before, in connection with the National Convention of 1896, so strong and flourishing that

PRESIDENT HARDING, CHRISTIAN ENDEAVOR ALUMNUS

Group of Endeavor leaders taken on the lawn of the White House after Dr. Clark had made President Harding a member of the Christian Endeavor Alumni Fellowship. President Harding is third in the back row. Next to him is Dr. Clark, and at his side Mrs. Harding.

we deemed it superfluous to plant another, but held a little service of rededication around the original tree.

The genial caretaker of the grounds remembered the former event and had done what he could to make the little sapling then planted vigorous and strong. A great tornado a few years before had wrought havoc among the old trees at Mount Vernon. Many of them had been mowed down by the hurricane, including all those in the vicinity of the Christian Endeavor Tree, which, young and supple, had bent without breaking, and not a limb had been lost. It stands in a commanding position, near the first tomb occupied by the body of President Washington before it was removed to the site which he had designated in his lifetime for his final resting-place.

The next day, Sunday, at the appointed time, some fifty Endeavorers, including a dozen of the most prominent ministers of Washington (our company had been limited by the President's secretary to fifty), were received in the great East Room of the White House. I said a few informal words about our joy in receiving the President into our fellowship, and alluded to the text in the book of Micah, which the President kissed as he took the oath on his Inauguration Day: "What doth the Lord require of thee but to do justly, to love mercy, and to walk humbly with thy God?" In his reply he referred to this, which he hoped would be the keynote of his administration. Then I gave him the little Christian Endeavor badge, whose minute and obstinate clasp refused to be easily pinned on his coat lapel. Mrs. Harding, however, after the vain attempt of myself as well as of Mr. Percy Foster, the president of the Washington alumni, to put it in its place, came to the rescue and promised to pin it on her husband's coat a little later. It was an unexpected pleasure to have Mrs. Harding with us. She is a most gracious lady, a beautiful, kindly American woman of the very best type.

We afterwards went out on the lawn of the East front of

the White House, and all had our pictures taken with the President and Mrs. Harding, an ordeal, undoubtedly, which the President frequently undergoes, but he could not have been more gracious about it, if this had been his first experience.

When we came away, Mrs. Harding said to us, with almost oriental courtesy, " You must come again. Remember this is not our house, but yours. We are only living here temporarily." However, none of us intend to abuse her hospitality by accepting her invitation too often or taking it too literally.

I was greatly impressed with the face and whole demeanor of the President. He has remarkably kind, benevolent features, and a beautifully expressive eye. He looks one squarely in the face and speaks with serious cordiality, and in a finely modulated voice. The whole impression is of a man who is anxious only to know his duty and to do it.

In the morning of that Sunday, I had spoken in the President's church, the Calvary Baptist, for a few moments before going to another church where my chief morning service had been arranged. The church was crowded in every part, and hundreds of people lined the curbs outside waiting to see the President approach, but he had motored into the country that morning to visit a friend, and was not at his own church as usual. But Secretary of State Hughes sat in his own accustomed place, and no preacher could ask for a more appreciative listener than he seemed to be. Calvary Baptist Church, long one of the leading Endeavor churches in Washington, while under the care of its long-time beloved pastor, Dr. S. G. Greene, who had recently died. Secretary Hughes and the President had for years attended this church, when in Washington, and the Secretary's daughter was a leading worker in the Endeavor society. Under its new pastor it sustains the same reputation.

A brief visit and a brief address at each of *five* other churches in the afternoon and evening of the same day, including a great mass meeting of Endeavorers in the First Congregational Church, finished a busy day, and I was quite tired enough to sleep well when I took the midnight train for Boston.

It is a fact of some interest in this connection that several members of the Cabinet are interested in the Christian Endeavor movement, sufficiently at least to become honorary members of the Alumni Association. Secretary Hughes, without solicitation, sent ten dollars to the Washington Endeavorers and asked to be enrolled as an alumnus. The President's secretary, Mr. Christian, has also joined the Washington Alumni, and the then Postmaster-General, Will Hays, was naturally elected to the Alumni fellowship, since in his younger years he had been active in the work, and the secretary of a local union in Indiana.

When the Washington Conference for the Limitation of Armaments was called by the President for November of 1921 I was naturally delighted, as were all my associates. We gave thanks to God, that the dream of the ages seemed likely soon to be realized, at least in a partial manner.

As we understood that President Harding and the Commissioners desired to know the sentiment of the public, and how far they would be backed up in proposing drastic reductions of naval armaments, I resolved that the constituency with which I had specially to do should not be backward in giving them this information. A petition, signed by a multitude of individual Endeavorers and many societies, and fairly representing three millions of young people, and millions more of former Endeavorers, went to the President, respectfully urging him to go to " the utmost limit " in urging world disarmament, except for police purposes. We reminded him at the same time that the Endeavorers had some right to be heard, since they are exactly in the age of enlistment and the draft, and that the young people of to-day, and their successors in the future, would have to bear the great burden of future wars. Also the patriotism of the young people could not be denied, since hundreds of thousands had responded to their country's call, in the late war.

Another petition, signed by fifty or more of the denominational trustees of the United Society, and by nearly as many more State presidents, who are also trustees, was sent to each one of the four commissioners, Secretary Hughes, Senators Lodge and Underwood, and Honorable Elihu Root. Both of these petitions were received very graciously. The following letter from the President's secretary speaks for itself:

<blockquote>
" THE WHITE HOUSE
" WASHINGTON

" November 2, 1921.

" My Dear Dr. Clark:

" The President has received your letter of October 31st with enclosure, and has read it with interest and appreciation. He asks me to assure you and all concerned that he is very much gratified by this expression of confidence.

" Sincerely yours,
" (signed) GEO. B. CHRISTIAN, JR.
" Secretary to the President."
</blockquote>

The Commissioners replied with equal cordiality.

Personal letters from the President, which I prize, tell of his interest in the Christian Endeavor Society, and of his warm appreciation of the prayers of the Endeavorers, who were called by telegram and through the newspapers, by Secretary Gates, to pray for the recovery of Mrs. Harding when it seemed that she was at the point of death in September, 1922.

THE FORTIETH ANNIVERSARY OF CHRISTIAN ENDEAVOR

IN PORTLAND — AYLMER SWEPT BY FIRE — WHY I AM STILL
PRESIDENT — A CROWNING CONVENTION — THE WON-
DERFUL PARADE — " A WARLESS WORLD BY 1923."

THE year 1921 was of special interest in Christian Endeavor circles, because on February 2 the movement had completed its fortieth year, and much was made of the occasion throughout America and in many other parts of the world. Naturally the societies in Portland, Me., were alive to the significance of the occasion.

I was in Portland on two occasions during the year, one of which was the installation of the new pastor, Rev. Morris H. Turk, my sixth successor in the Williston pastorate, and on another occasion I spoke in the fine new city hall whose municipal organ is the pride of Portland, as well it may be since it is surpassed in size and range by only one or two in the country. The Sunday-afternoon municipal concerts are truly religious in music and in the addresses that are provided. The little city that I knew forty-five years ago has doubled in population, and now numbers over 60,000, but it is as beautiful as in the olden days.

A little meeting of unusual interest was held at 62 Neal Street, on February 2, 1921, in the room where the first society was organized. Eight or ten of the original members were present. Mr. Granville Staples, who led the first Endeavor prayer meeting, also led this one, and many were the reminiscences of the old days. The lady who now with her husband and family occupies the old parsonage is a Roman Catholic, but she welcomed the little prayer meeting most heartily and told me with genuine appreciation about it in detail. "There stood Mr. Staples," she said, "just where he stood when the society was formed, and there sat one of the other old members, and there sat still another, and it was so good to have that little prayer meeting in our home." This, it seemed to me, was a remarkable concession on the part of a good Catholic, and, in a small way, foreshadowed an era of less bitterness between the dominant types of Christianity in America.

In the summer of this year, my birthplace, the town of Aylmer, in the Province of Quebec, was swept by one of those terrific fires for which the cities and villages of both the United States and Canada have long had such an unhappy pre-eminence. I was glad to be told that "Cherry Cottage," my boyhood home, being a little out of the centre, was spared, but the Presbyterian Church, the religious home of my father and mother, was burned, and the big stone house on Main Street, where many say that I was born and lived for a few weeks, was also destroyed. I was interested in a little controversy that appeared in the Ottawa papers on this point, some claiming that I was born in "Cherry Cottage," while others, among them a former mayor of Aylmer, who owned the house on Main Street, proved beyond a doubt, as they thought, that that was my birthplace. Of course that is a matter of little consequence. The good people of Aylmer, especially the Presbyterians, propose to build a fine edifice not only for worship but for community purposes as well. They have honored me undeservedly by desiring to call it by my name.

The great event of the year in Christian Endeavor circles was of course the World's Convention in New York, which

CHERRY COTTAGE

When visited by the delegates to the Ontario Provincial Christian Endeavor Convention who had come from Ottawa, eight miles away.

gathered into itself all the enthusiasms and the memories connected with the anniversary of two-score years of organized life. Great difficulties had to be overcome, financial and otherwise, for many smaller cities surpass New York in their interest in such matters, but these were gradually overcome. Hon. Frederick A. Wallis, Commissioner of Immigration at Ellis Island, an old-time Kentucky Endeavorer, was chosen chairman of the committee, and Rev. Harry A. Kinports and Mr. Marc Edmund Jones, his most efficient working assistants. The dates from July 5–11 proved to be the hottest of the year, and indeed of many years. Sultry and depressing, they would have ruined almost any other gathering, but the Endeavorers rose to the occasion, packed the big Armory on Park Avenue and 34th Street morning, afternoon, and evening with an inspiring as well as a perspiring audience.

It will be remembered, perhaps, that ten years before this, in 1911, when I completed my sixtieth year, I had fully intended to insist upon my resignation as president of the United Society, but was dissuaded by my colleagues from doing so. Ten years had passed and it seemed that now was of all others the time to insist upon carrying out my previous resolution. These ten years have been years of light and shadow, of sickness and health, of much travel and many activities. The United Society was now in splendid condition, the officers alert and efficient in the highest degree, and the prospects of the Christian Endeavor movement never were so bright either in America or the world around.

But again I was foiled in my design by the urgent entreaties and almost peremptory insistence of the trustees of the society and of the office force.

Though I could urge approaching old age, I did not have the excuse of shattered health, for as a matter of fact, I was healthier and stronger than a decade before. So I compromised with my persistent friends by saying in my annual report to the trustees that if they would relieve me of all financial responsibility for the United Society and the World's Union, I would not at that time resign the presidency. They at once agreed, and a financial committee of trustees was appointed, of which Dr. Hiram Foulkes, the very successful promoter of the New Era Movement of the Presbyterian Church, was chairman. Dr. Abraham Corey, equally eminent among the Disciples of Christ, Dr. Rufus Miller, publication manager of the Reformed Church, Dr. Haddaway, a well-known leader in all Methodist Protestant circles, and Mr. Fred Ball, one of the most influential young men of the Congregational denomination, were chosen to be the other members of the committee.

They at once went energetically to work to provide for a yearly budget of $75,000 for World-wide Endeavor. As I write, the prospects are bright for the complete success of this effort, and I am still President of the United Society and the World's Union of Christian Endeavor.

To return to the convention, I cannot recount the notable speakers whose words will long be remembered, the quiet devotional hours each morning, the schools of methods and of Bible study, or the hilarious banquets, which, either for Junior workers or Intermediates or the Alumni or the special groups of Endeavorers were held almost every day.

The most unique feature of the convention was an enormous procession of 15,000 delegates that marched up Fifth Avenue to the " Sheep Pasture " in Central Park, and there listened to one of the most rousing addresses ever given by Hon. William J. Bryan on World-Fellowship and Peace. Delegates from every State were in the line of the procession, and each delegate wore a simple costume featuring his own State colors. The near-by States, Pennsylvania, Connecticut, Massachusetts, and New Jersey, and, of course, up-state New York, had hundreds, and in one or two instances, thousands in costume. The police kept the beautiful avenue clear of all other traffic, and tens of thousands lined the sidewalks even up to the Park.

There were some unusually beautiful floats in the procession, several of particular significance representing scenes from Pilgrim's Progress.

A matter of most practical importance for the future was the launching of " The Four-Square Campaign," outlined in the annual message of the president, a campaign for construction, reconstruction, loyalty, and fellowship, a new campaign for old principles which naturally recognized the four divisions of Christian Endeavor, the four great purposes for which it stands, and the four special methods by which it accomplishes its work. " Never say ' no ' to God " was the motto suggested for the campaign.

It was taken up afterwards by all the State unions and many of the local unions, and I soon heard echoes of it from Great Britain and Australia, Germany and India, and other lands the world around.

Naturally world-fellowship and peace were the dominant notes in this World's Convention, with delegates representing many lands, races, and colors. Mr. Bryan, Dr. Landrith, and Fred B. Smith, Rev. John Pollock of Ireland, and others made tremendously powerful addresses on these subjects. Not only America, but all the world was ready to receive at this time such a message, so distressed and sick at heart had the nations become with the terrific struggle that had wrecked continental Europe and the civilization of the world.

Mr. Smith pleaded for a " warless world." Dr. Landrith in a remarkable set of resolutions voicing the opinion of the convention emphasized this idea with new vigor, and the president of the United Society in his closing five minutes ventured to propose the slogan " A Warless World by 1923."

This slogan gave big headlines to many papers throughout the country, and though it was considered by some daringly foolish, others commended it as not an impossibility, in view of the Conference for the Limitation of Armaments, which had been proposed that very week by President Harding.

Endeavorers, remembering that the war cry of the Atlantic City Convention in 1911, " A Saloonless Nation by 1920, the three hundredth anniversary of the Landing of the Pilgrims," had been realized, felt that the new date, which would coincide with the next international convention to be held at Des Moines, Io., was not too near for at least the beginning of a Warless World.

The only shadows upon this convention were the illnesses of former secretary Shaw, who was unable to attend the meetings, and a terrible accident to Dr. Daniel Poling and his family on their way by automobile from their summer home in New Hampshire to New York. For a time Dr. Poling's life was despaired of, and all the family had broken bones or bruises, but in a miraculously short time, considering the seriousness of the accident, Dr. Poling was able partly to resume his work, and the others wholly recovered from their breaks and bruises.

Not only was world-solidarity in the minds of all, but the thought that Christian Endeavor was now found in every land beneath the sun, bringing the young people of the world into a new fellowship was naturally dominant in the convention and afterwards. We had learned of societies in all the struggling new countries of Europe. In some of them they had existed before, while in others they were just being formed. Germany had more than doubled her Endeavor hosts; Latvia, Esthonia, Poland, Czecho-Slovakia, Hungary, Jugo-Slavia, Transylvania, were calling for financial help and sympathy from the United Society, and Mrs. Clark and I felt that we should strive to finish the European journey which we had begun nearly two years before, but which, by reason of revolutions and passport difficulties, we had not been able fully to accomplish. So on November 19, 1921, we bade adieu once more to our dear friends and kinsfolk and sailed for Havre on the French steamer " La Savoie."

FIVE MONTHS IN CENTRAL EUROPE

CLASSICAL FREIBURG — WITH OUR ARMY ON THE RHINE —
GERMANY IN 1922 —VICTORIOUS AND VIGOROUS CZECHO-
SLOVAKIA — DESPOILED HUNGARY — THE WONDERFUL
BETHANIA UNION — POLAND AND HER ENDEAVORERS —
DENMARK, HOLLAND, ENGLAND, WALES — HOME.

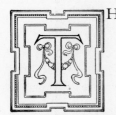HOUGH we landed in France our stay there was short because of the cold weather and the high prices. We could not keep warm in any hotel we could afford, for it was an unusually cold winter throughout Europe, and we found that prices had doubled since we were in Paris two years before. We soon made our way to Freiburg, the capital of the Black Forest of Baden, and here in a very comfortable hotel we stayed for two months, and I was able, with the help of Mrs. Clark's typewriter and her nimble fingers, to finish the last third of this volume.

We found Freiburg, as we had found it before in 1912, a very delightful little city, giving comparatively few evidences of the dreadful war through which it had passed. And yet it had by no means escaped the ravages of the conflict. More than three hundred bombs had fallen in the city during the war, the famous medical college had been destroyed, as well as a large theatre, and apartment houses in which many people had been killed. None of these bombings had been recorded in American or English papers. This was only one evidence of the way governments on both sides had tampered with the news, suppressing everything unfavorable and lauding everything that seemed to be of advantage to the side of the country that published the information.

SPIRE OF THE WONDERFUL CATHEDRAL IN FREIBERG

There were other signs of the effects of the war, which, though more prosaic than bombed buildings and slaughtered citizens were very practical evidences of war's horrors.   For instance we had no milk or butter during all our stay in Germany, and the tiniest lumps of sugar pretended to sweeten our coffee. The merest trickle of condensed milk thinned out to the *nth* degree, and different kinds of butter substitutes, graced the table, for most of the cows had been commandeered by France, and what little fresh milk there was, was reserved for infants and invalids and could be had only by a doctor's prescription.

It was a city of almost no automobiles and few horses, these means of transport having been sent across the border. Nevertheless, the city seemed to carry on its business and to be fairly prosperous, human muscle largely taking the place of horse flesh and electricity as a means of transportation. In some cases the poverty of the people was pathetic, especially of the aged and those dependent upon a small fixed income, which had been rendered almost worthless by the depreciation of the currency. When we first reached Germany the exchange rate was about 150 marks to the dollar, the normal value of the mark being twenty-four cents instead of three-quarters of a cent, to which it had dropped. When we left Germany five months later it had dropped to 330 marks to the dollar. I felt almost ashamed to take advantage of this terrible depreciation, though as a matter of fact the tradesmen and others were glad to get American money, whatever the premium might be. As I finish the proof-reading the rate is 5,700 marks to the dollar.

The surroundings of Freiburg, as I have remarked in another chapter, are ideal, and I took many a long walk into the Black Forest, along the lovely, well-beaten paths, greatly to the refreshment of soul and body. For the first month of our stay we had comparatively few interruptions, but then our Christian Endeavor friends found out where we were and many invitations were received, only a few of which we could accept, since we had gone to Freiburg especially as a quiet refuge for writing and for rest.

Early in February we left hospitable Freiburg, and after brief but very delightful visits to Liebenzell and Karlsruhe, reached Coblenz barely in advance of a universal railroad strike which kept us there for ten days.

Liebenzell is a gem of a place, also in the Black Forest, but in the kingdom of Würtemburg. Here has long been established a Faith Mission, which has sent out its missionaries to the ends of the earth. It is a health resort, with many springs of medicinal value, and two or three great hotels, but it has been made famous, not by its springs or its mountains, so much as by its noble mission training-school, and its godly leaders, like Dr. Körper, the head of the institution, and others whom I might mention.

Karlsruhe is the capital of Baden and a beautiful city, with one of the finest royal palaces and royal parks in all Germany. Here we met a fine assembly of Christian Endeavorers from all the vicinity, and had a meeting remarkable for its numbers and its cordiality. Before the meeting we were serenaded by an excellent Christian Endeavor brass band. During the progress of the evening a Christian Endeavor orchestra with the Christian Endeavor monogram on every instrument, and a mixed choir, furnished delightful music. One characteristic of Christian Endeavor in Germany is its consecrated music, both vocal and instrumental. Not only are the old German chorals splendidly sung, but many of the later gospel songs are also greatly enjoyed by the young people.

Karlsruhe, too, suffered greatly during the war. It is said to have been bombed every other day for two years. In one of the attacks of the French planes, thirty little children were killed, as they were enjoying a school holiday in one of the parks.

Our ten days in Coblenz (where, had it not been for the strike we should have enjoyed but one) furnished us with a unique experience. The leaders of the Endeavor society in the American Army of Occupation had told the senior chaplain,

THE GREAT MONUMENT OF KAISER WILLIAM THE FIRST AT THE JUNCTION OF THE RHINE
AND MOSELLE

In the distance, the great fortress of Ehrenbreitstein, with the American flag flying from the top. This castle was the
district headquarters of the American Army of Occupation.

Dr. Estabrook, of our expected visit. Whereupon he billeted us at the Coblenzerhof Hotel, the best in the city, which had been taken over by the American army. To that extent we were the guests of the Army of Occupation, and I was impressed into the service as a sort of assistant chaplain, preaching on the Sundays for the senior chaplain in the Palace Chapel, and speaking in the Y.M.C.A. huts, or to the soldiers in other groups almost every day.

I was glad to notice the friendliness and good will that existed between the German populace and the American soldiers. Our troops had been polite and considerate to the Germans, who reciprocated their good will. American officers and Y.M.C.A. secretaries were billeted in the best German houses, many of them genuine palaces, while the owners found refuge in the second or third story, yet I heard of no friction or ill feeling, but only of a genuine regret on the part of the inhabitants that the American troops must leave them so soon after our visit, to be replaced by the hated and hating French.

The last meeting that we attended, on the evening of our departure, was a joint Christian Endeavor meeting between the Endeavorers of Coblenz and the "American Society on the Rhine," as the soldiers' society was called. It was a most brotherly gathering. Cordial words were spoken in both languages, and before the meeting broke up that hymn which seems to be inevitable on such occasions, " Blest be the tie that binds," was sung.

I was glad to notice that after the American services in the Royal Chapel, where Emperor William's mother worshipped during her long residence in the city, several American flags which decorated the audience room were removed by the senior chaplain out of deference to the feelings of the Germans who occupied the chapel for an hour's service immediately after the Americans. Such considerateness was significant of the good feeling which had begun to prevail between the victors and the vanquished.

At last the long and disastrous railroad strike was over, and we took the first through train from Coblenz to Berlin. Here, too, our welcome was an extraordinary one. Though the great Christian Endeavor meeting which had been widely advertised had been postponed because of the strike that had suspended all travel, and the postponed meeting had to be held with very little advance notice, the beautiful hall in the Herrenhaus, the former House of the Lords of the Prussian

DR. AND MRS. CLARK WITH TWO ENDEAVOR SOLDIERS IN COBLENZ
President Fritz and Secretary Lanning of the Army Christian Endeavor Society, on either side.

parliament, was thronged with an enthusiastic crowd of young people, fully two thousand of them, it was said. No more cordial words could have been spoken by the director and secretary of the German union, and by the district and city unions as well. A fine luncheon had been served in the splendid banquet hall and everything was indicative of the strong place which Christian Endeavor held in the republican empire.

I learned that the societies had increased to more than 1,200, and that in a thousand more places a desire had been expressed for the formation of societies.

One pleasant feature of our stay was a visit to Friedrichs-hagen, the headquarters of Christian Endeavor in Germany, where Director Schürman, and Secretary Blecher have their homes, as well as some twenty more officers and employees of the Endeavor headquarters. Here a Christian Endeavor press

CHRISTIAN ENDEAVOR OFFICE STAFF AT GERMAN CHRISTIAN ENDEAVOR HEADQUARTERS, FRIEDRICHSHAGEN BEI BERLIN

Rev. Pastor Schürman, Director of German Christian Endeavor, stands at the right, his wife sits near him in the front row, their two children at their right. Mrs. Blecher, with her daughter standing beside her, at the left. The General Secretary of the German Union, Rev. F. Blecher, stands behind Dr. and Mrs. Clark. Mr. Wetsig, editor and publisher, is the fourth in the back row from the left. The others are in the secretarial and printing offices. A large publishing business in several languages is done in the building in the rear, which also is the home of the Director and Secretary.

prints and sends out a great amount of literature, and from here gracious influences extend to the farthest borders of the Fatherland, and into all the countries round about.

Our first side-journey from Berlin took us to Czecho-Slovakia and Hungary, two countries as much opposed to each other politically and racially as can well be imagined. The conqueror and the conquered, the Slav and the Magyar, the despoiled and the despoiler, were geographically divided only by an imaginary line, but really by an absolutely impassable line, so far as good feeling and kindly interest were concerned. Only in certain lines of religious activity was there any approach to each other by these antipathetic races.

Czecho-Slovakia had come out of the war with greatly enlarged boundaries and resources, free, and independent of her former rulers, and with high, not to say grandiloquent, hopes and aspirations to be the leader of the " Little Entente." Hungary had been despoiled by order of Versailles of two-thirds of her territory, not given to Czecho-Slovakia alone, but to all the immediately surrounding nations. She had lost her coal, her copper, and her salt, the great forests that covered her beloved ancestral mountains, and, in fact, all her resources except part of her agricultural lands.

The Czechs look back upon centuries of oppression under the Hapsburgs in which they believe that the Hungarians had had their full share. No wonder that the feeling between the two races was intensely bitter.

One way in which these feelings were manifested was in their different estimates of President Wilson. The Czechs lauded him to the skies, naming streets and parks and even railway stations after him in their larger cities, hanging his picture everywhere, as companion to the portrait of their beloved Masaryk, and placing him in the first rank of mortals as a defender of the rights of small nations.

The Magyars, on the other hand, regarded him as the betrayer of the old " enemy nations," declaring that he had led them to accept the armistice by proclaiming his " fourteen points," and then repudiating them when he had the conquered nations at his mercy. In vain I tried to persuade them that President Wilson alone did not engineer the Peace of Versailles, but that his benevolent intentions were largely thwarted by Clemenceau and other Allied leaders.

However, Christian Endeavor had an equally free course in both countries and the welcome we received was delightfully warm on both sides of the national boundary. The movement had naturally made little progress in Czecho-Slovakia because, until very recently, the comparatively few Protestants had had small opportunities to propagate their faith and

STATUE OF JOHN HUSS

Erected in the principal square of Prague after the fall of the Hapsburg dynasty.

methods of work. However, under the leadership and guidance of our good friend, Rev. J. S. Porter, of the American Congregational Mission Board, we had large and, I hope, fruitful meetings in Prague, Pilsen, Brno, Hradec, and Bratislava. All of these are most interesting cities, and are famous in the song and story of ancient times. The " *Los von Rom* " movement was at high tide when we were in the republic, and it was said that a million people, some said two millions, had left the ancient church to form a purely national Czecho-Slavic church.

It was not however so much a movement toward Protestantism as away from Rome. The forms and ceremonies of the Catholic church were largely retained, though the Pope was repudiated. The Czech Brethren Church, the devoted followers of John Huss, had gained somewhat in numbers, but the newcomers apparently knew little of the true tenets or spirit of Protestantism. It seemed to me that the movement had already begun to wane somewhat, partly because many of the four hundred priests who at first came out had gone back to Rome, and there were few to lead the multitudes, or to administer the sacraments, which the masses of the people still deemed essential. Nevertheless the movement had greatly stirred up the minds and consciences of the Czechs, and will doubtless result in largely increased intellectual and religious freedom.

In Hungary, as I have related in other chapters, Christian Endeavor has long had a strong foothold, and the Bethania Christian Endeavor Union has for years been famous for the quality of its leaders and for their complete consecration, a devotion to God's work which has enabled them to suffer and be strong in these days of tribulation and distress that have followed the World War. Hungary has indeed been one of the world's chief sufferers. She has not only lost most of her territory as well as her resources, but has suffered terribly from internal and external enemies. The Czechs on the West, the Roumanians on the East, the Jugo-Slavs on the South, and the Russians on the North have all had a hand in her sore affliction, while the four months' reign of the Communists under Bela Kun was the most tragic and disastrous era in her whole history. During this period, while the Bolshevists were intrenched in her magnificent capital, hundreds of Hungary's noblest men were murdered in cold blood, their bodies thrown into the Danube, which tells no tales.

The rich people were plundered, and even the homes of the poor were pillaged. The paper stock and all the literature of the Bethania Christian Endeavor Union were seized and carried off. Fortunately the rule of the Communists came to an end before the stock was destroyed, and the Endeavorers recovered most of it. So great became the distress because of the wholesale murder and thievery that prevailed, and because of the post-war poverty and the impossibility of trading with their neighbors, that many starved to death and a multitude committed suicide. I was told by Dr. Kiss, perhaps the most eminent professor of anatomy in all Europe, that even now, two years after the peak of their troubles had been passed, between five and six hundred people attempted suicide every month, a terrible testimony indeed to their destitution and hopelessness.

In the midst of this distressful gloom the zeal and untiring devotion of the Bethania Union shines out gloriously. Never have I seen more consecrated leaders, greater faith or more untiring energy than is displayed by this noble group. Many are men and women of eminence in other walks of life. Dr. Molnar, the president, is a distinguished lawyer and judge. Baron Podmanisky is a professor of Greek and Hebrew in the Reformed Theological Seminary. Dr. Csia is a well-known physician with a very large practice. Rev. Thomas Vargha is a successful pastor belonging to a distinguished family, his father, acknowledged as one of the most eminent poets of Hungary, having been one of the ministers of state in the old government. Dr. Kiss, to whom I have already alluded, is probably not surpassed by any anatomist in the world, while Fraulein Irma Pauer, the treasurer of the union, is known far and wide for her executive ability and her successes on the mission field as well as at home.

Before the war many societies existed in Budapest and vicinity, but they were scattered and peeled by the great conflict, and its worse aftermath of Bolshevism, so that now there are belonging to this union only some 250 members, but all of them stalwarts. Only those of consecrated lives and of willing hands are admitted, but these, small in numbers, have organized and carried on forty-eight Sunday schools. They hold nine evangelistic meetings every week, and as many more for the Juniors. They visit the three great prisons of Budapest every week, to which they now have free access; they have a mission for blind soldiers as well as for blind children; have meetings for fallen women, and also for the thousands of people who live in box cars in the outskirts of the city, because there are no homes for them in the terribly congested metropolis which shelters hundreds of thousands of refugees.

The most unique work of the Bethania Union is done by the so-called " suicide committee," the only committee of its kind, I venture to say, among all the millions of Endeavorers. This committee sends its members to seek out in the hospitals the would-be suicides who were not able fully to succeed in their design. The committee comforts them, gives them good cheer, tells them that heaven is not lost, and that they may still have hope in Jesus Christ, and brings them back to health and sanity.

After two or three days in the capital we visited Debreczen, the great centre of Protestantism in the republic, the cradle of Hungarian liberty, where Kossuth first proclaimed the national independence of Hungary. Afterwards we visited Nyiregy-haza, another leading city of the Magyars. Here we found the same untiring devotion as among the Endeavorers of Budapest, and here too, we were greeted by a great throng of interested workers. Such a crowd indeed, thronged the big hall that for some time we were unable to push our way through the crowd that blocked the aisles and passageways, until strenuous efforts had been made to force a passage for us to the platform. Here Endeavorers had a mission to crippled children, and had built *with their own hands* the modest building which already houses a few little unfortunates. If every community possessed a Madame Sholtess, the President of the union, who devotes her fortune as well as all her energies to the work, this world would indeed be a different place.

Going back to Germany for a short breathing spell, we soon started on another difficult journey, this time to the Free City of Danzig, and then on to Poland. As is well known, the treaty of Versailles cut Germany in two by decreeing a neutral corridor from central Poland to the sea, making Danzig a free city. This has naturally resulted in much heart-burning and many customs and passport complications, so that our passports were *viséd* and our baggage examined at least four times on this comparatively short journey.

A Junior Society in Viecbork (Vandsburg) Poland

The Free City of Danzig has a large commerce, and many substantial buildings and memorials of former greatness and present prosperity. During the Sunday that we spent there we met hundreds of friendly Endeavorers, and the next morning early started off in a cold and comfortless train for Vandsburg, or Viecbork, as it is now called in the Polish tongue. Formerly it was in the German province of Pomerania, and its people are largely German-speaking. It would be an unattractive little town were it not for the great Deaconess

Institution, which has made it famous religiously throughout Europe. Here a large number of deaconesses are trained, in a most devout and intense religious atmosphere, for helpful service of all kinds, as nurses and helpers of the poor. As spiritual guides and religious leaders they do a notable work throughout Germany and Poland.

This establishment is one of four under the same management, the headquarters being in Marburg in Germany. Every year a Christian Endeavor conference is held in Vandsburg, which brings together the young people from far and near. On account of the greatly depreciated currency, the poverty of the people, and the difficulties of travel we expected to see comparatively few young people at this meeting. What was our surprise to find that some 650 had gathered, many of them coming two hundred miles or more. As the number was far greater than had been anticipated the mission was hard put to it to accommodate so many, but the young men were willing to " endure hardness " for the sake of the religious uplift they received, and were ready to sleep in barns or open sheds on heaps of straw. In other ways, too, they showed their endurance and religious zeal, for they were willing to listen to three or four sermons in succession in a three hours' sitting of the convention, and they showed no signs of weariness.

What a sweet wholesome air of loving kindness pervaded this retreat on the wind-swept fields of Poland! The Sisters seemed to perform the humblest duties, actuated by the highest motives. They scrubbed the immaculate floors as though it was their greatest joy, and performed the meanest household duties with smiles on their faces and songs on their lips, and I believe in their hearts as well.

When we were ushered into the best room in the building, named " Thyatira," after one of the Seven Cities of Asia, we found our table heaped with flowers and fruits and delicious cakes, and also many hand-painted mottoes and pictures. One of these mottoes which they deemed peculiarly appropriate was a quotation from the Psalms, illuminated, and painted on a wide ribbon. It read in English:

> *" They shall still bring forth fruit in old age;*
> *They shall be fat and flourishing."*

We admitted the " old age " if not the " fat and flourishing." We shall long remember the kindness of Oberschwester Marie, and Schwester Marthe, a graduate nurse who assiduously dressed an infected felon on my finger, which had given me much trouble, and started it on the way to recovery. Indeed, all the sisters so ministered to our comfort and happiness that we can never forget their kindness.

Pastor Mund, the director of the work and the brotherhood which is established near-by, Pastor Stalder of Danzig, the president of the Christian Endeavor Union of Poland, Pastor Poppek, the secretary of the union, and many of the leading Protestant pastors of Poland, who had come to the gathering, all endeared themselves to us in our brief stay. We left Vandsburg with only happy memories, and with new courage for the future, since we have seen how those who have come out of great tribulation were able to maintain their faith and hope and good cheer, never slackening their zeal in the Lord's work.

An incident occurred on the way back to Germany which would have confirmed my faith in the goodness of human nature had it needed confirmation. We reached Konitz, on the border of Poland, after a long cold ride on a dilapidated, war-worn railway, riding in darkness the last half of the way, the train not being lighted at all. At the station we were met by two ladies, one a teacher of English, who conducted us, though absolute strangers, to one of the best homes in the town. Here a hot supper awaited us at ten o'clock in the evening, and later a comfortable bed, while the next morning, long before daylight, our hostess prepared a hot breakfast. Our host guided us to the station in the darkness of an intensely cold morning, smoothed the way for us with the crusty custom-house officers and the passport officer, and the one who searched me with conscientious care for any money I might have on my person, and started us off for Berlin with the cockles of our hearts warmed with a new admiration for the exceeding kindness of folks in strange and distant lands.

I must hurry over the rest of this journey, for this chapter is already too long. After a few more days in Germany our programme took us to Copenhagen, where a small but representative gathering of Scandinavian Endeavorers, under the leadership of Pastor Klaeboe of Christiania, and Pastor Kent of Copenhagen, sought to inaugurate plans for the development of the cause in Denmark, where Christian Endeavor has always lagged, as well as in the rest of Scandinavia. Representatives of Denmark, Norway, Sweden, Germany, and Esthonia came together for several days of helpful conference.

Then our journey led us back to Germany once more for a few hours, and then to Holland for a couple of meetings in The Helder and in Rotterdam. The currency difficulties were impressed upon us when I tried to get some German money exchanged for Dutch currency, which is nearer pre-war value than any other European country except Switzerland. Having 435 German marks in my pocket, the money changer would give me but two guilders and some odd Dutch cents for that amount.

Indeed, throughout all this journey currency difficulties beset us. When going to Hungary I received 92,000 crowns for twenty-five American dollars. In Czecho-Slovakia the exchange was much higher, but I received 3,400 crowns, if I remember rightly, for the same amount. In Germany the exchange varied all the way from 150 to 330 marks to the dollar.

The Helder is at the extreme tip of Holland, and here, some twenty years ago, the Christian Endeavor movement started, and here still are found its leading exponents in Mr. Tielrooij the founder of the first society and the present president of the union. Here lives also Mr. Storm, master of a large boys' school, lovingly called the " uncle " of Christian Endeavor in Holland.

In Rotterdam, we spent a delightful day with our friends Dr. and Mrs. Smitt, Mr. de Haring and Mr. Makreel, and other Endeavorers of the city. The Smitts entertained the one society in their own pleasant home, while they planned for larger things in the city and throughout Holland. The quality of the leaders whom I here met gave me assurance of a substantial future growth of the movement in the Netherlands.

I have so often in this narrative spoken of visits to Great Britain that a paragraph or two must suffice to tell of one of the most interesting of all my visits to the motherland of most Americans. Some new and eloquent leaders of the British pulpit have espoused the cause of Endeavor. Among them are Rev. Thomas Phillips of London, Rev. Lionel Fletcher of Cardiff, and others, while the old friends like Dr. Meyer, Dr. John Clifford, and scores of other leaders have lost none of their zeal for the cause. There has been a very decided advance in the numbers, confidence, and enthusiasm of the societies since the war, which in some places was quite disastrous to the movement, but to-day its prospects, and the hopes of its leaders, were never brighter.

This was attested over and over again by the great throngs which we met in Birmingham and Bristol, and at the great Good Friday meeting at the Metropolitan Tabernacle in London. The Endeavorers of England now have a comfortable and commodious home of their own on Denmark Hill, presided over by the general-secretary and his wife, Rev. and Mrs. Herbert Halliwell. Here an Endeavorer from the home-country or abroad, who is visiting London, will receive a hearty welcome, good bed and board, and find a delightful, homey, religious atmosphere, all for a very reasonable price. We tested the joys of this home off and on for a week, and then went on to Wales to attend the national convention in Swansea, which also was a cheering and hopeful one. As we left Swansea for the last meeting of our five months' stay in Europe the whole convention adjourned and went with us to the station to sing us off. They sang not only the dear old song, " God be with you till we meet again," which we had heard at so many railroad stations and steamship wharves in many lands the world around, but their own adaptation of an old church hymn which was the last strain we heard as the train moved away. Thus they sang:

> " Guide them, O Thou great Jehovah,
> Pilgrims through this barren land;
> They are weak but Thou are mighty
> Shield them with Thy powerful hand.
>   Bread of heaven,
> Feed them till they want no more.
>
> When they cross the stormy ocean,
> Bid their anxious fears subside,
> Bear them o'er the swelling current,
> Land them safe on America's side.
>   Strong Deliverer,
> Be Thou still their strength and shield."

I need only add that the prayer of their hymn was answered. In a day or two we sailed from the beautiful harbour of Plymouth, historically dear to every American, and after one of the most memorable of our tours, " landed safe on America's side."

SOME OTHER NOTED PERSONS I HAVE MET

DWIGHT L. MOODY — IRA D. SANKEY — THEODORE CUYLER —
T. DEWITT TALMAGE — HENRY WARD BEECHER —
PHILLIPS BROOKS — MALTBIE D. BABCOCK — EDWARD
EVERETT HALE — VICE-PRESIDENT FAIRBANKS — PRESI-
DENT TAFT — FRANCES E. WILLARD — ANNA GORDON —
" JOE " CANNON — CHAMP CLARK — J. H. KELLOGG —
JOHN WANAMAKER — WILLIAM J. BRYAN.

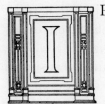

F MY readers have done me the honor of
perusing the many pages which precede this
chapter they have noted that as chronological opportunities have served, I have
spoken of many eminent persons whom my
little orbit has touched, but there are many
others whom I have met who are no less worthy of comment.
It has always seemed to me that contemporary pictures or
descriptions of leading men in different eras contribute much
to the value of any such book as this, for the impression men
make upon people of their own day is of value, whether the
future confirms the contemporary estimate or not.

I wish I were very much more of a Boswell, and sadly
acknowledge my limited powers in this direction. I have
never been a tuft-hunter, and shyness has kept me from making
the most of my opportunities on many occasions, but I have
had some unusual opportunities of meeting people of my day
and generation which ought not to be altogether left
unrecorded.

I believe that Dwight L. Moody will live long in the religious history of America, and indeed of the world.   His rare
common sense, his unswerving devotion to the Master, his deep
religious fervor, and the pithy pointedness and evident sincerity
of his addresses would have made him a marked man in any
generation.   He was accustomed to say " the world does not
yet know what God can make of a wholly consecrated man."
But Mr. Moody came as near showing what the Almighty
could accomplish with such a man as any one I ever met.   We
might add that he also showed us what God could do with a
consecrated man who was almost wholly uneducated, so far as
book learning went, except for the Book of books.

His schooling was of the scantiest.   His spelling was atro-
cious to the very end of his life, and I have had letters from
him in which half a dozen of the commonest words in the
language are most curiously mangled.   Yet this man could
move scholars and theologians to the depths of their natures.
He could bring such men as Henry Drummond and others
of that character to a deeper and stronger religious life.

He had no quavering doubts about the truth of his simple
creed, an indispensable equipment for a successful evangelist.
He declared at the Boston Endeavor convention of 1895 that
if the Bible declared that Jonah swallowed the whale he would
believe it just as he accepted the present record.   This, however, may have been an exaggeration for the sake of emphasis.
He was often imperious and brusque, but he was of tender
heart and humble before his God.   At his request I spoke at
some of his meetings in Northfield, and assisted for a few
days in the revival meetings in New York which were held
towards the end of his life.

I also knew Ira D. Sankey slightly, as he, too, was drawing
near the end of his notable career.   He was raised up by God,
like Moody, to drive home with the pathos and the winning
word of song the message which the great evangelist brought.
His rendering of " The Ninety and Nine," and other solos

which he composed and sang, doubtless led a multitude into the fold of the Good Shepherd of whom he sang. I happened to be attending a meeting of the Brooklyn Endeavorers in Dr. Cuyler's church in Brooklyn, when we heard that Mr. Sankey was living, or rather dying, in his home near-by. So after the meeting we all went to his house, and, standing on the side-walk and in the yard, the Endeavorers sang some of the hymns which he had made famous throughout the world. It greatly touched the sick man, and he sent for me to come up and re-ceive his thanks and benediction for the singers.

Dr. Cuyler was one of the great pastors and preachers of his day, and through his constant writings for religious publica-tions exerted a nation-wide influence. It was said that he had written more than three thousand helpful articles on religious themes, each of them bright, simple, and telling. I used to meet him at Lake Mohonk with the other worthies gathered there. He was so exceedingly deaf in his later years that it was almost impossible to talk with him. This, however, gave him no embarrassment, and his own voice, as is frequently the case with deaf people, seemed to drown out all other conversation in his vicinity. He was one of the cheeriest, happiest Christians I ever knew.

Though I did not know Dr. T. DeWitt Talmage personally, I heard him preach on two or three occasions. He was deemed by many a sensationalist, but he was certainly not of the offen-sive kind. His gospel message always rang true, and he doubt-less reached and helped a multitude in his vast Sunday congre-gation, who would not have been touched by a more quiet and restrained delivery.

The only time that I remember meeting Henry Ward Beecher was after a prayer meeting in his Brooklyn church. The large vestry was full, and Mr. Beecher's talk was spon-taneous and sparkling, and yet homely in its allusions to his early days and his father's home. After the meeting, when a large number of people had been propounded for admission to the church, I said to him, "It must be a great pleasure, Mr. Beecher, to receive such large accessions to your church month after month." " I ought to gather in a lot of fish," was his reply, " for I have a great big pond here in Brooklyn to fish in."

I did not tell him about it, but I had something to do with quashing a trial which some members of the church in Andover Seminary desired to subject him to, by reason of the scandal which clouded but did not embitter his later years. The civil trial had already taken place, and had resulted in the Scotch verdict of " not proven." Prof. Egbert Smyth and a few others in the Andover church were not satisfied with this, however, and desired to call an *ex-parte* council for the purpose of an ecclesiastical trial. As a member of the Seminary Church, I was put upon the committee to represent the student body. The other four members of the committee were professors. Professor Smyth was very ardent for the trial, as was also Prof. Meade. Prof. Churchill, and Dr. Bancroft, the principal of Phillips Academy, were more lukewarm, while Professors Park and Phelps opposed calling the council.

The affair dragged along until after I was settled in Portland. Two of the committee had come to feel that it was useless and unbrotherly to rake up the old coals of controversy and start a new fire. Having left Andover, my own attitude was not entirely known to the others, and I was earnestly besought by both parties to join their ranks. But I could not feel that it was right to prolong the scandal, and so voted with the two members of the committee who were against calling the council.

When the committee reported to the whole church, a majority of them being against further action, the whole matter died a natural death and was decently buried, greatly to Prof. Smyth's disappointment. Warm personal letters from Professors Park and Phelps, commending my action, compensated me for any loss of favor in other directions.

Mr. Beecher was undoubtedly America's greatest preacher. His naturalness and spontaneity, gave the impression of a great fountain of eloquence and wisdom, ever bubbling to the surface, and irrigating the parched fields of theology, causing flowers and fruits to grow up on every side.

The only American preacher likely to be compared with Mr. Beecher for power and eloquence was Phillips Brooks. I knew him slightly, and occasionally heard him preach, but the interview that I chiefly remember was in his study, near the end of his life. Never have I seen one who gave me such an impression of massiveness and yet gentleness. His great form towered a whole head above men who would ordinarily be called tall. His deep, cavernous eyes seemed to have the look of eternity in them. He could not grant my request that he would speak at a ministers' meeting for which I was responsible, but his refusal was as gracious as the acceptance of another would have been.

One of the most brilliant and devoted of America's great preachers died in his early prime, Maltbie D. Babcock, who left a deep impression on the country by his pastorates in Baltimore and New York. No one came within the circle of his influence who was not fascinated by his wit and charmed by his kindness of heart. His little poem on " School Days " is a gem which is set in the memory of many. He, too, was a trustee of the United Society, and went across the water in 1900 to speak at the World's Convention in London. Soon after that we were shocked and grieved to hear of his death by his own hands, in a fit of delirium resulting from typhoid fever.

Edward Everett Hale was another friend of whom no one could see too much. He was surely one of the most remarkable men whom New England has produced, more versatile in his gifts than any man I ever knew. Though called a Unitarian he was not far from the evangelical line, and I have heard him close his prayer with the words, " In the name of our Lord Jesus Christ." Someone has called him " a moth-eaten angel." His shaggy hair and unkempt beard and rather slouchy dress gave point to the appellation. If any one desires to see what may be truly called a speaking like-ness of this great Bostonian, let him look at his bronze statue just beside the Charles Street gate of the Public Garden.

His reading was omnivorous, and his knowledge encyclo-pedic. On one occasion I was telling him about our journey across Siberia, when he told me that he had a very rare book which I had never heard of, about Marco Polo's travels in Siberia. Later he sent it to me, and I found it of great interest. I have recently read in a Boston paper that I obtained the idea of Christian Endeavor from both Dr. Hale and Dr. Cuyler. I am not aware of it, but am glad to acknowledge my indebtedness to them both, and to many other Christian men of my acquaintance for inspiration and help. Horace Bushnell's book on " Christian Nurture " was more responsible for the idea than any other man or book.

My pen is anxious to record the names of a hundred other American preachers whom I have known and loved for their works' sake and for their personal congeniality, but there must be a limit to this chapter, and I forbear, especially since most of them are still living.

Among the public men of whom I have not spoken at length in previous chapters I esteemed vice-president Charles Fair-banks most highly. He was the leading national figure at the International Christian Endeavor convention in Seattle, and next to President Taft, at Atlantic City. It is strange how public men are maligned and their best characteristics ignored or twisted into faults. For years Mr. Fairbanks was always represented by his political opponents as cold and dis-tant, a stalactite in a cave, or a huge icicle endowed with a chilly life of its own. And yet, of all public men I have known, Mr. Fairbanks was one of the most kindly, generous, and genial. He was a strict temperance man, and the only prohibitionist, it is said, at that time in any high administration office, and yet he was libelled as "a wine-bibber," because on the occasion of the annual dinner which he gave to President Roosevelt, the caterer, to whom he had entrusted the banquet, without his knowledge in advance, served cocktails at the beginning of the feast. The opposition papers rang with denunciations of him as a hypocrite. His own denomination refused to send him as a delegate to its General Conference, and the country rang with a parody of a popular song, "Cocktail Charley was his name." To the above-mentioned banquet and reception he had invited Mrs. Clark and myself, but a sudden attack of influenza prevented me from accepting.

The last time I met him was in India in 1909. He had hoped to attend the Endeavor Convention in Agra, but could not make the connections, and at the last minute sent his address, a *thousand-word message by telegraph*. I have many letters of good cheer from him, which I highly prize.

A close rival in whole-hearted cordiality to Mr. Fairbanks is Chief Justice William Howard Taft. His jovial face expresses his kindly heart, and he is most punctilious in all the little courtesies of life. His address at the Atlantic City convention was the boldest utterance a president had ever made up to that time in favor of world peace, international arbitration, and conciliation. He advocated the submission of *all* questions, whether they affected the " *national honor* " or not, to a court of arbitration. I had the pleasure of introducing him to the great audience, not as " William the Conqueror," though his kindness had conquered many hearts, but as " William the Peacemaker." I do not think he has received the credit that should be his as our first Pacificist president, using the word in the best and largest sense of the term. His advocacy of the League to Enforce Peace, the League of Nations, and other measures of that sort in the years of controversy that preceded the Washington Conference on the Limitation of

Armaments, helped to clear the atmosphere of militarism and prepare the way for the better days that I believe are coming.

I must not forget to say a word about Miss Frances E. Willard. She deserves her high place as the noblest leader of America's womanhood. As a speaker she had a compelling power over her audiences by her gentle, womanly, but always persuasive speech. She was broad-minded and catholic in her views, and though at the head of the greatest of temperance organizations, did not allow it to consume all her energies. Woman's suffrage, higher education of women, evangelical religion in all its aspects, owe much to her, and her great heart took in all efforts for the uplift of mankind. Though a Methodist she liked the Christian Endeavor society for its interdenominational and international features, for its honoring both sexes equally, and for promoting an outspoken type of religion, and she was never unwilling to express her views in public or private. Her co-worker and worthy successor in the presidential chair of the W.C.T.U., Miss Anna Gordon, I also have known since she was a girl in Auburndale. She is a sister of that eminent missionary and educationalist, Mrs. Alice Gordon Gulick, of whom I have already written.

I happened to be in Washington just before the national conventions for nominating candidates for the election of 1912, and was introduced to Champ Clark, the Democratic leader of the House, and to Joe Cannon, the speaker. They both had in their bonnets presidential bees that were buzzing loudly, and both were very gracious to me as one who might possibly have some influence with a constituency which was worth cultivating. I hope I am not doing them an injustice.

After chatting with Mr. Cannon for a little while, and after I had moved away, not wishing to take more of his time, he called me back and said, " Mr. Clark, the papers say that I am a tough old reprobate, but don't you believe it. I wouldn't say d— to a mosquito if he bit me, and I never drank a glass of liquor in my life." The old Watch Dog of the Treasury was often accused of lurid language, but I will let his own testimony stand as he gave it to me.

Champ Clark spoke at one of our big conventions in that presidential year, but turned his speech into a political harangue, which I do not think did justice to his undoubted ability and force of character.

A friend whom I have learned to esteem most highly is Dr. J. H. Kellogg of Battle Creek, a truly remarkable character. The Battle Creek Sanitarium, the greatest institution of its kind in the world, is his own child. Far from being " a nest of faddists " as it is sometimes called, it is conducted on the most rigid scientific principles. Fifty specialists, each one an authority in his own domain, will, if desired, examine one for every ill to which flesh is heir. Dr. Kellogg's lectures on the preservation of health are as interesting as they are instructive, and the bigness of his heart is shown by the fact that he has adopted scores of orphans into his own family, giving to several of them his own name, and has started them on careers of usefulness. At one time thirty-nine orphan children sat around his private board in his great dining-room. It is true that no meat is allowed on the menu of the Sanitarium, but the food is so abundant, delicious, and well served that few miss their accustomed steaks and chops.

The doctor is not only a notable organizer, dietitian, and inventor of wholesome foods, but is one of the greatest surgeons in the country, and has successfully performed thousands of operations. His immaculate suit of white in summer and winter alike is a symbol and memory of purity and of good cheer to a multitude who have welcomed him to their sick beds.

America's foremost merchant prince, John Wanamaker, I am proud to number among my list of friends, and the affectionate letters I have received from him indicate that he has at least a little place in his heart for me. His career has been a marvellous one, but is too well-known to be recounted here.

In the midst of all his successes, he has retained a kindly democratic spirit, and a genial humor.

I remember a Sunday I spent with him many years ago, preaching in Bethany Church, which he has so long supported, and addressing his Sunday school of three thousand members. I had six services of one kind and another on that day, but my task was small compared with Mr. Wanamaker's. He attended eleven separate meetings, and as we were going back to the hotel where he was then living, for a late dinner, he said, " I missed one of my girls from Sunday school. She has been absent for several Sundays. I must look her up." So we toiled up three flights of stairs in a back street and found a poor family in the attic. When the door was opened the little girl rushed to him and threw her arms around his neck as though he were her own father.

He scolded her for not letting him know before that she had been ill. " Oh," said she, " I couldn't think of bothering you, Mr. Wanamaker." After more kindly chiding on that score, and pleasant conversation, we all knelt and Mr. Wanamaker prayed most earnestly for this one little lamb of his big flock, and for her mother, who was almost as much affected as the daughter. As we came out he said, " It is easy for a man with money to write a check, but what these people need is sympathy and the human touch." Mrs. Wanamaker, a gentle, gracious lady, was also a good friend of mine, whose cheering letters I greatly prized. In her last letter before her lamented death she enclosed a check for a thousand dollars, half of it for the work I was doing, and the other half that I might have more travelling comforts on the journey I was about to undertake.

I have already spoken of my admiration for Mr. William J. Bryan, but, in closing this wholly inadequate chapter about some of my most distinguished friends, I must add that I esteem him one of the greatest statesmen of his time, as well as one of the noblest of Christian men. I know that many

will scoff at the first statement, will throw " sixteen to one "
in my face, and perhaps rake up the criticisms of rancorous
opponents, but there is much truth in what Mr. Bryan himself
once said jocosely, that the Republicans have stolen most of
his old political clothes.   When we remember that he was
almost the first prominent statesman to advocate prohibition,
woman suffrage, an income tax, and other reforms, and that
he concluded a treaty with thirty nations during his brief term
as Secretary of State, treaties which would have prevented the
world war had two or three militarist nations accepted his
proposals, we can understand the point of his remark.   Whatever critics may say about his views on evolution he shines
even more luminously as a great preacher and a great Christian
than as a statesman, and his influence as an advocate of righteousness, temperance, and good will in his day and generation
has not been equalled I believe by that of any man of his time.

FIRST ARTICLES AND BOOKS ABOUT YOUNG PEOPLE'S WORK —
TRAVEL-BOOKS CONCERNING IMMIGRANTS — FIVE THOU-
SAND NEWSPAPER ARTICLES — MORE AMBITIOUS FLIGHTS
— MY PEN AS A TENT NEEDLE.

E READ of people who are born with silver spoons in their mouths. It is equally apposite to speak of other people who were born with a pen between their fingers. Without intending to boast at all of literary achievements, I think I may claim to belong to the latter class, certainly not to the former. I cannot remember a time when I did not like to write if I had anything to write about. Not that I belonged to the precocious type of children that has received so much attention of late years, like Opal Whiteley and Hilda Conkling, but it never seemed a task to me to write a letter, or a composition in school. When I had any special request to make of my parents, the granting of which was doubtful, seeming to need extended argument, I preferred to commit my plea to paper and ink.

I early aspired to the doubtful immortality of print, and have told in an early chapter about my first lucubration in a New Hampshire weekly and of other efforts which in my college and seminary days helped to pay my expenses.

Such an ambition is likely to grow by what it feeds on, and one little success often leads to another, while the usual disappointments of attempted authorship, although they discourage many from going far, do not put a permanent period to the pen of one who enjoys writing. I think I must have inherited this love from my mother, who, though she never published anything of note, showed by her carefully kept and beautifully written journal, a fine literary taste as well as an exalted but chastened spirit. Considering the work which has fallen to my lot to do, it was an exceedingly fortunate inheritance, for I have been able to do far more for the cause of Christian Endeavor by my pen than by my spoken words, even though these have been in the forty languages in which kind interpreters have enabled me to make myself understood.

The first articles about the Christian Endeavor movement I wrote for *The Congregationalist* and *The Sunday School Times,* within six months of the formation of the first society, when it was, as I called it, only a " hopeful experiment," and before it had been tried out in any other church than Williston. The first book, entitled, " The Children and the Church " was published the following year, 1882, and was the third book I had written up to that date. It was reviewed at length in many papers, and was afterwards republished in Great Britain, and the articles to which I have alluded were also copied in many papers.

If there ever was a psychological moment for the cause I had at heart, it was the moment when these articles and this book appeared in print. Rather let me say, it was God's moment, for throughout my whole life I have been impressed a hundred times over with the Divine leading in these matters. The right time, the right occasion, the right man, without any knowledge or planning on my part, seem to have been found; — the time, the occasion, the man, that of all others could promote this organized effort of Christian nurture.

Other bound volumes about religious work for young people with my name on the title page appeared in the earlier days of the movement, such as " Young People's Prayer Meetings," " Ways and Means," which told of different methods of committee work, and a " Manual of Christian Endeavor," which went at length into the whole matter of its principle and its endeavors.

Of late years I have felt that my gifted colleagues, Amos R. Wells and Robert P. Anderson, could write these technical books of methods and of inspiration for young people's work better than I could, and, having always much more work to engage my pen than I could find time for, I have left those subjects largely to them, and to other practical workers whose experience has fitted them for the task. Dr. Wells has been most prolific in his output of helpful Christian Endeavor literature. His volume on " Expert Endeavor " has been used as a text-book by tens of thousands. It was the result of his own thought that more well-equipped leaders, thoroughly acquainted with the fundamentals of the movement, should be developed. Mr. Anderson has also written many valuable Christian Endeavor books and booklets, and is constantly preparing others.

I have written besides the above, thirty or more bound volumes, a score or more of tracts or booklets on different phases of the work, some of which, like a little booklet called " Christian Endeavor in Principle and Practice," have been translated into many languages.

Two large volumes concerning the history of the movement, very fully illustrated, and which I hope may be of future value as telling more particularly about the work and workers of the first twenty-five years of the society, also bear my name.

Several somewhat elaborate volumes, not bearing upon the society, I have also found time to write, like " Our Journey Around the World," " A New Way Around an Old World," published in England under the title, " The Great Trans-Siberian Railway "; a volume on South America, " The Continent of Opportunity," and a book entitled, " In the Footsteps of St. Paul," describing our visit to thirty-one of the thirty-three cities with which the Apostle's name is connected. " The

Holy Land of Asia Minor" describes the present appearance of the Seven Cities of Asia. A couple of books deal with the immigration questions and are entitled, " Old Homes of New Americans," and " Our Italian Fellow Citizens." Three or four devotional books I have also written of which " The Great Secret " has been the most useful. A book on the joys of out-of-door life, especially the joys of the old farm at Sagamore, entitled, " The Gospel of Out-of-Doors," in a way, was a return to the theme of my first book, " Our Vacations," written nearly a half century before.

I have been more favored than most busy men in having opportunities for such literary work, because much of it has been done in what would otherwise have been largely wasted time, on steamers or railway trains. The work has beguiled the tedium of many long journeys.

By far the greater part of my literary work, if I may dignify it by that name, has consisted of fugitive articles, never collected, but contributed to *The Golden Rule* and its successor, *The Christian Endeavor World*, and to many other religious publications.

For more than thirty-five years I have contributed one or more articles and editorials to the Christian Endeavor weekly before mentioned, at least an average of two a week. In the early days of the paper, when I was more responsible for its contents than now, I used to contribute five or six articles, longer or shorter, to each issue. When I count up the appalling total of two articles a week for thirty-five years, and fifty-two weeks in the year, I find that the number of contributions amounts to more than 3,600. At least a third as many more must have appeared in other publications of which I can recall at least a score, like *The Christian Herald, The Youth's Companion*, and most of the leading denominational papers of American Protestantism.

Occasionally I have essayed a more ambitious flight, and have found my articles in such magazines as *The Century*,

The North American Review, Hibbert's Journal, Everybody's Magazine, The Atlantic Monthly, and *The Yale Review.*

Many of these articles have been toilsomely written with one of my many fountains pens that have been worn out in the service. Quite as many perhaps have been dictated to my secretary, or to my good wife, who on our many journeys together has carried her useful little Blickensderfer, otherwise known to her as "Kezia," in her trunk. I have never learned to use a typewriter myself, but why should I when I have such efficient and willing helpers in my office and my home? Moral: Young man, marry your stenographer, or get her to learn the art of typewriting after you are married, as I did.

I have never aspired to write a poem in my life, considering such literature quite beyond my powers, but I have especially enjoyed the writing of essays and descriptive articles, and other articles, which, though meant for print, were more of the nature of letters to my friends, among whom I have dared to count (perhaps too audaciously) the tens of thousands of subscribers to the paper with which my name has been so long associated.

In the earlier days I attempted a good many articles in a humorous or satirical vein, some of which were afterwards published in book form under the title, "The Mossback Correspondence," and, "Some Christian Endeavor Saints." In the days of a somewhat bitter theological controversy, forty years ago, some articles signed "Rusticus" were received with much applause by conservative theologians, though the author of them, so far as I know, was known only to the editors of the denominational paper in which they were published.

I have not taken myself as an author too seriously, and I do not claim any superior literary ability, but I am thankful to God that writing has been no ungrateful task. I think I can fairly say that though I may have written too much and too hastily, I have tried to express my views clearly and honestly, and have written little, however poor its literary merits, that

I would wish unwritten. Moreover, my pen has been to me what St. Paul's tent-needle was to him, and has largely paid my way in all my journeys, and has enabled me to give my life to the cause of Christian Endeavor, without salary or traveling expenses in foreign lands from the United Society or the World's Christian Endeavor Union. I would not say too much about this matter, but I am so often asked about it that a word of explanation is not out of place. My peculiar relation to the Christian Endeavor movement accounts for what may be considered an undue scrupulosity in this matter, as my friends have often called it.

I have wished to make sure in my own soul that no mercenary motive should ever influence me in doing my utmost for the cause which God seemed to have given to me to promote. Of course a laborer is worthy of his hire, and everyone who gives all his time to the promotion of such a cause as Christian Endeavor has a right to a good, living salary. But no one else can have the same relation to the movement as myself, nor has any one the same reason for refusing a salary or travelling expenses in missionary lands.

I remember that in the early days of the society it was reported to me on good authority that Dr.———— an eminent Boston minister, who looked askance at Christian Endeavor, said to an admirer of the society, " Oh, it may be well enough, and Clark must be making a good thing out of it." I resolved then that no one should ever be able *truthfully* to say that.

When, thirty-five years ago, I left the pastorate of Phillips Church in Boston, I was receiving a salary of $3,500 a year, a sum worth then nearly double what it would be now. After that, as editor of *The Christian Endeavor World*, I had a good salary for a number of years, but on the whole, have averaged during these five and thirty years, from this salary and other literary earnings, less than I received as a pastor.

Yet I have not suffered or " endured hardness " in thus

refusing much that I might have had, and have felt more free to go and come by not being dependent on the society for salary and for foreign travelling expenses. The Lord has provided enough and a little more than enough. In one respect I may have made a mistake in taking this course. If I were to live my life over I think I would take a comfortable salary and foreign travelling expenses, and then turn it all back into the Christian Endeavor treasury to be used for the world-wide work of the society. When one pursues the course I have taken, it soon becomes a matter of course that the president should have no salary. This would be unfair to those who will come after me.

Another reason for refusing a salary from the United Society is that I have desired to set an example of economy, which I think should be the aim of every organization that lives on the gifts of other people. Moreover the United Society of Christian Endeavor has never had any superfluous cash to expend on high salaries or on other matters. I am reminded of the minister who prayed that the Lord would make him humble and poor in spirit, and was told by his deacon that if the Lord would keep him humble the church would keep him poor. The Lord has certainly kept Christian Endeavor poor if not humble.

The chief reason for this poverty is that neither the United Society nor the World's Union has appealed for money to the local societies, their natural source of financial help, but rely upon individual givers who are friends of the movement. The United Society has said to the local societies, " Give through your own church and denominational missionary organizations." This principle has kept the United Society very short of funds, but it is far better that it should be so than not to emphasize, as it has, the loyalty of Christian Endeavor to its own church by this " self-denying ordinance."

One can easily reckon what a drain, in the course of thirty-five years, a salary of $3,500 a year, and perhaps $35,000 more all told during the thirty-five years, for travelling expenses in foreign lands, would have been upon the treasuries of the United Society and the World's Union. They simply could not have borne it.

Do not let me be understood as complaining in any way of financial distress. To keep " a shot in the locker " has kept my pen busy, to be sure, but it has not compelled me to face old age with anxiety. Agur's prayer, " Give me neither poverty nor riches," has been answered in my case. For fifty years I have been able to pay my bills regularly, to give my tenth, and lay aside a little every year for a rainy day. It is surprising how such a course maintained steadily for half a century, will accumulate a modest competence, however small the yearly savings. The money saved soon begins to work for its master.

A list of my bound books, omitting pamphlets and booklets, appears in the Appendix.

OUR HOME–LIFE

OUR SIX HOMES — MANY ABSENCES MAKE HOME MORE
PRECIOUS — OUR CHILDREN AND CHILDREN-IN-LAW —
PLEASANT HOME EVENINGS — HOME GAMES — HIKES
WITH MY BOYS — FAMILY PRAYERS.

T MAY seem, because of the many chapters
devoted to our travels, that our home-life
must have been very much abbreviated, and
its joys very scanty. Though it has been
often interrupted we have appreciated all the
more the home-life we have enjoyed, and in
some respects these many interregnums have made it more
precious. I have spoken in other chapters of my boyhood
homes. Since our marriage we have had six others, — in Portland, South Boston, Auburndale, summer homes at Grand
Beach and Sagamore, and, of late years, in a rooming-house
on Pinckney Street.

The first seven years were the quiet and comparatively uneventful years of a pastor in a small but charming city. The
next five in the throbbing heart of a large city, a section chiefly
given over to foreigners. Then for some twenty-five years,.
though with many long intervals of travel, in Auburndale,
one of the most beautiful suburbs of Boston, while our two
summer homes at Grand Beach and Sagamore have often been
havens of rest after a year of strenuous work or travel. The
Sagamore farmhouse is still the chief estate of our hearts,
though the Boston rooming-house has been a comfortable

winter resort for weeks at a time. Though our children's
doors are always wide open to us, and we often enjoy pleasant
days with them, we feel that we must keep our own separate
home as long as possible.

Our two older children were born in Portland, the next
two in Boston, and the youngest in suburban Auburndale.
Heaven called our little " Faith " home when she was only
one month old, but the other children have lived to grow up

OUR SUMMER HOME AT PINE POINT, ME., 1880 TO 1908

and have children of their own. All four of them over-top
their mother by many inches, and two of them, from their
superior height, look down upon their father.

I think few people have enjoyed a happier home-life than
ours has been, and every day I give thanks to God for this
great mercy. All our children are happily married. Our
oldest son, Eugene Francis, a professor of German in Dartmouth College, and now secretary of this great college, married
Martha G. Haskell of Auburndale, a poet of distinction, whose
poems have been welcomed by the best magazines, — *Scribners,*

Harpers, Good Housekeeping, and others. Harold Symmes, our second son, married Harriet S. Adams, a minister's daughter and a graduate of Mt. Holyoke, who has been prominent in the efforts for the upbuilding of her college. Sydney Aylmer, the youngest, a successful business man in Boston, married Margaret Elliott, a graduate of the Boston Conservatory of Music, who specialized, in her education, on the violin. My daughter, Maude Williston, married " the most popular young man in all Newton," so his neighbors say, who is active in church work, and a promoter of every good cause, while at the same time he is " not slothful in business," being connected with a large banking and brokerage firm. It has given me the greatest joy of all to know that all of my children and children-in-law are interested in the work of their churches, and are striving, each in his own way, to promote good will to men and the welfare of the churches to which they belong.

Among them they have presented us with nine grand-children, one or more being found in each family, while my daughter has given us three, two of them being twins. I have two namesakes, Francis Clark Chase, and Francis Edward Clark II. We have now seven, but two are in the churchyard laid.

No two of our children are alike, and yet, I think, in rather an unusual way, each one of the eight found his or her pe-culiar niche in the larger family circle. The two younger sons are good singers, and often with their music enliven the family circle, and are in demand at the little concerts and entertain-ments in our summer home. The rarest joy of our lives is when we all get together at Sagamore, as many as our house there will accommodate at one time, for the annual reunion.

One especially happy feature of our home-life has been the home evenings. Speaking for myself, these evenings have been especially precious to me, and no public entertainment, concert, lecture, or banquet can compare with them. We often

speak, when together, of anticipating a " P.M.E." or a
" P.S.E.," initials that would mean nothing to a stranger, but
which to us stand for a " Pleasant Monday Evening," or a

MRS. HARRIET A. CLARK
In her favorite attitude, knitting and reading. Taken
in 1920.

" Pleasant Saturday Evening," at home. The mother has a
special gift for reading aloud. She can take in a whole para-

graph at a glance, and, knowing what is coming, can give the right inflection, emphasis, and intonation, as few readers can, while at the same time she may be doing some embroidery work, darning stockings, or knitting. The most characteristic photograph taken of her shows her reading and knitting industriously at the same time.

For many years dominoes has been the favorite game with which to end up these home evenings. In these days when whist, bridge, and poker are considered the only worth-while

THE LIVING-ROOM IN THE OLD FARM HOUSE

Over thirty feet long. Sharp eyes can distinguish old-fashioned candlesticks and spirit-lamps, pewter plates, and the crane, and kettle in the big fireplace, the Dutch oven, huge andirons, and century-old rugs, chairs, etc. A warming-pan, hand bellows, and other antiques are there but undiscernible.

games for a social evening, I can see some lips curl in scorn at this statement. But there are certain games of dominoes, one of which, known among us as " The Gentleman's Game," is peculiarly a Clark family amusement. It requires a good deal of skill, foresight and applied mathematics to play it well, especially when double twelves and double fifteens are used instead of stopping at double sixes.

Let not the devotees of cards despise these old-fashioned

games of their forefathers, games that have never known the
hoof-prints of the evil one upon them. Of course I know
that many people play cards innocently and without any temp-
tation to gamble. Still I resent the sneer of those who see
no fun or profit in other games than cards. It is a significant
fact that in the great cosmopolitan City Club of Boston, with
its seven thousand members, no games of cards are ever
allowed. Checkers, backgammon, chess, and dominoes are
played, but never a game of cards within its walls. It used to
be said, and I suppose is true now, that in John Wanamaker's
store the only things, from pins to pianos, which could not
be bought, was a pack of cards. Is there not some ground
for this "taboo," more than the prejudices of old-fashioned
religionists?

I have alluded once or twice to the family hikes that I have
enjoyed with all my boys in the summer time, often in America,
and quite as often in foreign lands. Many places in Switzerland are dear to us all because of holidays spent there climbing
mountains, sailing on the beautiful lakes, or skirting their
shores. We have a store of memories connected with these
holidays, and many allusions known only to ourselves. Single
words or names of people flash upon memory's screen, as well
as long stories of happy days, or of people memorable for
their virtues or their idiosyncrasies.

Every summer when in America, up to my seventy-second
year, I have had, and I hope to have for years to come, if more
years are allotted to me, a glorious tramp with two or more of
my sons. Starting from Sagamore we have explored both sides
of Cape Cod on foot, walking from ten to twenty miles a day,
and putting up wherever night might find us. We have encircled beautiful Martha's Vineyard in this way, and quaint
old Nantucket, and have hiked down the Plymouth coast for
many miles to the south of Sagamore. I hope I am not merely
flattering myself in the belief that "the boys" enjoyed these
trips as much as the "elderly party" himself.

We have, of course, maintained the custom of family prayers during all these years, though we strive not to make it wearisome to the flesh or the spirit. I do not think that the value of this custom, not only as a religious exercise, but also as a promoter of the integrity and solidarity of family life, is sufficiently appreciated. The coming together once a day to listen to a passage from the word of God, or occasionally from some devout writer, while all together bend the knee in prayer, makes of family life something more precious

COLONY DAY IN SAGAMORE, MASS.
The colonists taken in Puritan costume in front of our old farmhouse.

than it could otherwise be, wholly apart from the religious value of the exercise. But of course religion cannot be left out. The thought of God, of our gratitude to Him, and of our dependence upon Him as individuals and as families, must lie at the very heart of devotion to one another and to the family as a whole.

I have hesitated to write this chapter, lest it seemed too intimate a story to share with the general public, but how can a man's life be known or recorded if he leaves out of it the largest part of that which makes it worth living?

Since the above was written, the first sad break in our family circle occurred, in the death of Martha Haskell Clark, the gifted poetess of whom I have written, the wife of our eldest son. It was a remarkable death-bed scene. Unable to recover from a serious operation, she lingered for three days and passed away not only peacefully but joyously, saying to her husband over and over again, as he held her hand, " Oh, this is a wonderful experience." These were her last words. Hundreds of letters to her husband and to me told what a place she had made by her poems in the hearts of many who have never seen her. I was assured by many in Hanover that no one could have left such a vacancy in the village community, chiefly made up of professors and their families. I will quote one little poem which was read at her funeral. It is from her pen.

THE VILLAGES

I cannot hope that Sorrow's feet forever and a day
Will pass my little House of Love where latticed sunbeams stray;
But when she lays her hand at last upon the swinging latch,
And steps where happy years have smiled beneath our spring-sweet
    thatch,
Grant me, O God, this heartfelt prayer, that somewhere it may be
Where little, small-town sympathy may fold and comfort me.

The little, small-town sympathy that runs across the fields
In blue-checked gingham aprons, and with flour upon its hands,
That bakes and brews, and sweeps and dusts, that wakeful serves
    and shields,
The little, small-town sympathy that knows and understands.

Thy cities, God, are builded high with carven stone on stone,
But hearts may ache, and lives may droop unheeded and alone,
And souls may dwell unknown, unloved, a single wall between —
Not so the quiet, home-sweet lives that fringe the village green.
Let others reap the splendors, Lord, but give instead to me
The homely round of living blent with small-town sympathy.

The little, small-town sympathy that steals on neighbor feet
From tiny lamp-lit houses, down a maple-shaded street,
That lends it strength on tear-dimmed ways its own bruised feet
    have trod;
The little small-town sympathy — the very soul of God.

WHAT MY RELIGION MEANS TO ME

HAVE some sympathy with the man who said, " I have no religion *to speak of*," not however, with the usual implied perversion of the words, that religion is not a thing to be openly and joyously avowed. Still, to open one's inmost heart concerning one's relation to God is a delicate matter, lest one speak insincerely or boastfully. Yet a book of this sort should scarcely be written without at least a short chapter of this nature.

Theology, being a matter of the head, rather than of the heart, is quite a different thing from religion. There is an evolution in God's providence from good to better, and there is also a devolution from bad to worse on the part of individuals and nations. It is only by His constant presence in the hearts of men and nations who receive Him that mankind and the world will grow better and more worthy of Him " whose right it is to rule."

I have never given much time or strength to theological controversy, feeling that I have other work to do in the world. Yet I honor the great theologians of the past and present days, and would not endorse the silly task indulged in by many, of belittling theology, the greatest of sciences, the science of God.

Fortunately the Christian Endeavor movement has never been involved in theological controversies, and there is no reason why it should be. It offers no creed to be fought over, for the creed of each society is the creed of its own church, the organization to which alone it is responsible, and by which alone it is governed. The corner stone of Christian Endeavor is not a theological *doctrine*, but a *covenant* of service: "*Trusting in the Lord Jesus Christ for strength, I promise Him that I will strive to do whatever He would like to have me do.*"

This keeps it on evangelical lines and in evangelical churches. Because of this pledge, no Unitarian church nor any other that leans far over to " the left " has ever formed such a society, or if it has formed one, has kept it up. Several Unitarian ministers have talked with me about it, but have found its pledge too evangelical to suit them. A few years after the Christian Endeavor movement started, Unitarians and Universalists formed young people's societies of their own, called " Christian Unions," which please them better and which have doubtless been most helpful along many lines of fellowship and social service.

Every earnest person, I suppose, must confess to ups and downs in his religious experience. Even St. Augustine, Jeremy Taylor, Edward Payson, and David Brainerd, acknowledge periods of emotional dearth and darkness. The greater the saints the more often these periods seem to be recorded in their biographies, because they are more sensitive than others, and more conscious of their ill-deserts.

My chief confession must be too great absorption in details, too little time given to things of the Spirit. The direction and development of the Christian Endeavor movement, so far as I have been responsible for it, has been such a continually pressing task, though for the most part a delightful one;

there have been so many States and countries to visit, so many letters and articles to be written, another one always pressing upon the heels of the last, that I have to confess, like one of old, that oftentimes, " While thy servant was busy here and there, He was gone."

Still, I do rejoice in many hours of communion with the Unseen, especially on some long voyages, such as the one from India to Africa, and often in the " night watches." Perhaps sleeplessness is sometimes sent to us that in the darkness and stillness we may see and hear God, whom the blazing daylight and the bustling world seem to put far away. My hours of prayer are not always so formal in time, or in attitude, as they were once, but there are more of them.

I have tried to give much of my belief and something of my own experience, in a little book called " The Great Secret," written, as I have heretofore mentioned, on a long voyage across the Indian Ocean. In this I said to the young people, for whom it was written: " Seek to realize this stupendous fact (of the immediate presence of God) for all Scripture is a lie if this is not true. Say to yourself over and over again: *God is Here. God is Here. God is Here. He is within Me. I am His Child. God is my Father. . . .*

" Little by little we shall go on to appreciate by such communion and meditation the deep truths of God's incarnation in Jesus Christ, of the Holy Spirit's indwelling, enlightening, witnessing, comforting power. But it will all be God, God within, God without, God here, God everywhere, God in His word, in His world, in history, in us. We come at last to realize, ' to *practise* (there is no other word so good as this of old Jeremy Taylor's) *the presence of God.*'

" We look forward to the hour of this practice with delight. It is refreshment, food, drink, clothing, health to the soul.

" Gradually the influence of this Quiet Hour goes with us through the day; every sorrow is sweetened, every joy doubled, every care lightened by His presence. Service becomes sweet, difficult tasks become light. Every hour has its song; life ' becomes worth living.' "

I was much impressed by a story of himself once told me by General O. O. Howard, the one-armed hero of Gettysburg. " My stump of an arm," said he, " used to give me a great deal of pain. When I was commander of the army and stationed at Governor's Island, I had occasion to be much in the crowded streets of New York, and I was frequently jostled by someone in the throng in such a way that my arm would throb with pain. I was getting to be cross and irritable, and was afraid I should become a testy old man, so I took to praying for the people who jostled against me: ' O Lord, bless that man,' ' Help this poor old beggar,' ' Comfort that one in widow's weeds.' This greatly helped me to forget my own aches and troubles."

Stonewall Jackson, it was said, used in a very real sense to " pray without ceasing." Before the Civil War he was a teacher in a military academy. When a new class came into his lecture room he would pray, " O God, help me to exert a good influence over these boys to-day! " When the class went out his prayer was, " Heavenly Father, go with them through the day." When he dropped a letter into the post-office box a little petition went with it, " Lord, bless this letter to the one who receives it "; and when he received a letter his petition was, " May I find in this letter some message from Thee, O Father! "

This is what I think the apostle meant by being " continually in prayer," not living apart as a hermit, or a monk, not being always in the attitude of prayer, but feeling the presence of God so near that it is never unnatural to lift up the heart to Him in thanksgiving or petition.

I do not mean to imply that I have attained to the company of these saints (though in all ages there have been some like them), but I press forward that I may attain.

Such prayerfulness and communion with God made these heroes no less active, energetic, sensible, and resourceful. Rather were their wits sharpened as their anxieties were soothed and their worries dissipated by the thought of God Himself as "nearer than breathing, closer than hands and feet."

In my own religious experience thanksgiving occupies constantly a larger place in my prayers than even petition. Every night I like to recount the blessings and joys that have come to me during the day, though they are always too many to be counted. Of course, too, there are always blessings to be asked for, blessings for children and grandchildren, for Endeavorers and their work in many lands, for our country, and especially, of late, for this distracted world, that peace and good will may come to it. But I feel that God knows so much better than I do what my children and my friends, my neighbors and my country need, — what may be real blessings, and what may be curses, — that I do not go into particulars as much as formerly, but leave them with Him, whose everlasting arms are underneath us all.

I am particularly impressed in my devotional moments with God's undeserved goodness in giving me my special work in the world. Realizing my limitations of intellect and soul, I wonder that He called me to start, and in some measure to develop, the work of the Christian Endeavor society. I see hundreds of my brother ministers more eloquent, more witty, more gifted in many ways than I. Why were they not chosen? Thousands of them were thinking along the same lines of Christian nurture in the early eighties. Why did He not give this honor to one of them? Why was the little experiment in Williston Church His chosen way of influencing millions in all lands for good?

This is no mock humility. The undeserved eulogies with which I am sometimes introduced on the platform, often make me cringe and cover my face, for I realize, as no one else can, how small has really been my part, and how all-embracing God's part has been in fitting the cause to the time, and in commissioning a multitude of young men and women for the special tasks He has given them through Christian Endeavor. Every month He has opened new doors; every month He has called young leaders to enter them, and they have responded, " Lord, here am I, send me! "

The voluntary, unpaid, and often inconspicuous endeavors of these millions of Endeavorers, whom God has called as really as He called Abraham or Moses or Luther or Moody, often amaze me. To them under God, belongs the credit, and it often makes me hot with a kind of shame to receive praise for what they, with God's help, have done.

I sum up in a sentence or two the religion of my later years: a growing sense of the immediate presence of God; a greater willingness to leave myself and my affairs in His hands; a feeling that Heaven is much nearer than we know; a sense that the clouds which often obscure our spiritual vision are merely earth-born mists which a breeze from the hills of God may at any moment blow away; and that the part of eternity in which we now live is but the fitting school for the everlasting days when God shall continually teach us new lessons, and give us new and joyful tasks, in the land where none shall say " I am sick."

If I should choose only one life-motto from the many I would like to live up to, it would be the same that I used to see on the stained glass door of the editorial office of the great author and reformer, W. T. Stead, of London.

> " Trust in the Lord with all thine heart,
> And lean not unto thine own understanding."

Chapter LXI

Years 1851–1922

CHANGES IN THREE–SCORE YEARS AND TEN

SEVEN WONDERFUL DECADES — MANY ADMINISTRATIONS — ANTI-SLAVERY — PROHIBITION — WOMAN SUFFRAGE — THE VICTORIAN ERA — MORALS AND RELIGION — MARVELLOUS INVENTIONS — THE WORLD WAR AND ITS EFFECTS — A CLOSING WORD OF OPTIMISM.

S WE live our quiet or eventful lives one day glides so imperceptibly into another that it is difficult to realize what momentous changes are really taking place in the world. One has to look back over a lifetime to note them. The hour hand of a clock does not seem to move, but after twelve hours have passed, we see that it has circled the whole disk. The springing blade of corn seems no taller to-day than it was yesterday, but after three months we visit our garden and find that the stalks measure ten feet. So with human life, and the life of nations.

In many respects I think the last seven decades of the world's history have marked the most astounding progress and most momentous happenings of any seven decades since the world began, always excepting of course the first decades of the Christian Era. I was born in 1851. Then slavery was thoroughly intrenched in the United States and in many other parts of the world. Pro-slavery Franklin Pierce of New Hampshire was in a few weeks to be elected president by an overwhelming majority in the electoral college. It looked as though the anti-slavery cause was forever doomed, and even in radical Boston its advocates were almost hounded to death. Yet ten years later slavery itself, and not the anti-slavery cause, received its death blow. I have lived through the administrations of Pierce, Buchanan, Lincoln, Johnson, Grant, Hayes, Garfield, Arthur, Cleveland, Harrison, McKinley, Roosevelt, Taft, Wilson, and well on into Harding's administration.

Each one of these four or eight year periods has been marked with political and economic changes of great moment to the nation and the world, though I have not room to speak of them in detail.

After our terrible Civil War, which stirred my imagination, as it must have stirred every boy of that period, our country settled down to fifty years of peace, except for the comparatively unimportant Spanish War, justified to our consciences by the barbarities of Spain in Cuba, though it is still doubtful if the Spaniards had anything to do with blowing up the "Maine." Yet the results of that little war proved momentous, for it made the United States an Asiatic power, and saddled upon us responsibilities for a great archipelago, a responsibility from which most Americans, I imagine, would be glad to be released.

Alaska, Hawaii, and shortly before my day, great Texas, golden California, and indeed the whole Southwest were added to our ever-expanding territory, largely through a war with Mexico which it is difficult for us now to justify, and which, indeed, at the time, was opposed by a large minority of the American people.

Still more unbelievable than the success of the anti-slavery campaign was the long prohibition campaign of education and agitation. The unspeakable saloon wrought out its own doom and dug its own grave. It had become so vile, catering to the worst elements in public life which it centred in itself; it had become such a hot-bed, or rather ten thousand hot-beds of political intrigue and corruption, that even people who saw no harm in moderate drinking joined the teetotalers and swept the country for drastic prohibition. I realize that the battle is not yet fully won, and that the country still has to fight bootleggers and law-breakers in high places and low; yet, that Prohibition has been a great boon to millions in removing daily temptations to drunkenness, has made the lives of millions of women and children brighter and more comfortable, and has greatly reduced drunkenness, poverty and wretchedness, only Prejudice will deny.

Another great reform resulted in the passage of the Nineteenth Amendment, granting to every woman of legal age and American citizenship a right to vote. The good results of this reform it is too early yet to measure, but I believe it will make a better and purer America.

Think how the scorners would have scoffed at any one who in the middle of the last century had predicted these reforms! Even their advocates would have said, as Israel's captain said to the Prophet Elisha, " Behold, if the Lord would make windows in heaven might this thing be! "

When we come to the domain of science and invention it would take an encyclopedia to tell of the changes and improvements that have taken place. In 1851 the world was just emerging from the tallow-candle era, though whale oil was used to some extent, and gas had been installed in the larger cities. The vast reservoirs of oil, waiting for man to tap, were still unknown. Coal was mined to a very limited extent, and four-foot logs, which required so much muscle to chop, saw, and split were exclusively used in country places. Modern sewage, the modern bathroom, water-pipes all over the house, were all undreamed of in the great majority of homes. The old oaken bucket and the Saturday-night tub still held sway. The world had to wait many years, of course, for the electric light, the telephone, the trolley-car, and the automobile, while wireless-telegraphy, and the aëroplane come within the memory of the schoolboys of to-day.

What a marvellous thing was the first horseless carriage that

I saw bumping and swerving along the streets to the dismay of all pedestrians! How gloriously bright seemed the first electric light that I saw installed! I still cannot conquer my amazement as I think of wireless telegraphy and telephony, the phonograph, the moving-picture film, and the marvels of the radio outfit.

When we turn our eyes abroad, the changes that have occurred, even within a dozen years, in the rest of the world have been much more startling than in America. In the nineteenth century most nations thought they could no more get along without kings and nobles than that the world could exist without the sun, moon, and stars. Now, by a vast majority the nations are republican, at least nominally, kings, queens, and emperors have been abolished, and the principle of the right of the people to govern themselves if they can has been established even in the few so-called monarchies that are left.

Who could have dreamed, even at the beginning of this century that monarchical China, Russia, Germany, Austria-Hungary, and a dozen smaller nations would ever elect their own rulers and join the ranks of the republics.

I think I have been fortunate to have lived through most of the so-called Victorian Era, scoffed at though it is in these days by many of the impressionists and the free versifiers. It was for the most part an era of decency and comparative peace, and until modernists can produce other writers and leaders of public thought like Carlyle, Ruskin, Thackeray, Dickens, Trollope, Gladstone, and many others in England, and men like Lincoln, Grant, Hawthorne, Emerson, Longfellow, Lowell, Whittier, Garrison, Webster, and Beecher in America, they may well withhold their jibes concerning " the tepid mid-Victorian Era."

In the domain of morals and religion, I cannot speak with so much confidence concerning the progress of these last seventy years. The Darwinian theory, whatever it may be called to-day, has doubtless unsettled many minds. This would not matter so much if some positive system of truth had been wrought out to take the place of the old theology in these wavering souls. Many have concluded that since the doctors of religion and ethics disagree, no one can believe anything for a certainty, and a good-natured, lazy optimism, and a hazy agnosticism have often taken the place of strenuous belief.

After all, one must believe something strongly enough to live and die for it before one can do much for the world. A period when most people are careless concerning their belief, and are content to be agnostic, can never be a great historic era.

Especially in academic circles is this prevailing agnosticism and indifference to an earnest faith felt. I believe that the students in our higher universities are more gentlemanly and courteous in their manners than formerly. There are fewer " roughs " and " toughs " than in the olden days, but I also fear that there is less religion and earnest devotion than a half century ago. The line was more distinctly drawn then between Christians and unbelievers. The professors of religion really believed something and believed it very heartily. Presidents of colleges and teachers, in America at least, thought it was part of their business to make Christian believers as well as scholars. Now, religion, as well as church if not chapel services are quite optional, except in the smaller denominational colleges, and a few larger ones.

The great World War was undoubtedly followed by a period of irreligion and lax morals. Since it had become right to kill your enemy scarcely anything could be wrong. The massing of millions in camps and trenches, the upsetting of the old social order all over the world, was followed by indecent dress, indecent dances, and a general lowering of the conventional standard of conduct. It became much harder for young Christians to take a decided stand against the evils of the day and to maintain it. Christian Endeavorers as a whole have struggled against the tide, but have not been wholly successful in maintaining their old standards.

Yet I am glad to be able to close my book with words of hope and optimism. Post-war indifference and indecency have reached their climax. A reaction is already taking place. The church, the Sunday school, and the young people's societies are coming into their own again. The nations are realizing as never before in all the history of the world, the folly, the wickedness, the wastefulness, and the uselessness of war and of international hate and suspicion.

The Conference at Washington for the Limitation of Armaments, has, I believe, begun a new era in the checkered life-story of this old world, and the year of 1922, in which this book has been finished, is, it seems to me, brighter than any other recent year with the dawn of a new hope, the hope of the era sung by the angels at the birth of Him who alone can bring it about, the era of

"PEACE ON EARTH, GOOD WILL TOWARD MEN."

THE WIDER INFLUENCE OF CHRISTIAN ENDEAVOR

The influence of Christian Endeavor is not by any means confined to the eighty thousand organizations that bear its name. This is indicated by the number of societies with which Dr. Clark is more or less officially connected, because of his relation to the Christian Endeavor society. Many other positions of this sort he has been obliged to decline.

Aside from the United Society of Christian Endeavor and the World's Christian Endeavor Union, and some local clubs and organ-ganizations, he is a corporate member of the American Board and was formerly on its Prudential Committee, a member of the Child-Conservation League of America, of the Massachusetts Civic Alliance, a director in the World's Morning Watch, honorary vice-president of the American Peace Society, vice-president of the American Humane Education Society, a member of the National Society for the Upbuilding of the Wards of the Nation, a member of the advisory board of the World's Purity Federation, on the advisory board of the Family Altar League, also of the Biblical Department of the Church and School Social Service Bureau, a vice-president of the Evangelical Alliance of Greater Boston, a trustee of the Church Peace Union and a member of the Continuation Committee of the same, on the advisory committee of the American Institute of Social Service, on the Commission on Christian Education of the Federal Council of the Churches, and a corresponding member of the ex-ecutive committee of the Council, a member of the Council of One Hundred, a member of the advisory council of the World Peace Foundation, a member of the Education Commission of the National Congregational Council, a member of the National Insti-tute of Social Science and of the National Committee of Studies in Social Christianity, a trustee of Kimball Union Academy, a vice-president of the Massachusetts Peace Society, a member of the Massa-chusetts Child-Labor Commission, and a vice-president of the National Evangelical Alliance, a member of the National Council for Prevention of War, a member of the Executive committee of the World Alliance for International Friendship through the Churches, and also a member of its international committee. Several other organizations might be added, for this is by no means a complete list of organizations which through Dr. Clark have sought or are now seeking the recognition of the Christian Endeavor movement.

Some of these organizations take considerable time, while others are chiefly honorary in their character; but they indicate in some degree the number of good causes that are being promoted, and, as has already been said, the desire on the part of their promoters to interest the young people of the land in their enterprises.

APPENDIX

List of books by FRANCIS E. CLARK,
with date of issue, name of publisher, and brief comments.

1. "Our Vacations," 1874. Estes and Lauriat.
   His first book, written while in the theological seminary.
2. "Life of William E. Harwood," Portland, 1877. Hoyt, Fogg, and Dunham.
   The story of a brilliant young man who died in early life, much lamented.
3. "The Children and the Church," 1882. Congregational Publishing Society.
   The first book about the Christian Endeavor society. Passed through several editions. Republished in London. 2,000 copies of the first edition of this book were bought for free distribution by Hon. W. J. Van Patten, of Burlington, Vt., the first president of the United Society of Christian Endeavor, and were largely responsible for introducing the movement to the public.
4. "Our Business Boys," 1883. Lothrop.
   Based on the replies of many business men of Portland to questions sent them about true success in life.
5. "Looking Out on Life," 1883. Lothrop.
   A book for girls of a somewhat similar character.
6. "Danger Signals," 1884. Lee and Shepard.
   A book for young people, compiled from a series of Sunday-morning talks in Phillips Church, South Boston.
7. "Young People's Prayer Meetings," 1887. Funk and Wagnalls.
   This book covers the field of young people's prayer meetings, suggesting many lists of topics. Reprinted in England.
8. "Ways and Means," 1890. Lothrop.
   The best plans as then understood for Christian Endeavor societies.
9. "Christian Endeavor Saints," 1890. Pilgrim Press.
   A semi-humorous book about young people's characteristics.

10. "Our Journey Around the World," 1894. Worthington.
    A subscription book about their first journey around the world. 50,000 or more copies sold. Illustrated.

11. "The Mossback Correspondence," 1889. Lothrop.
    The views of "Old Father Mossback" on various subjects.

12. "The Everlasting Arms," 1898. Crowell.
    A book intended to bring comfort to the distressed.

13. "The Great Secret," 1898. United Society of Christian Endeavor.
    The secret of health, beauty, happiness, etc. A devotional book, many thousands sold.

14. "Fellow Travellers," illustrated, 1898. Fleming H. Revell Company.
    Chapters of travel in various countries.

15. "World-Wide Endeavor," 1895. Gillespie and Metzgar.
    The story of the beginning and early years of Christian Endeavor. Fully illustrated.

16. "Old Lanterns for New Paths," 1898. United Society of Christian Endeavor.
    A devotional book based on the life of Jeremiah.

17. "A New Way Around an Old World," illustrated, 1900. Harper Brothers. Published in England with title "The Great Siberian Railway." Several editions.
    The story of our journey across Siberia. Illustrated by original photographs, taken by Mrs. Clark.

18. "My Mother's Journal," 1900.
    Extracts from the journal of Lydia F. Symmes. Printed for private distribution. United Society of Christian Endeavor.

19. "Training the Church of the Future," 1902. Funk and Wagnalls.
    A series of lectures given in nine of the leading theological seminaries of the country.

20. "Christian Endeavor Manual," 1903. United Society of Christian Endeavor.
    A text-book of Christian Endeavor.

21. "The Presence of God" (Bishop Jeremy Taylor), 1899. United Society of Christian Endeavor.

22. "Living and Loving" (Prof. A. Tholuck), 1899. United Society of Christian Endeavor.

23. "The Kingdom Within" (Thomas à Kempis), 1899. United Society of Christian Endeavor.

24. " The Golden Alphabet " (Master John Tauler), 1899. United Society of Christian Endeavor.
   These four books of some fifty pages each, contain selections from eminent devotional authors, each edited and with introduction.
25. " Christian Endeavor in All Lands," 1906. Winston.
   A complete history of the first twenty-five years of Christian Endeavor, very fully illustrated.
26. " The Gospel in Latin Lands " (A mission-study book, jointly with Mrs. Clark), 1907. Macmillan.
27. " The Continent of Opportunity," illustrated, 1917. Revell.
   The history and present condition of South America, with the story of a journey with his daughter to nine South American republics. Five editions printed.
28. " Similes and Figures from Alexander Maclaren," 1910. Revell.
   Including brief biography of Dr. Maclaren by Dr. Meyer, and with introduction by Dr. Clark.
29. " Old Homes of New Americans," illustrated, 1912. Houghton Mifflin Company.
   A book about our immigrants from the countries of the then Austria-Hungarian monarchy.
30. " The Holy Land of Asia Minor," 1912. Scribners. Illustrated by original photographs.
   Describing visits to the " Seven Cities of Asia."
31. " In Christ's Own Country," illustrated, 1914. Christian Herald.
   Describing a journey in the Holy Land.
32. " The Charm of Scandinavia," illustrated, 1914. (Jointly with Sydney A. Clark), Little, Brown, and Company.
   Describing Norway, Sweden, Denmark, and Finland in " letters to Judicia."
33. " Christ and the Young People," 1916. Revell. Fourteen chapters about Jesus Christ and his relation to young people.
34. " In the Footsteps of St. Paul," illustrated, 1917. Putnam.
   A book describing visits with Mrs. Clark to thirty-one of the thirty-three cities St. Paul is known to have visited.
35. " Our Italian Fellow Citizens," illustrated, 1919. Small, Maynard, and Co.
   About our immigrants from Italy, based on visits to many Italian cities.

36. "The Gospel of Out-of-Doors," 1920. Chiefly about the trees, birds, weeds, hens, rainy days, etc., on the old farm at Sagamore Beach.

37. "Memories of Many Men in Many Lands," illustrated, 1922. United Society of Christian Endeavor. An autobiography.

Also many booklets, leaflets, sermons, etc. One or more sermons in "Sermons by the Monday Club," on the Sunday-school lessons, each year for forty years. Many introductions for, and special articles in, books written by others.